S0-AEZ-053

THE WORLD THROUGH MAPS

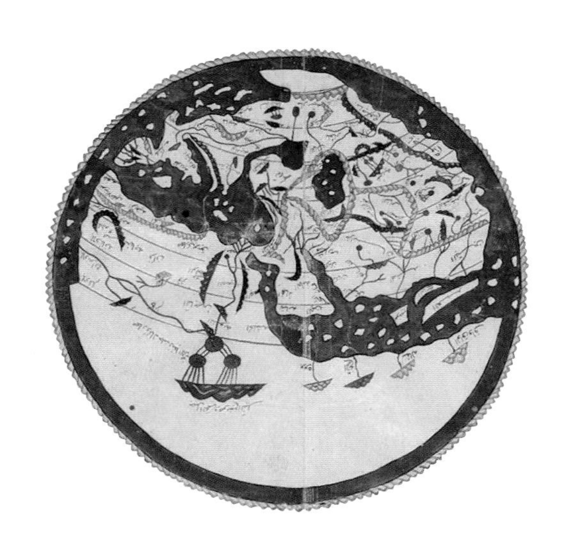

Circulus Arcticus
Obila flu.
Canaoga
Obila flu.
Zubilaga
Chiagiga
Cogib flu.
California regio sola fama Hispanis nota
Vng quae a nostris Gog dicitur
Tubicines aerei
Tartar villa
Polus magnetis respectu insularu capitis Viridis
Polus magnetis respectu Corui insule
Bargu campestria quorum incole vocan. tur Mecriti
Oceanus 19 ostijs inter has insulas irrumpens 4 euripos facit quibus indesinenter sub septentrionem fertur, atq3 ibi in viscera terre absorbetur. Rupes que sub polo est ambitu circiter 33 leucarum habet.
In septentrionalibus partibus Bargu insule sunt inquit M. Paulus Ven. lib. 3 cap. 5, que tantum vergunt ad aquilonem, ut polus arcticus illis videatur ad meridiem deflectere
OCEANUS SCYTHI et Mare T
Gradus 75 latitudinis 80 85 90
Rupes nigra et altissima
POLUS ARCTICUS
Hic euripus 5 habet ostia et propter angustiam ac celerem fluxum nunquam congelatur.
Hec insula optima est et saluberrima totius septentrionis.
Hic euripus 3 ingreditur ostys, et quotannis ad 3 circiter menses congelatus manet latitudinem habet 37 leucarum
Pygmei hic habitant 4 ad summum pedes longi, quem admodum illi quos in Gronlandia Screlingers vocant.
3 Eylanden
Yshouck
NOVA ZEMBL
Mare gla.
Groclant
t Nieulant
Gebroke land
Inwijck
Sr Hugo Willoughbes land
PETZO MARE
MYRMANSKOI MARE
Hit als Sandersons Hope prom
Na prom
Neum pro.
Beeren eylandt
Wardhuys
Nort cape
S. Thome cenobium
Alba
GROENLAND
Sammawik
Lappia
Muyaster insula
ciale
OCEANUS SEPTEN
Lofot
Varo
Finmarch
Berg
Rust
Hales iland
Elizabe.
Circulus Arc

THE WORLD THROUGH MAPS

A History of Cartography

John Rennie Short

FIREFLY BOOKS

Published by Firefly Books Ltd. 2003

First printing 2003

National Library of Canada Cataloguing in Publication Data
Short, John Rennie
The world through maps : a history of cartography / John Rennie Short.
Includes index.
ISBN 1-55297-811-7
1. Cartography—History. I. Title.
GA201.S46 2003 912'.09 C2003-900400-7

Publisher in Cataloguing-in-Publication Data (U.S.)
(Library of Congress Standards)
Short, John Rennie
The world through maps : a history of cartography / John Rennie Short.
[224] p. : photos. , maps ; cm.
Includes index.
Summary: An illustrated history of maps and mapmaking, including reproductions of 200 antique maps.
ISBN 1-55297-811-7
1. Cartography—History. 2. Maps. I. Title.
526/.09 21 GA105.6.S59 2003

Published in Canada in 2003 by
Firefly Books Ltd.
3680 Victoria Park Avenue
Toronto, Ontario, M2H 3K1

Published in the United States in 2003 by
Firefly Books (U.S.) Inc.
P.O. Box 1338, Ellicott Station
Buffalo, New York 14205

Conceived and produced by Andromeda Oxford Limited
Kimber House
1 Kimber Road, Abingdon
Oxon OX14 1BZ
www.andromeda.co.uk

PROJECT DIRECTOR Graham Bateman
MANAGING EDITORS Susan Kennedy and Shaun Barrington
PROJECT EDITOR Hazel Songhurst
ART DIRECTOR Michael Whitehead
DESIGNERS Jane and Chris Lanaway
PICTURE MANAGER Claire Turner
PICTURE RESEARCHER Alison Floyd
PRODUCTION Clive Sparling

Printed in Italy

Contents

AMERICA
Anno Domini 1492 a Christophoro Columbo nomine Regis Castellæ primum detecta, et ab Americo Vesputio nomen sortita 1499.
L.S.
Varias a varijs et antehac editas esse, et quotidie edi tabulas totius Mundi situm depingentes, cuiq; notum est: hac tamen nullam accuratiorem elegantioremq; esse libere dico: quippe quæ succinctius quam omnes aliæ singula depingit, multosque errores aliarum tabular. corrigit. Imprimis vero in Oceano Tartarico et circa illum, multa aliter meliusq; delineat: nec non in nova Guinea, et India Orientali, ut et in America Sept. et Mar del Zur, ac versus Fretum Magellanicũ plurima innovat mutatque vale et fruere.
Quicquid habet Ganges et Dives America quicquid,
Quas et opes mittunt Arabes, Indi, Africa, Seres,
Per maria et terras ad publica commoda quævis,
Huc fert Mercator; paucis, ut plurima dicam,
Pars tenet hæc mundi reliquas celeberrima partes.
Septentrio
Circul.s Arctic.s
SEPTENTRIO
NALIS
MAR DEL NORT
Tropicus Cancri
Circulus Æquinoctialis
MAR DEL ZVR
Tropicus Capricorni
MARE PACIFICVM
OCEANVS PERVVIANSIS
AMERICA MERIDIONALIS
Circulus Antarcticus
LIS INCOGNITA
Meridies
AQVA
Nova Britannia
Nova Anglia
Nov. Belgium
Virginia
Florida
Granada
Nova Hispania
SINVS MEXICANVS
Hispaniola
Cuba
Jamaica
Acores Ins
Terra nova
Frisland
Fretum Davis
Groenland
I de Cabo Verde
Caribana
Guiana
Brasilia
Chili
Rio d la Plata
Fretum Magellanicum
Fretum le Maire
Staten landt

PART I

Introduction

LEFT *Henricus Hondius's world map, 1630*

1

INTRODUCING MAPS

The Language of Maps

Maps are central to the human experience and mapmaking is a major social achievement. In many ways, the history of maps and mapmaking is the history of human society. This book explores this most human of enterprises by looking at the evolution of maps through history, and the major developments in mapmaking.

MAPS REPRESENT a vital form of human communication. Like all systems of communication we can identify different elements: the producer, the medium, the message, and the consumer. The producers of maps are called mapmakers. They range from highly skilled specialists to the person who sketches a rough route map for friends coming to dinner. Through the ages most mapmakers have remained anonymous. This book will look at many of the maps created by these unknown people. It will also consider maps that are the work of known individuals who gave maps and mapmaking a distinctive signature, from the early cartographic works of the 2nd century C.E. geographer Claudius Ptolemy, to the 20th-century maps of Richard Edes Harrison, the US cartographer whose striking maps were published in *Time* magazine during the Second World

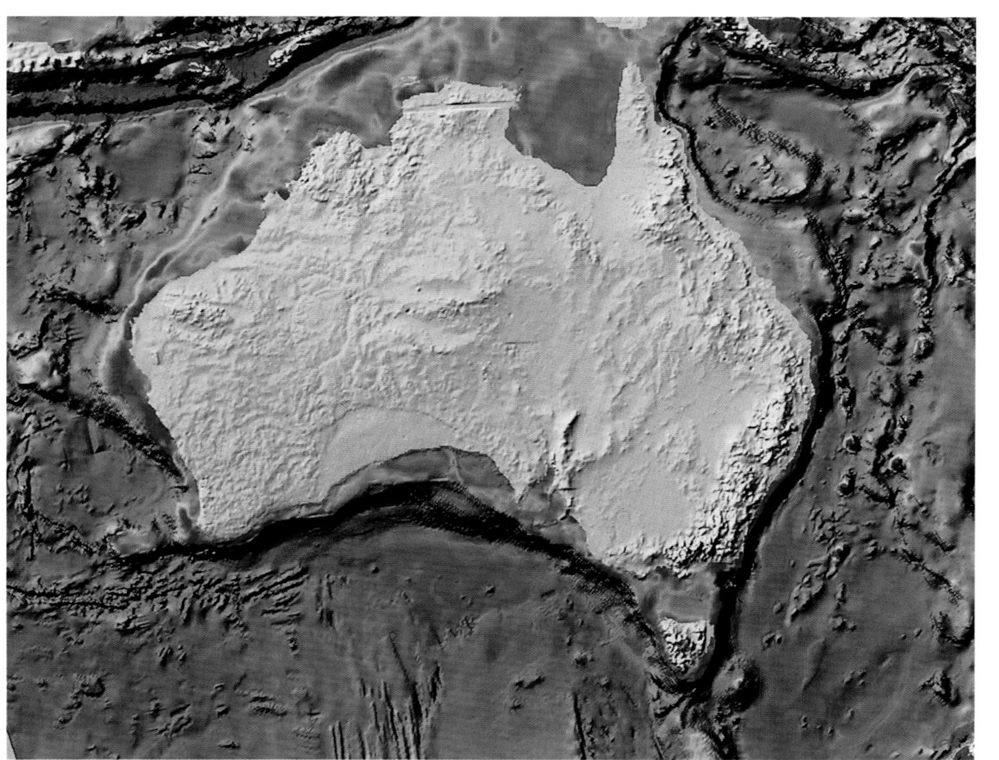

LEFT ***Modern computer-generated map of Australia***
This map of Australia shows relief on land and below the sea. The shallowness of the sea between the north of the island continent and New Guinea indicates the land bridge that was available to people and animals before the most recent raising of sea level. Along the eastern coast, the map picks out the narrow range of mountains as well as the shallow seas that allow the growth of the coral reefs of the Great Barrier Reef.

RIGHT ***Petroglyphs, Bishop, California, date unknown***
There are many petroglyphs located in the volcanic tablelands around Bishop, California, created by the Paiute-Shoshone Native Americans. Could they be cosmological symbols, or depictions of rich hunting areas? The exact meaning of the signs remains a mystery.

War, to the demands of Arno Peters that the world look at itself anew, with a different map projection.

The term "map" comes from the Latin *mappa*, meaning "cloth." Over the centuries, maps have been (and still are) produced in many different forms. They have been carved in stone, painted on silk, printed on paper, inscribed on wax tablets and stored as computer images. There are common maps, and there are rare maps, either the few remaining examples of multiple copies or unique maps, made with one viewer in mind.

There are many different types of map, from simple route maps to maps of countries of the world. Their uses also differ: to plot a journey, to claim territory, or to locate phenomena as varied as air temperature and variations in human health. Maps are used to describe the world, to explain history, to guide action, and to justify events. Like language itself, maps are called upon to perform a variety of roles, and they embody a variety of messages. There are obvious messages, such as "this is the location of Toronto" and more complex ones. For example, 18th-century English and French maps of North America were not just depictions of land; they were acts of colonial assumption.

Consumers of maps can be specific audiences as well as more general readers. Access to maps produced in time of

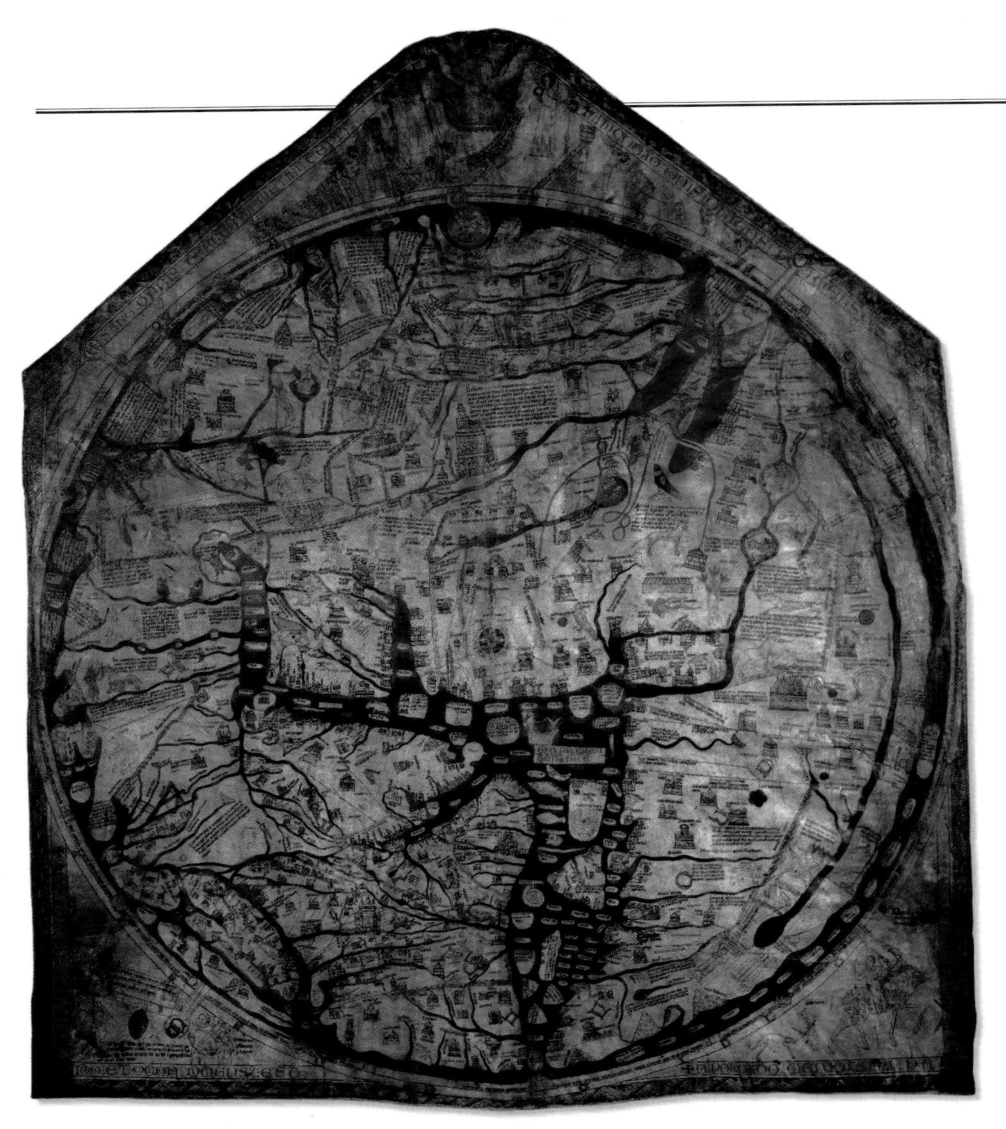

LEFT ***Hereford mappa mundi, c.1300***
The Hereford mappa mundi is one of the largest medieval world maps at over 5 feet high by 4 feet wide (1.58 by 1.33 meters). It shows the eastern hemisphere north of the equator before European knowledge of the New World (see page 58).

RIGHT ***Jigsaw puzzle map, 1766, by John Spilsbury***
During the mid-18th century, the first English board games for children began to be produced by commercial firms. The games included dissected puzzles. These were invariably maps that had been cut into pieces around political borders and then pasted on to boards. They were intended for use as aids in teaching geography.

BELOW ***Portrait of Ptolemy, 1630, by Henricus Hondius***
This fanciful portrait of Ptolemy on a world map is anachronistic. It uses 16th-century costume for a 2nd-century person. There are no accurate portraits of the great mapmaker, but his presence on later maps is a sign of respect for his work and cartographic achievements.

war, for example, is usually restricted for fear that vital information will fall into enemy hands. Military maps convey a great deal about the mindset and objectives of the producers of the map, and hence about their attitudes, actions, and conduct during the war. But when the war is over, restricted maps can have a wider circulation and their message changes for the reader.

Maps have always had a symbolic importance. The first maps, carved in stone and drawn in sand, had as much a symbolic as a practical value. They gave meaning to life as well as direction, by locating, or "centering" people. And even today contemporary maps reveal just as much about ourselves as inhabitants of the world as they do about the geography of the world. When we use national boundaries, for example as important elements in map design, we signal the importance of nationalism to individual and group identity.

Maps also have a decorative purpose. Many maps are extremely beautiful and intricate. Some are designed specifically as art objects, but even the most practical have an esthetic quality to which many people are instinctively

drawn. Maps are as much works of art as they are products of technical achievement.

Maps are pictures of the world that embody changes in artistic depiction, scientific inquiry, and the way we view and understand the land around us. They are material objects, social documents, and historical artefacts. The history of cartography is a complex story of changes in artistic representation, technical progress, and social construction, all of which bear the mark of economic and political power.

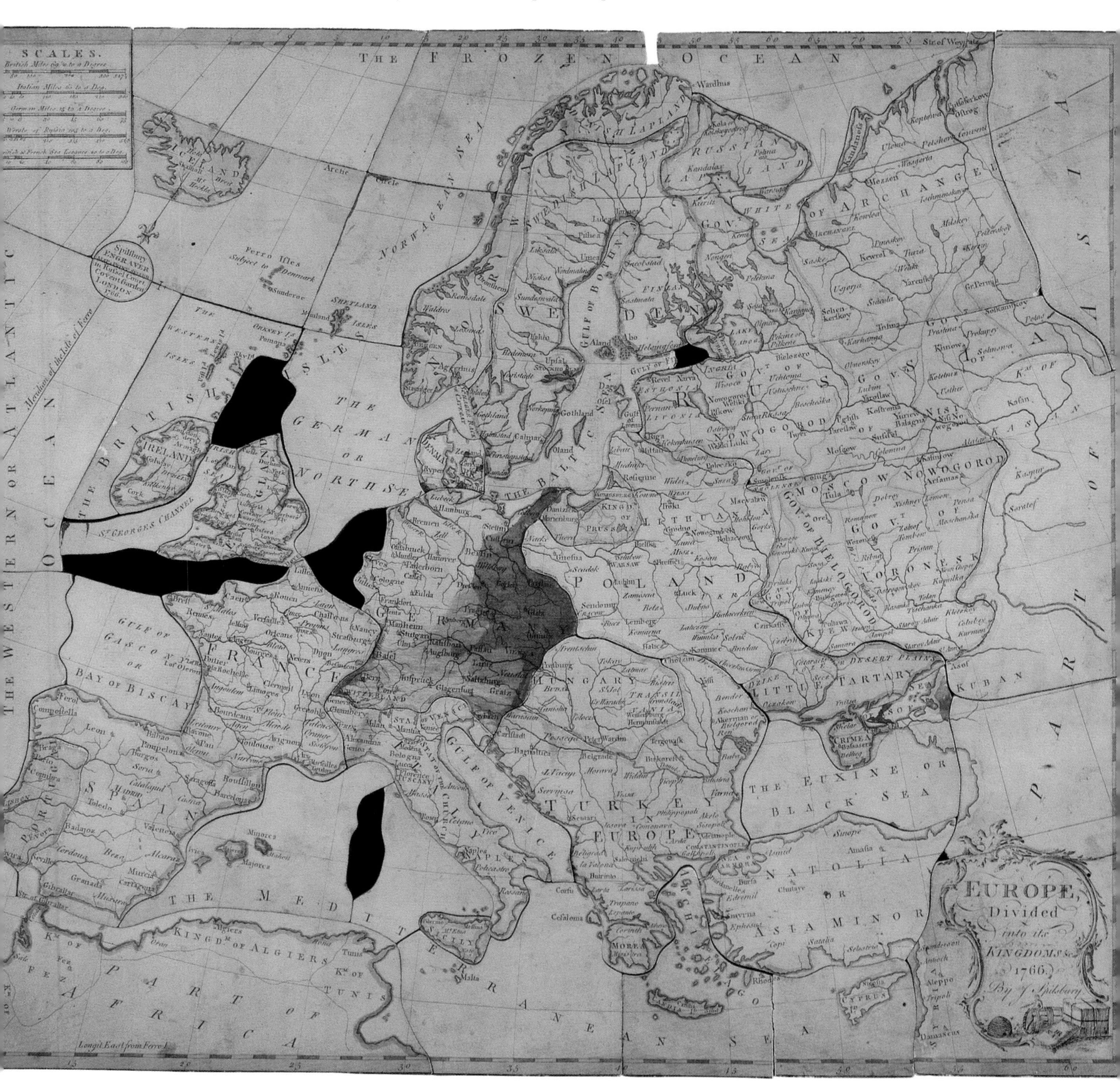

Scale and Projection

To understand maps it is important to be familiar with two important terms: scale and projection. Maps represent the world. In effect, they represent a large area on a smaller surface. The precise relationship between the world and the map is called "scale." Maps have to compress the area of the world onto the surface of the map, which may be no larger than a postcard or an A4 piece of paper. "Scale" is the measure of compression. For example, 150 miles (250 km) of the world may be represented by 1 inch (2.5 cm) on the map. This can be represented mathematically as 1/15,000,000. This is called a "small-scale" map, as the fraction is small. A "large-scale" map, of 1/250 for example, shows much more detail. Maps come in a variety of scales. Think of the different scales as if they were photographic lenses: large-scale maps are the close-ups of the world, small-scale maps are the wide-angle shots.

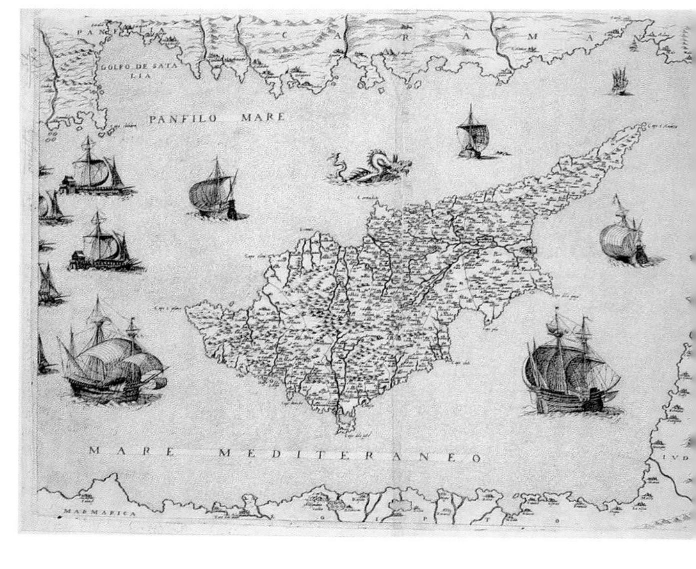

ABOVE *Map of Cyprus, c.1570*
This map has two scales: one to show the coastline of the eastern Mediterranean and another to depict the island of Cyprus. The size of the island is exaggerated compared to the coastal areas, allowing us to see the overall context but also to gain more detail of the island.

Scale is shown on maps in a number of ways, as a fraction and as a measuring rule. Understanding the scale of a map is important when reading the map. Distortions of scale should also be looked for, since they will exaggerate some features and minimize others.

The larger the territory covered by a map, the greater becomes the problem of the earth's shape. The world is spherical, while maps are flat. When the mapmaker represents a very small piece of the world on a map—say a city—then the spherical nature of the earth is not an important issue. However, the more territory that is covered on a map, the greater the distortion. In representing the whole world on a flat surface the mapmaker distorts a spherical object by making it flat. The best solution is to represent the world as a globe, which retains the reality of the sphere. However, globes can be expensive to make and cumbersome to use, and so flat maps of the world are still necessary.

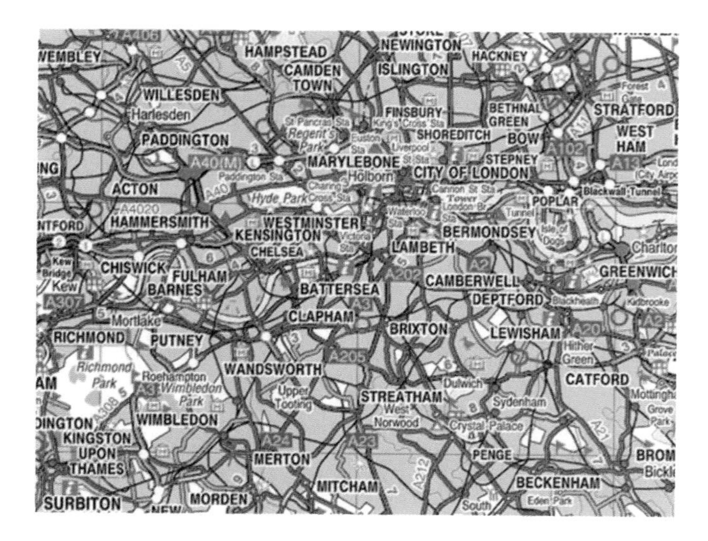

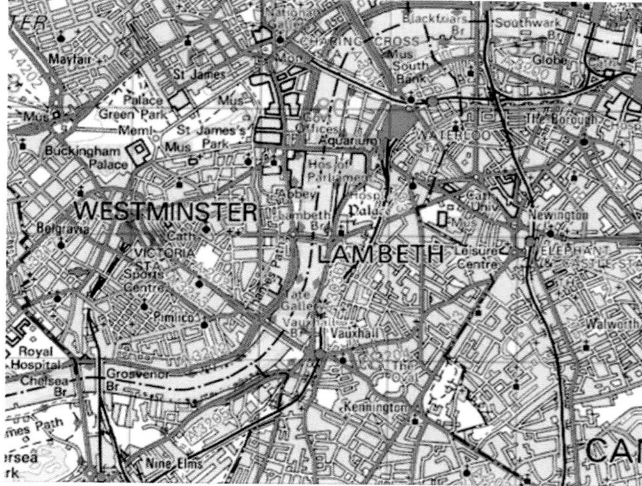

Map "projections" are the formal representation of the round world on a flat surface. All map projections are distortions, but they differ in what they distort. Perhaps the most famous projection of them all, the Mercator projection (named for the 16th-century Flemish geographer who invented it) distorts the size of the polar regions, making them appear as large as the equatorial areas of the world. Mercator devised his projection as an aid to navigation. An alternative projection, first devised by the Scotsman James Gall in 1871, distorts the shape but keeps the land mass sizes closer to reality. There are many other types of projection, ranging from the more hemispheric Goode projection to the "squashed orange" shape of the Robinson projection, the curvy sinusoidal equal area projection. All maps are a trade off among the competing desires for accurate area size, location and direction.

While the distortions are most apparent in small-scale world maps, all maps are distortions. Whenever we represent part of the world on a piece of paper or on a computer screen, we create a distortion. Oddly, distortions can be used to good effect. The Lambert conformal conical projection, for example, which was first developed in 1772, more accurately portrays regions of the world that are more east to west in extent, such as Russia. On the other hand, regions that are more north to south in extent, such as continental America, are more accurately portrayed by the polyconic projection, which was devised in 1820.

BELOW ***Three scale maps of an area of London***
The three maps demonstrate the degree of precision available at different scales. (From left to right these are 1:250,000, 1:50,000, and 1:10,000.) As if seen through a lens, more and more details are revealed as the scale increases.

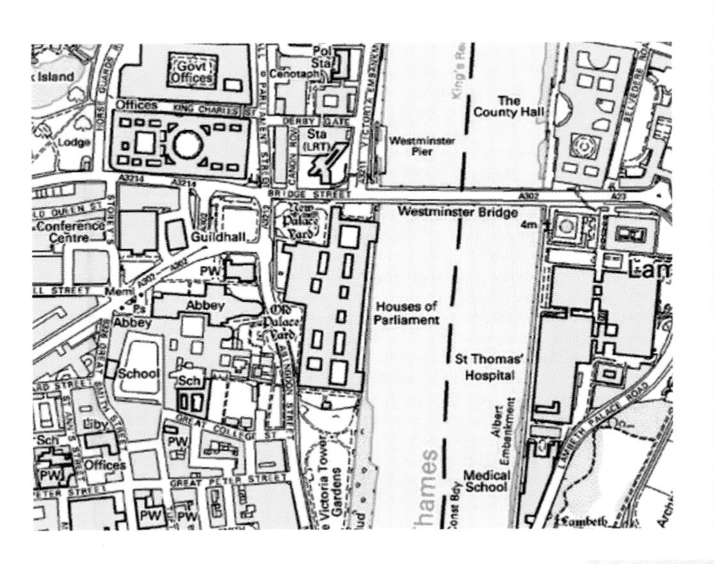

PROJECTIONS

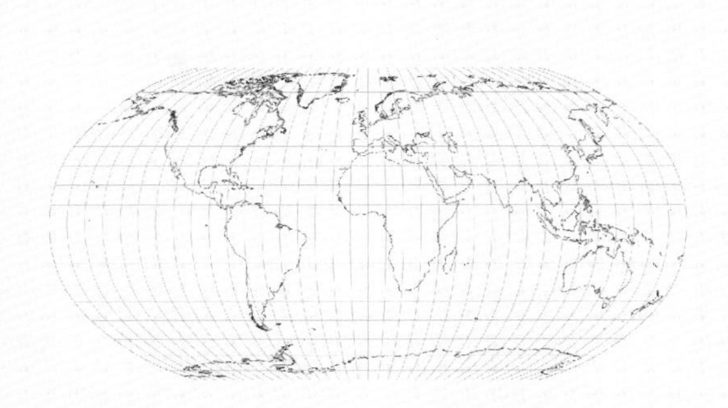

ROBINSON PROJECTION

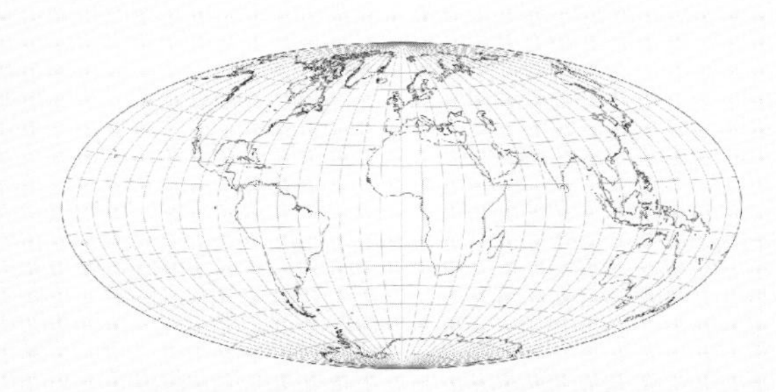

HAMMER PROJECTION

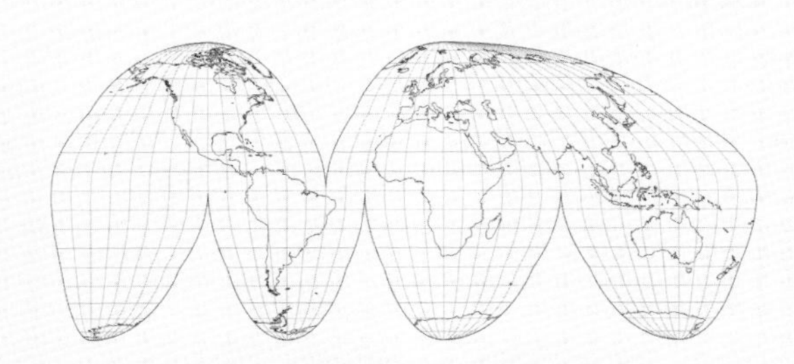

GOODE PROJECTION

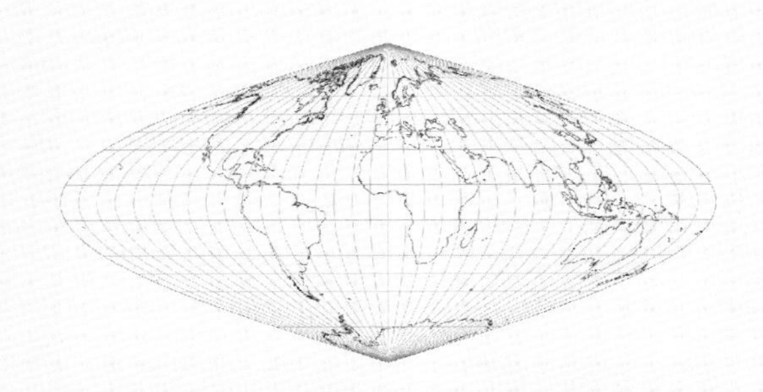

SINUSOIDAL PROJECTION

Orientation

Maps represent the world, or parts of the world, but they do so from particular directions. The directionality of a map is referred to as its "orientation." Many people consider north as the top of a map and south as the bottom, and indeed the majority of contemporary maps are orientated with north at the top. However, this is a relatively recent convention—and not a necessity. We live in a spherical world where there is no obvious top or bottom and in a universe where the terms "top" and "bottom" have no intrinsic meaning.

Using north as the principal point of orientation is no simple matter. First of all, there are two types of north: "magnetic" north and "true" north. True north is the direction of the North Pole, an imaginary, though fixed, location, the northernmost point on the earth's axis. Magnetic north is the direction in which a compass needle lies. While true north is unchanging, magnetic north varies over time—as magnetic orientation changes—and in different parts of the world. Over the history of the earth there

OPPOSITE, TOP ***Medieval T-O mappa mundi***
This medieval world map is orientated with east at the top and north on the left. The map divides the world into the three continents of Asia, Africa, and Europe. The world is centered on Jerusalem.

OPPOSITE, BELOW ***Vale of Kashmir, 1836, by Addhur Rakim***
This map has a multiple of orientations rather than just one. It is a map that provides travelers with the view in front of them as they meander along the roads.

BELOW ***Universal Corrective Map of the World, 1979, by Stuart McArthur***
There is no reason why maps should be orientated with north at the top. We are so used to it, however, that this world map by McArthur of Melbourne, Australia looks odd.

has been marked magnetic variation; at times magnetic north has been located close to the South Pole rather than the North Pole. The exact reasons behind magnetic reversal and magnetic change are not known.

We are so used to seeing maps orientated toward the north that when we see one with alternative orientation, it comes as a great surprise. The Islamic mapmaker Al Idrisi's early map of the world uses the typical south orientation of many early Islamic maps. More recent examples include the "upside down" map of Australia. Medieval cartographers often placed Jerusalem, the place of Christ's death and resurrection, at the center of their maps, which were orientated toward the Holy Land in the east—i.e. they had east at the top. In fact, the term "orientation" is derived from this fact, *oriens* being the Latin for "east." To orientate a map initially meant placing east at the top.

Religious doctrine also influenced map orientation in other belief systems. Many older Islamic maps, for example, were created with religious observance in mind. Muslims pray toward Mecca—toward the sacred rock, the *Kaaba*, to be precise. They do this five times a day as part of their daily prayer cycle and also whenever they are reciting the Koran and when a person is laid to rest. Therefore, it is vitally important to know in which direction the *Kaaba* lies. Hence, maps were made to show this direction from most places in the known Muslim world. Two brass scientific instruments have recently been discovered dating from the late 17th century but representative of cartographic knowledge and expertise in the period 800 to 1500 C.E. The instruments contained maps of the world with a list of cities situated on a grid. Practitioners could use the grid to plot direction and distance to the *Kaaba* from a range of different cities.

Map orientations are often the result of implicit judgments and particular perspectives on the world. For example, in medieval maps of the world, the British Isles looks as if it is located on the edge. This is because, for medieval European scholars, it was an accurate location for a peripheral (and hence relatively unimportant) part of Europe. A Dutch map of the New England area of North America in the 17th century is orientated with west at the top, because this is the way the coast was encountered by sailors coming from Europe.

Orientation can change within maps. This was a common feature of Indian maps of the 19th century. For example, an 1836 map of the Vale of Kashmir now housed in the British Library shows buildings and features from a variety of orientations; they are mainly shown along the border of the map. The images are presented from the changing perspective of travelers as they approached the different places by the most obvious route, rather than from a standard centered orientation.

The center of maps also plays an important role in guiding our perceptions of the world. The standard Mercator projection is often presented centered on the prime meridian, which passes through Greenwich, UK. As this projection placed the British Isles at the center of the world, it is clear why the Mercator projection was such a favorite of British imperial mapmakers. It reflects the significance of Britain in colonial times.

But imagine what would happen if we centered the map at 180° and turned it the other way around? Then Australia would be portrayed in a more significant position. So map orientations structure how we see the map, and hence, the perspective from which we see the world.

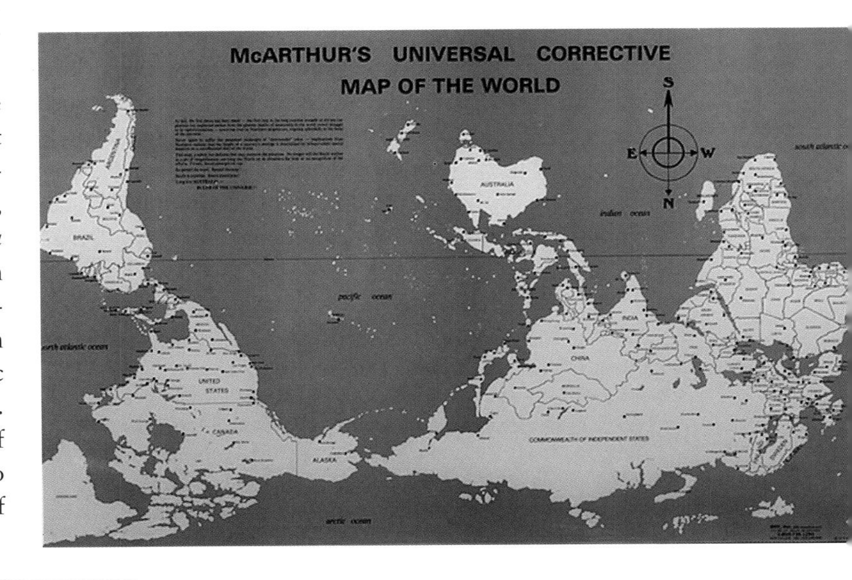

Symbols, Pictures, and Plans

There are, very broadly, three different ways to represent the world in maps: through symbols, pictures, and plans. Very early and more recent maps use symbols to represent things in the world as things on the map. For example, maps carved in rock use symbols to represent people, places, and animals. Australian Aboriginal sand painting maps use distinctive circular motifs to represent camps, water holes, and meeting places. Drawing a line to represent a river, a circle to signify a town, or a stick figure to represent a person are all symbols employed in maps.

Most modern maps use a complex array of symbols to represent a variety of phenomena. A contour line, for example, is a symbol used to represent altitude, while the hierarchy of towns can be represented with different-sized urban symbols. While picture maps are often immediately obvious, maps that use symbols are often complex enough to need a key to make sense of them—they are in a form of code. Another term for the key or code breaker that explains the meaning of the symbols is the "legend." Both names are evocatively accurate. The key unlocks the meaning of the map. Without a key the symbols may be hard (or impossible) to decode. The legend implies something that has to be read, a story.

Picture maps can be found throughout history, and embody artistic as well as cartographic skills. Maps from 18th-century China, for example, are as much works of art as they are cartographic achievements. Picture maps show altitude and places using the visual tricks of the artist, such as perspective and foreshortening. They are immediately accessible and very often do not need a key.

There are different picture maps depending on the viewpoint of the artist. A "panorama" or "view" map

RIGHT ***Map showing administrative divisions in Jiangxi Province, China, 18th century***
The map from an atlas depicts relief with both pictures and colors, giving the viewer an immediate sense of the physical geography of the area. The towns and cities are clearly visible as are individual buildings. This map is pleasing to the eye, with a subtle color palette, and also gives a detailed sense of the relief and settlement patterns of the region.

MAPPING ALTITUDE

Maps that show topographic relief have a problem. They are trying to show a third dimension in a two-dimensional object. One way out of this is to create three-dimensional relief models of the world. But for those making two-dimensional maps the representation of relief presents a challenge. Mapmakers have overcome this in a variety of ways. First, they may make pictorial representations of relief—many older maps, for example, have little pictures of hills. Second, they can show altitude in symbolic form. Contour lines depict altitude by linking places of similar altitude. The reading of contour lines takes some practice, and they are more useful on large-scale maps. Mapmakers can also show relief by patterns of shading. In this case, a light source from a single direction is assumed to highlight altitude. Shaded relief maps have reached a high level of sophistication in Swiss maps. Hachure maps use a system of line spacing that is part shading and part pictorial to represent altitude. Color coding is also used, especially in small-scale world maps where contour lines would create too much information. Some maps use several techniques to represent relief, including hachures, contours, shading, and color.

ABOVE ***Modern computer-generated relief map***
This large-scale map covers part of California, Nevada, Utah, and Arizona. It provides a very detailed sense of relief showing both flat surfaces and complicated folds in the earth's surface. The computer software has generated shadows as if the sun were in the northeast.

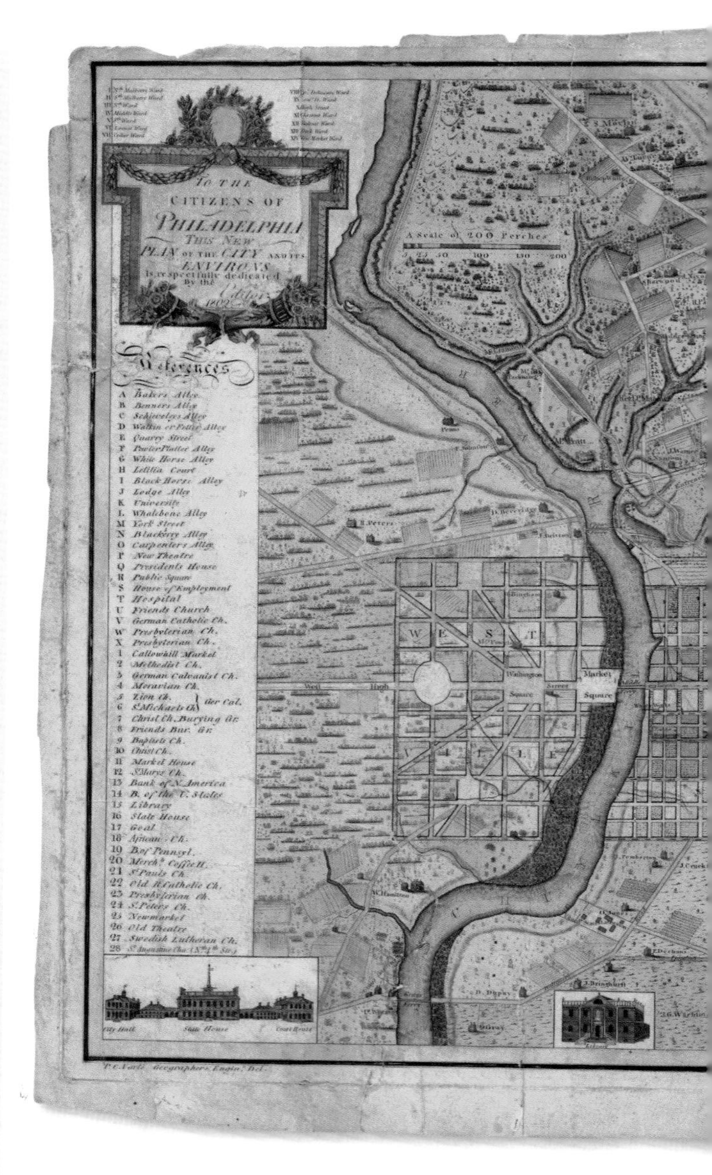

presents the vision of someone at ground level looking at the prospect or vista in front of him or her. Such maps give a sense of the landscape from a ground-level perspective and are often used to present a picture of the landscape as a tableau.

The "bird's-eye view" represents the world from an oblique, aerial perspective, and is particularly good at depicting the height of buildings and landforms. This technique is common in urban mapping, where the perspective allows the mapreader to see the relative height of buildings as well as their location. The bird's-eye view is found in maps from all over the world over the past thousand years. Its evolution is closely related to artistic developments such as perspective drawing and three-dimensional esthetic representation. In all picture maps,

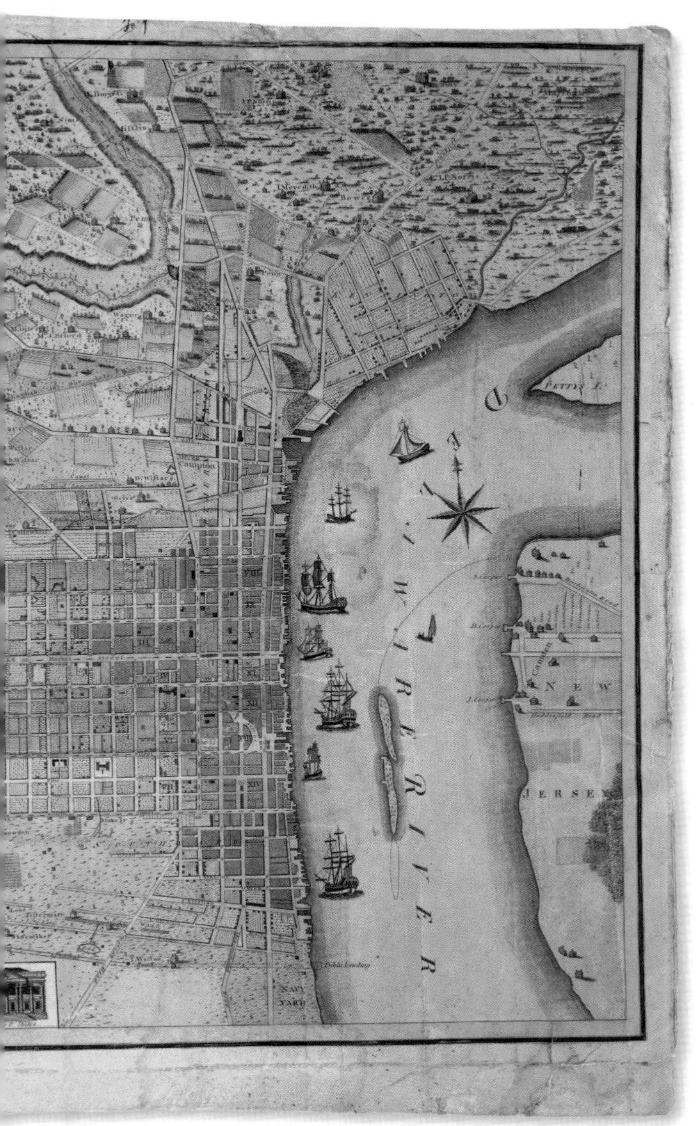

LEFT *Map of Philadelphia, 1802, by Charles Varle*
This is a complex map that uses both symbols and pictures. The city streets are shown as a plan, assuming the viewer is directly above the city; the countryside is shown as a bird's-eye view, assuming the viewer is at an oblique high angle. Many objects in the map are shown in three dimensions.

BELOW *North Wales County, 1579, by John Saxton*
In this map, relief is shown pictorially as a series of small molehills. Their size is proportional to the height on the ground, and while charming in appearance, the result is not very accurate.

but particularly bird's-eye view maps, art and cartography are indistinguishable.

An aerial view taken from directly overhead is often called a "plan view." Some of the earliest maps were drawn in this way. For example, many Australian Aboriginal sand painting maps are drawn as if the viewer is looking straight down at the landscape.

A "scale plan view" is a plan view drawn true to scale. Accurate plans depend on careful measurement and recording. Most official maps produced by national planning agencies are scale plan maps.

Many maps contain elements of all three types: symbolic, picture, and plan. The map of Philadelphia made in 1802 by Charles Varle (above) combines the scale plan with pictures. The map is both pictorial and symbolic. There are pictures of things, such as ships, and symbols for buildings and vegetation. There is a plan view of Philadelphia and a bird's-eye view of the local countryside. Pictures, symbols, and plans intersect in the same cartographic representation.

The history of cartography on the past four hundred years has been a shift from pictorial representation to symbolic representation. Most national mapping agencies use symbols such as contours to show relief rather than little pictures. While we have gained accuracy we have perhaps lost the easy accessibility of pictorial maps. There has also been a shift from panoramic and bird's eye views to plan views. It is easy to "read" molehills as hills and to "see" the city shown as a bird's-eye diagram rather than a plan diagram. We have lost as well as gained by shifts in cartographic representation.

The Grid

A fundamental element of maps and mapmaking is the "grid." The accuracy of maps, the relationship between the map and the real world, is based on the use of a grid. When someone draws a map of a room freehand, he or she will probably exaggerate or reduce areas of floorspace by drawing the walls too long or too short. With a grid system the length and breadth of the room are measured accurately and the mapmaker translates these measurements to draw the room at the correct scale.

A grid is a system of vertical and horizontal lines that structures the way we see and represent space. To locate objects on the latticelike grid pattern of a map seems such a natural thing for us to do that we take it for granted. Yet it has not always been so. The grid had to be invented. To see the world enmeshed in a grid implies a sophisticated grasp of mathematics. But more than an understanding of mathematics was involved. The grid implied a conceptual ability to imagine the world in purely spatial terms. By

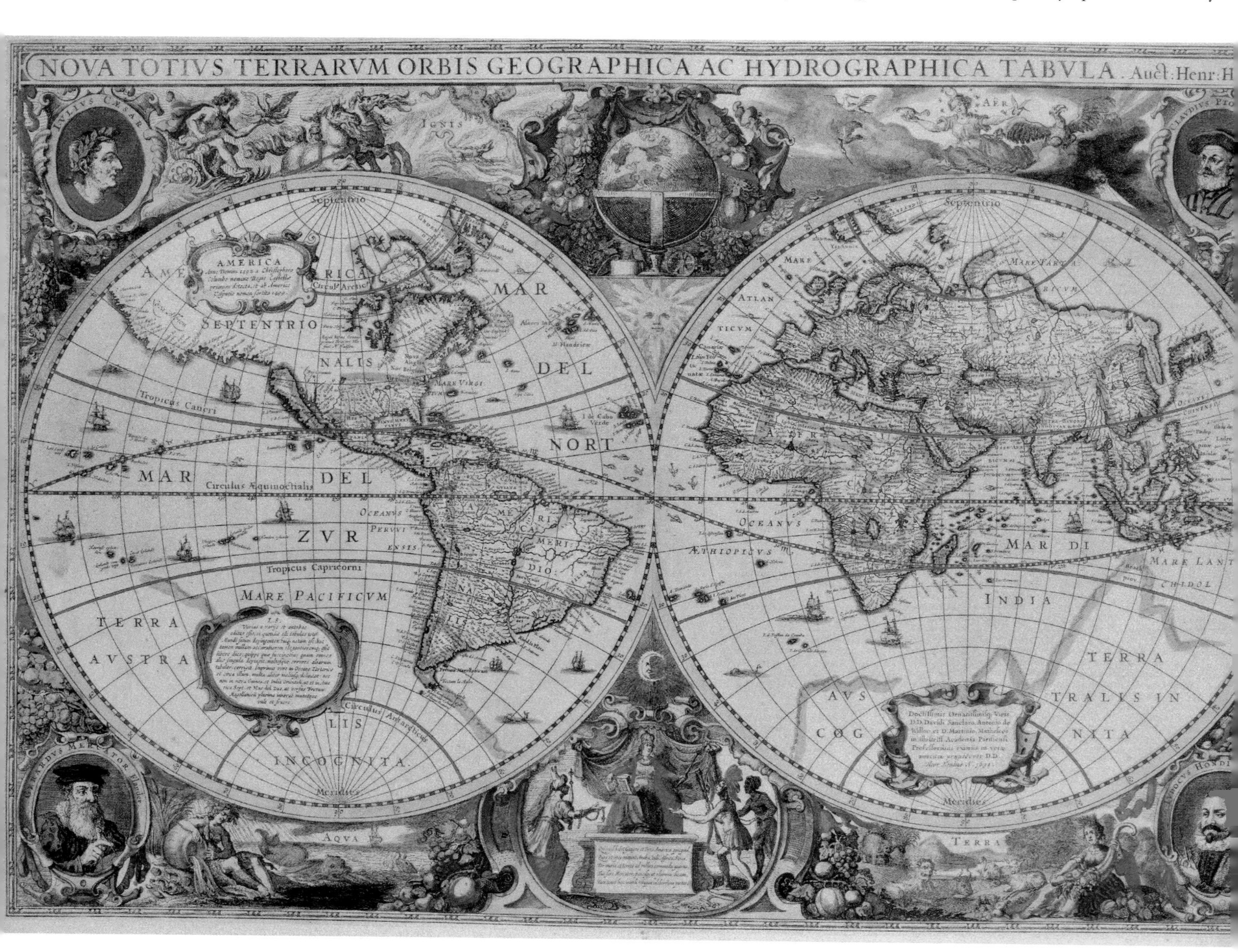

simplifying the representation of the world to the abstractly geometric, a major revolution was wrought. The grid transformed the rough terrain of the world into a pure geometry, and allowed the world to be plotted and replotted, mapped and remapped, represented and reimagined.

Large-scale maps use a grid of "latitude" and "longitude." These are imaginary lines drawn respectively east to west and north to south over the globe. Latitude measures places north and south of the equator. The scale used is degrees, minutes, and seconds—either north or south of the equator, which is set at zero degrees. The north and south poles are set at 90°. Latitude can be determined by using astronomical data. The height of the sun in the sky varies by latitude, and the same applies to all other visible stars. The position in the sky of the North Star, often called the pole star, also varies by latitude. Navigators in the past determined the height of either the sun or the pole star (one could be measured by day, the other by night) to fix their latitude at sea. Persian, Muslim, and European astronomers and navigators invented a variety of devices including the astrolabe, quadrant, sextant, and octant, as well as the cross-staff and back-staff, to determine latitude.

Latitude is closely connected to climate, since the closer you get to the equator, generally, the hotter the location. Climate is in fact an ancient Greek word, simply meaning region or zone. Terms often used in understanding the weather, such as "polar," "temperate," "subtropical," and "tropical" derive from zones of latitude that were first identified in the 2nd century C.E. by the geographer Claudius Ptolemy (see page 52).

Longitude is a measure of the location of a place east or west of an imaginary line called the prime meridian. Values are given as degrees east or west of the prime meridian, which is set at 0° up to 180° east or west. Unlike latitude, which has an obvious starting point of the equator, one line of longitude is no more significant than any other. Greek scientists and geographers who started to "grid" the world almost 2,000 years ago used a variety of prime meridians: Hipparchos used the Aegean island of Rhodes as

LEFT *World map, 1630, by Henricus Hondius*
At first glance, this map of the world looks more decorative than accurate. The borders are filled with elaborate decoration and portraits of famous people, as well as illustrations depicting the seasons of the year and the personification of the continents in the bottom middle. But the map is also finely gridded. Lines of latitude and longitude criss-cross this double hemispheric world map in a mesh of mathematical precision.

MEASURING LONGITUDE

ABOVE ***John Harrison***

Lines of latitude run east to west parallel to the equator and the location of any place can be fixed with reference to how far north or south you are from the equator. Lines of longitude, in contrast, run north to south, and allow locations to be fixed east or west of a prime meridian. While latitude could be determined with reference to the sun and the stars, the measurement of longitude was much more difficult. The solution lay in accurate timekeeping and sophisticated chronological equipment.

The world is a giant clock that keeps on turning around its own axis as well as around the sun. If we measure time in a particular place by the moment when the sun is highest in the sky, then different places in the world will always have different times according to their position east or west of the prime meridian. In order to find your longitude, you need to know the time in two different places: the time where you are at the moment and the time in the place from where you started your journey.

In 1714, the British Parliament offered a huge reward to anyone who could come up with the answer to the problem of accurately measuring longitude at sea. Many of the scientists of the day sought to solve the problem by astronomical observations. The solution, however, came from a clockmaker, John Harrison, who created a timepiece that could accurately keep time on board a ship. This was no mean feat given the swell and roll experienced on the open sea by most ships of the day. (The swell and roll were a problem because at the time all clocks were pendulum clocks: the key was to design a clock that did not require a pendulum.) Harrison experimented with numerous devices and, finally, in 1762, his timepiece was effectively tested to be an accurate timekeeper and measurement of longitude.

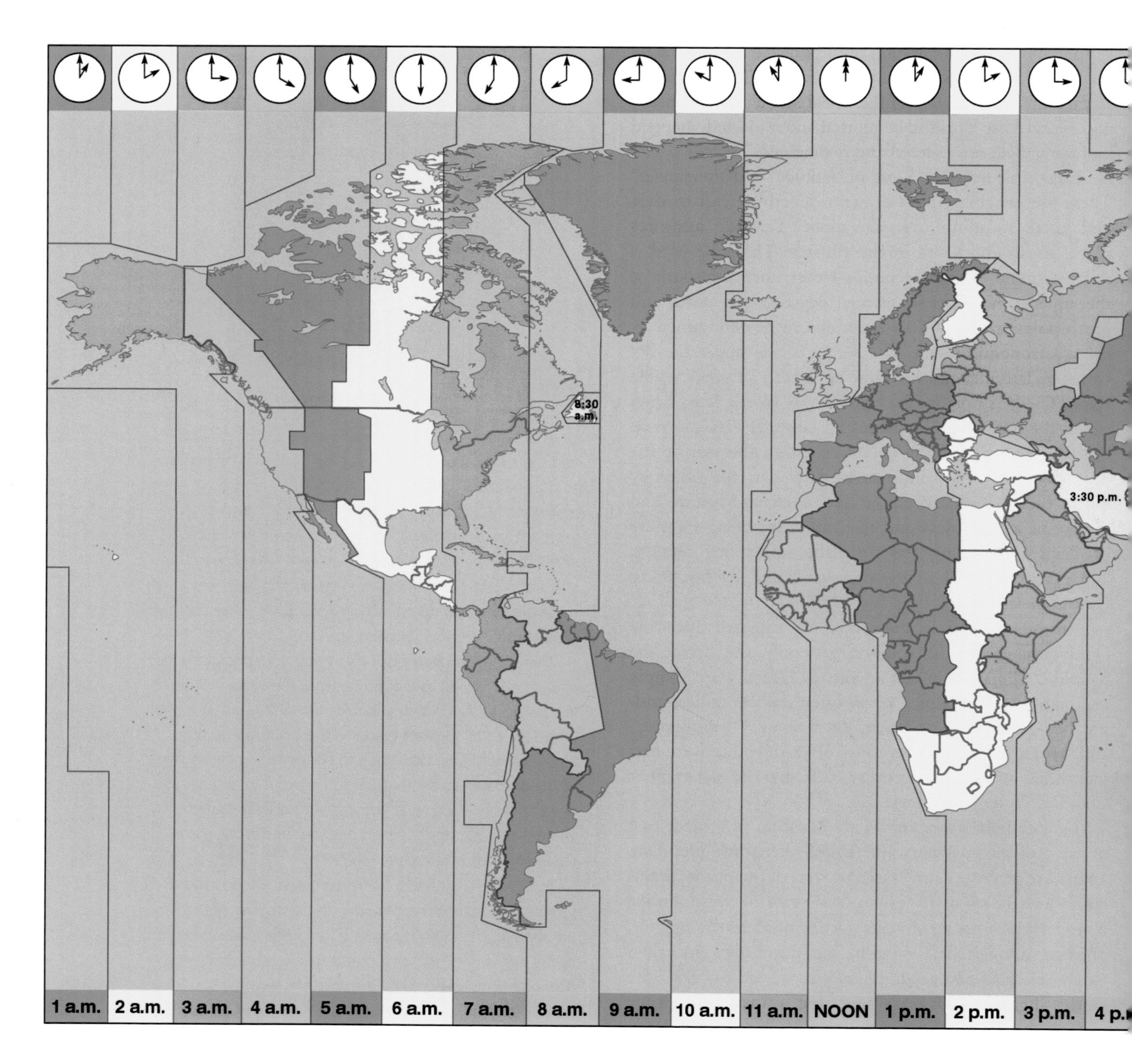

his prime meridian, while both Ptolemy and Marinus used the Canary Islands in the Atlantic. From the Renaissance to 1884 a variety of prime meridians were used. Each country used its own capital. For example, the French used Paris, the English used Greenwich in London, the Dutch used Amsterdam, the Belgians used Brussels, and the Portuguese used Lisbon. After the American Revolution (1775–83), mapmakers in the United States changed the prime meridian from London to Philadelphia (the capital from 1790–1800) and then to Washington. Throughout the 19th century, many US maps would use a double system on the same page, with longitude from Washington at the bottom and from Greenwich at the top.

This meant that during the 19th century, maps gave the spatial location of places in the world at different longitudes depending on whether the map had been prepared

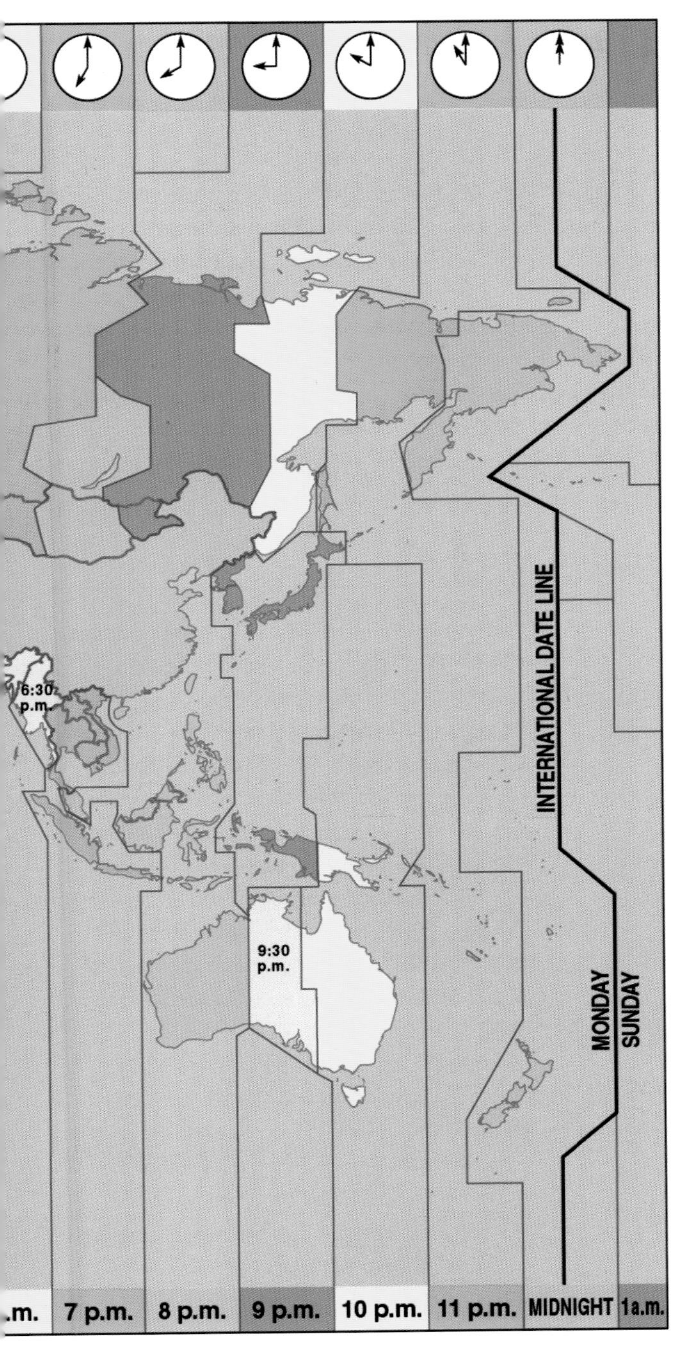

ABOVE ***The western hemisphere as a spherical grid***
This depiction of the world is now a commonly used symbol; the grid has become an expected part of the image. No such lines exist on the ground but they nevertheless remain vital in determining accurate location.

LEFT ***Modern world map showing longitude and time zones***
The earth spins by 15° of longitude every hour; anyone traveling west gains an hour for every 15° of longitude traveled. To overcome the problem, in 1884 Canadian engineer Sir Sandford Fleming suggested a system of time zones and proposed the International Date Line, running north-south through the Pacific Ocean and avoiding major land masses.

by a French, English, Dutch, or American mapmaker. In 1871 an International Geographical Congress meeting in Antwerp, Belgium, decided that sea charts should use the same prime meridian of Greenwich. It was to become obligatory within 15 years. By the early 1880s most countries had adopted the new system, although the French still used Paris, the Spanish used Cadiz, and the Portuguese used Lisbon. The Brazilians used both Greenwich and Rio de Janeiro, and the Swedes, always polite and unwilling to offend anyone, used Stockholm, Greenwich, and Paris. At the second International Geographical Conference in Rome in 1875 it was agreed to use Greenwich as the prime meridian on land maps and in 1884 it was agreed that Greenwich would become the prime meridian on all maps. The world now had a global standard; local time had been replaced by a standard time centered on Greenwich.

Silences and Lies

Maps are texts that tell us important stories. They represent a form of communication that can speak across the centuries. We have to listen with a careful ear because their messages are rarely simple or clear. Maps are often unwitting witnesses because they tell two stories: the story in the map and the story of the map. The story in the map is the physical, social, and political depictions it contains. The story of the map is the history of its production and consumption.

Maps are neither mirrors of nature nor neutral transmitters of universal truths. They are narratives with a purpose, stories with an agenda. They contain silences as well as articulations, secrets as well as knowledge, lies as well as truth. They are biased, partial, and selective. Traditional histories of maps and mapmaking have always tended to focus on the increasing accuracy of maps. In recent years the history of mapmaking has been enlivened and enlarged by scholars who view maps as texts to be

SECRET MAP OF LONDON, 1926

The General Strike of May 1926 was the closest Britain came to an insurrection in the 20th century. Called by the Trades Union Congress in support of the coal-miners, the Strike lasted only nine days but brought large parts of Britain, including London, to a standstill. The military was called in—armored cars were seen in the capital. The Government feared the outbreak of complete anarchy and class war. Secret correspondence between the War Office and Ordnance Survey indicated that a special map of London had been prepared beforehand to show facilities that authorities considered "vulnerable," as well as "control" points in case of trouble—although these could indeed be one and the same. Even the existence of this map itself was kept secret, and all copies of it were believed to have been destroyed until this copy was presented to the British Library by the Ministry of Defence in 1995. (Key to secret map below.)

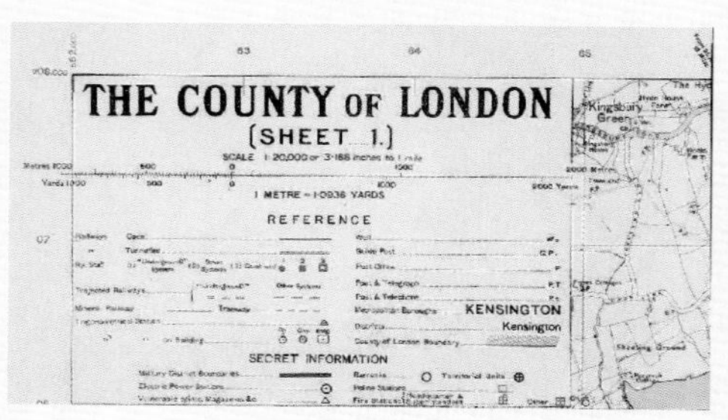

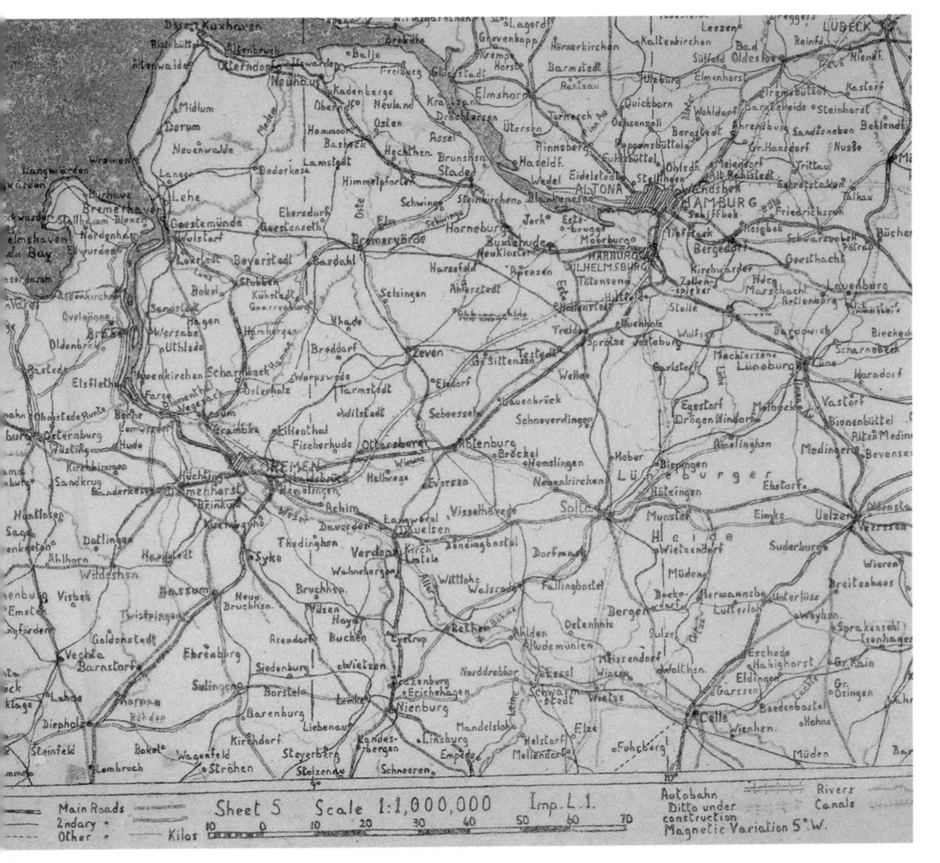

LEFT ***Map of Hamburg, Germany, 1944, by British prisoners of war***
This map was made in secret by British prisoners of war Wallis Heath and Philip Evans, and was to be used by those trying to escape. The map details roads, rivers, and canals—all likely routes of escape. It is remarkably accurate for a map made in very difficult conditions. More than 500 copies of four different maps were produced.

decoded. Maps are no longer seen as value-free, socially neutral depictions of the earth, but rather as social constructions that bear the marks of power and legitimation, conflict and compromise. Maps are social as well as technical products, and mapping is not only a technical exercise, but also a social and political act.

Let us look in detail at the notion of map secrets and map lies. Maps in themselves can be secret—they may be restricted in usage and readership. Most military maps are classified as secret, some of the more sensitive are top secret. Maps made by prisoners are also secret maps. British prisoners of war in a camp near Brunswick in Germany in 1944 made a sophisticated set of maps of the surrounding area of northern Germany so that those lucky enough to escape could find their way back to Britain. The enterprising prisoners used tiles from a building in the camp as printing plates. They drew the maps by hand and made a printing press from floorboards, using tar from the pavements as ink.

Government maps often contain secret information. Maps of sensitive installations, secret organizations, and clandestine operations rarely become public knowledge. During the General Strike in Britain in May 1926, the government feared an insurrection from organized labor. The military was mobilized to counter such action. A secret map of London was prepared by the government that showed "vulnerable" sites and "control points" to be used in the event of civil unrest.

But even so-called "ordinary" maps have secrets. In fact, all maps have secrets because they tell us only part of the story. For example, a road map that does not show relief features gives a subtle (and false) impression that the area it maps is perfectly flat. A geographically challenged acquaintance of mine once traveled from the American Midwest to San Francisco using only a road map. This meant that he was unprepared for the effect of steep hills on his car engine especially when crossing the high peaks of the Rockies.

Many maps have calculated secrets. For example, a map of the world centered on Greenwich, UK, glosses over the fact that there is no "natural prime meridian point," no top and bottom to the world. When calculated secrets turn into calculated misrepresentations, then we can speak of "cartographic lies." When maps are used as propaganda, then the misrepresentation and cartographic lies are more obvious. German maps of the British Empire in the late 19th and early 20th centuries played up British expansionism to emphasize the need for Germany to catch up in the imperial stakes.

All maps, in one sense, are lies since they involve a massive partial (mis)representation of the solid world on to a smaller object. The round world is turned into a flat piece of paper at the cost of incredible selectivity and bias. Maps do show us the lie of the land, in the multiple sense of the word "lie."

2

THE EARLIEST MAPS

Maps Carved on Rocks

Most maps are transient things. Traced in sand, painted on hide, or made of paper they do not generally last for very long. They are fragile and easily lost or destroyed. The oldest extant maps, which have stood the test of time, are carved in rock and reflect the very beginnings of human society.

INTERPRETING PREHISTORIC rock maps poses considerable problems. The first is the basic question of "Why?" The earliest human societies were nomadic, constantly on the move. What practical use would a map of a specific area have been to a mobile people? The answer leads us to a sense of the earliest rock maps as symbolic interpretations rather than practical objects for wayfinding. Rock maps, like rock art in general, were primarily associated with belief and ritual. The carvings on the rock were not meant as everyday messages but were connected with wider cosmologies. Often inscribed during ritual times and in sacred places, such maps have a symbolic importance; they are part of a deeper religious symbolism and we can only hazard a guess as to their full meaning.

The second problem is that we lack a key to these ancient maps. Does a stick figure mean a specific person, people in general, or something completely different? Do the circles represent water, the earth, or a mandala-type symbolic pattern? Without a key we have absolutely no way of knowing for sure. The third problem is just as basic: are the designs that we see really maps at all? Without a key or a context are we simply assuming these patterns are maps when in fact they are something else? There is a hazy uncertainty between maps and non-maps in rock art.

The fourth problem is dating rock art. When was a design carved on a rock? The estimates are just that—rough guesses, made all the more vague by the fact that rock maps, like rock art in general, are often assemblages of work done over the centuries by many different hands. Sites would be carved and recarved over decades, centuries and perhaps thousands of years. What is the date of such a rock map?

The earliest rock maps were most likely created in the upper paleolithic period around 40,000 years ago. This

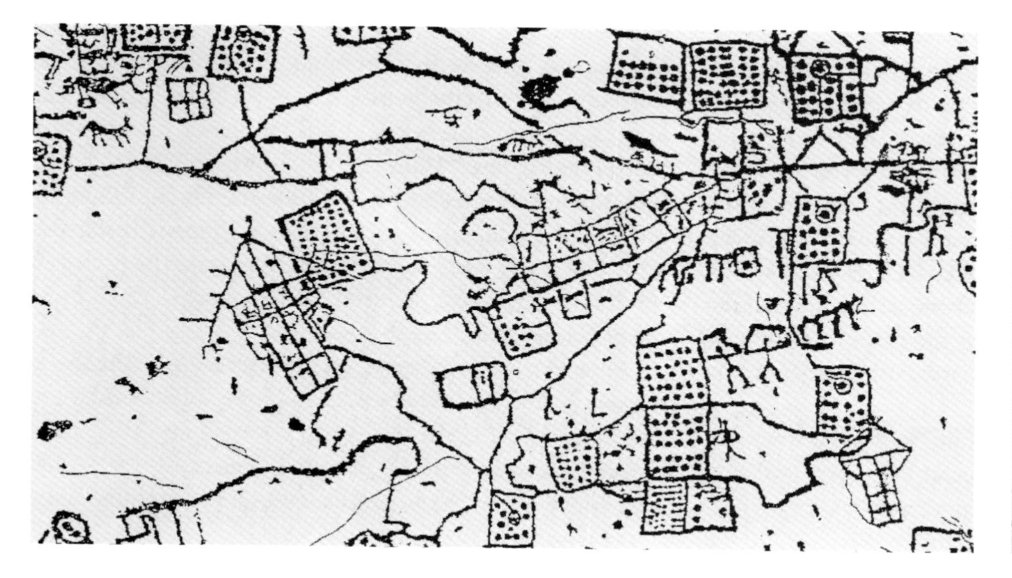

was a time that saw a considerable flowering of artistic expression, especially in the carving of small sculptures and in rock art. The rock art from this period consisted of paintings, incised designs, and relief carvings. There has been no simple explanation of the designs, motivations, or purposes of this art, but it seems clear that it was more significant to its creators than a simple recording of facts. The time taken to carve in rock suggests that these images represent something of extreme importance.

Despite the problems in interpreting rock maps, different rock maps have been identified: topographical maps, celestial maps, and cosmological maps. Topographical maps depict the countryside, land use, and even individual buildings. Celestial maps indicate the location of stars, while cosmological maps are models of the entire universe. Both picture maps and plan maps have been discovered. The conclusion we can draw is that mapmaking was an important part of early human society; it was part recording of the world and part symbolic gesture—an attempt to give meaning and significance to the world and the heavens. It seems highly likely that maps were closely connected to religious beliefs and cosmological understanding.

Complex topographical maps have been found throughout European paleolithic sites. In the area around Valcamonica and Mt. Bego in the French-Italian Alps, a number of later topographic maps carved 2,000 years ago have been discovered. They are renditions of topography that recently have been interpreted as forms of offering to the gods asking for rich harvests.

Above the Italian town of Capo di Ponte, situated between Lake Garda and Lake Como, is the site of one of the oldest maps in the history of cartography. Dated at the middle Bronze Age (around 1900 to 1200 B.C.E.), it is an assemblage that now covers a rock surface measuring 13.5 x 7.5 feet (4.1 x 2.3 m). This surface was "written" on right into the late Iron Age, but the oldest section reveals a complex pattern of points, lines, and surfaces. It is a plan map, a view directly from above. What do the signs mean? It has been suggested that the lines indicate paths, the points and circles show springs while the stippled areas indicate land use types – perhaps orchards and fields. With its range of symbols and plan view it is an extremely complex, sophisticated map.

LEFT *Topographic map, Iron Age*
This map from Valcamonica in Italy, probably created during the Iron Age, shows an agricultural landscape of fields and villages. Scholars suggest that the engraving was a form of offering to the gods to provide good harvests and healthy animals.

THE EARLIEST STAR CHARTS

Since the beginning of human history, people have looked up at the stars. It is only comparatively recently that electric light has blocked out the night sky for many urban dwellers, and in much of the modern world light pollution has closed off the wonderful sight of the true night sky.

Observed from the earliest times, the night sky inevitably became a fitting subject for what are known as "celestial" maps. Such maps, of varying degrees of sophistication, have been found carved on, or made from, rocks in Europe, Africa, and the New World.

Early celestial maps took two main forms: those drawn on stone, skin, or bark, and those made to interact actively with the movement of the sun and stars—the best-known example of which is the Stonehenge stone circle in southern England. Here, no less than 12 major alignments of sun- and moonrise are marked out by the relative positions of the stones. At sunrise on the summer solstice, the sun passes through a carved hole in one of the stones and light floods along the central avenue. Stonehenge is a celestial clock but it is also a map in the sense that it stands as a guide to the lives and customs of the people who used it.

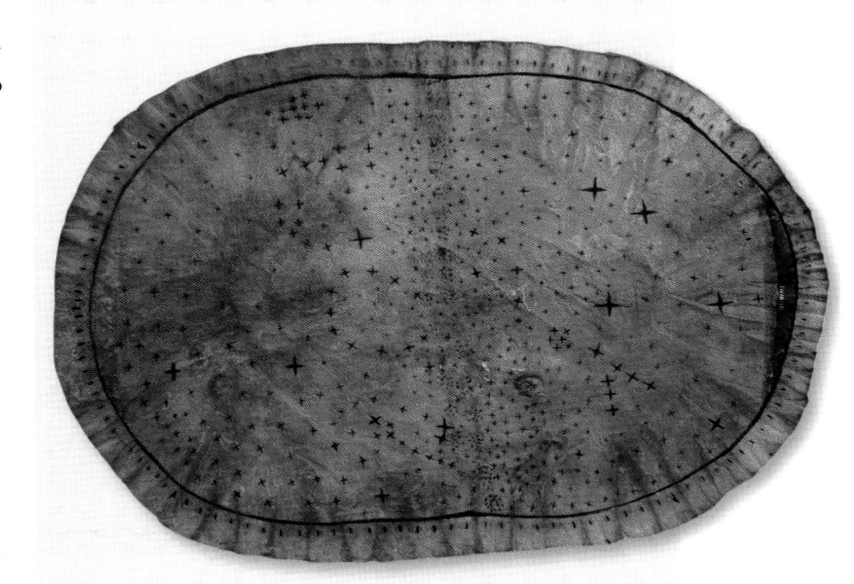

ABOVE ***Pawnee star chart, c.17th-19th century***
This celestial chart, on elkskin, was made by the Pawnee Indians of the Nebraska great plains. The oval represents the horizon, the Milky Way is delineated down through the center, the summer sky is shown on the left and the winter sky on the right.

Early Rock Maps in Africa

The earliest examples of cartography in Africa are rock "maps." The earliest rock art was created by hunter-gatherer peoples around 40,000 years ago, and represents a milestone in social evolution. Although human beings (*Homo sapiens*) are believed to have first appeared in central southern Africa around 100,00–130,000 years ago, their behavior was still premodern—that is, they left no evidence of art, they buried their dead simply, made a limited range of tools, hunted for small, docile mammals such as antelope, lived in caves, and had limited technological development. Then we reach the milestone: around 40,000 years ago, beginning in Africa, humans began to demonstrate distinctly modern trends. Early forms of art appeared, along with more elaborate burial rituals, and a variety of new tools such as sophisticated digging sticks and knives. Larger animals were hunted and the first examples of constructed settlements (huts rather than caves) began to appear. There are competing explanations of this crucial evolution of human behavior. Some argue that it was the result of a slow process of technological improvement, while others say that it was the result of a genetic mutation that led to an improvement in the organizational capacity of the brain. One thing, however, is not in doubt: modern behavior began with the *Homo sapiens* of Africa, and rock art is one of their first important achievements.

The early rock art of the African hunter-gatherers is figurative, consisting of pictures of people and animals, and an overwhelmingly common theme is the hunt. Hunts, we learn from the rock art, were collective endeavors. We can regard the rock art of prehistoric Africa as "records" of actual events, and as symbolic "diagrams" drawn to celebrate the hunt and promote continued success. Whether these depictions constitute mapping is open to question.

Around ten thousand years ago a shift occurred from hunting and gathering to agricultural-based societies (see page 38). The importance of the hunt gave way to that of the settled home, the seeded earth, and the domesticated animal. The new cosmologies were embodied in rock art. While the hunter-gatherers depicted animals and bands of hunters, the agriculturalists engraved houses and cattle.

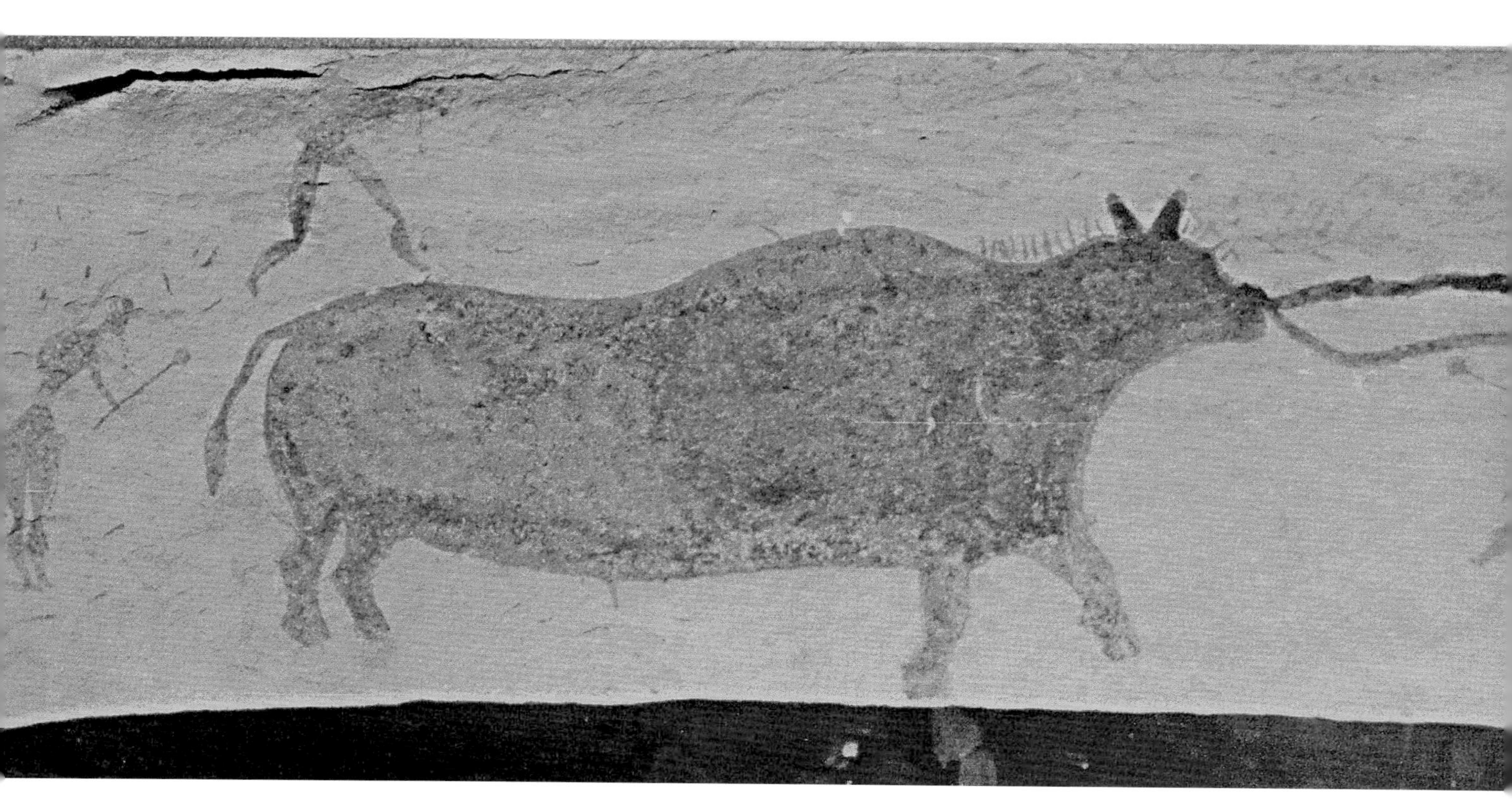

There are some good examples of agricultural rock art in West Africa. For example, symbols painted in caves in Mali have been interpreted as cosmological maps showing the cardinal directions. These directions are mirrored in the layout of villages and individual dwellings of the Dogon people. However, most of the rock art of agricultural societies in Africa is restricted to a relatively small region in the eastern half of South Africa, close to grassland vegetation. Rock maps can be found in areas characterized by stone structures that were first built around 1,000 years ago (rock was used simply because of the lack of trees in this region). From around 500 years ago, the rock art of this area depicts cattle, homesteads, pathways, and settlements shown in a plan view. Engravers, believed by some archeologists to have been young males, also used the natural indentations in the rock to represent topography.

RIGHT ***Kwazulu-Natal rock engraving***
Cattle formed an important element in the life of the early hunter-farmers. This rock engraving depicts cattle pens.

BELOW ***Portion of bamboo mountain panel rock art, Natal***
This engraving depicts the hunt. The hunters' camp is shown on the right.

Interpreting Rock Art Maps Around the World

Rock maps have been discovered wherever rock art has been identified. Here we will look at some examples from North and South America, the Arctic, and Australia.

Numerous maps carved in rock have been found in South America. Although subject to the problems of interpretation there is good evidence that petroglyphs (symbols carved in rock) found in the Andean part of Peru and in Argentina are maps of villages, mountains, streams, and agricultural landholdings. The maps (if this is what they are) contain complex systems of representation with plan views of river drainage and bird's-eye views of human and cultural elements, such as people and settlements. Some petroglyphs in Argentina may represent maps, calendars, and solar charts on the same stone, and tell of a culture familiar with both the terrestrial and the celestial realms.

At least 1,000 years ago, cultures began to flourish in the region of the Nazca plain of South America. The so-called "Nazca lines," located near the modern town of Nazca on the south coast of Peru, were created by people who removed weathered rocks to reveal the lighter deposits underneath. The resultant lines stretch for miles and cover about 200 square miles (518 sq km), in places showing straight lines emanating from a central point. These lines on the desiccated plains of Nazca have been interpreted as maps, but are they? Could they in fact be plans of irrigation systems? Or offerings to the sky and mountain gods that controlled precious water in the coastal desert? The room for speculation is immense, which makes the interpretation of these lines all the more intriguing.

A variety of rock maps have been identified in North America. The different types include maps as designs, hunting trails, plans of dwellings, and astronomical charts. One of the earliest rock map sites in North America is a series of designs carved on a large basalt rock surface in Idaho. It was called "Map Rock" by the early white settlers because the design looked rather like a map. Some interpretations suggest that it is a large-scale map of an extensive area of the Snake River Valley. The main motif is a long, snakelike line that may represent the course of the Snake River. The lines off this main river are its tributaries. The round figures represent peaks and mountains. The

RIGHT *Nazca Lines, date unknown.*
A typical Nazca figure in the landscape, this geometric figure also conjures up the image of a bird. The Nazca lines could have been drawn as early a 200 B.C.E. or as late as 1000 C.E.

BELOW *Map Rock, Idaho*
Map Rock is situated on the north side of the Snake River in Idaho, USA. For hundreds of years indigenous people carved maps on the surface of the basalt rock. This rock map plots the course of the Snake River.

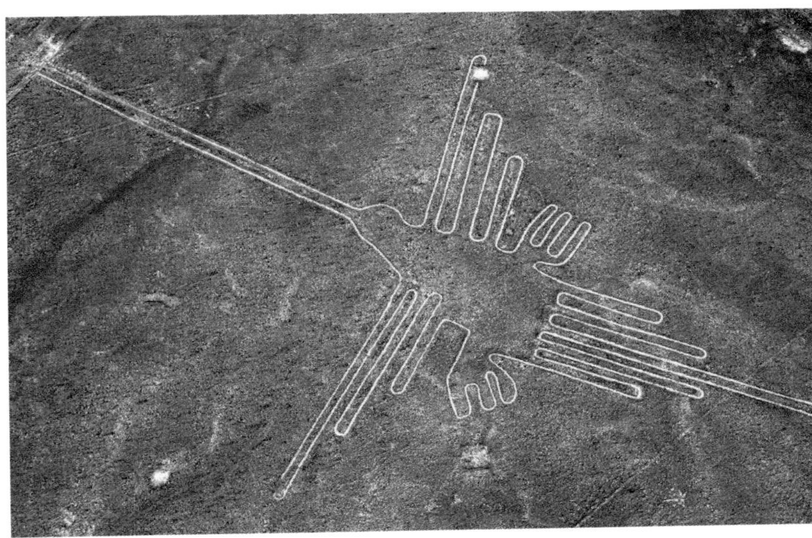

geographer G. Malcolm Lewis has redrawn the map to pick out significant features and compared it with a topographical map of the area. The results are convincing. Map Rock seems to have been correctly named. It is in all probability a map of an entire river basin covering almost 32,000 square miles (82,880 sq km).

The tradition of rock maps has lasted for thousands of years, and some examples are relatively recent. For example, a petroglyph in Pinyon Canyon, Colorado, shows animals being herded by stick-like people with outstretched arms. Dating of the site suggests that it is not more than 500 years old. However, this dating measures the most recent activity, which may be the end of a long unbroken line of ritual that stretches much farther back in time.

The most likely prehistoric rock maps found in the Arctic and subarctic Eurasia refer to hunting. People and animals are shown in profile against a plan view. Petroglyphs in the Karelia region of Russia have been dated as being between 3,000 and 5,000 years old. They show the path of an elk and hunters on skis.

Rock art is common in Australia, where the Aboriginal people have been living for between 45,000 and 60,000 years. Motifs and designs can be found incised and painted on rock walls, surfaces, and boulders. Some of the oldest examples of rock art on the continent are the Panaramitee-style engravings discovered at Yunta, in South Australia. They depict circular designs and the tracks of birds and animals. As maps, these engravings have a deep spiritual meaning. They relate to the Aboriginal creation myth of the Dreamtime (see page 34) and are also a partial representation of the surrounding landscape. Hence, these maps have to be read as religious as well as cartographic texts.

The Maps of Hunter-Gatherers

Some of the oldest maps were produced by hunter-gatherer societies around 40,000 years ago. There was a practical purpose to these maps. The location of succulent berries, the routes of migratory animals, and the best places to hunt animals rich in protein were all important sources of spatial knowledge, and were passed down by word of mouth as well as being recorded in various forms, including maps. Again, there was a link with spiritual beliefs. To note places rich in resources was also an attempt to secure their continued existence and benefit. In a pantheistic world, where gods inhabit every grove, rock, river, and plain, depicting places and animals was an act of supplication as well as of practical value.

A more modern link with the maps created by the oldest hunter-gatherer peoples can be found in Siberia. The hunting cultures of this region had a sophisticated ability to both make and read maps. Scientists and ethnographers of the 18th, 19th, and 20th centuries were surprised at the ability of the local peoples to outline the shape of their country on paper when requested, and also to interpret Russian maps. Their cartographic ability was based on a need to move around the vast region of Siberia. Traditional maps from this area took a number of forms: the local people would draw ephemeral maps in the snow to arrange meetings, and more permanent maps were also inscribed and painted on wood and bark.

The Chukchi are a people who live in the far northeast of Russia, which borders on the Arctic Ocean. They made maps on wooden boards, drawn with deer or reindeer blood. There are written reports of explorers as early as 1705 noting the existence of these mapboards. The Chukchi mapboards are now in a museum in St. Petersburg, Russia, and were probably created in the 19th century. There are nine boards, which together form a detailed map of a river course. The complete map is 14 feet long (4.25m), representing a substantial piece of cartography. The boards show the course of the river in some detail as well as depicting life along the river. Vegetation, animals, and hunters' cabins are also shown. Rivers were the original "highways" of this inhospitable land, allowing people to travel over great distances, as well as being a source of food. The Chukchi map may even have had trade value as local peoples realized that this spatial information was valued by other peoples, especially the foreign explorers and Russian administrators.

Maps and cartographic motifs figure in the everyday material culture of hunter-gatherer societies. They appear on paddles, canoe seats, clothes, wooden plates, trees, and on the body. The cartographic richness is a function of the material and symbolic importance of spatial information in hunter-gatherer societies. To stay alive and in tune with the material and the spiritual worlds, you had to "know your place," and these ancient maps performed a key role in achieving this.

LEFT ***Chukchi sealskin map, 19th century***
This map was drawn on a piece of bleached sealskin. It was traded to US whalers by the Chukchi people in the 1860s or 1870s. It shows rivers, ships, hunting scenes, and pictures of everyday Chukchi life.

The Chukchi people also drew their maps on skins. A large sealskin pictographic map was obtained by the crew of an American whaleboat in the late 19th century, and is now on display in the Pitt Rivers Museum in Oxford, England. It depicts different animals including whales, deer, and bears along with hunting scenes, shamans (witch doctors), and villages. It shows not only the indigenous peoples but also Russians, Europeans, and Americans. Various geographic locations have been read off from the shoreline around the edge of the sealskin, including St. Lawrence Bay. The map may represent a calendar of events covering a year, although it has also been suggested that it was made specifically to trade with foreign sailors in return for money and goods. Look again at the map. Is it just a map? Or is it a calendar, or a commodity? We will never be certain, but of one thing there is no doubt: it shows indigenous people and outsiders sharing the same space. In this sense it also records the beginning of the end for traditional ways and the ancient cultures of indigenous peoples.

ABOVE ***Chukchi sealskin map (detail)***
A closer look at the Chukchi sealskin map shows a shared space of exchange. Foreign ships are shown beside indigenous canoes; note that there are pairs of people trading goods. The Chukchi people were trading with the people of the outside world and this map is a record of this economic and cultural exchange, as well as being traded goods itself.

Indigenous Cartographies

Remnants of old forms of mapmaking abound in museums and libraries. But there are also living examples of indigenous cartography. For example, Hugh Brody, in his book *Maps and Dreams* (see bibliography), shows the spatial knowledge of the Beaver people of northwest British Columbia. They mapped their land use and travels in the fall and winter of 1978–9. Their spatial knowledge was mapped onto standard 1:250,000 topographic maps to give a juxtaposition of alternative mappings of the world—new and old, premodern and modern cartographic sensibilities on the same page.

However, we should be wary of looking for, or indeed finding, "pure" indigenous maps in the contemporary world. The level of contact between indigenous people and outsiders has created a rich mix of old and new, indigenous and non-indigenous in hybrid forms. Today's world is one of hybridity rather than purity. In this section we will look at Aboriginal Australian cartography as an example of contemporary indigenous mapping with the proviso that the term "indigenous" needs to be read as a qualified and potentially misleading term, to remind us of the hybrid nature of contemporary cultural forms.

ABOVE **Honey Ant Dreaming** *by Old Mick Walankari Tjakamarra, 1973*
The Aboriginal artist has primary spiritual responsibility for the area of territory depicted on the map. The painting of the area is a way to maintain this spiritual connection.

The term "Aboriginal" is a generic one; in reality there are many different kinship groups living in different parts of Australia. While there are examples of maps and mapmaking from the precolonial period in the late 18th century there is also a rich contemporary tradition. Two main forms can be identified. The first is the bark painting of the tropical northeastern and northern parts of Australia, and the second is the so-called "dot painting" maps of the interior, especially the area in central Australia around the town of Alice Springs in the Northern Territory. Both forms share a common pattern.

Australian Aboriginal maps are part of a broader system of meaning that ties group identity to particular places and times. There is no sharp division between then and now, the past and the present. The Aboriginal "Dreamtime" was the time when the world was created by mythic figures. Individual parts of the landscape, such as a water hole or a rock outcrop, are associated with particular Dreamtime stories that tell how the world was made by the giant wallaby, the serpent, or the caterpillars and birds. The spiritual ancestors of the Aborigines tried to give order and form to the universe in the original Dreamtime. The intense sense of place that characterizes the Dreaming means that its art is topographical, cartographic. Individual Aborigines keep these stories alive, through song, dance, and paintings.

Different types of bark paintings can be identified, from the wholly abstract to the much more figurative. While some of them refer to general cosmologies of the universe, many of them contain reference to particular places. In that sense they are maps, but they are maps with a particular purpose: they do not simply say where things are, but celebrate their deeper meaning. Sometimes only part of this meaning is ever revealed.

Sand paintings of the central Australian desert were

ABOVE *Aboriginal map mosaic, 1988, by Michael Jagamara Nelson*
Nelson is an Aboriginal artist. His mosaic is set in the middle of an "island" to represent the island continent of Australia.

INDIGENOUS MAPS AND CONTEMPORARY LAND CLAIMS IN AUSTRALIA

Britain colonized Australia from 1788. Land was a central issue in the contact between the two cultures. The British declared *terra nullis*—that the land was empty—and no land treaties were signed with indigenous peoples. Their land was simply taken away from them. It was only in 1976 that Aboriginal land claims began to be recognized by the federal government. Under new legislation Ayers Rock was renamed Uluru and returned to the indigenous Anangu people. In 1992 the Australian High Court ruled that so-called "native title" did exist. The land was not *terra nullis*. Since then land claims have been an important and politically charged theme in Australian politics at both state and federal level.

"Maps" in the form of bark paintings and sand dot paintings have been a central part of the land claims and have been used in numerous legal cases to "prove" that certain communities own the land. Since there is no legal documentation, "proof of spiritual responsibility," one of the terms and criteria of the legislation, was derived from these maps. Communities petitioned the federal parliament and the courts with indigenous maps. Maps produced as part of a deeper spiritual exercise as well as in the context of a growing commercialization were also called upon to bolster land claims.

originally just that: figures and patterns drawn in the sand. However, since the 1970s, at the prompting of non-Aborigines, they have been reworked as oil paintings on canvas. The patterns again range from the abstract to the more figurative, but most often the land is represented as a plan view with circles indicating camps and water holes, and half-circles representing meeting places. These are maps in that they signify specific places, but they also tell the story of Dreamtime sites. They contain many levels of meaning. At one level they are esthetic patternings. At another level, once the key is revealed, they become maps. At deeper levels they tell a secret story known only to initiates and often only to the mapmakers themselves.

In recent years Aboriginal esthetics have become an important part of the Australian national identity. A sand painting motif now stands at the entrance of Parliament House in Canberra, a modern reminder of the continuing presence of Aborigines and their commitment to the land. However, we should be wary of seeing bark painting and sand painting maps as part of an ancient, unbroken tradition. They are in fact "invented" traditions: many of the tools used are modern, and there is a self-conscious marketing and promotion of the "Aboriginality" of such art. Most works are made for a non-Aboriginal audience. They have become commodities rather than religious artefacts.

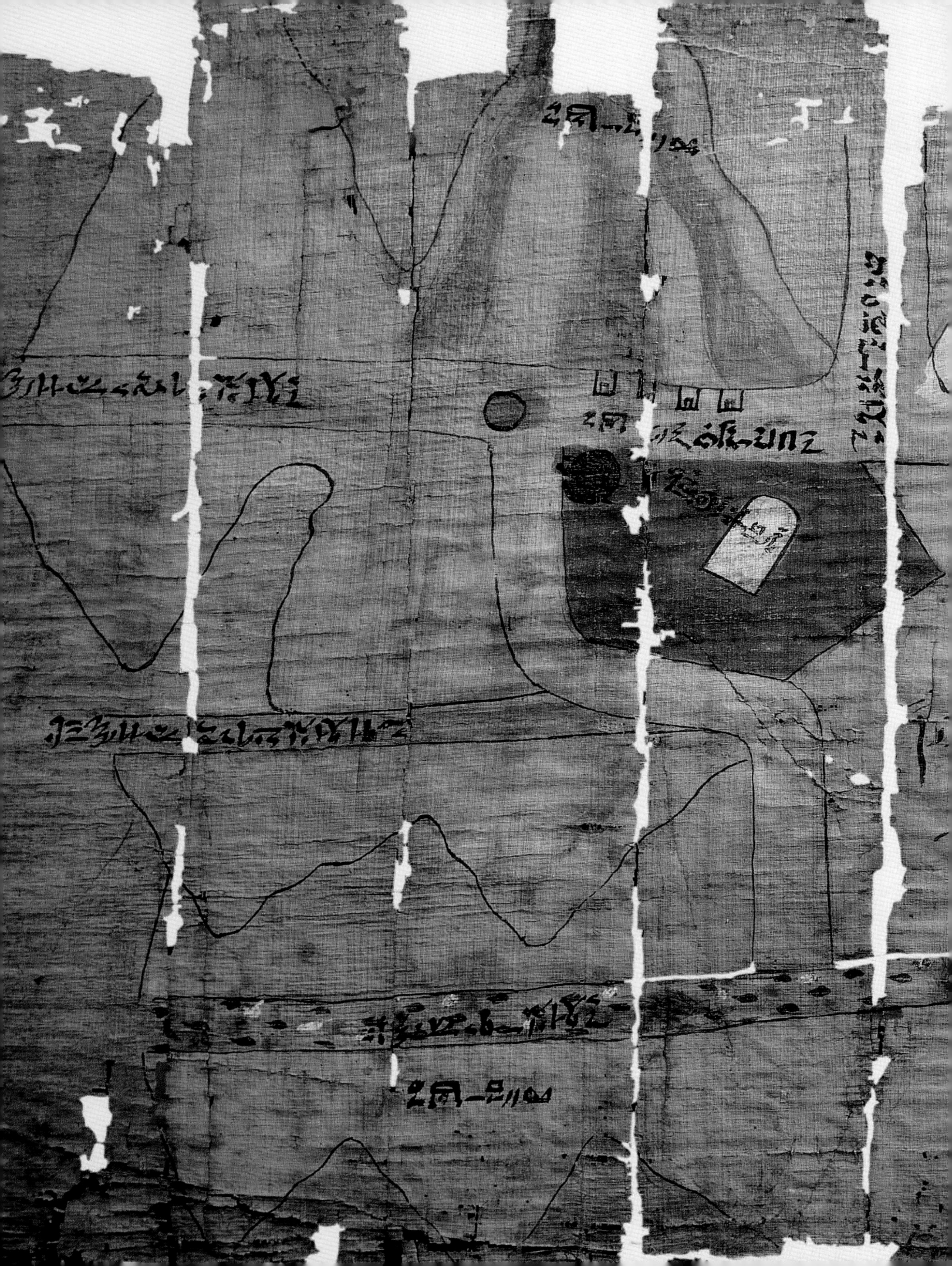

PART II

The Ancient World

LEFT *Papyrus map of the Red Sea hills of Egypt, showing roads and gold mines, c.1250 B.C.E.*

3

MAPS IN THE ANCIENT WORLD

Maps and the Rise of Agriculture

The agricultural revolution grew out of centralized authority and concentrated power. Maps and mapping were important tools in the management of agricultural lands and irrigation systems. Mapping the land was a way to control the land.

THE SHIFT FROM a hunting-gathering mode of production to one of settled agriculture occurred independently in Africa, Asia, Europe, and the Americas. In each case the shift was marked by the rise of a cartographic tradition that focused on field systems more than hunting trails, and on property relations more than animal habitats. Mapping was dominated by landholdings, land management, and urban centers.

The rise of cities used to be explained as being the result of agricultural surplus. Until recently it was believed that people developed crops so that more of them could be supported, giving rise to permanent settlements, towns, and eventually cities. According to the theory, this led to more complex and more organized societies; the continued cultivation of crops enabled sufficient food to be produced to allow some people to be released from food production and become scribes, priests, and administrators. In recent years this theory has been turned on its head. Agricultural surplus, it is now argued, did not create cities. Rather, centralized control systems forced people to generate an agricultural surplus.

The relationship between settled agriculture and centralized, hierarchical societies can be found in Egypt, China, the Indus Valley, the Central Andes, Mesoamerica, and southwest Nigeria. One of the oldest sites is in Mesopotamia, between the Tigris and Euphrates rivers, where between 5,000 and 6,000 years ago urban-based societies grew up beside an organized system of irrigated agriculture. The societies of ancient Mesopotamia underwent a concentration of power and organized knowledge and witnessed developments in writing, literature, and science. Mapmaking was part of this intellectual revolution.

Mesopotamian maps etched in clay have been found that are estimated to be around 3,500 years old. While some are maps of the world (as it was known at that time), the vast majority are large-scale maps of small areas, drawn as plans. The map of the fields from the city of Nippur, the Sumerian capital just south of Babylon, is typical. Made around 3,500 years ago, it records the estates of the political and religious élites alongside the curve of the river. Irrigation channels separate the different estates. This map embodies the centrality of land, irrigation, and power in Mesopotamian mappings.

Agricultural productivity was boosted by centralized water management schemes that in turn reinforced central political control. Field patterns, landholdings, and irrigation systems were key elements of Mesopotamian society and thus the subject of most of the maps. The Nippur map also contains some of the earliest writing, and indeed the culture of Mesopotamia is credited with the invention of the written form. Maps had now become part of a wider textual description of the world, with words and symbols joining together in the same document, perhaps for the first time.

Small-scale maps of larger areas were also produced in Mesopotamia. The town of Sippar, located just north of Babylon on the banks of the Euphrates, is depicted on a 2,500-year-old clay tablet. The town is shown as a rectangle beside the river and irrigation channels. The basis of Mesopotamian society was the fertile fields produced by irrigation. Hence, as the source of life the irrigation channels were a prime area of cartographic concern.

RIGHT ***Mesopotamian clay map of Sippar, c.500 B.C.E.***
This clay tablet map marks out the town of Sippar as the rectangular figure at the top of the tablet. The intricate canal system is shown coursing its way over the landscape. These canals allowed large agricultural yields.

While the scribes of Mesopotamia etched on clay, the scribes of ancient Egypt made maps in different forms: as motifs on pottery, and on papyrus, which was a form of paper made from an aquatic reedlike plant, Cyperus papyrus, cultivated in the Nile Delta. Papyrus maps of gold mines, canals, and temples have all been discovered; the survival of such fragile material is remarkable in itself. In both Mesopotamia and ancient Egypt, maps shared a concern with land, irrigation, city plans, and land ownership. In both societies, as in the other centrally organized agricultural systems of the ancient world, maps recorded important information relating to the land. For example, it was vital to know who owned what land for tax purposes, to ascertain ownership rights, and demarcate boundaries.

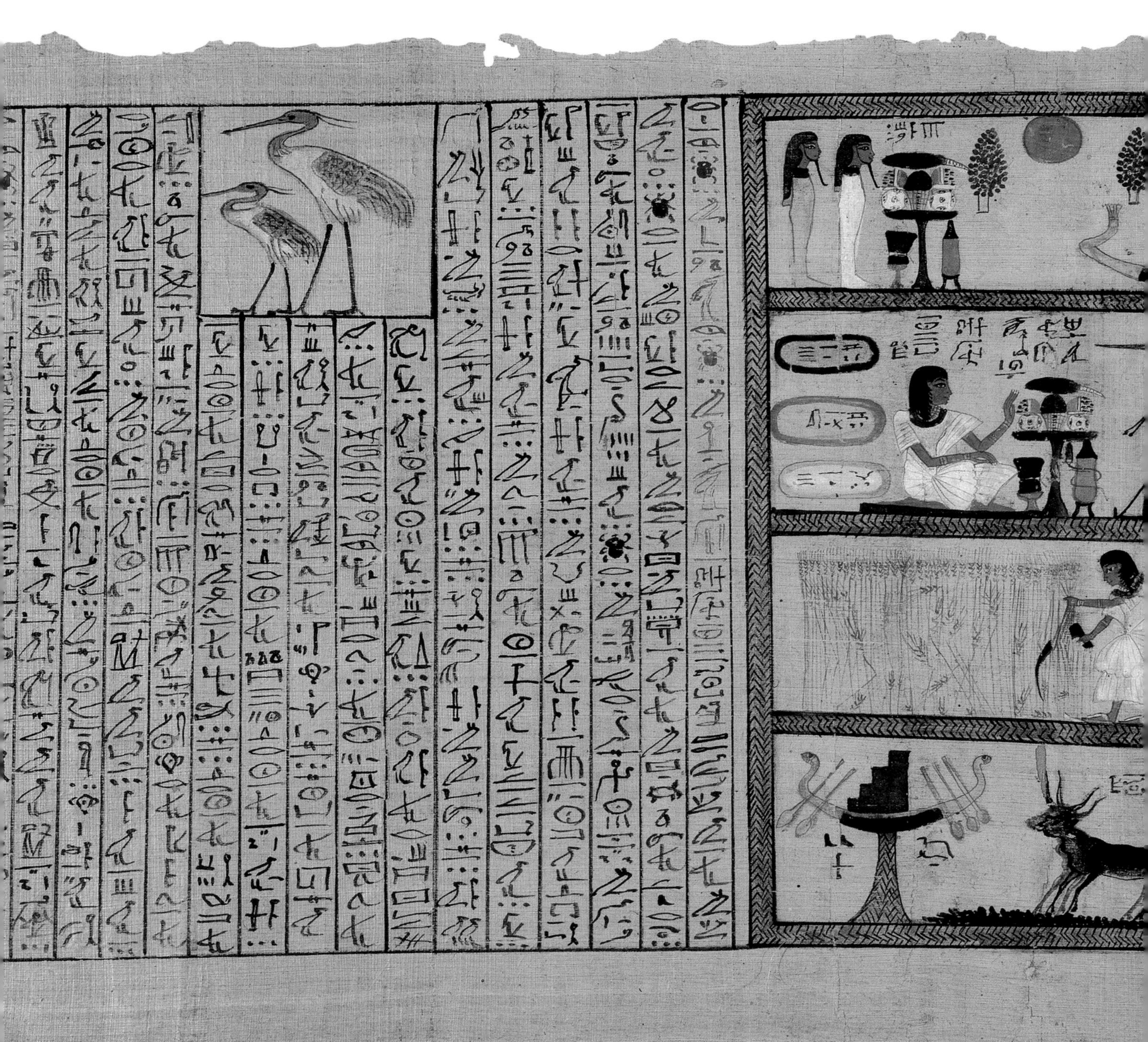

In all the great agricultural centers of the ancient world, sophisticated mapping emerged at the same time as forms of writing and mathematics. The organized power associated with these hierarchical societies enabled the development of systems of technical knowledge and information recording. The collection of data became an essential part of maintaining social control and political power.

CLAY TABLET MAPS OF MESOPOTAMIA

The maps of Mesopotamia were part of a more general type of communication in the form of water-cleaned clay tablets. The oldest surviving examples of writing are on these tablets. The majority of them were thin tiles only about 5 inches (13 cm) in length. While the clay was still moist, a scribe would mark small characters and figures on to it using a stylus. Longer texts would consist of a number of tablets. The clay was then hardened by being left in the sun or baked in an oven, leaving a permanent record. Full-time scribes were able to record a great deal of information, and the tablets were used for government records as well as recording commercial transactions, land ownership deeds, and maps.

The script on the tablets is called "cuneiform." It marks a shift from the previous pictorial methods of representation to an alphabetic system and is one of the greatest of human achievements. The use of clay tablets as a writing material persisted for almost 2,000 years.

ABOVE ***The Gasur map, c.2300 B.C.E.***
This clay tablet map was discovered near the city of Kirkuk in present-day Iraq, in 1930–31. It is one of the oldest extant maps in the world.

LEFT ***Ancient Egyptian papyrus map of the afterlife***
The ancient Egyptians made a variety of maps. This depiction of an ideal landscape in the mythical afterlife of Osiris, draws upon contemporary agricultural practices; it is a kind of map for the dead that is actually a record of the living. It is a record of the good life in the afterlife.

Maps and the Development of Urban Civilization

Prehistory becomes history with the rise of urban civilizations, beginning first in Mesopotamia around 6,000 years ago. The rise of cities is associated with the development of highly centralized political power, marked social hierarchies, and improved forms of technical knowledge—including astronomical observations, formal mathematics, writing, and cartographic sophistication. In the kingdoms of ancient Egypt, China, Nigeria, and South America, new forms of agricultural production and urban development went hand in hand.

Cities were important in these ancient societies. They were the center of social control and housed the political élite and the religious functionaries. The cities contained the palaces and the temples. They were the centers of religious worship, the point of contact between the sacred and the profane. The bond between the people and their leaders and gods was cemented in the urban landscape of giant temples and sumptuous palaces, and in the regular rituals of worship.

Babylon is one of the most famous cities in antiquity. It was the capital of Mesopotamia from around 1,000 B.C.E. to the time of Christ. According to the Greek historian Herodotus (*c.* 484–*c.* 425 B.C.E.) it was the most splendid city in the world. Around 2,500 years ago, under King Nebuchadnezzar, the city became the center of a great empire. It was the largest city in the world, covering around 2,500 acres (10 sq km). It housed temples, ziggurats (brick-built temple towers), and palaces. The Tower of Babel and the famous Hanging Gardens of Babylon were also built in the city. A small clay tablet map, a fragment of a larger map of the city, shows the temple of Marduk and the processional path that wound past the Ishtar Gate to a small temple outside the city.

One of the earliest city plan maps was made around 3,500 years ago. The plan of the city of Nippur (as mentioned on page 38) is arguably one of the earliest city plans to be drawn to scale. The map shows the temple of Enlil on the right-hand side in a square enclosure. Like all Mesopotamian maps the canals are clearly shown.

Some city maps tell stories of time as well as space. One example of a terrestrial map that is also a cartographical history is the map of the city of Tenochtitlán, painted in about the year 1541. It depicts the establishment of the city. Around the border the symbols represent different years. The beginning year, the symbol in the upper-left, represents a picture of a house to signify the establishment of the city 216 years earlier. The cross in the middle of the map represents the four canals of the city surrounded by depictions of its founders. Hence, the complex iconography maps a place and tells a story.

ABOVE ***Mesopotamian clay tablet map (city fragment)***
This plan map of Babylon that has survived the ravages of time shows in geometric precision the temple of Marduk and processional roads.

RIGHT ***Map of Tenochtitlán, Codex Mendoza, c.1541***
This complex map tells the history as well as the geography of the city. The large blue cross signifies the four canals that divided the city into socially distinct areas.

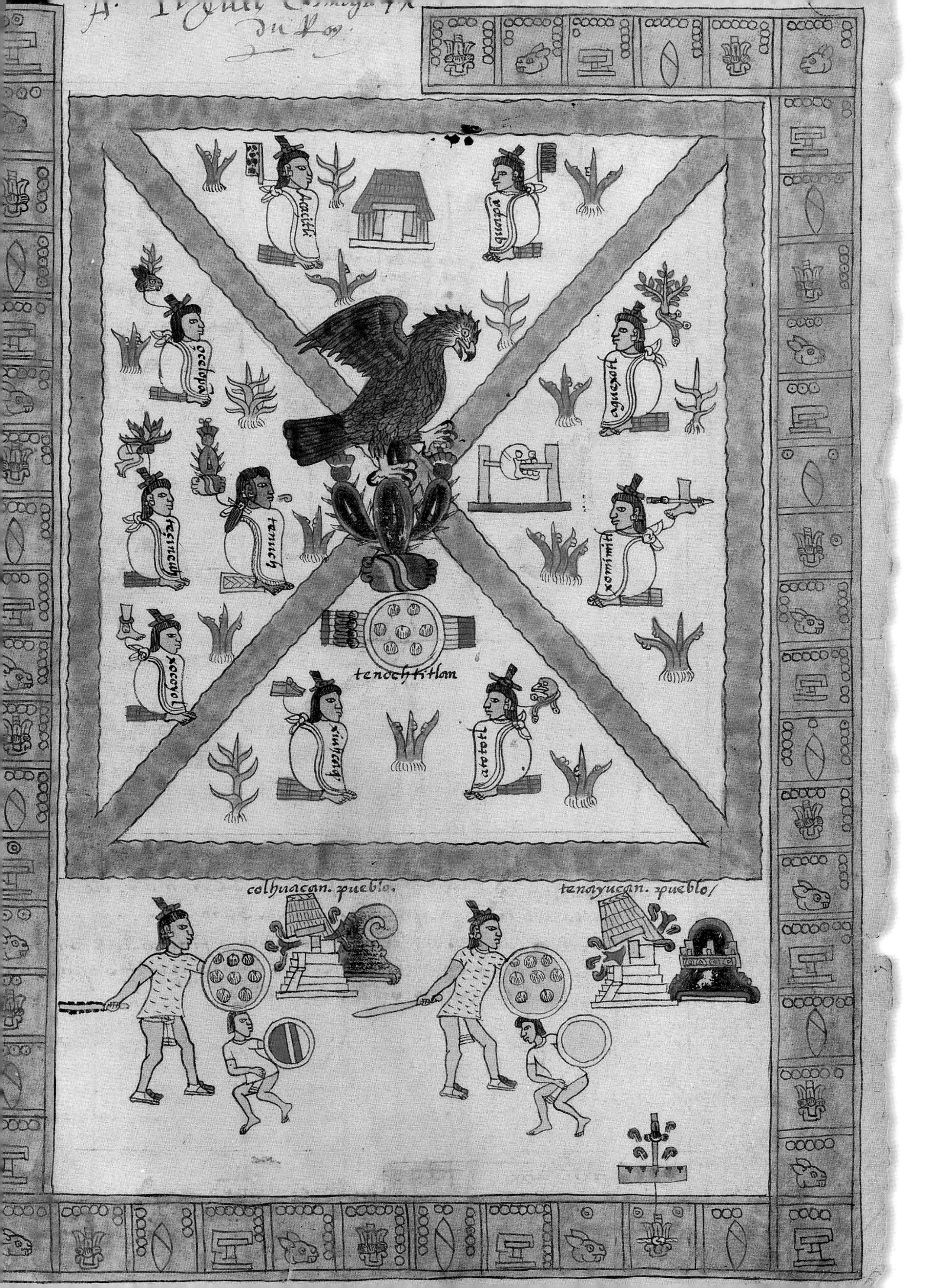
tenochtitlan
colhuacan. pueblo.
tenayucan. pueblo.

Maps of South Asia

While the cultures of South Asia are very old, most existing maps are relatively recent, few dating from more than 800 years ago. However, since some are part of a much longer historical tradition we can make some "back projections" in time from relatively recent examples.

There are a variety of pre-European maps in South Asia. One of the largest categories consists of cosmological maps that depict the universe in a symbolic, cartographic form. Cosmologies are the order given to our understanding of both the practicalities and the mysteries of life. They are particularly apparent in the Jain religious tradition. Founded over 2,500 years ago, its central preoccupation is the prevention of injury to all living things. Jainism, like Buddhism and Hinduism, aims at the perfection of the soul and karmic evolution. It preaches universal tolerance and is noncritical of other religions. The Jain cosmological text shows a central continent surrounded by successive rings of ocean and mountains. Produced in the 15th century, it is less a map of the cosmos, more a meditation on the world.

There was a concern in South Asian civilizations with geographical as well as cosmological knowledge. Geography is richly detailed in the great Hindu literary classics. The world's longest poem, the *Mahabharata*, was composed over a period of some 1,000 years, beginning around 2,500 years ago. It contains rich geographic detail, including descriptions of pilgrimages and rivers, which have a special significance for Hindus. However, despite such obvious concerns with geography, there is much less evidence of actual mapmaking in ancient South Asian civilizations. South Asian map expert Joseph Schwartzberg suggests that the paucity of maps is mainly due to the hot, humid environment of the region. Mildew, damp, termites, and ants all take their toll on fragile maps. Other reasons cited include the active destruction of maps by the early Muslim invaders of northern India. Schwartzberg also suggests a deep lack of interest in terrestrial mapping among South Asian peoples. Cosmologies were more important than either histories or geographies to the cultured élite.

Nevertheless, there are some examples of geographical as well as cosmological mapping from the region. Consider two examples of both large-scale and small-scale maps. The Marathi world map is a geographical and a cosmological map. The circle at the top is the cosmography, being a conception of the world shared with the Hindu, Jain, and Buddhist traditions. The circle encompasses the universe, the continents are set in seas, and the world is centered on Mount Meru. Below the cosmographical circle the map depicts India, orientated with north at the top. The rope-like lines at the top of the geographical map are the Himalayan mountain ranges, the Arabian Sea is shown as an oblong of water running north to south on the left-hand side; the other symbols represent rivers and hills in the subcontinent. At the bottom, the Indian Ocean is shown.

Jainism has a long practice of drawing cosmographical charts. A 15th-century example, now in the Victoria and Albert Museum in London, UK, shows a three-continent world centered on Mount Meru, sacred for Jains and Hindus. The chart is highly symmetrical. A central circular continent is surrounded by two other continents shown as

LEFT ***Mughal map of Srinagar, Kashmir, late 19th century***
This wool embroidered map provides a vivid picture of the city. It is full of life and energy, and shows rivers and lakes teeming with water craft.

RIGHT ***Jain cosmographical chart of the world, 15th century***
This Jain cosmographical chart of the world combines more religious imagery than actual geography. The circle is a recurring image in Jain charts.

concentric circles separated by oceans. The symmetry is less about geography and more about the Jain sense of order. This map contains both very ancient and relatively recent knowledge: the cosmographical circle derives from similar figures produced over 1,500 years ago, while the depiction of the Himalayas probably draws upon knowledge gained from Europeans. While the map compresses space and the geography is more abstract than topographical, the juxtaposition of older cosmography and newer forms of geographical representation suggests a type of mapping poised between old and new forms of spatial representation.

South Asia has a rich tradition of religious diversity. In northern India, there was also a strong Islamic presence, especially from the time of the Mughal Empire (16th–18th centuries). Mughal art was much more figurative and secular than that of other Islamic societies, and this is evident in its mappings. The Mughal map of Srinagar, in Kashmir, is embroidered in wool on cloth. Exceptionally detailed, it shows rivers and lakes flowing through the city, bridges, and individual houses. It is presented both as a plan view and as a bird's-eye view, which allows the shape of the city to be documented.

4

MAPS OF THE CLASSICAL WORLD

Cartography in Ancient Greece

The ravages of time have left us only a small cartographic legacy from ancient Greece, a civilization that reached its zenith between 600 B.C.E. and 200 B.C.E. Ancient Greece was a society that made and used maps extensively for exploration, conquest, trade, and intellectual curiosity. The Greeks developed many of the theoretical principles that underlie contemporary cartography.

ONE OF THE EARLIEST records of an ancient Greek map dates from the 8th century B.C.E. and appears in Homer's *Iliad* where there is a description of the shield of Achilles on which is a map of the world surrounded by water. Around the cosmos in the center of the shield are depicted a city at war and a city at peace, along with pastoral and farming scenes. Homer is describing a cosmological map showing the earth as an island that is maintained and defined by human activity. The Greeks believed that civilization was intimately linked with the development of the city. Urban social life and settled agriculture were regarded as the basis for human advancement.

Anaximander of Miletus (610–546 B.C.E.) drew one of the earliest maps of the world as then known to the Greeks and constructed a globe. Ancient Greek maps of the world were drawn or carved on wooden panels and bronze tablets. They were circular in design, and centered on the village of Delphi in central Greece. Delphi was important because in antiquity it was the main sanctuary and oracle of Apollo. The oracle's advice about religion, morality, commerce, and colonial projects, spoken by a priestess in a trance, was widely sought.

Beginning around 600 B.C.E. there was an incredible burst of intellectual creativity in ancient Greece. The mathematician Pythagoras (588–*c.* 500 B.C.E.) envisaged the world as a perfect sphere; the astronomer Aristarchus (310–230 B.C.E.) proclaimed that the universe was heliocentric—that its center was the sun—and Eratosthenes (276–194 B.C.E.), a Greek who worked at the Great Library of Alexandria, was one of the first to measure the earth.

Eratosthenes wrote two works: the *Measurement of the Earth* and *Geographica*, in which he respectively outlined a method to measure the circumference of the earth, and how to make a map of the known world. Both works are now lost, but the arguments were repeated by later writers. Eratosthenes' technique of measurement was brilliant. He knew that at the city of Syene on the Tropic of Cancer, the sun was directly overhead at noon on the date of the summer solstice. At the same time he ordered that the angle of the sun be measured in Alexandria, which lay on the same meridian, 500 miles (800 km) away. The angle turned out to be one-fiftieth of a circle. Hence, Eratosthenes assumed that the distance between the two cities was one-fiftieth of the circumference of the earth. Since one-fiftieth equaled 500 miles, the total circumference must, he reasoned, be 50 times 500, which is 25,000 miles (40,000 km). From this measurement Eratosthenes made some upward estimates to arrive at a figure of around 25,200 miles Astonishingly, his calculations were relatively accurate, and only his assumption, based on the theories of Pythagoras, that the world was a perfect sphere, skewed the result. In fact, the shape of the world is of a flattened sphere: around the equator the circumference is about 24,899 miles. From this base measurement, Eratosthenes was able to create a more precise map of the world than had previously been

RIGHT ***Spain and Portugal, 15th century, after Ptolemy***
This richly illustrated manuscript map, illuminated and made on vellum, was a prized possession. The map is more of a rough chart than an accurate map and it reflects the ancient Greeks' sketchy knowledge of a peripheral part of Europe.

ΩΚΕΑΝΟΣ ΚΑΝΤΑΒΡΙΟΣ
ΑΥΤΙΚΟΣ ΩΚΕΑ
ΙΣΠΑΝΙΑ
ΛΥΣΙΤΑΝΙ
ΙΣΠΑΝΙΑ ΒΑΙΤΙΚΗ
ΕΚ ΤΟΣ ΘΑ ΛΑΣ ΣΑ
ΙΒΗΡΙΚΟΝ ΠΕΛΑΓ
ΗΡΑΚΛΕΙ ΠΟΡΘΜΟΣ

THE LEGACY OF EUCLID

ABOVE *Euclid*

The development of a formal mathematics was one of the great achievements of the classical world. The mathematicians of ancient Greece drew upon Babylonian mathematical expertise, but gave a greater clarity and elegance to mathematical propositions that has stood the test of time. There was a connection between mathematics and cartography. The basic mathematics for Ptolemy's work was that of Euclid, as described in his *Elements*. Euclid gave definitions of points, lines, triangles, circles, and other basic shapes. He then outlined ten basic axioms—for example, that it is possible to draw a straight line between any two points. From these deceptively simple building blocks, Euclid constructed what we now understand as "geometry" (which literally means "measuring the earth": geo = earth, metry = measure).

Euclid created an abstract space, a pure world of lines, points, triangles, circles, and spheres. This rational geometry was then mapped on to the physical world.

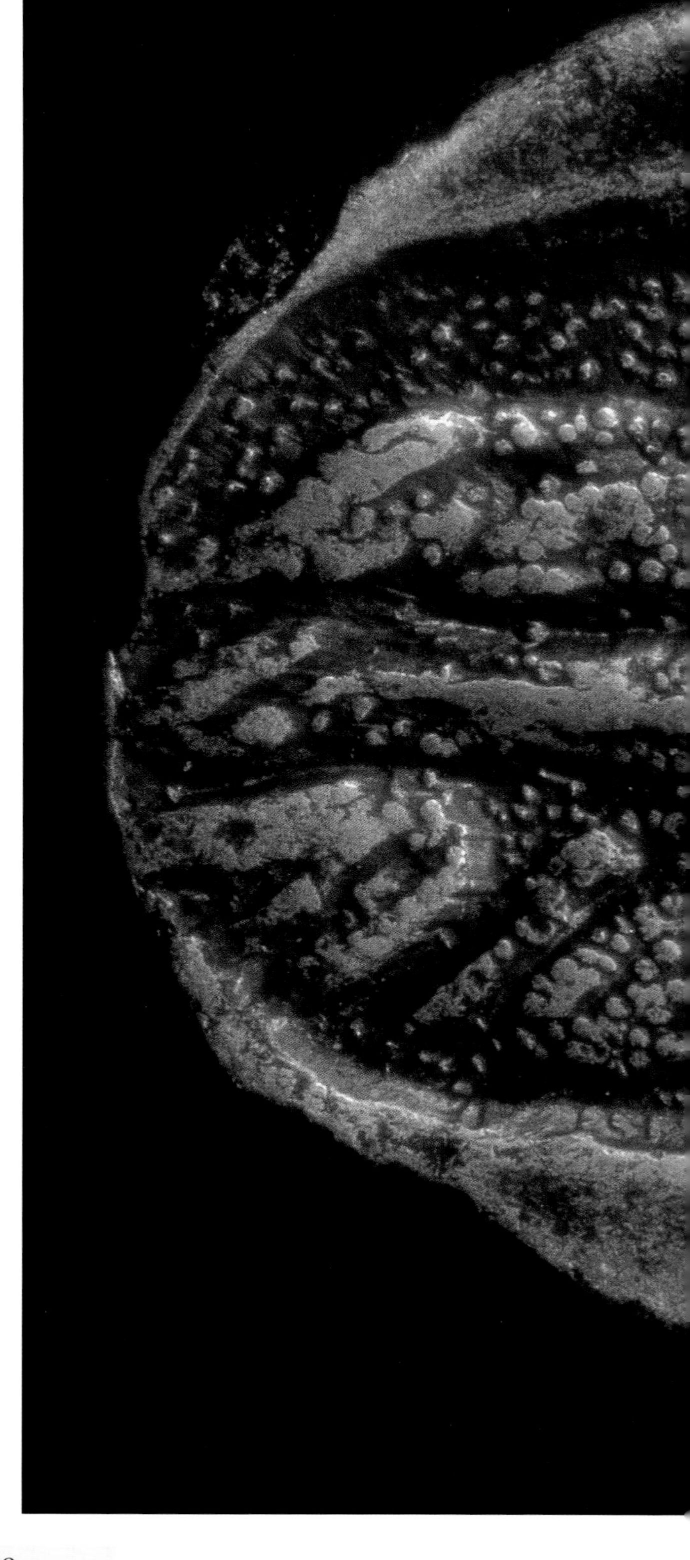

RIGHT *Ionian coin map, c.330 B.C.E.*
This map, on the reverse side of a silver coin, a tetradrachm, shows an area in modern-day Turkey near the city of Ephesus.

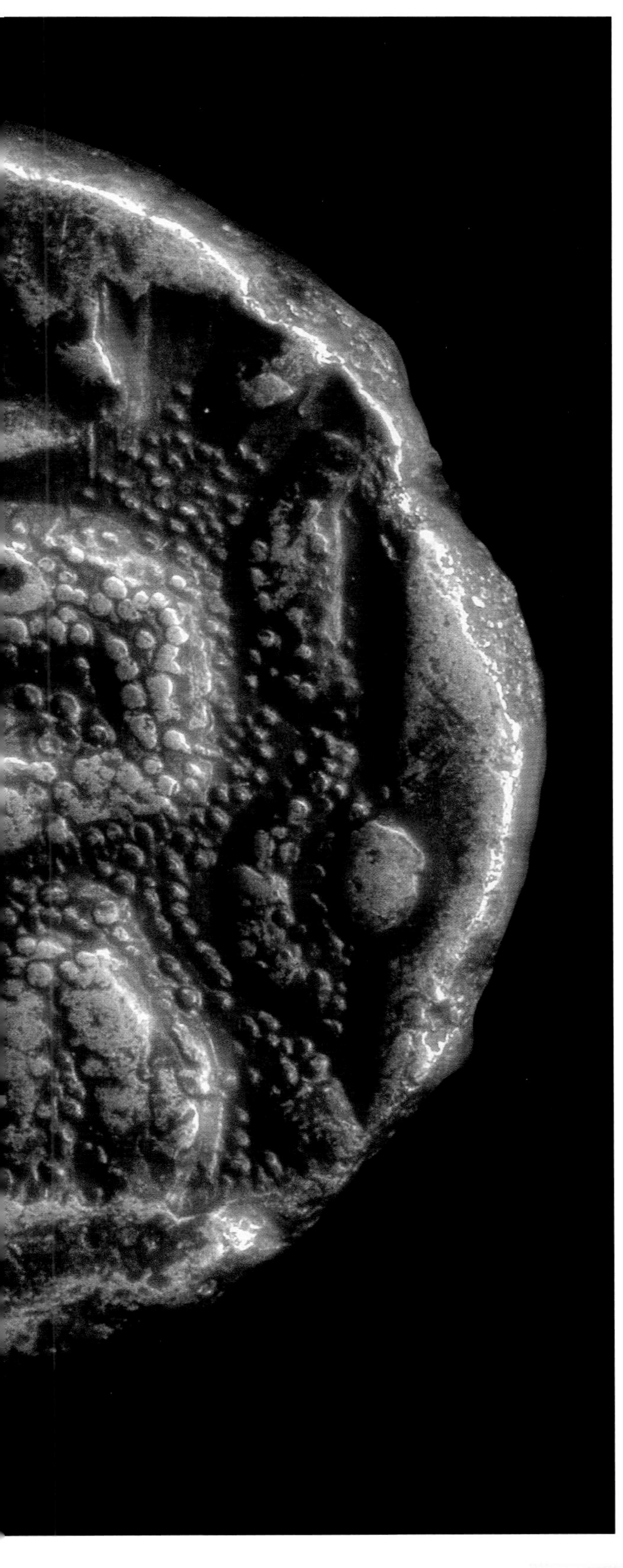

CLASSICAL CIVILIZATIONS

The classical civilizations developed in ancient Greece and Rome between about 500 B.C.E. and 500 C.E. Together these cultures have exerted a profound and enduring influence on the Western world, especially in the areas of language, politics, philosophy, art, drama, and science.

Beginning in the 5th century B.C.E., the city-states of Greece—particularly Athens—enjoyed a period of remarkable intellectual and political development. The Greeks pioneered the democratic system of government, their dramatic performances foreshadowed modern theatre, and their sculpture inspired the artists of the Renaissance 1,500 years later. Through the conquests of the Macedonian king Alexander the Great in the 4th century B.C.E., Greek culture spread throughout much of Asia and the Middle East.

Roman civilization began around 510 B.C.E. As well as building a vast empire, the Romans also had a lasting impact in the fields of engineering, art, and culture. They built a network of roads across Europe, and beautiful cities with temples, theatres, baths, libraries, and aqueducts.

The Roman Empire in the west collapsed in 476 C.E. However, its eastern half continued for another thousand years, and was known as the Byzantine Empire. This Christian empire had its capital at Constantinople, and ruled over Asia Minor, the Balkans, and Greece. It was finally conquered by the Ottoman Turks in 1453.

drawn. He was the first person to locate the inhabited world on a globe with some degree of accuracy.

Cartographic imagery became a common theme in Greek art. Coins have been discovered dating from the third century B.C.E. that show maps of regions of Asia Minor on their surfaces. Globes, both terrestrial and celestial, were used for teaching and decoration. One of the largest known examples was a terrestrial globe measuring some 10 feet (3 m) in diameter, made by Crates of Mallus in around 150 B.C.E. Drawing upon the writings of Homer, Crates identified four inhabitable zones on his globe: two in the northern hemisphere and two in the south. The Greeks inhabited the northern zones, known as the *Oikoumene*, and named one of the southern zones the *Antipodes* (which in Greek literally means "having the feet opposite"). This name is still used today by people living in the northern hemisphere to describe Australasia.

Maps of Ancient Rome

Spatial knowledge was vital to the creation and maintenance of the Roman Empire. A survey of the world was initiated by Julius Caesar (100–44 B.C.E.) to provide geopolitical information about the empire. Four geographers surveyed the four quarters of the known world; it took them over 30 years. The result was known as the "Agrippa Map" as it was Marcus Agrippa (*c.* 63–12 B.C.E.), lifelong friend of the Emperor Augustus (63 B.C.E.–14 C.E.) and his chief military commander, who oversaw the making of the map. The Agrippa Map was either carved in or painted on marble in a colonnade in Rome.

Large-scale mapping—the mapping of relatively small areas and regions to a large scale—was a major cartographic feature of the Roman Empire. The mapping of cities was a major preoccupation. One of the most impressive urban maps is the *Forma Urbis Romae*. This map was engraved on marble between 203 C.E. and 208 and created under the rule of Septimius Severus (146–211 C.E.). It was carved on 151 slabs of marble and was attached to a wall near the Library of Peace in the Forum of Vespasian. The map shows details of private and public buildings, including shops, streets, and staircases. It seems likely that the map was commissioned by Severus, who undertook major rebuilding and restoration work in Rome after the fire of 191. The scale is approximately 1:250, although important buildings are shown larger than they actually were. The map was not only a useful tool for administration, it was also a celebration of the rebuilt Rome.

ABOVE ***Detail from the Peutinger map, c.400 C.E.***
This part of the Peutinger map shows the eastern Mediterranean. The island of Cyprus is clearly visible in the middle of the sea. To the right of the island, the city of Antioch is shown as a human figure holding a long spear and shield.

LEFT **Formis Urbis Romae *urban map, 203–208 C.E.***
From small fragments such as this, it has been possible to reconstruct the giant map of Rome. Originally, stone cutters engraved the map in marble. This fragment shows buildings, roads, and the course of the Tiber River.

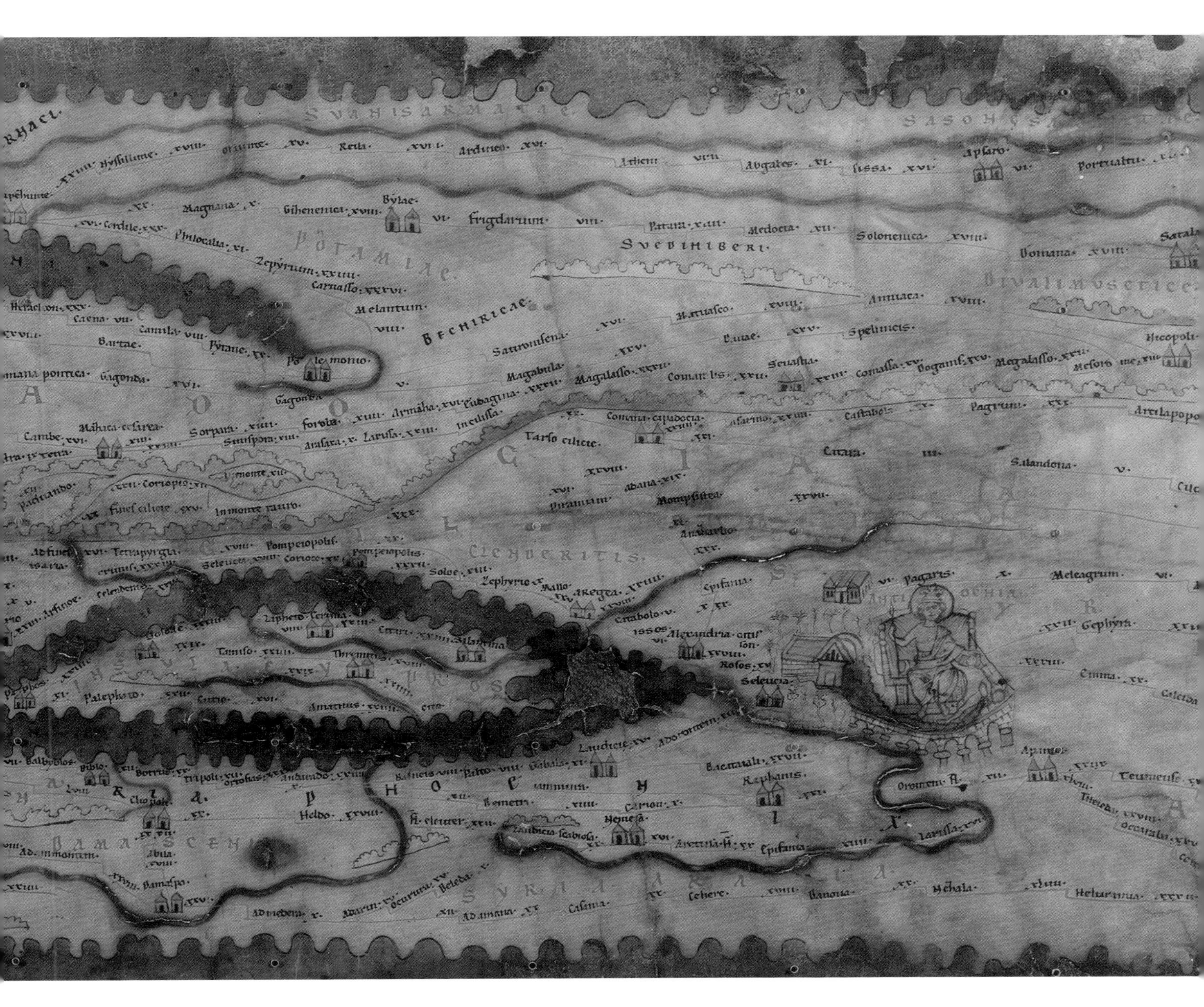

The ancient Romans also used maps as a means of recording landholdings, and Roman surveys of individual properties and groups of landholdings have been found in a variety of forms. For example, property maps carved in stone were discovered in the Rhone Valley in France. They were most likely used for tax purposes, or possibly to assist in the regulation of water use: many farms throughout the empire were irrigated by water supplied via aqueducts, and tablet maps have been found that show the location of landholdings in relation to water supplies.

As for the Inca Empire, the smooth running of the Roman Empire relied upon its roads, and at its height the empire boasted some 53,000 miles (85,000 km) of road. Extensive lists, or "itineraries" of all Roman roads were made, and some of them included maps of the road system. The most impressive itinerary map is the "Peutinger" map, which is drawn on a piece of parchment some 22 feet (6.75 m) long by 13 inches (34 cm) wide, and dates from the 4th century C.E. The map represents the empire at its height and includes India, Persia, Gaul, and Britain. The original map has been lost, but fortunately it was copied in the 13th century, and the copy has survived. It is a remarkable piece of work, showing Rome depicted as a woman holding a globe, shield, and spear.

Claudius Ptolemy

Greek and Roman cartography reached a culmination with Claudius Ptolemaeus (known as Claudius Ptolemy). Ptolemy (127–145 C.E.) was a Greek-Egyptian who worked in the Great Library of Alexandria in the 2nd century C.E. He spent his adult life in Alexandria, a Greek city in Egypt, founded in 332 B.C.E. After the death of its founder, Alexander the Great, the city became the capital of an empire ruled by one of Alexander's generals, also called Ptolemy (366–283 B.C.E.) He created a dynasty that lasted seven generations until the time of Queen Cleopatra (69–30 B.C.E.). Alexandria became one of the wonders of the classical world, competing with Rome and Constantinople (modern Istanbul) for size and grandeur.

At the heart of the intellectual life of the city was the Great Library. Established by the early Ptolemies, the library eventually held over 700,000 volumes, including copies of the great Greek tragedies of Sophocles and ancient Buddhist texts from India. Much Greek and Babylonian learning was transcribed, discussed, amended, and improved there. It was here that the astronomer Aristarchus argued that the earth was heliocentric (see page

BELOW *World map from Ptolemy's* Geography, *c. 1500s*
This manuscript map is an example of Ptolemy's conic projection. Europe is in the top left corner, Africa in the bottom left. Sri Lanka is the large island at the bottom right.

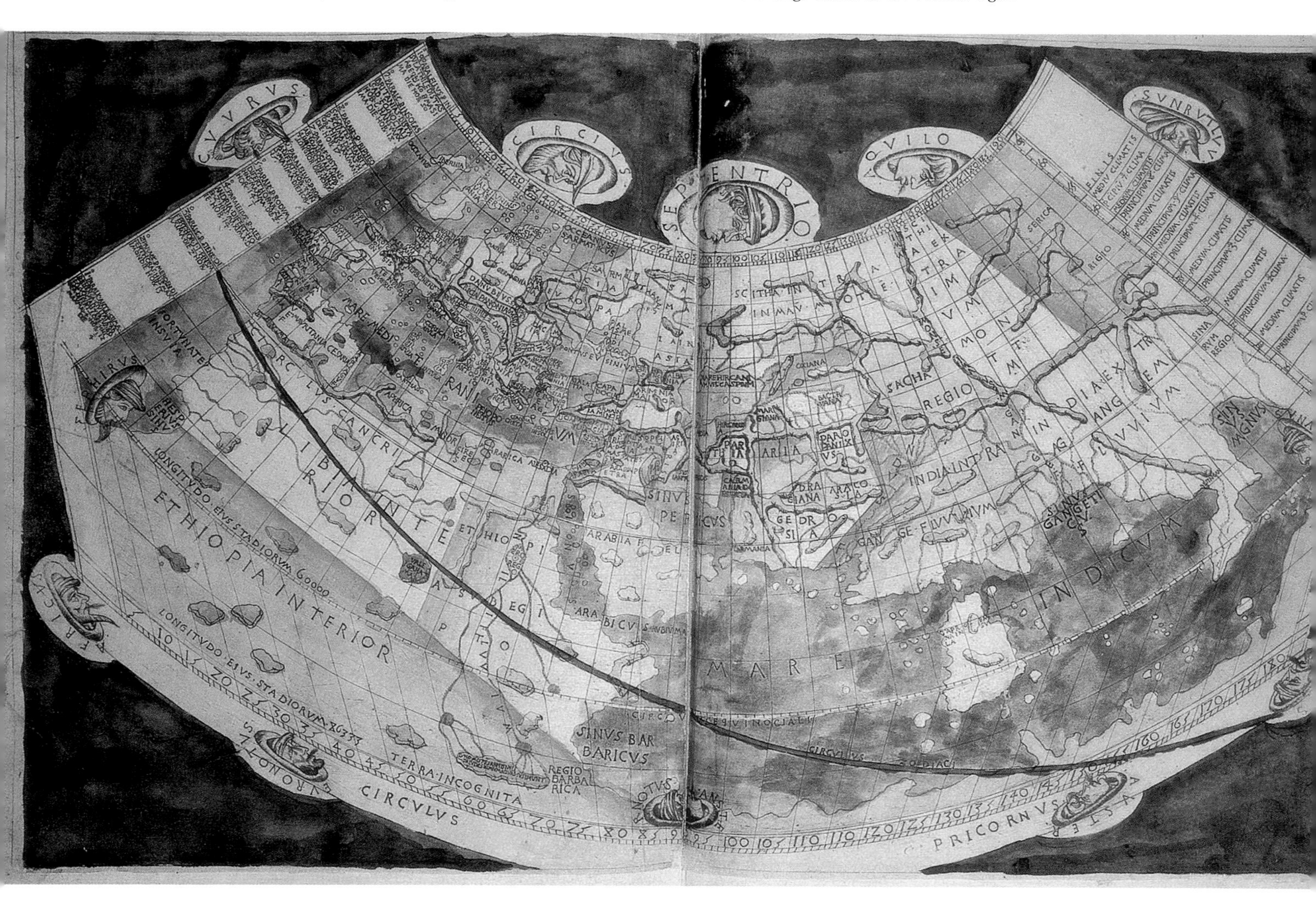

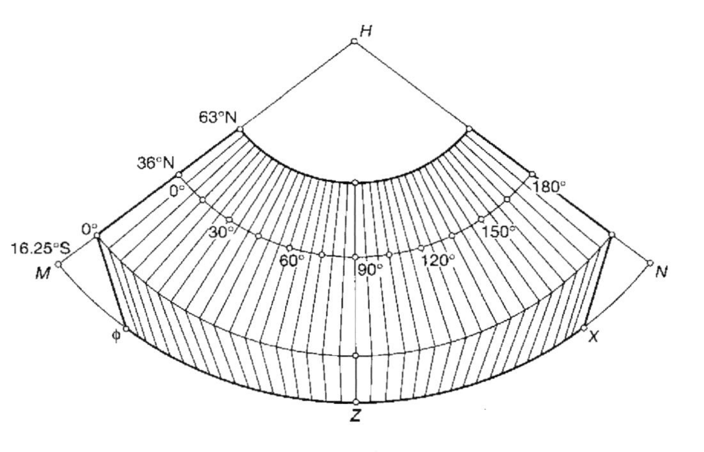

ABOVE ***Ptolemy's conic projection***
Ptolemy's simple but ingenious device was to have straight lines of longitude converge at the North Pole. This enabled mapmakers to make allowance for the curvature of the earth.

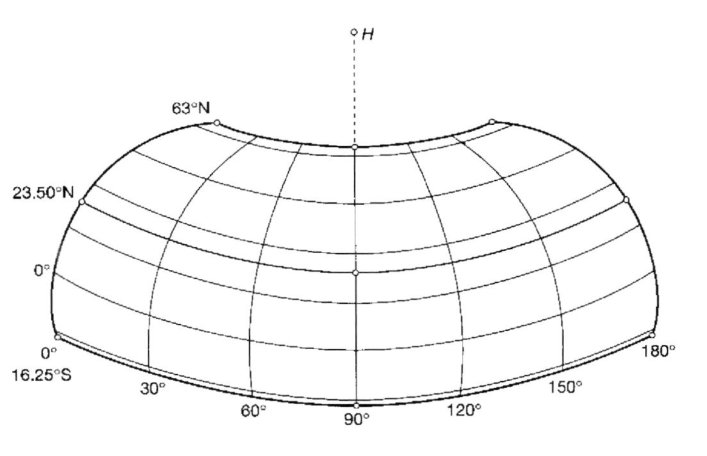

ABOVE ***Ptolemy's pseudoconic projection***
On Ptolemy's pseudoconic, or spherical projection, the lines of longitude curve toward the pole. This was a far harder projection to construct, but gave a more accurate result.

ASTROLOGY AND CARTOGRAPHY

In addition to his famous *Guide to Geography (Geographike hyphygesis),* Claudius Ptolemy also wrote the *Almagest*, a work of astronomy, and the *Tetrabiblos*, which is an extended astrological treatise. That one scholar could write about geography and astronomy on the one hand, and astrology on the other, may seem strange to contemporary readers, used to a scientific division between these areas. However, astrology was considered an important and legitimate area of scholarship in the West until as late as the 18th century.

Ptolemy had a unified vision of the world, and his three books mapped the earth (the *Guide*) and the heavens (the *Almagest*), and then examined the connection between the two (the *Tetrabiblos*). Nowadays astrology is generally considered to be unscientific, and yet there is still something deeply attractive about looking to the stars to guide, or predict our actions on earth. Who has never looked at their stars in a newspaper or magazine?

46), and Euclid completed his *Elements* (see page 48). One of the chief librarians was Eratosthenes (see page 46), and his world map formed the basis for Ptolemy's work.

Ptolemy wrote on a variety of topics: music, optics, astronomy, and astrology. One of his major works was his eight-volume *Guide to Geography* (C.E. 127–155). Volume 1 begins with a general description of latitude and longitude and their measurement. Earlier writers such as Eratosthenes and Hipparchus, had suggested the idea of imaginary lines drawn across the surface of the earth. Ptolemy developed their work, proposing that lines of latitude parallel to the equator should be divided into degrees and minutes, with 0 degrees at the equator and 90 degrees north at the North Pole. Lines of longitude were divided into 180 degrees east and west of a prime meridian, which Ptolemy set in the Fortunate Islands, the present-day Canary Islands.

Ptolemy thus cast a grid over the surface of the globe that allowed places to be identified by their coordinates of latitude and longitude, and to be plotted relative to each other and to the whole earth. The lines of latitude and longitude could be bent into all kinds of wonderful shapes, now called map projections (see page 12). In Volume 1 of his *Guide to Geography*, Ptolemy outlined two projections: a regular, conic projection in which the lines of latitude are shown as concentric, circular arcs, and a pseudoconic projection, in which the lines of longitude are circular rather than straight. Volumes 2–7 contain tables of latitude and longitude relating to sites in different parts of the known world, including Europe, Africa, and Asia. In Book 8 Ptolemy made some general comments on map construction and listed 10 maps for Europe, 4 for Africa, and 12 for Asia. These maps did not survive, but Ptolemy provided the key to successful mapmaking with his general model and specific coordinated data, and this allowed later scholars to make increasingly accurate world and regional maps.

Maps of Byzantium

Cartography in the Byzantine Empire played an important role in the development of contemporary mapmaking, connecting the knowledge of the classical world to that of the Renaissance. Unfortunately, very few examples of Byzantine cartography have survived.

The early Christian Church exerted a great influence on Byzantine society and culture. As a result, surviving cosmographical maps include significant religious iconography. The best-known examples come from a book by the Alexandrian scholar Cosmas, called the *Cosmas Indicopleustes*. Cosmas was an autodidact who had traveled widely. Some of the maps of the universe in his *Cosmas Indicopleustes* depict a rectangular world, with paradise in the east beyond the ocean. In another work, the *Christian Topography*, of which only fragments remain, Cosmas included maps showing a flat earth.

The most important Byzantine maps survive in the form of mosaics and frescoes. The best example of Byzantine cartography is the Madaba map, discovered in the old church of Madaba in Jordan, in 1884. A mosaic map of Palestine and parts of Egypt, it includes a distinctive pictorial representation of Jerusalem. Only a small part of the whole has survived, but scholars believe that the complete mosaic measured about 80 feet (24 m) in length and 20 feet (6 m) in height, and was made between 542 and 565. Some 2 million mosaic fragments would have been needed to complete the map. Another good example of a Byzantine mosaic map is the Nicopolis map, made in the 6th century C.E., which shows a general representation of the world.

In the later Byzantine Empire there was a revival of interest in classical literature, and many geographic texts were preserved and restored. The scholar-monk, Maximus Planudes (1260–*c.*1310), acquired and restored manuscripts by Claudius Ptolemy. Many Byzantine manuscripts were taken to Italy in the 15th century. Thus, the greatest cartographic legacy of the Byzantine Empire was to transmit knowledge from the classical to the "modern" world.

RIGHT ***The Madaba mosaic map, 542–565 C.E.***
This is one of the oldest Christian maps. The city of Jerusalem is shown in the bottom right.

ΒΗΘΑΓΛΑ
ΓΟΦΝΑ
ΒΕΝΙΑΜΙΝ
ΤΩΝΟΡΙΩΝ
ΒΕΘΩΡΩΝ

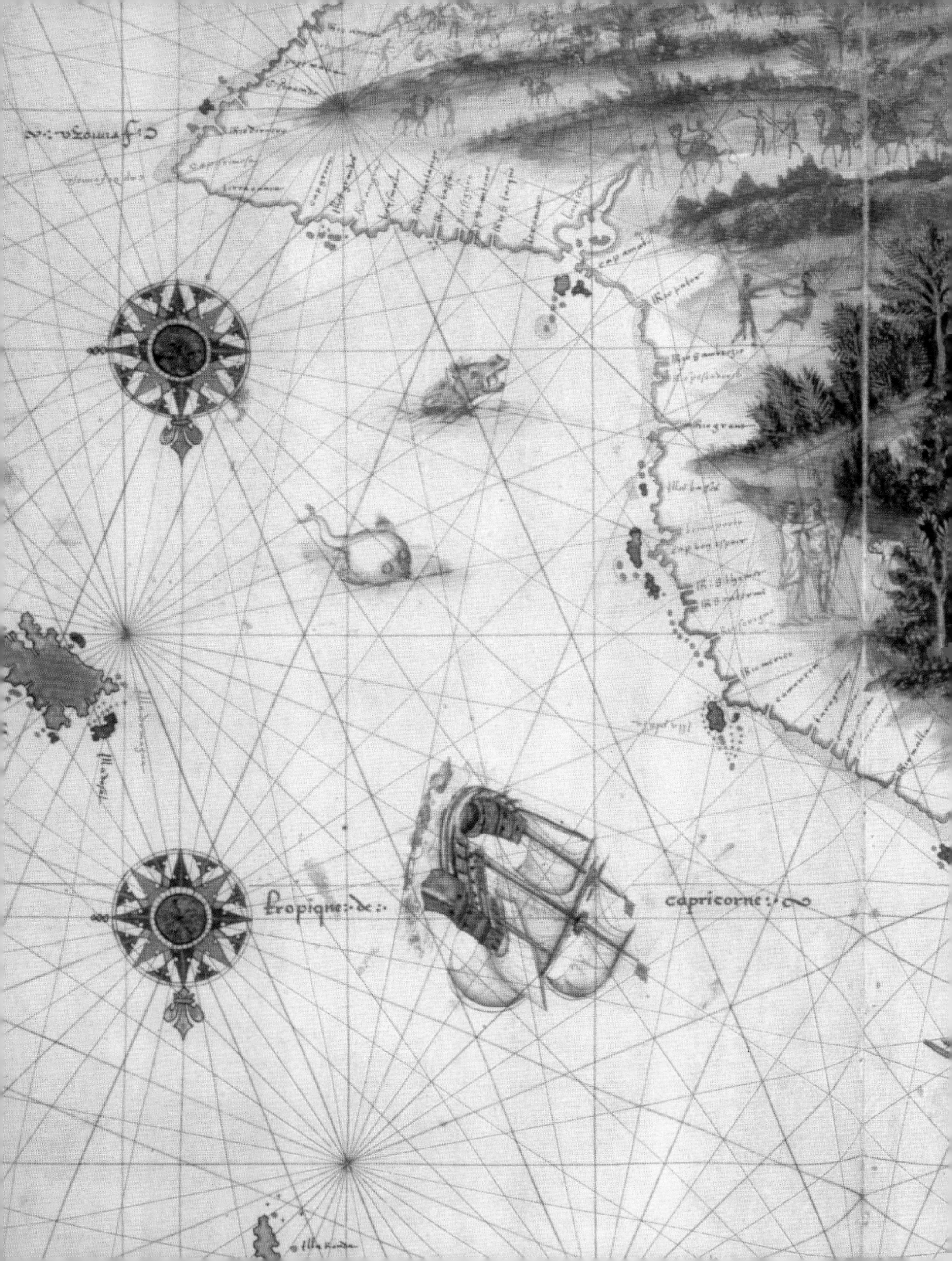
tropique: de :
capricorne :

PART III

The Medieval World

LEFT *Detail of a map from the Vallard Atlas, 1547*

5

THE MAPS OF MEDIEVAL EUROPE

Mappaemundi

Terrestrial mapping in medieval Europe was a minor activity. Surveying techniques were only rudimentary, and geographical knowledge in general was fragmentary and incomplete. However, three main types of maps were produced in this era: "mappaemundi," "portolan charts," and regional maps.

THE TERM "MAPPAMUNDI" comes from the Latin *mappa*, meaning "cloth" and *mundus*, meaning "the world." Hence, mappaemundi (the plural of mappamundi) are maps of the world. They were often very small, frequently appearing in the margins of illuminated manuscripts. Some, however, were much larger, designed for public display. The largest medieval map was a mappamundi called the "Ebstorf Map," which measured over 9 feet (3 m) across and was the cartographic equivalent of a rose window in a church, providing a religious image of the world.

Mappaemundi were not just maps—they were cosmologies that reflected a deeply religious-based view of the world. There are three known styles: "tripartite," "zonal," and "transitional."

The tripartite is the most common form of mappamundi, and there are over 600 surviving examples. Tripartite maps are circular and are divided into three land areas. A typical pattern is to have Asia at the top, Africa in the east, and Europe in the west. In a small number of cases a fourth area (the Antipodes) is included.

In many of these maps the tripartite structure is obvious, and symbolizes the division of the world by God to the three sons of Noah: Shem, Ham, and Japheth. Tripartite maps are sometimes called "T-O maps," because their outline combines a "T" shape inside an "O" shape, and they have been seen as representing the Christian cross. In other tripartite maps this division into three is less obvious. A good example of this is the 13th-century "Psalter Map," which is a classic example of medieval cartography. It is centered on Jerusalem and is full of details from biblical stories. Standing over the world is Christ, who holds a T-O globe in his left hand.

THE HEREFORD MAPPAMUNDI, C. 1300

This parchment medieval map, which was made by Richard of Holdingham around 1300, now hangs in Hereford Cathedral in the west of England (see page 10.) it is full of religious symbolism. Christ sits in judgment at the top of the map; on his right hand the saved are raised up by angels, while on his left the damned are led by demons down into hell. Around the map biblical scenes such as the Tower of Babel are represented. Unfortunately, the original rich and vibrant colors have been dimmed by time, so that, for example, the original bright greens and blues have become shades of dark brown.

The Hereford Mappamundi is a large, T-O map, with Jerusalem shown at the center of the world. East is at the top with a terrestrial paradise shown on the easternmost edge. The map is rich in geographical details, drawn from the Bible, Roman itineraries, and some travel reports. Picture maps of individual cities, battle scenes, monstrous peoples, and mythic animals are everywhere. The map is an eclectic mix of fact and fancy, myth and reality, all held together by a Christian cartographic iconography.

RIGHT ***The psalter map, c.1260***
The map is only 4 in (9 cm) wide. Jesus Christ sits at the top of the world and Jerusalem is at the very center of the map. East is at the top of the map. The Red Sea is clearly identifiable; it was invariably colored red in medieval world maps.

egiptus
albania
grecia
roma

Zonal mappamundi maps are circular and divided into five or seven climatic zones. Over 150 copies have survived. With their emphasis on climatic divisions, zonal maps represent an early form of thematic mapping (see page 198).

Transitional mappaemundi date from the 14th century and reflect the more accurate knowledge of the world gained by that time, largely due to maritime exploration and the resulting sea maps that could be consulted. These maps are called "transitional" because they represent the transition from medieval to Renaissance mapmaking styles, and mark a shift from a religious to a more humanist, and Renaissance-inspired, iconography.

ABOVE ***Mappa mundi, c.1320, by Pietro Vesconte***
This small map of the world, which measures no more than 14 inches (35 cm), is part of a written manuscript. It was made by the Genoese mapmaker Vesconte, probably in Venice. He made a number of charts and atlases between 1310 and 1330.

RIGHT ***Higden mappa mundi, c.1350***
The Benedictine monk Ranulf Higden (1299–1363) has given his name to over 20 world maps produced between 1340 and 1400. Oval, circular, and mandorla world maps have been identified. This oval map of the world is orientated with east at the top and Jerusalem at the center. Mappaemundi were produced—not by the monk himself—for copies of his popular history of the world, the Polychronicon.

earth was visualized as a perfect circle divided into seven climatic zones.

Celestial mapping was also an important element in Islamic science. The construction of astronomical measuring instruments such as "planispheric astrolabes" allowed Islamic scholars to make accurate astronomical observations. Refined in the Arab world between the 7th and the 17th centuries, the astrolabe was a device for measuring the location of stars. Maps of the celestial universe were etched into these brass instruments, reflecting their practical purpose.

A number of cosmographical maps were produced by Islamic scholars of the occult. For example, at the end of the 11th century, Jabir ibn Hayyan produced circular models of the universe that identified the world of substance surrounded by the world of the soul—the world of the intellect. Islamic mysticism was the fertile context for the cosmographical maps produced by Ibn al-Arabi and by his interpreters, who sought to translate his dense mystical-philosophical writings into diagrammatic simplicity.

ABOVE ***Signs of the Zodiac***
Celestial mapping was an important part of Islamic science. In this example from an early 19th-century Sanskrit manuscript, the constellations have been delightfully illustrated.

One such illustration shows a model of the universe devised by Ibrahim Hakki (d. 1195) that contains the four elements, seven planets, and twelve signs of the zodiac.

Cosmographical maps such as these were used not only to summarize a cosmology, but also to provide initiated scholars with an opportunity for mystical contemplation. They link the world of outer reality with the spiritual truths of the inner world. In his religious work *Ma'rifetname* (*The Book of Gnosis*) Hakki outlined a topography of the cosmos with a fiery seven-layered hell located at the bottom. Only those who led a good life were thought able to leave hell via the "straight road." In the middle of the diagram, earth is surrounded by seven spheres and above is paradise, showing the heavenly tree, Tuba.

Islamic World Maps

Islamic world maps share four main characteristics. First, they are meant as general representations of the world, being drawn at such a scale that only the general picture, rather than a detail, is revealed. Second, the world is centered on what we now call the Middle East. Third, they draw heavily upon the tradition of Ptolemy, although the later 14th-century maps begin to identify new features. Fourth, while some of their stark geometry may be explained with reference to the Islamic proscription of some kinds of images and image making, they are as much inspired by mathematics as by religion.

Many Islamic world maps were built upon latitude and longitude tables of places in the known world. Both al-Battani (*c.* 880) and al-Khwarazmi (*c.* 820) constructed geographical tables listing the features, climatic zone, latitude, and longitude of known countries. While al-Battani drew upon Ptolemy's measurements, al-Khwarazmi drew upon other sources. However, it was not until the 14th century that Islamic mapmakers used a grid to represent longitude and latitude on their maps, despite the fact that knowledge of these concepts had been widely known for hundreds of years.

The earliest existing Islamic world maps come from the "Balkhi School" of geographers, which takes its name from Abu Zayd Ahmad ibn Sal al-Balkhi (d. 934), a scholar who wrote a commentary on a set of maps. A number of geographers have been grouped under the name of this school including al-Istakhri (10th century), Ibn Hawqal (d. *c.* 977), and al-Muqaddasi (d. 1000). World maps made by al-Istakhri are typical of the style of that time: the world is presented as a sphere, surrounded by a sea, with the earth's surface divided by two further seas, the Mediterranean and the Indian Ocean. These world maps are centered in the Middle East, and are projected with south at the top.

One of the best-known Islamic world maps is by al-Idrisi, a scholar who traveled throughout Europe and North Africa. Around 1140 he was employed by King Roger II of Sicily to make a world map, of which a 15th-century copy survives. It is one of the most interesting maps in the history of cartography. While drawing upon the Ptolemaic understanding of the world and being based firmly in the tradition of Islamic world maps, it is also a very fresh representation. Europe and Asia are geometrically represented and the Nile River is shown. The map combines the traditions of the East and the West, Islamic and Christian. Drawn by a Muslim for a Christian king, and drawing on Ptolemy as well as contemporary travel reports, this world map represents a highly unusual melding of cultures and traditions.

AL-IDRISI

Al-Idrisi (1100–*c.* 66) was born in Ceuta, Morocco. He studied at Córdoba in Spain, then an Arab city that was a center of scholarship for Jews, Christians, and Muslims. While still only a teenager he traveled widely through Asia, North Africa, and Europe. His work developed and he made use of the writings of Ptolemy, Arab scholars, and information from European travelers. He was an early example of a cosmopolitan scholar who drew upon diverse cartographic traditions to make his maps. While he had an enormous impact on Arab scholars, his effect on European cartography was indirect. It is only recently that the quality of his work has been fully appreciated in the West.

LEFT *World map, 1456, by Al-Idrisi*
This is a more geometric representation of the world compared to the generally religious maps produced in Europe at the time. The mountains appear ropelike while the inland lake that is the source of the Nile looks like little boats.

RIGHT *Islamic world map, 1571–2, by the al-Sharafi al-Sifaqsi family*
This world map was part of a portolan atlas, made in the Tunisian town of Sfax. The map is sometimes orientated with south at the top.

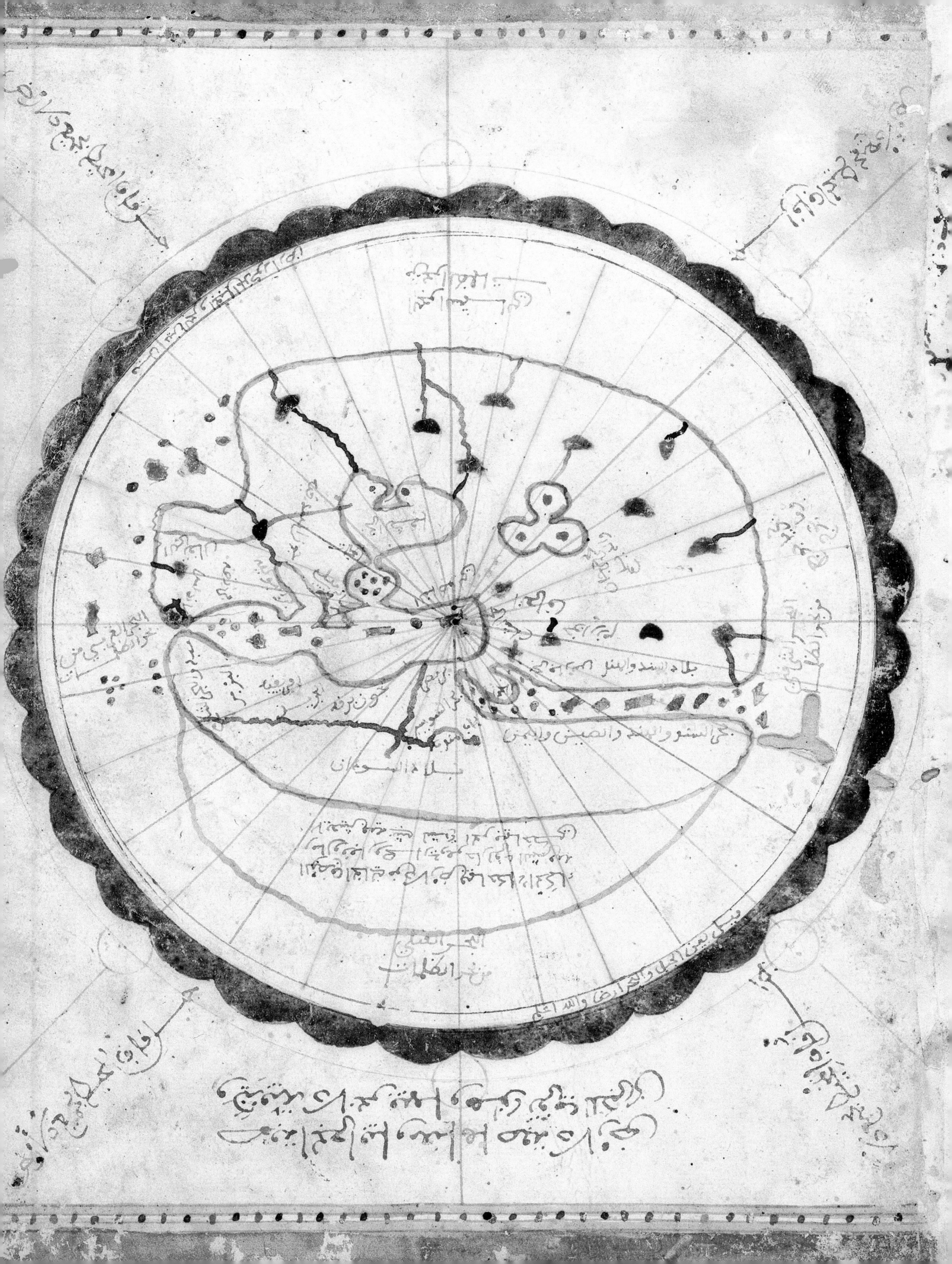

بلاد السند والهند

بحر السند والهند والصين واليمن

بلاد السودان

والله اعلم

Islamic Regional Mappings

A wide variety of maps were produced during the Islamic Renaissance (800–1400). As the heart of the Islamic Empire, the Middle East and North Africa were the most easily and most frequently mapped areas. The River Nile in particular was cartographically recorded from at least the 9th century. The scholar al-Khwarazmi (d. 847) produced numerous regional maps, and his map of the Nile is a very geometric representation of the great river rising from the Mountains of the Moon in central Africa and flowing into the Mediterranean.

The Balkhi School of geographers (see page 70) produced a number of regional maps that constitute an Islamic atlas, consisting of a world map, maps of the Mediterranean Sea, the Indian Ocean and the Caspian Sea, along with maps of 17 provinces of the Islamic Empire in the 10th century. The maps are geometric in design, with rivers represented as straight lines and lakes shown as perfect circles. They depict routes, towns, and mountains, and it has been suggested that they show caravan routes across the Islamic Empire. Careful examination reveals that the maps of the western, Arab-speaking provinces, in contrast to the eastern, Persian-speaking provinces, were drawn in a freer style, with more attention being paid to details on the ground.

More extensive Islamic regional maps were produced in the 12th century. A compendium produced around 1154 by al-Idrisi called *Nuzhat al-Mushtaq* (*The Book of Pleasant Journeys into Faraway Lands*) contains a world map and 70 regional maps. These maps are accompanied by a text that explains the human geography of the region. Unlike the earlier Balkhi maps, these maps contain information on latitude and longitude, as well as the location of towns and mountains, and represent a very sophisticated level of cartography.

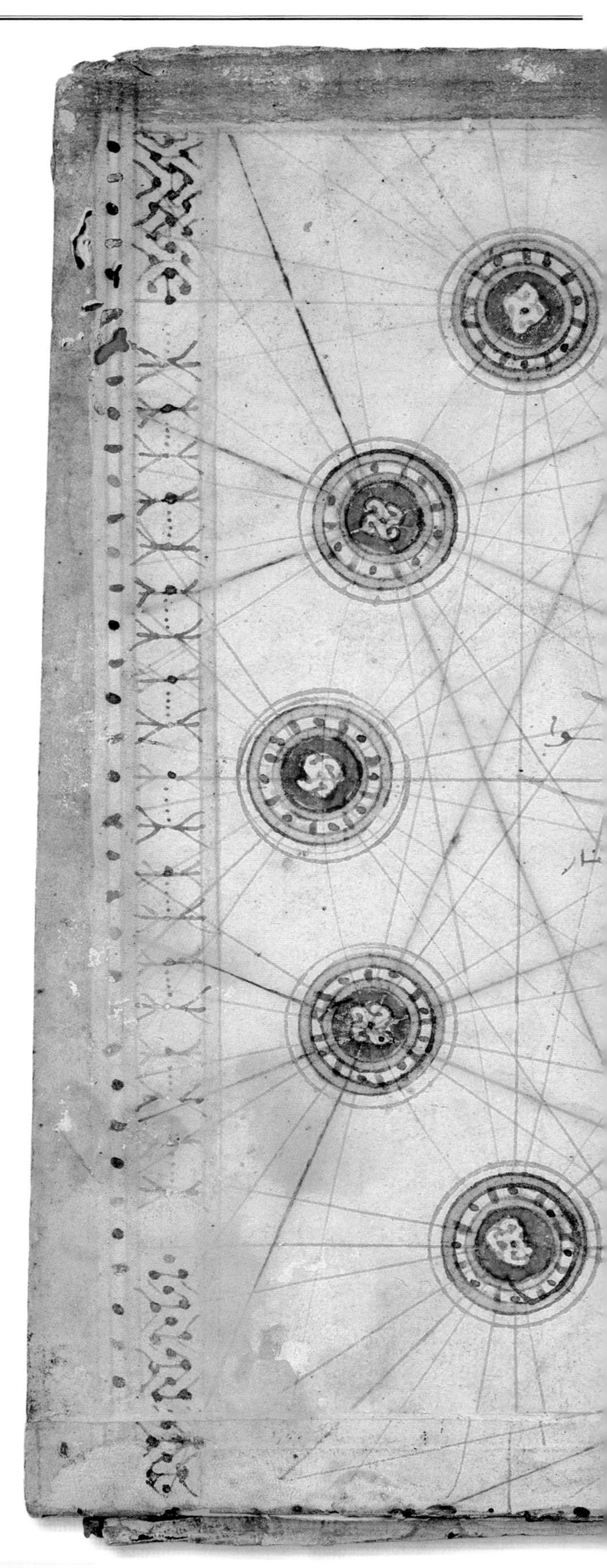

RIGHT ***Islamic maritime chart, 1571–2, by a member of the al-Sharafi al-Sifaqsi family***
This portolan chart depicts the Gulf of Sidra in the Mediterranean. The coastal features and ports are clearly marked to enable easier navigation.

Islamic Astronomy

The development of celestial cartography owes much to the early Islamic astronomers who made various astronomical instruments to assist in a more accurate mapping of the stars. The astrolabe, for example, was a small handheld instrument that fixed stars in a celestial grid. One of the earliest examples was made in the late 9th century for Ahmad, the astronomer of the city of Sinjar, by the master astrolabe maker Ali ibn Isa on the orders of Caliph al-Ma'mun. Astrolabes were made throughout the Islamic world in Moorish Spain, Syria, and what is now Pakistan.

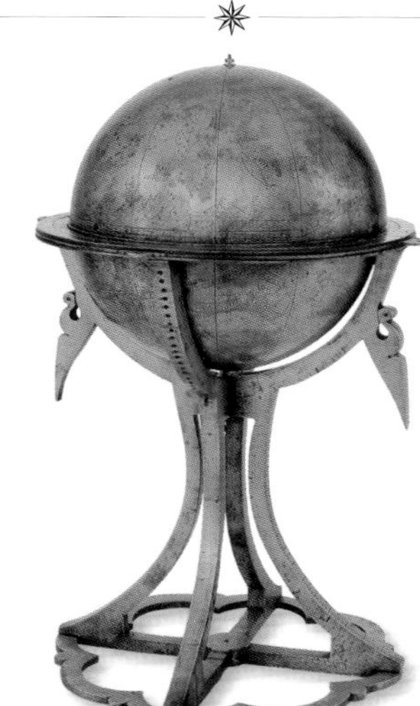

Celestial globes were models of the night sky. Although developed in ancient Greece and Rome, they became an important part of Islamic celestial mapping. The earliest known globe was made in Valencia, Spain, by al-Wazzan toward the end of the 11th century.

The armillary sphere was a small globe representing the earth, surrounded by metal bands that represented the celestial equator and polar circles. The sphere became a popular symbol of science during the European Renaissance and can be seen illustrated in many Renaissance books on astronomy, cosmography, and more general humanistic subjects.

Islamic science led to the cataloguing and mapping of hundreds of stars. *The Book of the Constellations of the Fixed Stars*, for example, was written in the 10th century C.E. by al-Sufi, who was the court astronomer in Isfahan, in contemporary Iran. It plots the location of over 1,000 stars and was the basis for many of the early astrolabes and celestial globes.

The constellations were also mapped by Islamic scholars. Drawing on Babylonian, Indian, and Bedouin traditions, al-Sufi noted 48 constellations in his *Book of the Constellations of the Fixed Stars.* The Bedouin influence is apparent in the representation of the constellation Cassiopeia as a woman with a camel beside her. Al-Sufi was enormously influential, not only in the Islamic world, but also in Christian Europe. The *Book of the Constellations of the Fixed Stars* was translated into Latin in 1270 and into Italian in 1341, and its legacy of knowledge endured throughout the period of the European Renaissance.

ABOVE ***Islamic celestial globe***
Celestial globes, one of the oldest forms of celestial mapping, were made throughout the Islamic world.

LEFT ***Construction of the astrolabe, 11th century***
For Muslims it was, and is, necessary to know in which direction to pray. Islamic cartography thus paid special attention to calculating accurate directions to Mecca.

RIGHT ***Detail from* The Book of Fixed Stars, *10th century, by al-Sufi***
Maps of star constellations become the raw material for flights of fancy, as shown by this celestial map of fanciful designs based around stellar coordinates.

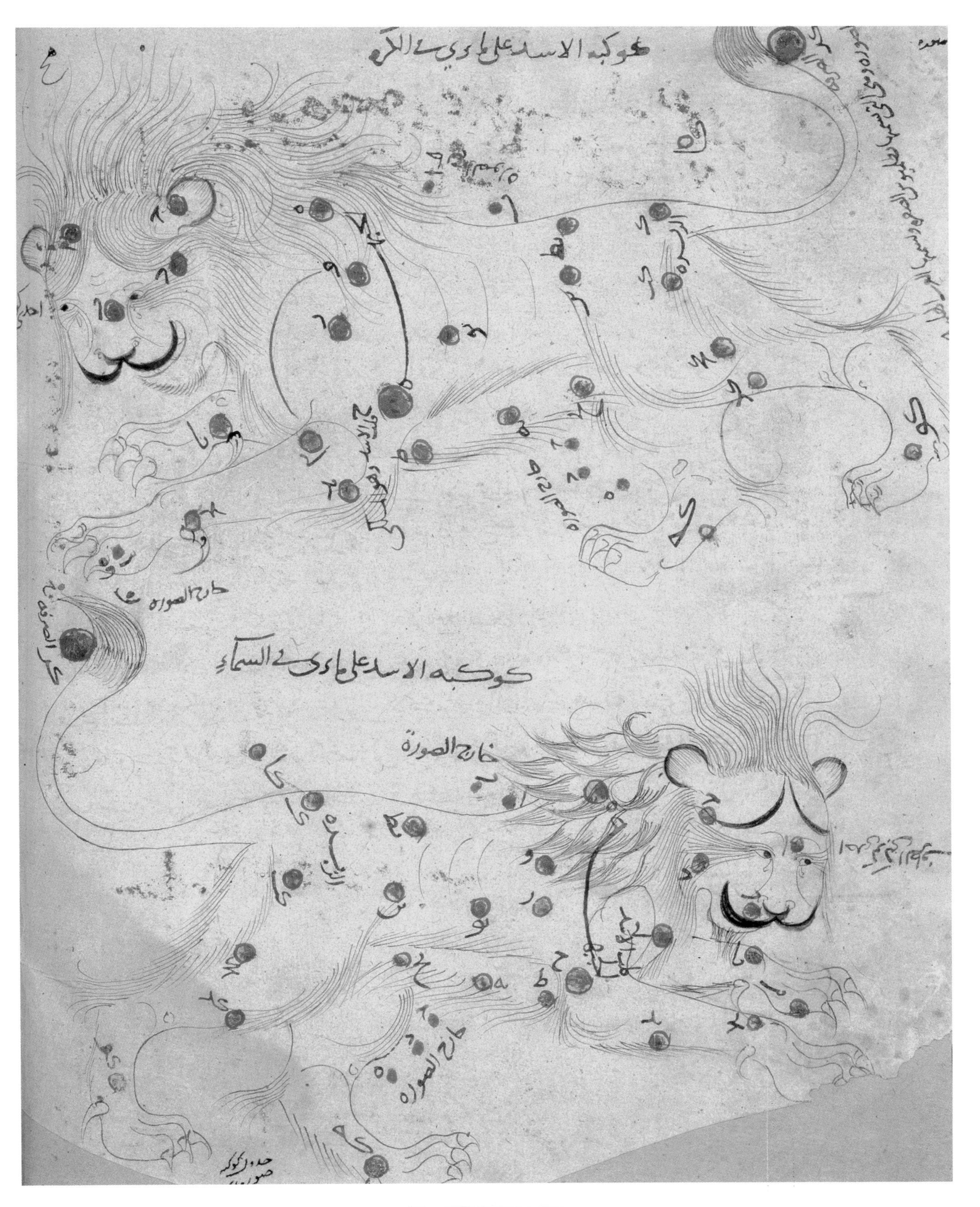
كوكبة الاسد على ما يرى في الكرة
كوكبة الاسد على ما يرى في السماء
خارج الصورة
خارج الصورة
خارج الصورة

Maps of China

China has a rich and long cartographic tradition. One of the earliest maps was discovered in a tomb in Hebei province. Engraved in bronze and depicting a plan map of a mausoleum, it dates from around 400 B.C.E. There are many examples of other early Chinese maps.

EARLY CHINESE MAPS inked onto wooden boards have been dated as early as 200 B.C.E. Maps were also made on paper, wood, silk, and stone. They were sophisticated, being drawn to scale and using abstract symbols.

Pei Xion (224–71 C.E.), a Chinese scholar, was responsible for many of the principles of Chinese mapmaking. He identified scale, location, distance, elevation, and gradient as important considerations when making maps. He is credited as being the father of Chinese cartography, just as Claudius Ptolemy is regarded as the father of western cartography. Pei Xion outlined the need for careful measurement and attention to geographic detail in mapmaking. A later mapmaker, Jai Dan (730–805 C.E.), is credited with using a grid in constructing maps, and subsequent Chinese maps are characterized by grid mapping and mathematical sophistication. The Hua Yi Tu stone map of 1136 is based on a map made by Jai Dan.

During the Tang (618–907 C.E.) and Song (960–1279 C.E.) dynasties, local Chinese governments drew up and submitted maps to the central authorities on a regular three- or five-year basis. Since there were almost 300 local governments, a large number of maps were produced over the years. Those made using bamboo, paper, and silk had limited lifespans, so the ones that have survived for us to see today are those maps that were made on rocks or carved on tombs.

RIGHT ***Map of China and its empire, Korea, 19th century***
Mapmaking in Asia was intimately related to the business of bureaucratic control of the empire. Maps of local areas, provinces, and the expanding empire became an important tool that enabled political leaders to envision and manage the vast territory.

SOCIETY IN MEDIEVAL CHINA AND THE FAR EAST

The early Medieval period under the Tang dynasty (618–97 C.E.) witnessed a flowering of Chinese civilization, with significant advances in technology, art, literature, and administration. Block printing was invented, making books available to much wider audiences. There were also great advances in farming throughout the Far East. The main crop was rice, and the spread of a fast-growing Vietnamese strain helped to develop a very efficient food supply, providing an economically self-sustaining system that survived in some areas until the 20th century.

In China, government civil servants were selected through an examination system that attracted the most talented people from all levels of society. This system helped to break the power of the established aristocratic families. Senior civil servants, known as scholar-officials, acquired a special status in their local communities. They became an important binding influence in Chinese society, acting as intermediaries between the imperial court and the mass of the population. As printing and education spread, a new merchant class arose, rivaling the landowners and government employees in their wealth.

In most Far Eastern medieval societies, people followed three main religions or philosophies: Confucianism, Taoism, and Buddhism. They were known as the "three ways;" most people practiced elements of all three. During the medieval period, a revival of Confucianism—Neo-Confucianism—reinforced a rigid acceptance of authority, which maintained political stability, but impeded social and cultural progress in China, Korea, Vietnam, and Japan until the 19th century.

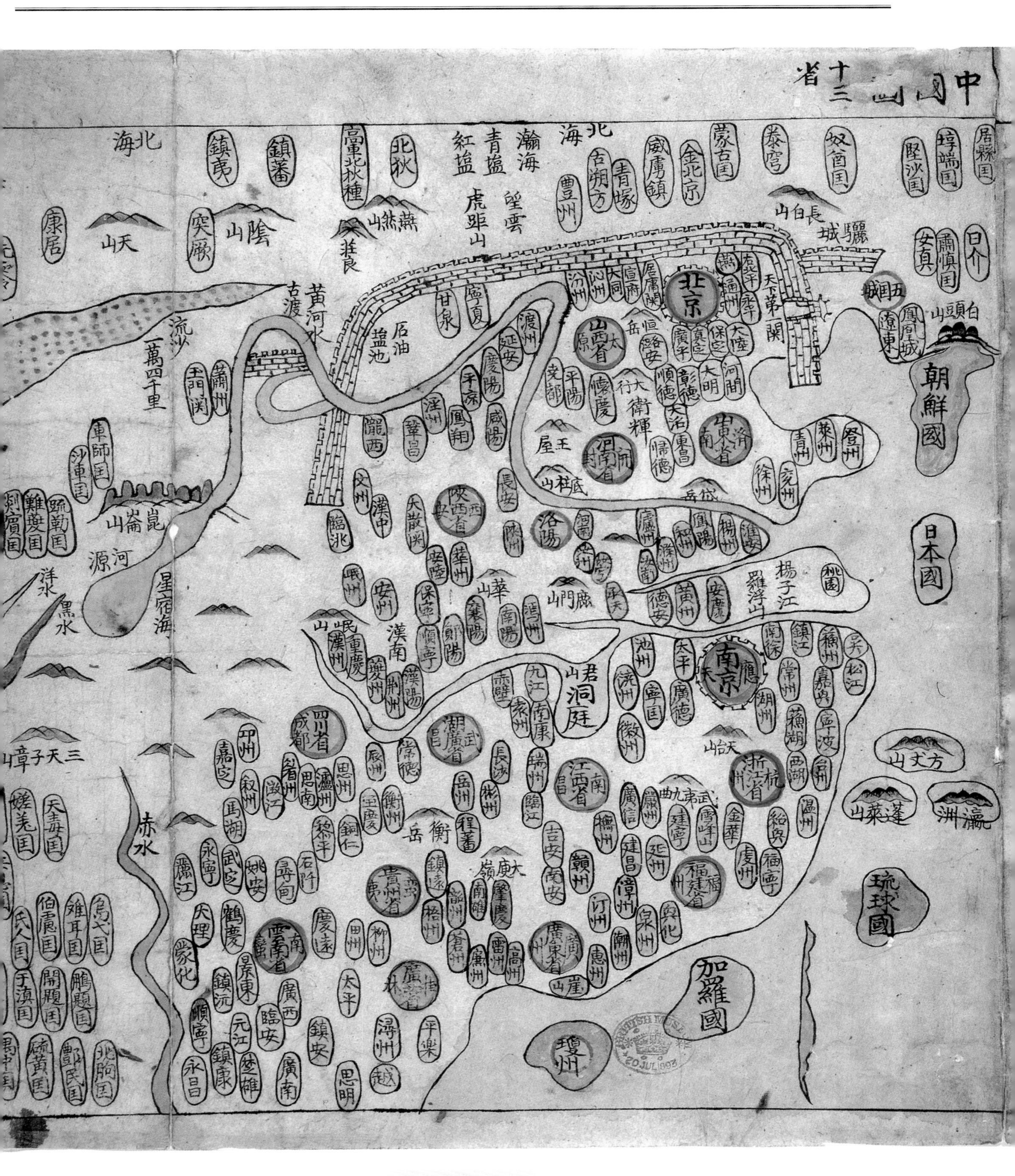
中國十三省
北京
南京
山西省
山東省
河南省
陝西省
四川省
湖廣省
江西省
浙江省
福建省
廣東省
雲南省
貴州省
朝鮮國
日本國
琉球國
加羅國
瓊州
天下第一關
黃河水
揚子江
洞庭
一萬四千里
星宿海
北海
瀚海
崑崙山
長白山
白頭山
方丈山
蓬萊山
瀛洲
赤水
黑水

The atlas of China and the surrounding areas compiled by Chu Ssu Pen (1273–1335) reveals the richness of Chinese cartography. Most of the country was mapped at a detailed scale, and the atlas also reveals an accurate knowledge of the South China Sea and the Indian Ocean. Africa is understood in general outline, and the locations of the Congo and Nile rivers are shown.

Maps and power went hand in hand in medieval China. The earliest Chinese maps were produced by the central authorities, either for military, political, or administrative purposes. Careful mapping and cartographic knowledge were seen as important elements of political power and military intelligence. Later, in 1579 the Chinese produced a complete atlas of their empire, called the *Guang yutu*. The maps in the atlas show boundaries, roads, cities, administrative units, postal stations, and military posts, demonstrating that what was cartographically important at that time was the political structure of the country, its military presence, and the centers of civilized society.

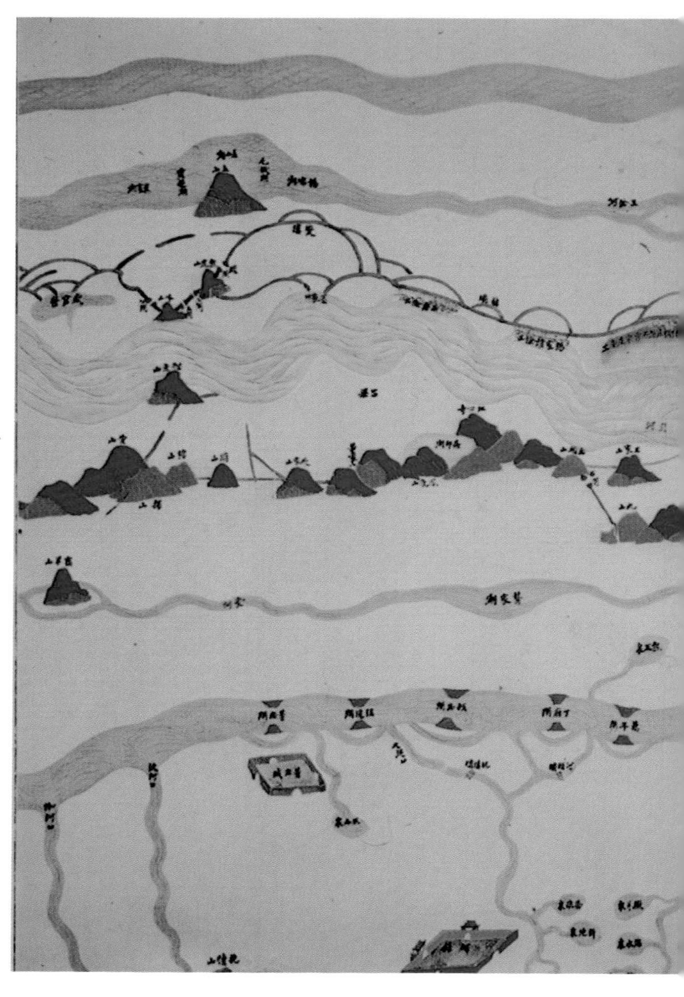

ABOVE ***Map of Grand Canal, China, 18th century***
This is a more figurative large-scale Chinese map than the one on the previous page. Relief is shown as little molehills, and villages are identified. Most of the villages are walled. This is as much a painting as a map.

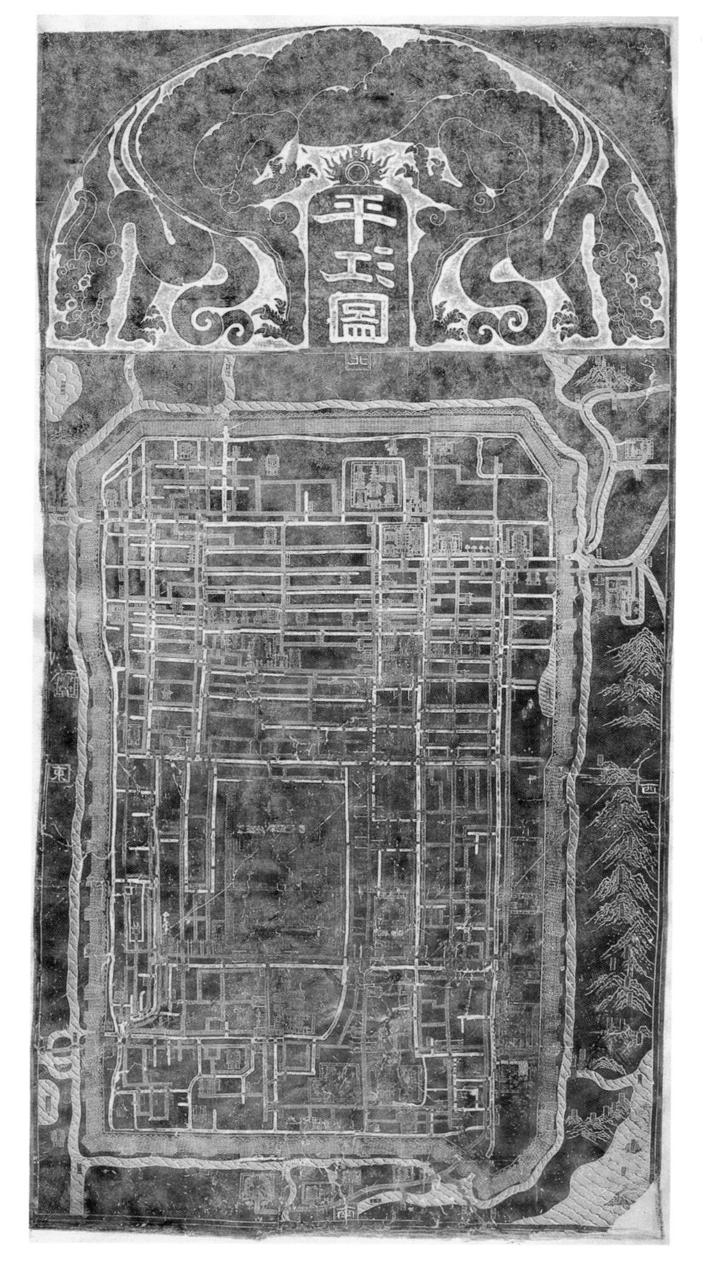

LEFT ***Stone-carved map, c.1229***
This map of Pingjiang province is a rubbing from a stone carving. It shows a gridded city with rich variety of features including temples, bridges, and roads, surrounded by rivers and hills.

While gridded maps were an important element in Chinese cartography, pictorial maps were also important. The map of the Grand Canal, for example, represents the waterway in plan form while other physical features and cities are shown from a bird's-eye perspective. The Chinese Empire was a hydrological society, dependent on the great river systems of the country for transport and agricultural productivity. Hence, mapping the waterways was of vital importance to the economy.

Like European cartography, Chinese mapmaking was affected by outside influences. Between 1405 and 1433, the Chinese maritime explorer Chen Ho led seven expeditions to the Pacific and Indian Oceans, greatly expanding the empire's geographical knowledge. In addition, the arrival of the Jesuit missionary Matteo Ricci in 1582 marked a significant development in Chinese cartography, bringing with him as he did a new way of looking at the world. Ricci was a point of transmission between Chinese and western cartography. He showed the Chinese the principles of latitude and longitude and introduced them to a less Sinocentric view of the world. He also introduced Chinese geographical knowledge to the West, providing a more accurate picture of Asia for western mapmakers.

Subsequent official Chinese mapping was influenced by the European cartographic tradition, and in the 18th century ground surveys using latitude and longitude were employed by the central Chinese authorities. While some indigenous mappings remained resistant to foreign influences, Chinese mapping increasingly became part of a more universal cartographic tradition.

MATTEO RICCI (1552–1610)

ABOVE *Matteo Ricci*

Matteo Ricci was born in Macerata, Italy, on October 6, 1552. He joined the Jesuit order when he was only 19 and 11 years later he was posted to the mission station in the Portuguese province of Macao. He eventually gained permission to enter China in 1582, and by 1601 he had reached the imperial capital of Beijing. Although he was a zealous missionary eager to make Catholic converts (it was rumored that he converted 2,000 high-ranking Chinese officials), he was also an intellectual who was interested in cartography, and his knowledge had an important influence on the tradition of Chinese mapmaking.

Ricci was able to exert such an influence because he was sensitive to local traditions and respectful of Chinese culture. He took the trouble to learn Chinese, which many foreigners did not do, and adopted some of the clothes and language of a traditional Chinese scholar. A transcultural intellectual, Ricci succeeded in bringing the East and West closer together, a remarkable achievement.

Maps of the Far East

While Chinese cartography exercised a great deal of influence on mapmaking throughout the Far East, there were other independent centers of the craft, notably Japan and Korea.

Maps played an extremely important role in traditional Japanese society both as practical devices and as decorative pieces. They were used as part of a centralized hierarchical system of control and surveillance. In the 8th century C.E. the central government of Japan ordered maps to be made of the various provinces. These maps were drawn in a distinctive style and became known as the "Gyoki maps." The name comes from a Buddhist priest, Gyoki Bosatsu (670–749 C.E.), who came from Korea and practiced mapmaking. Gyoki maps generally show provinces, roads, and cities. They are usually orientated with south at the top, and they dominated Japanese cartography from the 8th to the 19th centuries. When another survey of provinces was commissioned by the central authorities in the 17th century, another series of Gyoki maps was produced.

Much of the mapping of the country and its cartographic representation was undertaken for administrative political purposes. The schematic map of Japan in the encyclopedia *Nichureki* is an abstracted representation of routes and towns, and was probably drawn up to help tax collection.

Japanese society was deeply dependent on the rice crop, which provided the staple diet of the people. Grid maps of rice paddy fields date from the 8th century C.E. and were important records of the ownership of a very important resource. Accurate mapping of the land also helped to minimize disputes over land ownership.

Japanese cartography was heavily influenced by the Europeans. The early European traders were called *nanbanjin*, meaning "southern barbarians." The name was used when the Japanese produced world maps on the European model. Nanban maps, produced in the first half of the twentieth century, show the world on projections that had been learned from the Europeans, such as the Mercator projection. In a fusion of East and West the Nanban maps are an example of cross-cultural cartography, as indeed are Japanese marine charts from the 17th century onward, which were influenced by Portuguese maritime cartography.

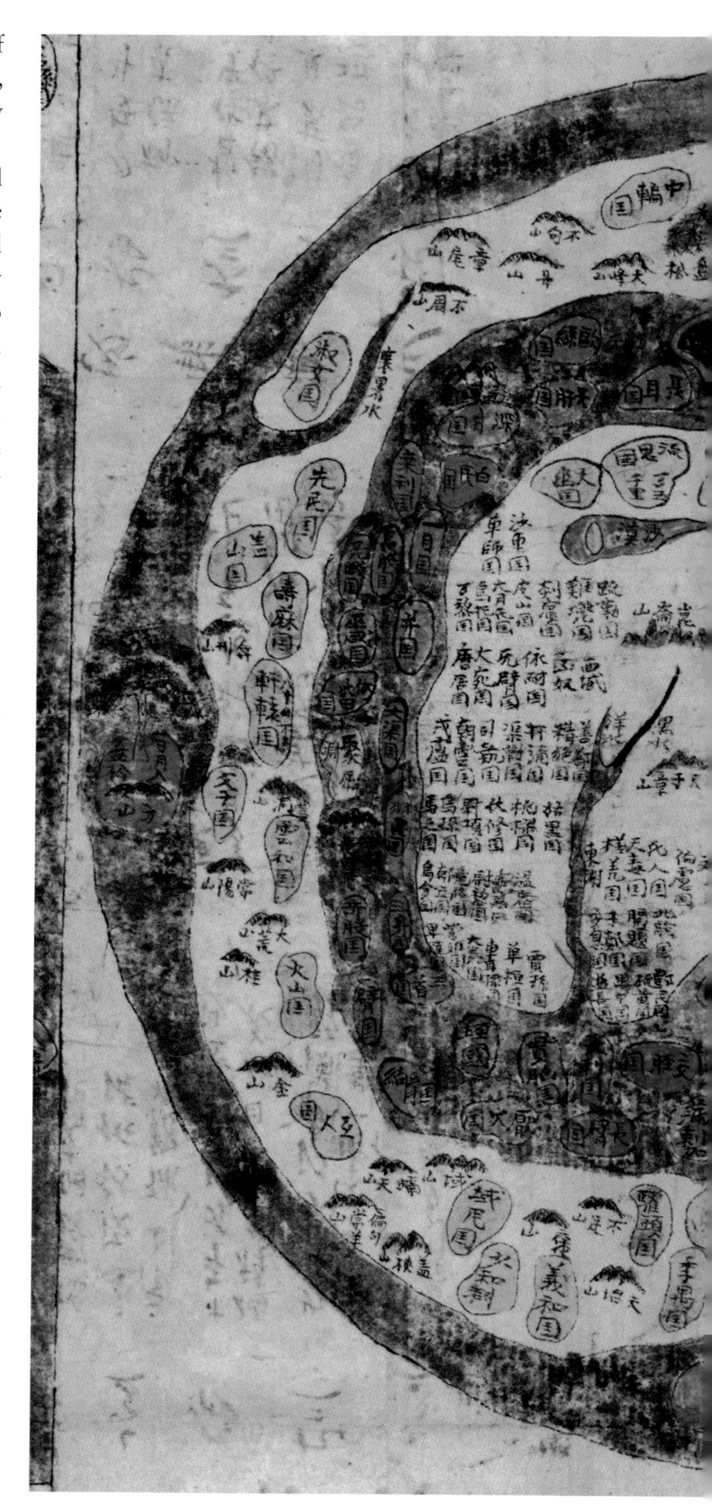

BELOW **Ch'onhado** ***(map of the world), Korea, 19th century***
World maps, called Ch'onhado, depict a circular world centered on Korea. The rest of the world is presented in the margins. These maps were very popular during the 18th and 19th centuries.

The Korean word for map, *chida*, can be translated as "land picture." The oldest surviving Korean map is a world map that was produced around 1402. There is a long tradition of world maps in Korea that show the country as the center of the world, with little regard for geographic accuracy. Such maps, which were extremely popular during the 18th and 19th centuries, are known as *Ch'onhado*. They depict a circular world that is centered on the Far East. The rest of the world is presented on the margins.

Large-scale maps had a much more pragmatic purpose in Korean society. Maps of the provinces were made to assist administrative control. Systematic mapping of these regions began in the late 15th century and was standardized to a common scale in the 18th century. One important variant of official large-scale maps was the production of *kwanbangdo* maps. These were drawn up with an emphasis on terrain and military communications in order to assist with the country's defense. They were produced in a variety of forms, from long scrolls showing boundary regions to detailed mappings of fortresses and coastal defenses. *Kwanbangdo* maps were often painted on screens or drawn on portable scrolls so that they could be taken for use in the field by military officers and commanders. Local maps of towns and the surrounding areas were undertaken on a much less systematic and professional basis.

One distinctive type of Korean map is the *hyongsedo* map, which can be translated as a "shapes-and-forces" map. Such maps first appeared in the late 14th century. They have a forceful energy to them, drawing as they do upon the rich tradition of geomancy, which sees the landscape as alive with energy or life force, known as *chi* in Chinese. A correct reading of the landscape to maximize positive energy was essential for the proper location of buildings, houses, temples, palaces, and shrines. In this tradition landscape is not inert, but a vital living force. The *hyongsedo* maps emphasize the vitality of the land. An important figure in the development of Korean cartography was the 15th-century court official, Chong Ch'ok (1390–1475), who was ordered to survey three provinces. His 1463 map of Korea is in the *hyongsedo* style.

By the 17th century, Korean cartography was being influenced by western cartographers, especially the Jesuits working in China. By the 19th century Korean mapmaking was fully integrated into a more general scientific form of mapping. While something was gained in accuracy, the vitality of the *hyongsedo* maps was replaced with a less vital and energized depiction of the land.

B
A
Q
B
S
S
P
M
O
N
X
S
D
E
F
X

PART IV

The First Age of Exploration

LEFT *Detail of the Champlain map of New France, 1612*

Maps of Mesoamerica

The region known as Mesoamerica runs from the Mexican border with the United States down to the northern border of Honduras, embracing much of modern Mexico and Guatemala. The best-known ancient cultures of the region are those of the Aztecs and the Maya but many others flourished in Mesoamerica.

OTHER ANCIENT CULTURES in Mesoamerica included the Olmecs, Mixtecs, Toltecs, and Zapotecs. These peoples were responsible for producing some of the most sophisticated maps in the New World.

Four different types of Mesoamerican map have been identified: terrestrial maps with and without a historical narrative, cosmographical maps, and celestial maps.

Maps with a historical narrative, which we can also call "cartographic histories," have been found throughout Mesoamerica. Communities made maps depicting their own geographical region and its history, including data like the date the community was founded and the sites of important battles. Such maps represented a celebration of a people's culture and a record of their lands. A good example of the way in which such maps combined place and time is a 16th-century map, now in the British Museum, which shows an area around the town of Metlatoyuca in southeastern Mexico: in the middle are a series of human figures linked by a rope, believed to be an early form of family tree.

Numerous examples of the second type of Mesoamerican map—terrestrial maps without a narrative—have been discovered. For example, the "Codex Kingsborough" (see page 86) map shows the territory around the town of Tepetlaoztec, in southeastern Mexico. The map shows trees, rivers with eddies, and paths with footprints. Around the border are little hieroglyphs giving the names of places and settlements. Hieroglyphs are typical of Mesoamerican maps.

A good example of the third type, the cosmographical maps, is the "Codex Fejervary-Mayer." In pre-Columbian

Mesoamerica, the cosmos was represented in illustrations that showed strong horizontal and vertical components. Such maps represent the cosmos as three primary layers: earth, sky, and the underworld, sometimes further broken down into sublayers. The earth is further divided into four quadrants. At the center is the "world tree," the vertical axis of which runs through all three layers. The map of the cosmos in the Fejervary-Mayer Codex shows the cosmos stretching out along four axes to the four trees of life. Embodied in this map is a representation of the creator god Tezcatlipoca, whose dismembered body is stretched diagonally with the head in the top right-hand quadrant and a hand in the upper left. Bone fragments can be seen in the lower right and left quadrants. The map therefore represents a complicated cosmology that depicts creation myths as well as the passage of time.

Mesoamerican societies had an intense interest in the movement of the stars. The Maya, for example, relied on the stars and the sun in particular to create their calendar. They had a sophisticated understanding of the solar year and their calendar was more accurate than the one used by the Spaniards who invaded them. They recorded the exact day, hour, and even minute of important acts of their rulers and other significant events. According to their religious beliefs, certain ceremonies had to be performed on a specific date. This was a particular feature of Aztec culture. They made many sacrifices to their sun god, Tonatiuh, believing that this was necessary in order to make sure he rose and crossed the sky each day. As a result celestial maps were drawn with incredible accuracy. Particular attention was paid to the movement of Venus, as this planet was believed to be the god Quetzalcoatl, a symbol of death and resurrection.

Unfortunately, there are very few surviving examples of Mesoamerican maps produced prior to the arrival of the Spanish in the first half of the 16th century. The "Codex Nuttall" is a famous map that shows a U-shaped valley with two rivers running along its floor, combining topography and symbols in a rich design.

The arrival of the Spanish conquistadors in Central and South America proved catastrophic to the indigenous peoples and their ancient cultures. The Spanish brought disease, and modern weapons against which the Indians could not compete. However, the invasion also brought about a cartographic encounter between the New and the Old Worlds. We can see the result in the so-called Cortés map of the city of Tenochtitlán, named after Hernán Cortés (1485–1547), destroyer of this, the capital of the Aztec Empire. In this map, European and indigenous forms of mapmaking are employed in a complex juxtaposition of plan, bird's-eye view, and pictorial representation. The map was printed in 1526, but by the time European readers had a chance to examine it, Tenochtitlán had been reduced to ruins by the Spanish, and 3,000 years of Mesoamerican civilization had come to an end. The remnants form the foundations of modern Mexico City.

LEFT ***Mixtec map, Codex Nuttall, 16th century***
This is a rare Mixtec map of the Apoala Valley. The walls of the valley are represented by a large U-shape. The left wall ends in the mouth of a giant snake, probably a cave, while the right wall ends with a tree and an emerging human figure, which suggests the beginning of family lineages. On the valley floor there are two smaller U-shapes that represent rivers.

MESOAMERICAN SOCIETIES

The Mesoamerican societies were the indigenous cultures that developed in parts of Mexico and Central America before the arrival of the Spanish in the 16th century. The complex organization of these societies, and the impressive nature of their buildings and cities, rival the eastern hemisphere civilizations of ancient Egypt and Mesopotamia.

The first human presence in this region has been dated to around 21,000 B.C.E. Village farming life began around 1500 B.C.E., and with it came the first signs of civilization in the form of art and trade. The first great Mesoamerican civilization was that of the Olmecs, beginning around 1150 B.C.E. The Olmecs were famous for their extraordinary stone monuments, which included colossal stone heads measuring up to 9 feet (3 m) in height.

Between 900 and 300 B.C.E., the Zapotec people achieved a high level of development at Monte Albán in southern Mexico, producing the first writing and calendars in Mesoamerica.

The classic period of Mesoamerican history occurred between about 300 B.C.E. and 900 C.E. During this phase, the Maya, Zapotec, Totonac, and Teotihuacán cultures developed both technologically and artistically. The Maya were especially creative, introducing astronomy, mathematics, calendar-making, and hieroglyphic writing, as well as producing some great monumental architecture. The great political and commercial power of this period lay in Teotihuacán, in the Valley of Mexico.

The Toltecs came to dominate Mesoamerica between 900 and 1200, ruling from Tula in central Mexico. The final great Mesoamerican power was the Aztecs, who controlled central Mexico from around 1428 until their defeat by the Spanish in 1521. The Aztecs themselves had predicted the death of their civilization. A coincidence of their complex calendar calculations and the cycle of the planet Venus indicated the return of the vengeful Quetzalcoatl, the "Feathered Serpent." Cortés was quick to identify himself with the deity and exploit Aztec despair.

LEFT ***Tepetlaoztoc, Codex Kingsborough, c.1555***
This map is of the region around the town of Tepetlaoztoc. Both indigenous and European map styles are evident. The open-mouthed hill represents a cave, a standard pre-Conquest design, while the map-maker has also used European symbols such as little hills and trees to represent relief and forests. Roads are marked with footprints.

Maps of South America

Three types of indigenous mapping can be found in South America: celestial maps, maps made at the behest of Europeans by indigenous people, and maps made by Europeans but influenced by local conceptions of space.

When the Europeans came to the New World they needed geographical information in order to get around, identify the local peoples, and locate resources. Many maps were drawn, most of them in the form of quick sketches in the sand or hand gestures in the air. Only a very few were made as permanent records.

European maps of the region were influenced by native mapmaking techniques. One of the most famous examples of this is the map of Guyana made by Sir Walter Raleigh (1554–1618) around 1595. Raleigh was searching for the mythical region of Eldorado, where it was said great wealth could be found, and he relied on the knowledge of the local American Indians to draw his map. The mythical city is shown, on the edge of the equally mythical Lake Manoa. There is an obvious South American Indian influence to the map: south is at the top and many native settlements are shown. The lake at the center is full of animistic conceptions of places as alive, a characteristic of traditional South American mapmaking. Even the lake itself looks animal-like. Drawn to a consistent scale of 1 inch to 50 miles (2.5 cm to 80 km), but of fanciful geography, the map is both a scientific document and an act of willful imagination.

In the 15th century, the upland zone of South America was dominated by the Inca people who, from their capital Cuzco, ruled an empire that stretched from modern Ecuador to Chile. From around 900 B.C.E. to 1532 C.E. numerous spatial representations were made by the Incas. Many of these "maps" represented *ayllu*—local communities based in particular territories. The fields in these communities were arranged in a fixed radial pattern, emanating from a central settlement point, with parallel strips of land. These same patterns formed the basis of repeated designs on Inca ceramics, stoneware, and textiles.

RIGHT *Map of Guyana, 1595, by Sir Walter Raleigh*
This map was made by Sir Walter Raleigh with the help of local people. The place names were most likely written in his hand. The map depicts the Orinoco river system. The lake at the center of the map has a curiously animated look, as if it was a wriggling insect.

The Incas had an elaborate and remarkably sophisticated road system, which was essential to the maintenance of such a large empire. There were four main roads, carefully measured out, and places were represented on maps in relative location to the road system.

A variety of maps were drawn by the Incas. One of the most fascinating is the *khipu*, a knotted rope composed of a primary cord and secondary strings, used as a counting and mapping system. The different pendants represent kin groups associated with different parts of the valley.

Maps of North America

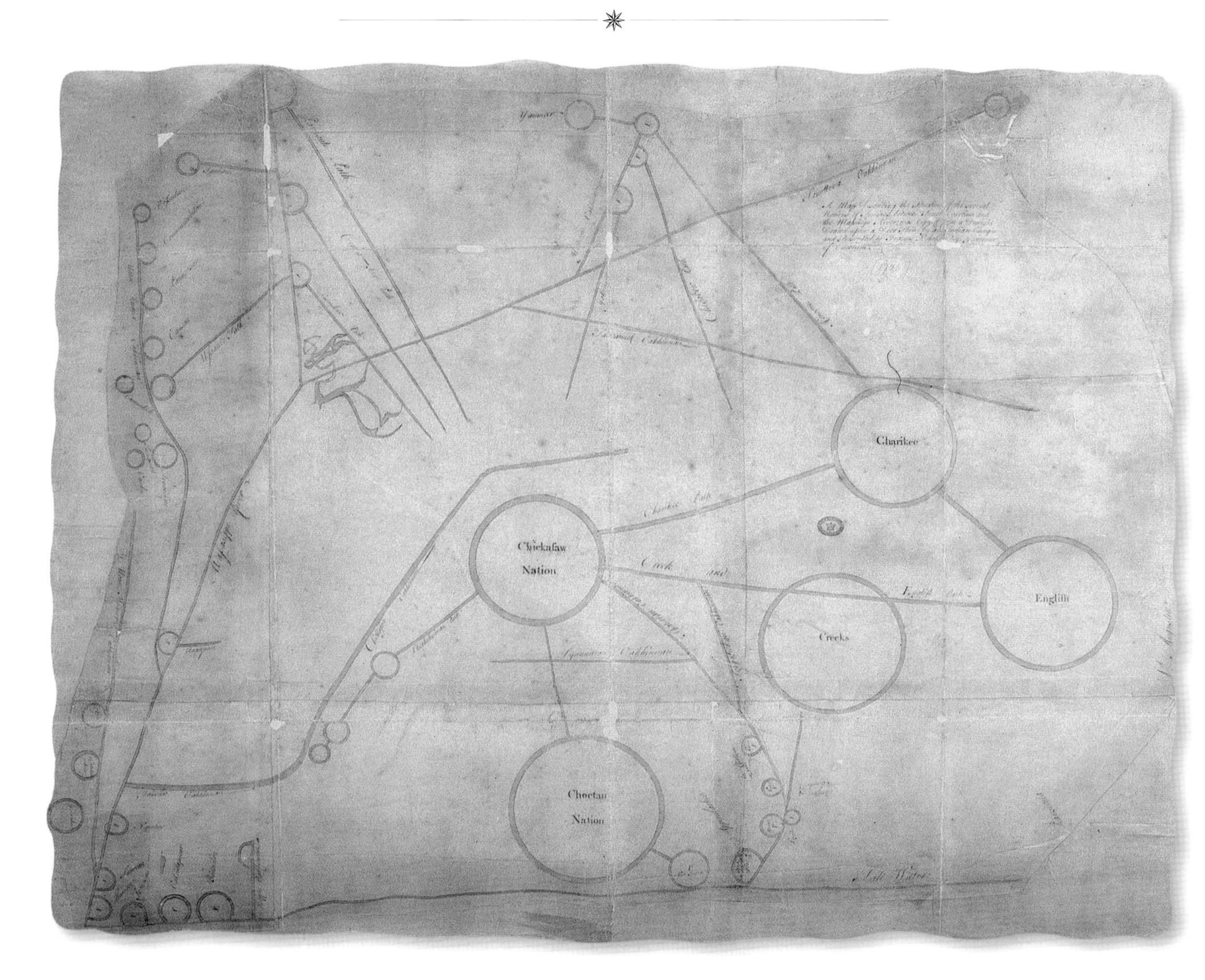

ABOVE ***The Chickasaw map, 1723***
This manuscript is a copy of a map drawn on deerskin by an unnamed Native American. Depicting an area about 700,000 square miles from Texas to New York, it was probably intended to illustrate the relative positions of the pro-English Chickasaw tribe and pro-French tribes.

North America covers a vast area, from the searing heat of the Mexican desert in the southwest to the permanent cold of Alaska in the north. There are few examples of maps made in North America before contact with the Europeans. The evidence is restricted to cartographic representations in rock art, such as the rock paintings in Baja, California, and the petroglyphs in Colorado, Nevada, and Arizona. As with all rock art, the identification of map-related representations is sometimes difficult. The best-known example is the Map Rock petroglyph in Idaho (see p. 30). However, many examples survive from the postcontact era. They are made from a variety of materials, including paper, animal skin, ivory, and birch bark. In Canada, for example, the Inuit people engraved maps into the ivory tusks of walrus; a walrus-tusk souvenir dating from the late 19th century shows an Inuit map of Alaska. While the engraving draws upon traditional crafts and indigenous knowledge, the production of such items was stimulated by non-native buyers.

In the forested areas of the northeast in present-day Canada and USA, native peoples painted and inscribed maps on the inside of birch bark. These maps were used to assist in navigating along rivers and waterways—the easiest and quickest routes though the dense forest regions. They were sometimes left as cartographic messages along the trail, attached to sticks. These maps are a practical demonstration of function following form, as it was easier to represent linear patterns on birch bark (the grain prevented the drawing of sinuous lines or complex crosshatching). One of the oldest examples was preserved because it was mounted and framed soon after it was made. The inscription above the map tells the reader that it was "made by Indians on birch-bark and attached to a tree to show their route to others following them." The map was found between Ottawa and Lake Huron in May 1841 by Captain Bainbridge of the British Royal Engineers.

As with the South American experience, many North American maps were produced specifically for the early European settlers, and for the same reasons: in order to gain control of territory, the invaders needed to know where they were and what lay around them. In 1683 the English trader Robert Livingston obtained a map of the Susquehanna River from three Native Americans. The map depicts a section of the river that was well-known to the indigenous people and proved invaluable to the colonists as a result, allowing them to expand their influence and area of trade.

Maps of North America made for the colonial authorities also drew upon the knowledge of indigenous cartographers. Francis Nicholson, the governor of Maryland, South Carolina, and Virginia from 1721 to 1728, took a great interest in the cartographic knowledge of the Native Americans. As a result in 1721 and 1723 respectively he was presented with two indigenous maps: a Catawba map that showed the Native American peoples in South Carolina, and a Chickasaw map on deer skin that depicted the Indian nations between South Carolina and the Mississippi. The cartographer of the Chickasaw map, an unnamed "Indian Caicique," produced highly abstracted depictions of intertribal connections. In this way, indigenous mapmakers assisted the colonizers in their enterprise.

A HOMELY COSMOLOGY

Maps of the cosmos can come in many forms, even in the way homes are designed. The traditional houses of the Navajo Native Americans are circular, with the door facing east and a fire in the center. Hence, the sun circles around the house, and the house represents the cosmos, mapped into the fabric of everyday life.

RIGHT ***Prehistoric rock carvings, Nootka Canada***
Exposed walls proved a blank page for indigenous people to write messages. Some of the messages were highly symbolic maps of the cosmos and the local area. Finding the key to these maps is an intriguing puzzle.

Mapping South America

Maps have played an important role in the exploration and discovery of New Lands. Cartography became an essential element in the European incorporation and appropriation of overseas territory. The mapping of new territory was a vital part of political control as well as scientific understanding. The New World was mapped in order to be understood as well as subordinated.

IN 1492, MARTIN BEHAIM made a globe of the world and Christopher Columbus landed in what he thought was Asia. We do not have a copy of the map Columbus used, but it was probably similar to Behaim's globe in its depiction of the world. While Behaim's globe does not show the New World, it does show China at about the same distance from Europe as the Americas, with the island of Cipangu (Japan) situated just to the west of the mid-Atlantic. According to Columbus, Asia was within reasonable sailing distance.

After its discovery, the New World was gradually described and represented in map form. Columbus' pilot, Juan de la Cosa, made a chart of the world in around 1500 showing some of the islands of the Caribbean, with Cuba's distinctive outline clearly visible, plus a large landmass north and south of the islands (see page 63). Portugal and Spain were extremely active in the exploration of the New World. One of the earliest maps of those lands is the "Cantino Planisphere," drawn around 1502. Cantino was an Italian living in Portugal, who smuggled the map out of the country to present to his superior, the Duke of Ferrara. The map shows the outline of the coast of Brazil

RIGHT *World map* (mundu spericum), *c.1506, by Giovanni Contarini*

This fan-shaped map is one of the first maps to include Columbus's discoveries. However, the mapmaker believed that the islands on which Columbus landed, shown in the middle left of this map, were off the coast of Asia. The new islands are portrayed as part of an old world view.

with Portuguese flags dotting the coastline, and is interesting for several reasons. For example, the flags on the coastline make it clear that the mapping of the New World was considered to be part of the process of claiming these new lands for western nations.

The oldest printed map of the New World is by Giovanni Matteo Contarini. Completed around 1506 it shows the Caribbean islands in the middle of the ocean with a vast unknown continent to the south and no North America at all. Contarini believed that Columbus had landed in Indo-China. The text claims that the place "holds a great store of gold."

By 1507 a map by Martin Waldseemuller showed North America as a separate continent. The map is crude, and North and South America are shown as separated by a small strait of water. However, this map is the first printed representation of the New World as an identifiably separate territory, and is also the first map to use the name "America", in honor of Amerigo Vespucci.

In 1576, Philip Apian, a skilled map- and globemaker, was commissioned by Duke Albrecht V to make a map of Bavaria and a globe of the world. The resulting globe shows a quite different world from that of the Behaim globe made 84 years earlier. North and South America are joined by a narrow isthmus, and the river systems in South America are a rough but true representation of the courses of the Amazon and the Plate. Florida is clearly shown in North America, but little else is recognizable. The coastlines are reasonably accurate, but the interior of these huge continents is hardly mapped at all.

EUROPEAN DISCOVERY AND EXPLORATION OF THE AMERICAS

The first Europeans to reach the Americas were Norsemen who settled in Iceland and Greenland between the 9th and 15th centuries, from where limited contacts were made with some coastal regions of North America. However, any settlements there were soon abandoned, and never reported in Europe.

The real European discovery of the Americas occurred in the late 15th century with the voyages of Christopher Columbus to the Caribbean, and John Cabot to Newfoundland. At first these lands were thought to be part of Asia, but it soon became clear that a "New World" had been discovered. In the centuries that followed, several European nations, notably Spain, Britain, and France, sought to gain control of the Americas. Military expeditions were sent to claim the land as theirs, and in their wake, especially in the French and Spanish territories, went missionaries intent on converting the native peoples to Christianity. Settlements were built, and adventurers and explorers began to chart the newly conquered territories.

In 1521, Spanish forces under Cortés conquered the Aztecs, and Spain took control of Mexico. This success inspired other conquistadors, such as Pizarro, to venture to the New World, and during the 16th century, Spain grew to dominate large parts of Central and South America.

The exploration of the east coast of North America by the British and French was dominated by attempts to find a navigable sea route to the profitable markets of Asia. This "Northwest Passage" proved elusive, but the search for it led to the mapping of large areas of the new continent. Colonization followed slowly, and it was only in the early 17th century that the French, Dutch, and English established permanent settlements in North America.

Mapping North America

While the Spanish and Portuguese laid large claim to South America and were responsible for the early western mappings of that land, the mapping of North America was mainly left to the Italians, Dutch, French, and English.

In May 1497 the Venetian explorer John Cabot sailed from Bristol, England, and within a month landed in what is now Newfoundland. Like Columbus, Cabot thought he had landed in Asia, and he claimed the territory for the English king, Henry VII. His son Sebastian also sailed west, on behalf of the English as well as the Spanish. His world map, the "Cabot Mappemonde" was completed in 1544 and can be seen today in the National Library in Paris.

The French were actively involved in exploring along the St. Lawrence River. Jacques Cartier (1491–1557) explored the region between 1534 and 1541 searching for a way to the Orient, and his discoveries were incorporated into many subsequent maps of the area. Sixty years later, another Frenchman, Samuel de Champlain (1567–1635), made his first expedition to North America. On his return to France he suggested that the region could, and should, be settled and colonized. With this idea in mind, he returned to North America and traveled throughout eastern Canada and New England, producing a number of important maps along the way. In 1612 he produced a map that promoted his ideas of colonization and was clearly

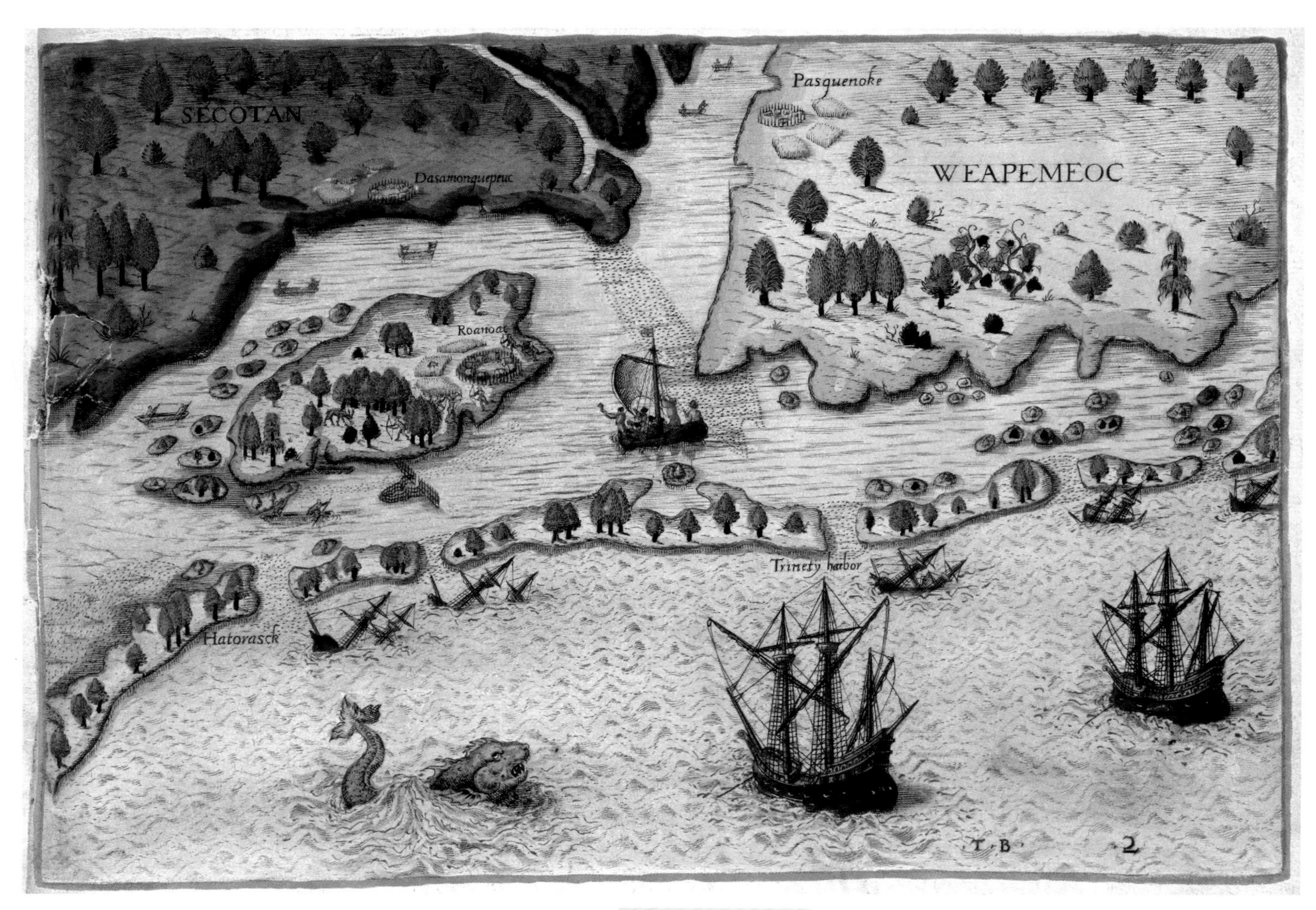

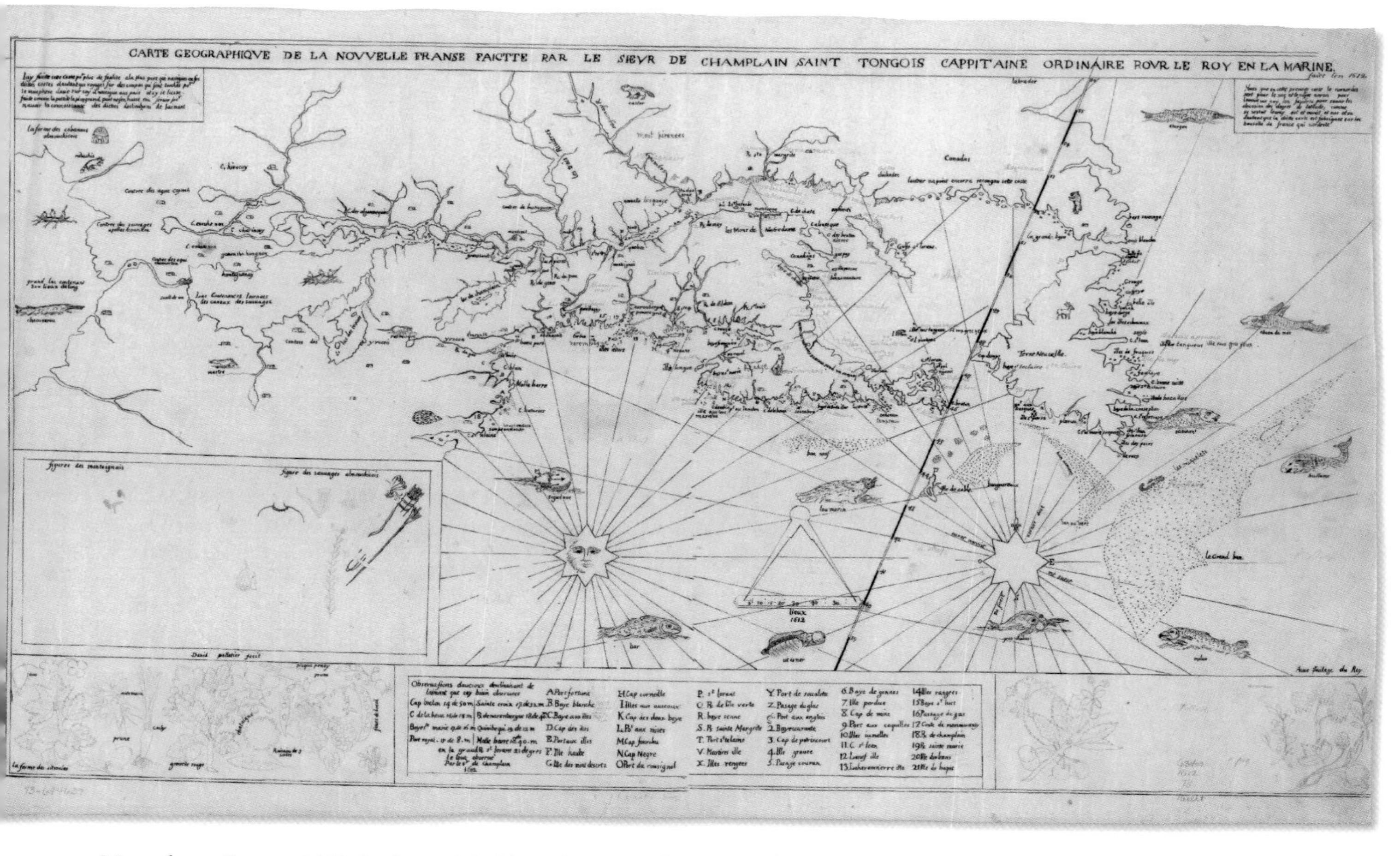

ABOVE ***Map of new France, 1612, by Samuel de Champlain***
Champlain's knowledge of the new land of North America, like the other early European explorers, was biased in favor of the coastal areas. The interior was less well known. Rivers were an important access into the interior. In this map the river routes and their interconnections are clearly shown.

LEFT ***Map of the arrival of the English in Virginia, c.1585, by John White***
The sunken ships along the barrier islands tell of the navigational dangers. Native American canoes are shown and native American names, such as Secotan and Weapemeoc, are given. The English were arriving in a land already occupied.

designed with prospective settlers in mind. The bounty of the region was represented by scantily clad natives, a dazzling array of natural products, and the prospect of easy movement farther west—perhaps even to Asia.

The English were also eager to claim territory in the New World. Unable to compete with the Spanish and Portuguese in the south they instead looked to the north. Sir Walter Raleigh was a keen promoter of—and participant in—English overseas expansion, and in March 1584 he received permission from Queen Elizabeth I to make voyages to the New World. His second expedition left Plymouth on April 9, 1585. On board were Thomas Harriot, the principal navigator, and John White, who had been given special responsibility to note down and draw all they saw, to survey the ground, and make a general map. Harriot took a variety of instruments with him including compasses and clocks. On June 30, the fleet anchored at Roanoke Island and Harriot and White began work. They surveyed the entire coastline from Ocracoke to Cape Henry and westward up the Roanoke and Chowan Rivers. Harriot fixed exact locations with his astronomical instruments and survey equipment and conducted studies of the local people and their language. White painted 63 watercolors of flora, fauna, and the native peoples. The result was one of the most comprehensive surveys of North America by the early Europeans. On his return to England in 1586, Harriot wrote *A Briefe and True Report of the New Found Land of Virginia* (1588), which was later republished by the Flemish publisher Theodore de Bry with the addition of beautifully illustrated engravings from John White's watercolors.

Mapping the Pacific

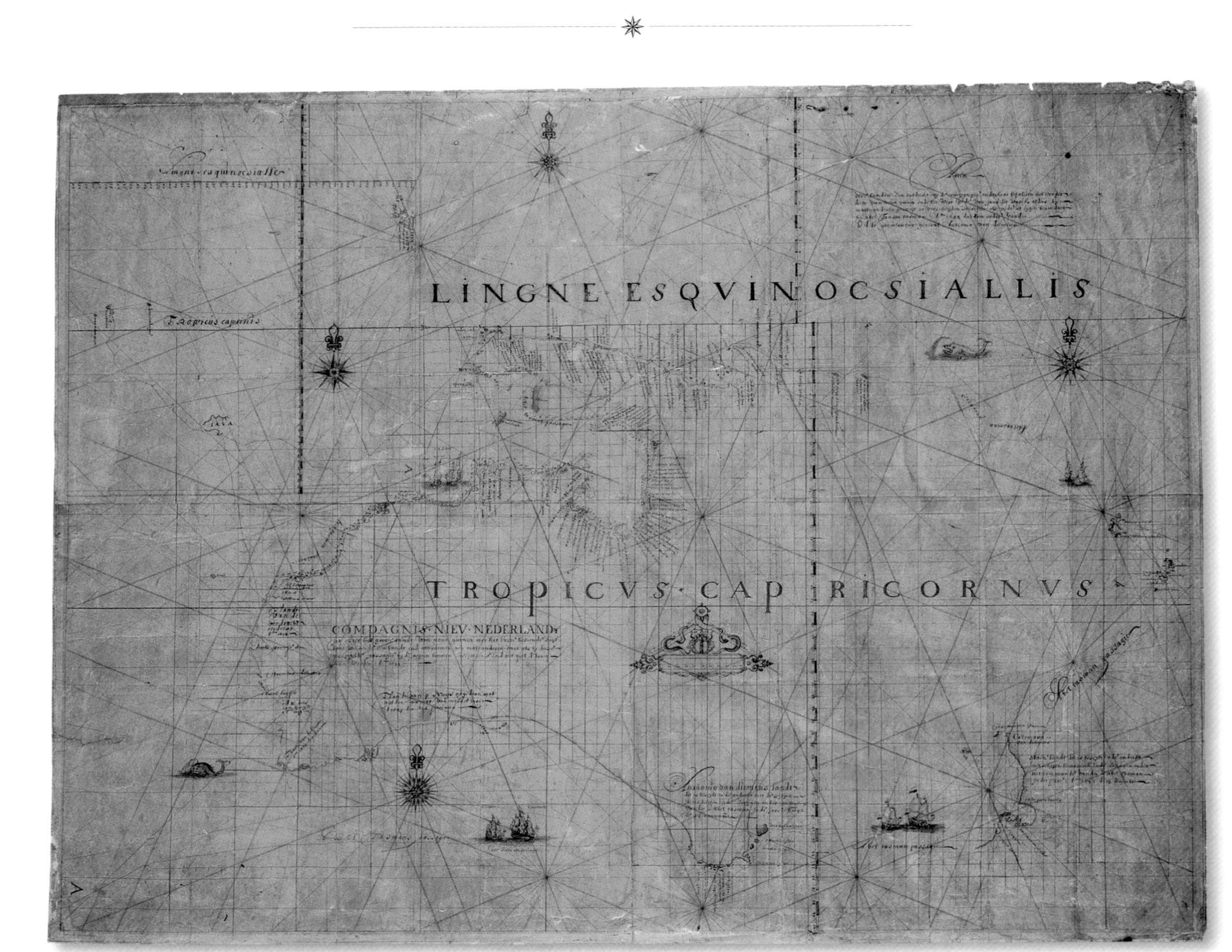

In many 16th-century European maps of the world the Pacific Ocean is shown as a blank space between the barely known America and the only slightly better-known Asia. Exploring this vast ocean presented a huge challenge to explorers and mariners.

The Portuguese explorer Ferdinand Magellan (*c.* 1480–1521) was one of the first sailors to chart the Pacific. In 1519 he headed a Spanish expedition seeking a passage west to the Indonesian Molucca Islands—then known as the Spice Islands. He sailed across the Atlantic, round the southern tip of South America (through what is now known as the Strait of Magellan), and into the Pacific. He was then killed by hostile local people in the Philippines.

ABOVE ***Map of the South Pacific, early 17th century, by Abel Tasman***
In 1639, the Dutch navigator Tasman was sent by the Dutch Governor General of the East Indies to search for islands of gold and silver east of Japan. The five-month journey was the first that Tasman made to the south Pacific. His journeys produced some of the first detailed European maps of the coastal areas.

RIGHT ***Chart of New Zealand, late 18th century, by Captain James Cook***
Captain Cook led three expeditions to the Pacific and southern oceans. He sighted the coast of New Zealand on October 6, 1769. Cook was not just a brilliant navigator but also an accomplished map- and chartmaker. He made some of the earliest European maps of Hawaii, Australia, and New Zealand.

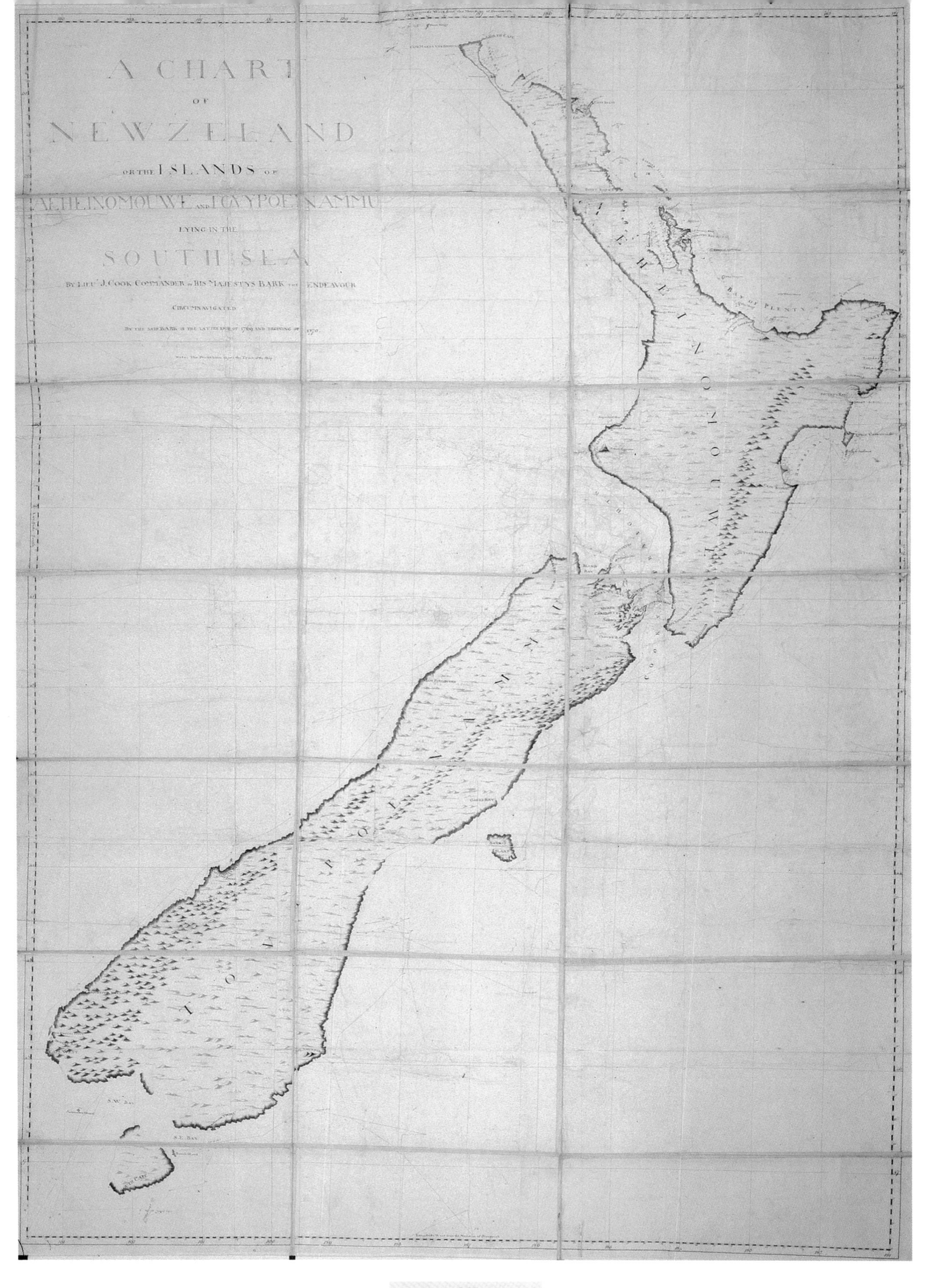
A CHART
OF
NEWZELAND
OR THE ISLANDS OF
AEHEINOMOUWE AND TOVYPOENAMMU
LYING IN THE
SOUTH SEA
BY LIEUT. J. COOK COMMANDER of HIS MAJESTYS BARK the ENDEAVOUR
CIRCUMNAVIGATED
BY THE SAID BARK IN THE LATTER END OF 1769 AND BEGINING OF 1770.
BAY OF PLENTY
S.W. BAY
S.E. BAY

Eight of Magellan's men were also murdered. The survivors continued the journey and arrived back in Spain in September 1522. Only 18 of the original 270 crew survived, but they had achieved the first circumnavigation of the globe, and identified islands that would be useful as "stepping stones" for crossing the vast Pacific. Keen not to be outdone, between 1577 and 1580 the Englishman Sir Francis Drake (*c.* 1540–96) also managed to circumnavigate the globe, landing en route on the coast of northern California and claiming it for the English. For 200 years many maps marked this area as "New Albion."

In the 17th century, the Dutch replaced the Spanish and Portuguese as the most active European explorers of the Pacific. The Dutch navigator Abel Tasman (*c.* 1603–59) sailed right around Australia and was the first European to visit Tasmania, New Zealand, Tonga, and Fiji. In a later voyage of 1644, he visited Australia itself, calling it "New Holland," a name that stuck for another 150 years. Many Dutch maps of the mid- to late 17th century incorporated and built upon Tasman's amazing discoveries and achievements.

In the 18th and early 19th centuries, the mapping of the Pacific was undertaken mainly by the French and British. A period of intense rivalry began with a British expedition that sailed in June 1764 under the command of Commodore John Byron. The expedition was commissioned by the Admiralty to find possible bases for the English navy in the Pacific and South Atlantic. A second expedition set out in 1766 under the command of Captain Samuel Wallis and discovered islands in the Tahiti group.

In the same year, the first French expedition to the South Seas left Nantes with Louis-Antoine de Bougainville in command. Later, Jean François Marie de Surville, la Perouse, and Entrecasteaux, in separate voyages, extended French understanding of Pacific geography. Accurate maps were made of coastlines, islands, and maritime regions; this new and improved cartographic knowledge was quickly incorporated into printed maps. By 1810 the Pacific was no longer a blank canvas but had been successfully gridded and mapped.

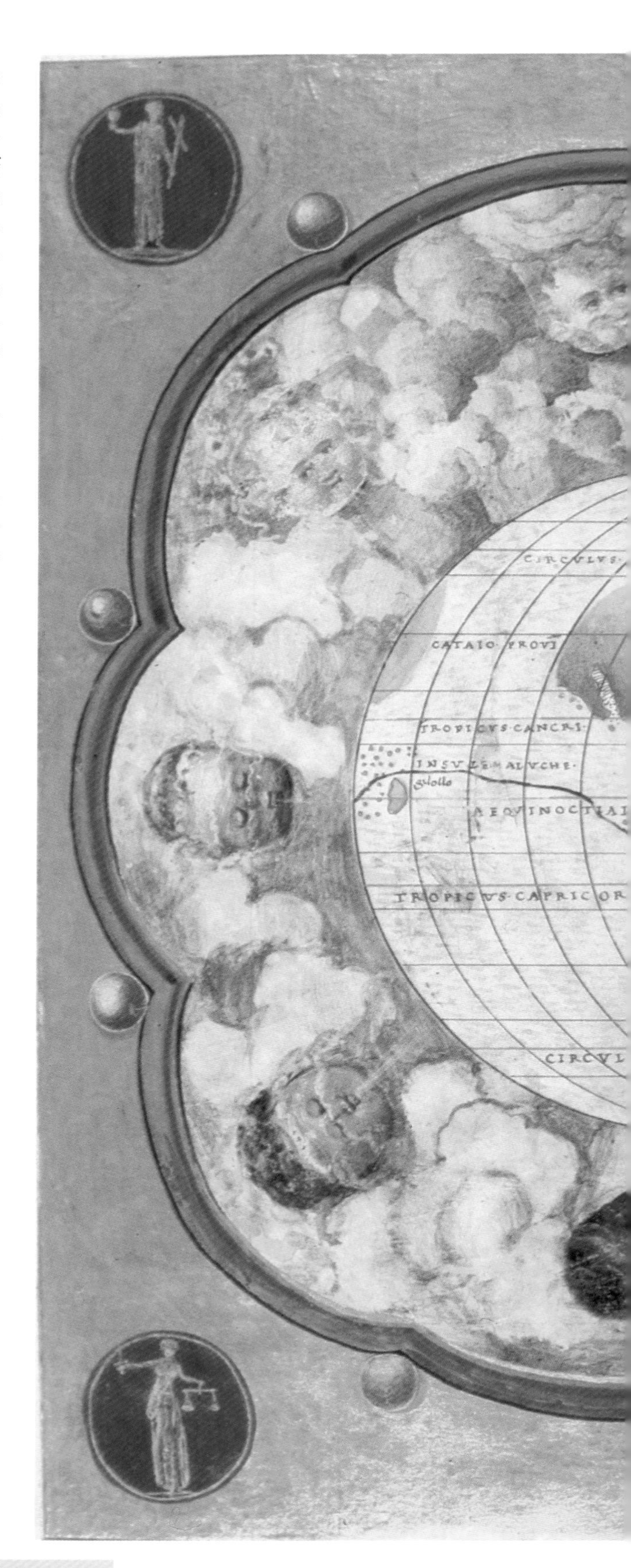

RIGHT ***World map showing Magellan's voyage, 1544, by Battista Agnese***
This world map is from a portolan atlas produced in the workshop of the Italian mapmaker Agnese. There are many editions of this map, but on this particular one the cartographer has plotted Magellan's circumnavigation of the world.

TERRA DE BACALAO
CATAIO
ASIA
LIBIA INFERIOR
AEGIPTVS
PERV
MVDVS NOVVS
BRAZIL
RIO DE LA PLATA
INDICV MARE
C·DE BONA SPERANZA

The Development of the Sea Atlas

A cheaper alternative to the "Dieppe atlases" were those made by Battista Agnese, a prolific Venetian chart-maker whose workshop produced over 60 different sea atlases between 1534 and 1564. "Agnese atlases" are smaller than the Dieppe versions (see page 64), and were aimed at a less affluent market; nevertheless they remain beautiful pieces of craftsmanship. The charts are all gridded and plotted with latitude but no longitude, and each atlas typically contains a calendar, a table of declinations, a picture of an armillary sphere, a zodiac, nine sea charts, and an oval map of the world. The charts are full of vignettes of cities, forests, mountains, and rivers, and the lettering along the coasts is consecutively red and black, to make reading easier.

By the late 16th century, a wider range of more reasonably priced sea atlases was becoming available. A good example is the *Spieghel der Zeevaerdt*, published in two parts in 1584 and 1585. Its English title is the *Mariner's Mirrour*, and it contains sea charts of the coastal waters of western Europe from Cadiz to the Baltic. The author was a Dutchman, Lucas Janszoon Waghenaer (1534–1606), who had been a sea pilot in his youth. *Spieghel der Zeevaerdt* was his "magnum opus," and provided a manual of navigation as well as printed charts on a common scale covering the coasts of northern and western Europe. Part 1 begins with material on navigation, and tables of the sun's declination and lunar risings. It is a practical guide that gives detailed instructions on how to navigate by the stars. The first map is a portolan chart of northwest Europe, the area covered in the atlas, followed by 23 further detailed charts. Volume 2 contains 22 charts to the scale 1:370,000, showing profiles of the coast, compass roses, depths around

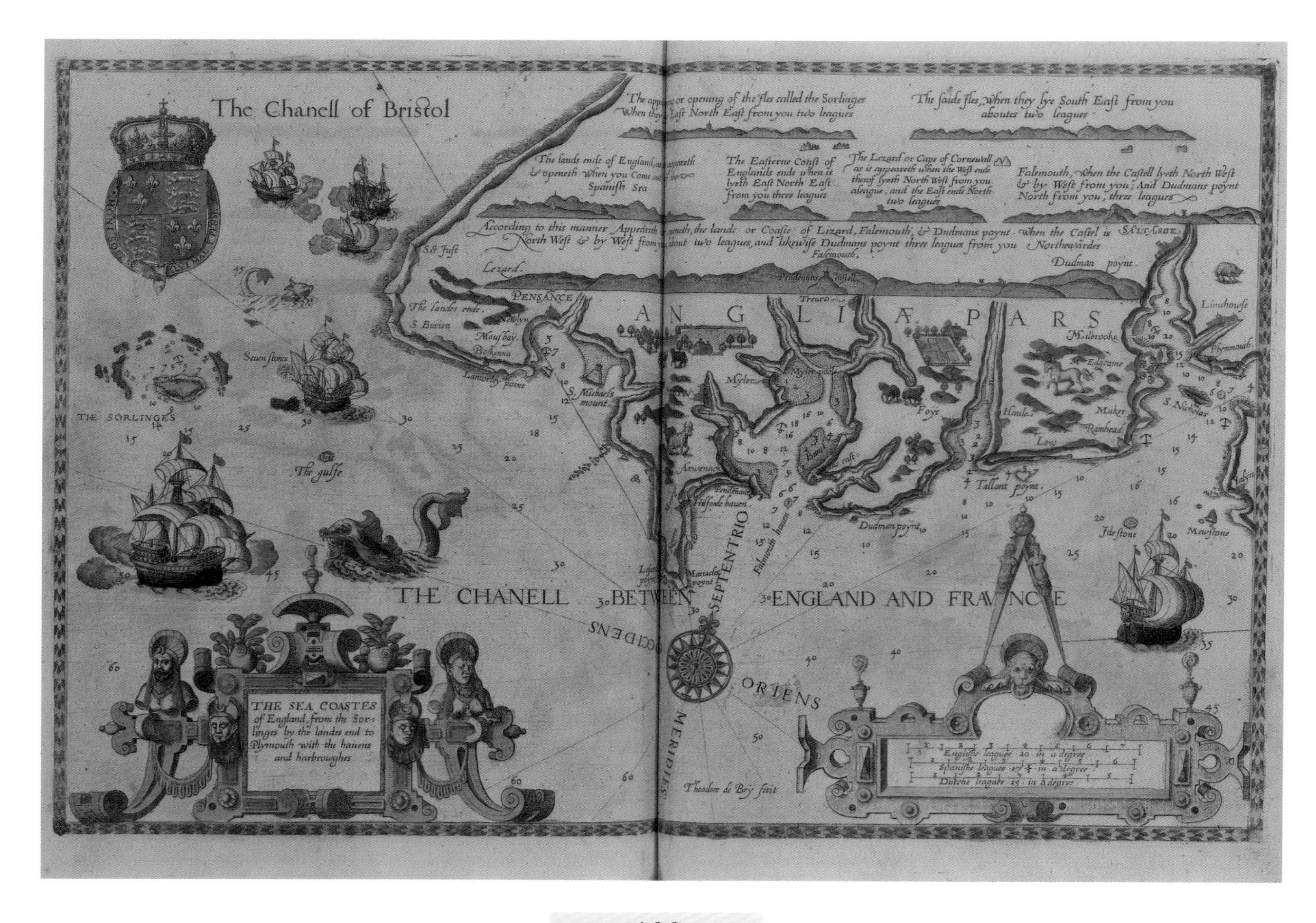

river mouths, and the location of sandbanks, towns, and rivers. In taking this approach, Waghenaer was the first to show sea charts and coastal profiles on the same map. Not surprisingly, the atlas was a great success, and by 1592 was available in five languages. Eighteen Dutch editions had been published by 1620.

Waghenaer went on to produce other navigational texts. His *Thresoor der Zeevaerdt* (*Mariner's Treasure*) of 1592 was a detailed set of sailing directions, more precise than the *Spieghel* and including charts for northern Scotland, the Baltic Sea, and the Mediterranean. In this book Waghenaer chose the uniform scale of 1: 600,000, and chose to place the profiles of the coasts in the text rather than on the charts.

Waghenaer's work was the template for subsequent publications. In 1606 Willem Blaeu (1571–1638), a nautical instrument- and mapmaker, published *Licht der Zeevaerdt*, which updated Waghenaer's *Spieghel* and contained more charts of southeast England and the Low Countries. In 1612 it was translated into English as *The Light of Navigation*. Blaeu went on to publish *Eeste deel der Zeespiegel* in 1623, which was translated two years later as *The Sea-Mirrour*, and subtitled, *Containing a briefe instruction in the art of navigation and a description of seas and costs of the Easterne, Northerne and Westerne navigation.*

The popularity of the atlases produced by cartographers such as Waghenaer and Blaeu was a direct reflection of the status of the Dutch as a major maritime power in the 16th century. When dominance of the sea was transferred to the British in the 17th century, it was English mapmakers who provided the maritime atlases to guide English shipping all over the world.

BELOW LEFT ***Sea atlas, by Waghenaer***
This is an English version of Waghenaer's innovative sea atlas. The transects in the interior were snapshots of the terrain visible to mariners and thus were helpful to seamen looking at the coast and trying to estimate where they were.

BELOW ***A Dutch chart, by Lucas Jans***
The sea atlases rarely depicted territory very far inland. Their concern was with the land-sea littoral. The charts give estimates of coastal water depths so that ships would avoid the risk of grounding.

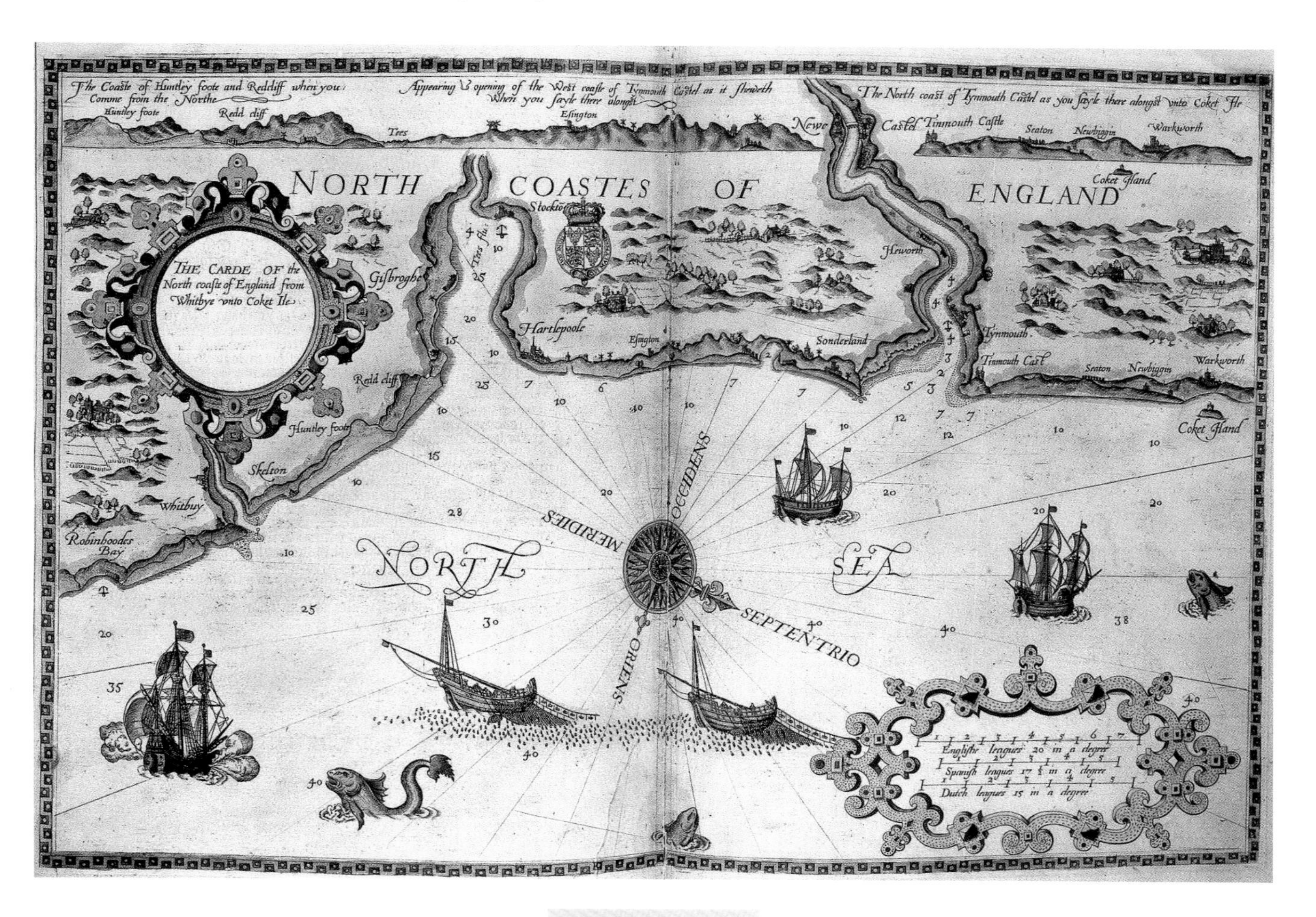

10

MAPS OF THE EUROPEAN RENAISSANCE

Ptolemy and the Renaissance

By the early 1400s, Byzantine scholars had begun to bring their Greek manuscripts, including Ptolemy's writings, to Italy (see page 54). A translation of Ptolemy's Guide to Geography *into Latin was begun by Emanuel Chrysoloras and completed by Jacopo d'Angolo of Tuscany in 1406, after which it was widely distributed.*

BEFORE PRINTING BECAME widespread, manuscripts were first translated and then copied by hand. In the case of Ptolemy's *Guide to Geography*, as with other texts, the various translations involved changes and amendments, and were hence not straight translations at all. They are better thought of as "updated editions." In 1427 for example, Guillaume Fillastre, the Canon of Rheims, France, told his copying scribe to add a map of northern Europe by the Danish geographer Claudius Clavus to the *Guide*. In 1466, Donnus Nicolaus Germanus presented the Duke of Ferrara, Italy, with a copy of the *Guide* that included further new map projections

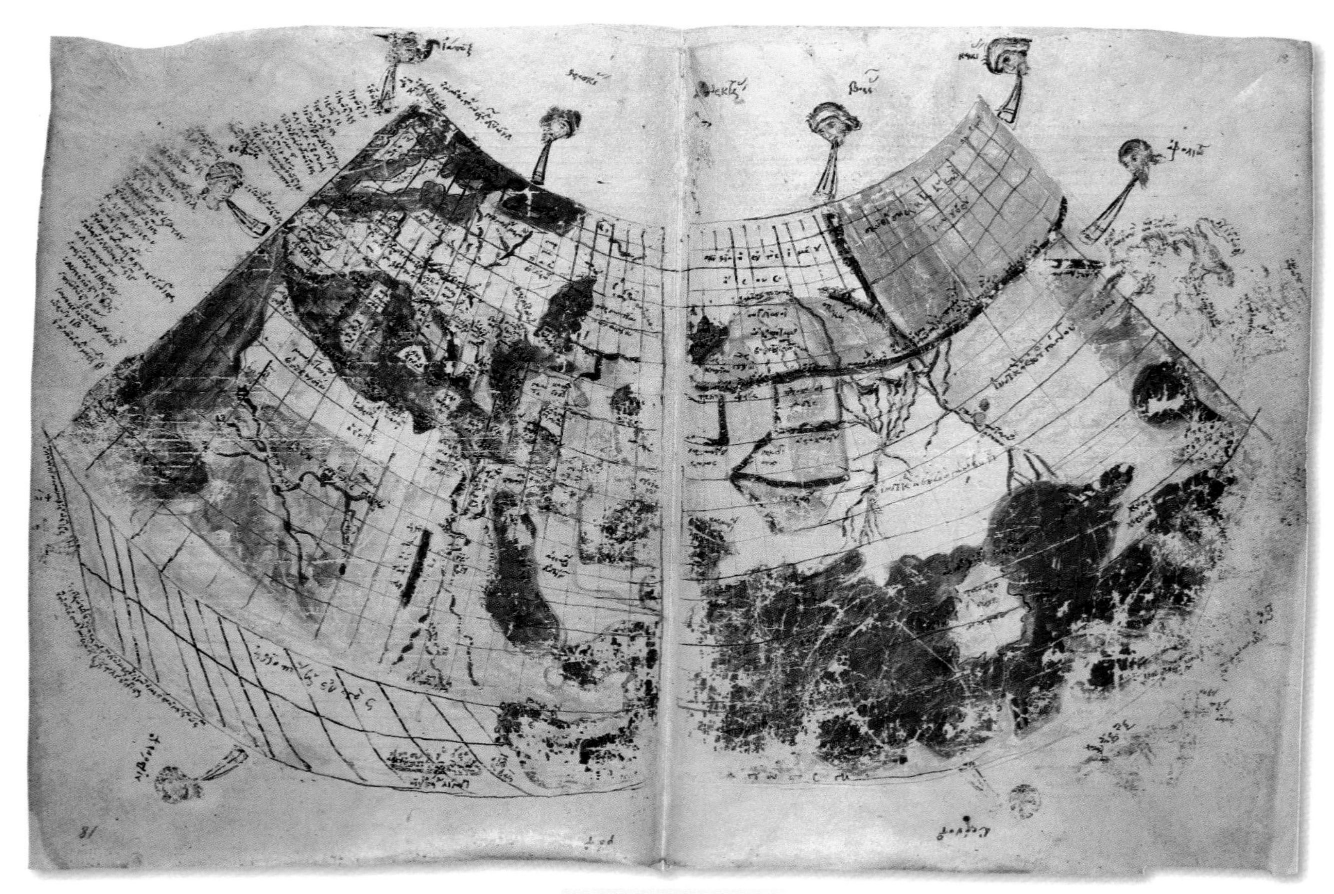

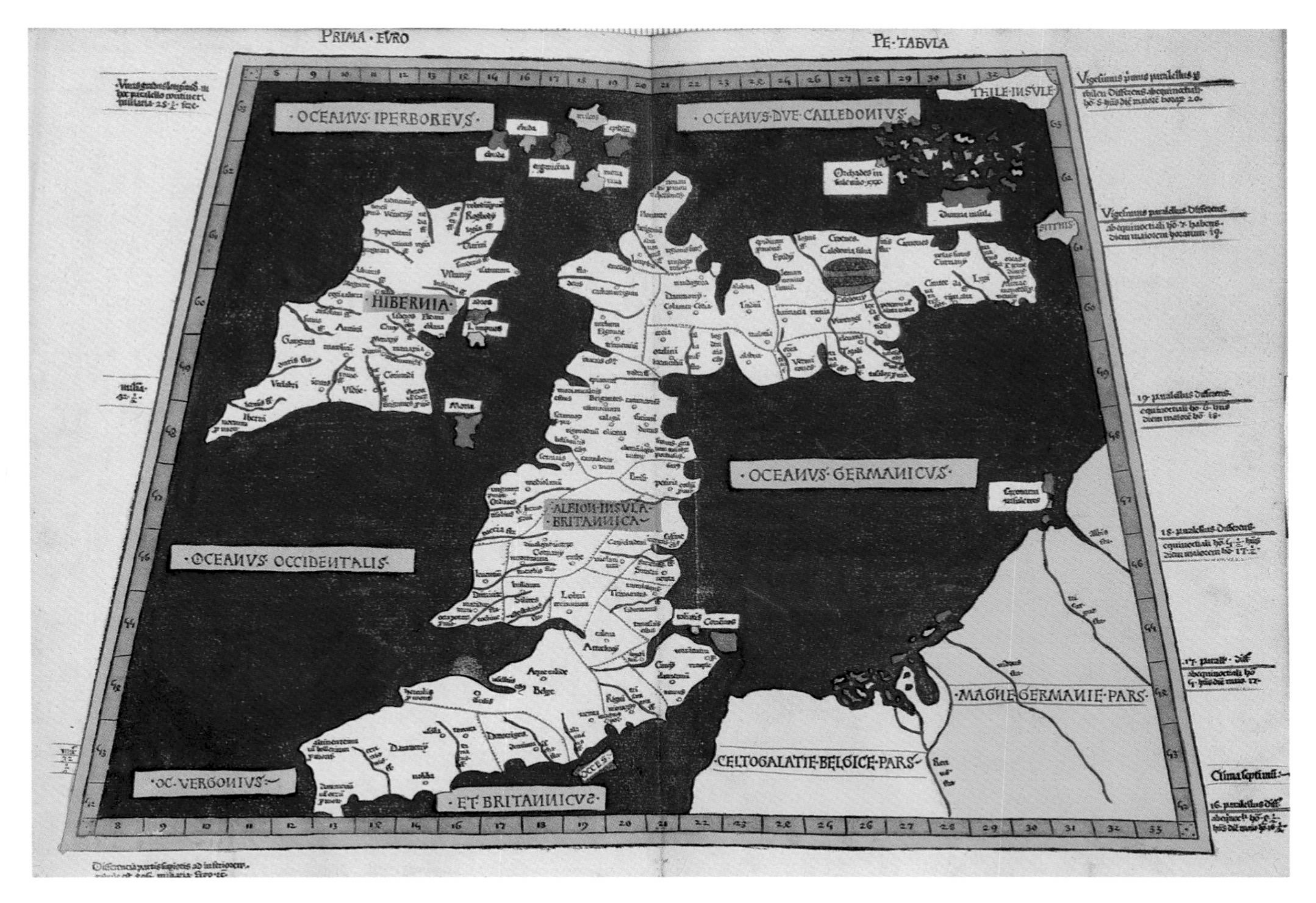

ABOVE ***Prima Europa Tabula*, *1482, from Claudius Ptolemy's* Guide to Geography**

This early Renaissance Ptolemaic map of the British Isles shows a very distorted Scotland that lies east to west rather than north to south. On the remote edge of the Roman Empire, it was one of the least known provinces of the continent. The woodcut map pinpoints major cities such as London, St. Albans, Colchester, and York.

LEFT ***World map after Ptolemy***

Ptolemy outlined two world projections, including this fan-shaped design. It shows the world as then known to classical scholars: Europe and Asia as far as the borders with China and north and central Africa. The New World was unknown. The large island at the bottom right, now known as Sri Lanka, was an important island for spice traders.

and a cartographic key for representing physical features and boundaries. The Florentine painter Piero del Massaio designed two manuscript copies of the *Guide* in 1469 and 1472, which contained contemporary maps of Spain, France, and Italy as well as perspective views of the major cities of the Mediterranean. Thus, working on Ptolemy's text was a wonderful opportunity to bring this great work right up to date, and hence make it a practical tool as well as a scholarly tome.

The history of the printing of the *Guide* reflects the early history of printing in Europe. The first printed copy appeared in Vicenza, Italy, in 1475. It contained no maps, but had two diagrams of map projections. At about the same time, other editions appeared in Rome (1478), Florence (1480), and Ulm, in Germany (1482). The Ulm edition has richly colored woodblock maps with deep-blue seas and yellow borders, and is arguably one of the most beautiful of all (see page 105).

More than 50 editions of the *Guide* appeared in cities all over Europe between 1475 and 1730 in a variety of forms. The text was published in lavish editions for wealthy patrons, such as the beautiful Ulm edition, as well as in smaller, more modest volumes meant for wider circulation to the less wealthy, such as the 1548 and 1561 editions. After 1508, editions of the *Guide* included maps incorporating the discovery of the New World.

Those who worked on the various editions of the *Guide* constitute a "who's who" of Renaissance cartographers: Nicolaus and Jodocus Hondius, Gerardus Mercator, Sebastian Munster, Johan Ruysch, Bernardus Sylvanus, and Martin Waldseemuller. Ptolemy's great work provided an opportunity for successive generations of mapmakers to try out their skills and test themselves against a common standard. The *Guide* was a publishing phenomenon that allowed scholars to work on an old theme while developing new twists: new projections, new maps, new ways of looking at a new world. The publishing of Ptolemy was, after the Bible, one of the most important printing ventures of the Renaissance, and the primary impulse to creative cartography in the 16th century. Ptolemy's influence on Renaissance mapmaking was sufficient for Giovanni Matteo Contarini to describe himself, on his 1506 world map, as "famed in the Ptolemaen art."

Successive 16th-century editions of the *Guide* give us a remarkably detailed picture of an expanding world. For example, while a 1513 edition by Martin Waldseemuller had 20 maps, a 1548 edition by Giacomo Gastadi had 33.

THE RENAISSANCE

The term Renaissance means "rebirth." It describes the period of intellectual, artistic, and cultural awakening in Europe that characterized the change from the medieval period to the modern era. The Renaissance originated in Italy during the 14th century and reached its height in the 15th and 16th centuries. In other parts of Europe it occurred between the 15th and mid-16th centuries.

The Renaissance was a time of great achievements in learning, literature, science, and the arts. It found its first expression in Italy, where relative political stability and economic growth led to the establishment of libraries and universities. Scholars, poets, craftsmen, and artists were supported by great patrons such as the Medici family of Florence and the Sforza of Milan. Interest in the classical civilizations was reawakened during this era, reflected in the writings of Francesco Petrarca and Pierre de Ronsard, the art of Michelangelo, and the architecture of Alberti and Brunelleschi.

The philosophy of humanism, which placed secular, human values at its center, challenged medieval religious authority and called for a return to classical ideals. The most notable humanist was the Dutch scholar Erasmus. Humanism led to a more realistic depiction of nature in art, as can be seen in the works of Leonardo da Vinci and Raphael. It also inspired the romantic and sensual writings of Boccaccio and Rabelais.

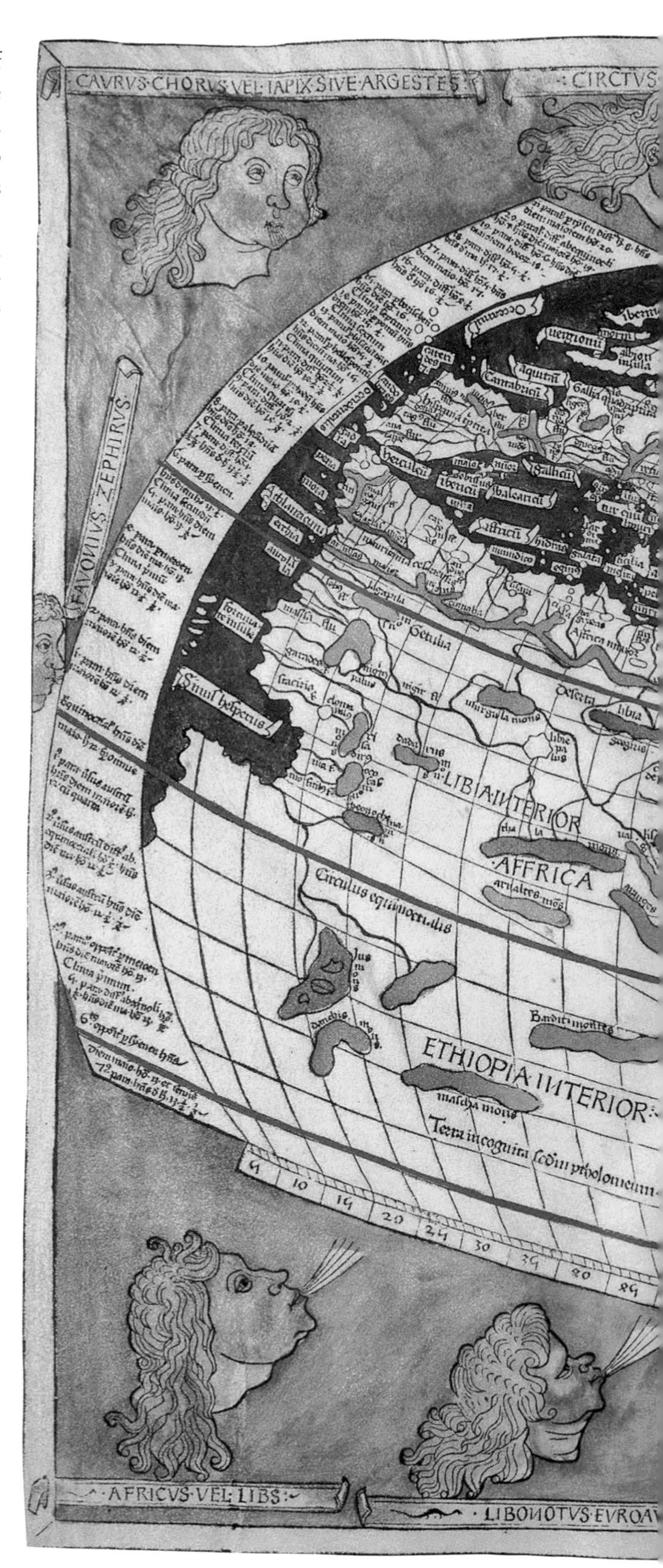

RIGHT ***World map by Ptolemy***
This world map is drawn to the second projection suggested by Ptolemy, the pseudoconic projection (see page 53). It reveals the world known to European scholars before the discovery of the New World. This map is from the beautiful Renaissance Ulm edition.

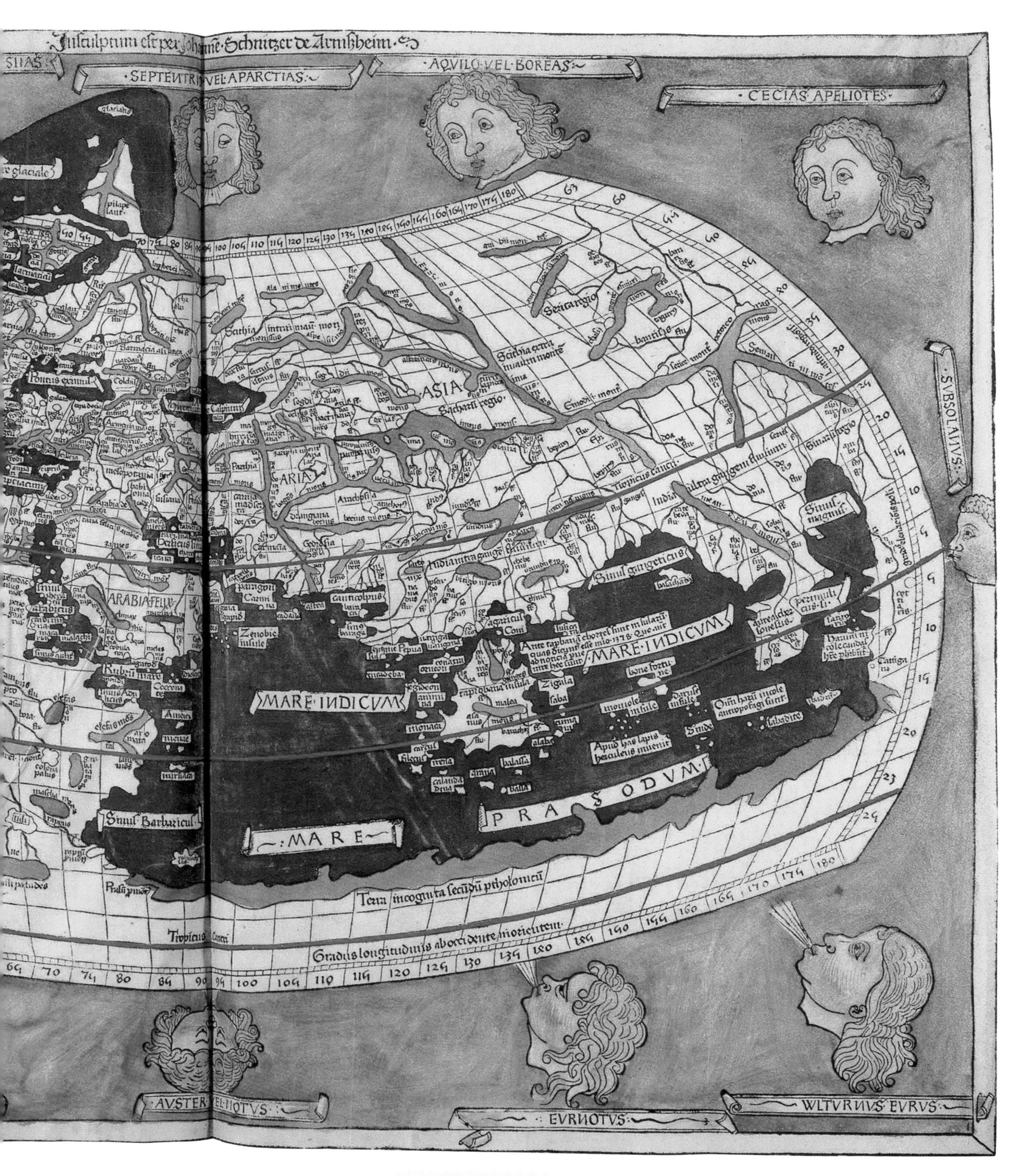
SEPTENTRI VEL APARCTIAS
AQVILO VEL BOREAS
CECIAS APELIOTES
SVBSOLANVS
ASIA
MARE INDICVM
PRASODVM
MARE
AVSTER VEL NOTVS
EVRNOTVS
WLTVRNVS EVRVS

Cosmography

In his book *Cosmographia*, Peter Apian (1495–1552), drawing on Ptolemy, made a distinction between cosmography, geography, and chorography: cosmography was the study of the universe, geography was the examination of the earth, and chorography looked at parts of the earth. The terms were fluid rather than fixed; for example, the *Guide* was sometimes translated as the *Guide to Geography* and sometimes as the *Guide to Cosmography*.

Throughout the 16th century, a number of influential books were published that outlined the new cosmography. The most influential work was certainly Apian's *Cosmographia*. Apian was born in Lesinig, Germany, on

Hoc Schema demonstrat terram esse Globosam.

Si terra esset Tetragonica /vmbra quoqꝫ tetragonalis figurae in eclypsatione lunari appareret.

Si terra esset Trigonica :vmbra quoqꝫ trian/gularem haberet formulam.

Si terra hexagonalis esset figure:eius quoqꝫ vmbra in defectu lunari hexagonalis appareret. que tamen rotunda cernitur.

ABOVE *from Apian's* Cosmographia
Apian's book is full of delightful illustrations such as this one that explains the principle of solar and lunar eclipses. The diagrams tend to personalize and humanize scientific facts.

RENAISSANCE MAN LOOKS TO THE STARS

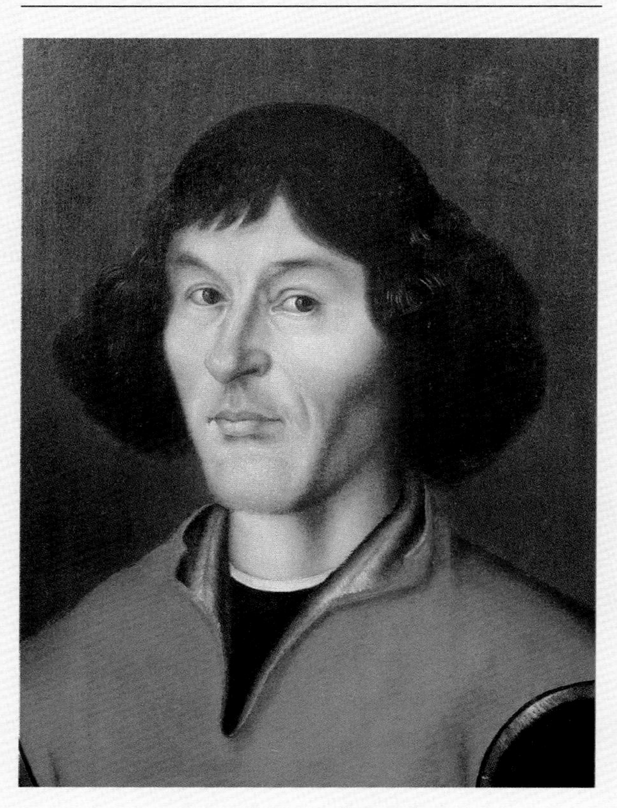

ABOVE *Nicolaus Copernicus*

The mapping of the heavens was an important part of the "humanist project" of the European Renaissance. While the less precise "science" of astrology had maintained a strong influence from the time of the Roman Empire, a true attempt to map the heavens accurately was not made in Europe until the 16th century, when there was a renewed interest in astronomy. In 1543, Nicolaus Copernicus (1473–1543) published his book *De Revolutionibus Orbium Coelestium* (*On The Revolutions of the Heavenly Spheres*), in which he proposed that the sun, rather than the earth, was the center of the universe, contradicting Ptolemy (see page 46). By doing this, Copernicus found that it was easier to do the calculations required to establish the positions of the planets.

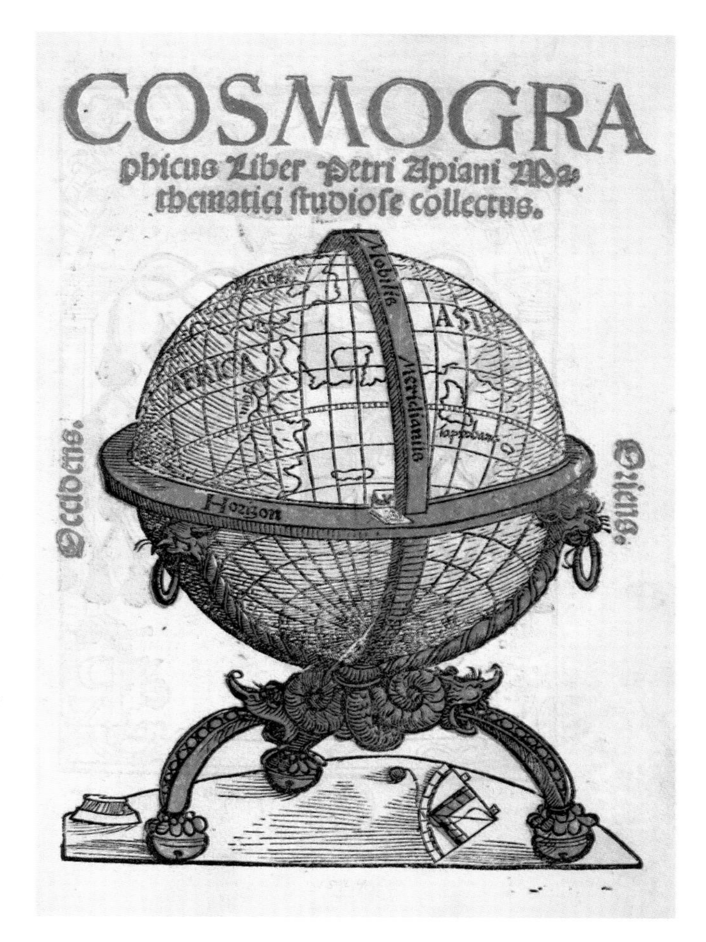

RIGHT *From Apian's* Cosmographia, *1524*
This illustration depicts an armillary sphere. Originally intended for measurement, it was mainly used as a teaching device to show students the structure of the universe.

BELOW *A volvelle from Apian's* Cosmographia
Apian's book is filled with little paper moveable instruments, volvelles that allow the reader to pull a string and make observations. This delicately illustrated volvelle allowed the reader to make connections between months and astrological signs.

April 16, 1495. He studied at Leipzig and Vienna and was considered an outstanding mathematician, astronomer-astrologer, and instrument maker.

The first edition of the *Cosmographia* was published in 1524. It was a general introduction to cosmography and included subjects that we would now call astronomy, geography, surveying, navigation, and instrument making and design. Five years later the cartographer-surveyor Gemma Frisius (1508–55) produced a corrected, amended version, which was published in Antwerp (now in Belgium). The work subsequently became *the* handbook of Renaissance cosmography.

A key illustration in the *Cosmographia*, which can be found in most of the various editions, is a depiction of an armillary sphere, an instrument first outlined by Ptolemy in his *Guide*. The world is held in a cradle of measurements, surrounded by a celestial heaven. Everything is bound in a perfect sphere and is susceptible to measurement and observation. The earth is firmly placed in a wider universe, and its tilt is used to explain the different climatic zones.

The movement of the sun and the moon are used to explain seasonal and daily variations in daylight hours.

A central feature of the *Cosmographia* is measurement: the correct way to measure latitude and longitude, to calculate the times of sunrise and sunset around the world, to ascertain the correct height and distance of far-away objects, and to establish the position of celestial bodies. There are hundreds of detailed diagrams and illustrations showing observers looking at the world through a variety of instruments in order to calculate accurate measurements. The world is an object of technical analysis, seen through the eyeholes of astrolabes, quadrants, nocturnals, and telescopes.

One of Apian's greatest achievements was the *Astronomicum Caesareum* (1540). It is one of the most lavish books that was published in the 16th century, consisting of large, six-layered volvelles (little paper devices that allowed computations to be made) hand colored and beautifully illustrated, which allowed complex, accurate astronomical calculations to be made within 1°. The book is full of star charts and new projections, allowing the northern and southern spheres to be mapped on one page.

Map Miscellanies

The Renaissance project of understanding the world embraced both history and geography. This fusion is apparent in the great chronicle of the world printed in Nuremberg in 1493. The *Nuremberg Chronicle* was history and geography combined in a great rolling epic of some 600 folio pages. It was produced on the cusp between the medieval and the early modern periods and was called by its creators *The Book of Chronicles from the Beginning of the World*. It is one of the greatest picture books ever produced. Unlike those of its medieval predecessors, the illustrations are not small inserts or marginal flourishes, but major enhancements to the text. There are 1,809 prints taken from 645 woodcut blocks, including illustrations of 598 notable people, scenes from the Bible, maps, and city views. As befits an enterprise that was in part a patriotic attempt to show the dominance of Nuremberg over the rival towns of Augsburg and Ulm, the view of the city of Nuremberg is the largest woodcut.

One of the most important writers in the Renaissance cosmogeographical tradition was Sebastian Munster. Born near Mainz, Germany, in 1505 he went to Heidelberg to enter a Franciscan order. Two years later he traveled to Louvain to study mathematics, geography, and astronomy, and in 1509 his order sent him to the monastery of St. Katharina in Rufach in the Vosges Mountains, France, to study geography, mathematics, cosmology, and Hebrew with Konrad Pelikan. Munster was a prolific writer, and published 80 books on theological subjects as well as translating a Hebrew text of the Bible into Latin. Like all cosmographers and mapmakers, he was in thrall to Ptolemy. His *Ptolemy's Geography* first appeared in 1540 and went through numerous editions with added notes and new woodcut maps.

Munster's most important work from the point of view of the history of cartography was his *Cosmography*, first

BELOW ***Nuremberg, from the* Nuremberg Chronicle, *1495***
The Nuremberg Chronicle was conceived, designed, and printed in the German city of Nuremberg. The makers of the book made the largest and most detailed city illustration that of their own city.

published in Geneva in 1544. This was a massive work: the first edition had 659 pages with 520 woodcut maps and illustrations, and subsequent editions increased in size. By 1548, the *Cosmography* had 818 pages and 725 woodcuts, and by 1550 had reached gargantuan proportions, with 1,233 pages and 910 woodcuts! For much of the 16th century it was one of the most important sources of geographical, historical, and scientific knowledge.

The *Cosmography* is an eclectic collection of material—some old, some new, part myth, part fact. It contains diverse information, from surveying and mining techniques to discussions of mythical creatures such as the phoenix, goblins, and spirits. It details the reasons why sugar was grown in parts of Italy, and includes an interesting discussion about the one-eyed and large-eared people who were supposed to inhabit parts of India. Discussions of latitude and longitude sit side by side with genealogies of long-dead European monarchies. It is also full of maps: maps of the world, maps of whole countries, regional maps, and many city views.

THE STRANGE LIFE OF JOHN DEE

John Dee (1527–1608) was one of the most fascinating figures of the 16th century. Born in Wales, his father was well connected at the court of Henry VIII and sent him to Cambridge in 1542. Five years later he went to Louvain (now in Belgium) and studied with Gemma Frisius (1508–55) who was then cosmographer to the emperor and the reviser of Apian's *Cosmographia*. Dee brought back scientific instruments made by Frisius, including the cross-staff and globes as well as knowledge of the triangulation method of surveying. Dee invented a compass that allowed mariners to follow a route across a great circle, the line of minimum distance across the surface of the globe. He was actively involved in exploration and discovery, giving technical advice to Drake, Frobisher, Gilbert, and Raleigh, and instructing many seamen in navigational techniques. He knew the English metaphysical poet John Donne (1572–1631), the dramatist and poet Christopher Marlowe (1564–93), and William Shakespeare (1564–1616).

John Dee tutored and advised some of the most important and powerful people in the land. His mathematical and astrological knowledge was used in the casting of horoscopes to find the most propitious days for events and actions. He was also interested in the occult, and believed he could speak to angels. In his later life he lost his influence and died in poverty in 1608.

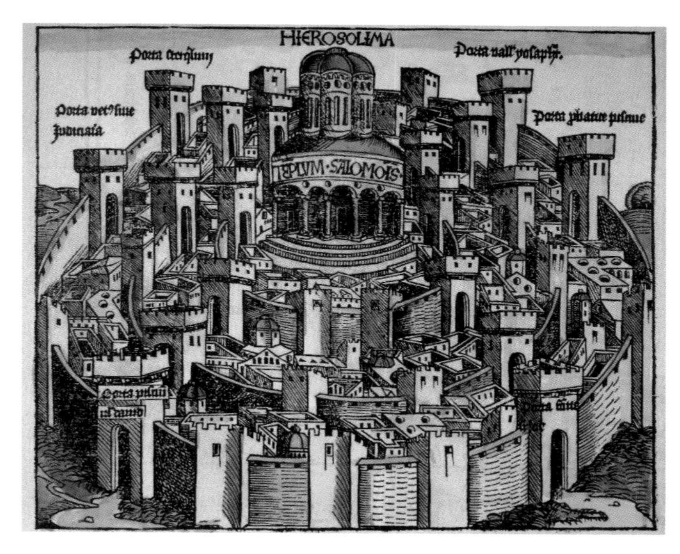

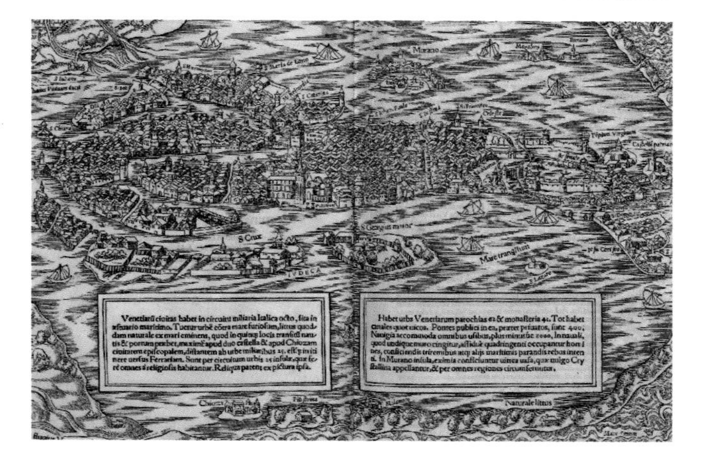

ABOVE, TOP TO BOTTOM **Jerusalem, Babylon,** ***and*** **Venice** ***from Munster's*** **Cosmography,** ***1544***

In the earliest editions of Munster's Cosmography *many of the woodcuts of cities were generic rather than specific; some images were used for more than one city and some images ascribed to a particular city did not show the city at all. In contrast, these three images are much more honest to the real cities of the time. Munster died of the plague shortly after the publication of the definitive 1550 edition.*

Cartography and Surveying

In the early part of the 16th century most land surveys were recorded as written documents. Land was yet to be spatially coordinated, mapped, or plotted. By the end of the century, however, surveys invariably involved maps, and the word "survey" began to mean a mapping exercise. Surveying was discussed by Gemma Frisius (1508–55) in his book *Libellus*, which in 1533 he had bound to the Flemish edition of Apian's *Cosmographia*. Frisius was adept at instrumentation and measurement: he made globes and in 1540 published a world map and an influential work on arithmetic. In 1545 he published a book on the cross-staff, making it a more accurate tool for surveying. The remarkable flowering of large-scale maps that occurred in Europe in the mid-1500s is in part due to Frisius and his influence.

Unsurprisingly, there was a close connection between mapmaking and surveying. The mapmaker Christopher Saxton (born *c.*1542) was also a surveyor. His *Atlas of the counties of England and Wales* was published in 1579. Saxton was employed as an estate surveyor from 1587 to 1608, performing about four surveys a year. He made about 25 estate maps and produced 14 written surveys (see page 119). Like other surveyors, Saxton produced a variety of survey maps designed for different purposes—for example to resolve boundary disputes and disputes over water rights—as well as general estate maps.

TOP RIGHT ***Circumferentor, 1601–30***
This instrument is inscribed with the scale, punched on the circle, by degrees. It has only one pair of fixed sights and the compass is missing. Circumferentors were commonly used during the 17th and 18th centuries to compare angles, enabling the user to work out how far away a distant object was.

CENTER RIGHT ***Circumferentor,1676***
This circumferentor was made by the architect Johannes Macarius of Modena, Italy, in 1676. The joint on the support allowed for both vertical and horizontal use.

BOTTOM RIGHT ***Surveyor's Folding Rule, 1574***
This brass folding rule was made by Humfrey Cole (1530?–91). He was the first craftsman of the English instrument-making trade, which became established in the 16th century. The folding rule is a surveyor's compendium. It is fitted with sights so that it can be used to measure and draw land surveys to scale. On the other side the instrument carries mathematical tables, a quadrant, and a sundial. This instrument was probably bought by gentlemen and wealthy practitioners who wanted to show off their mathematical skills.

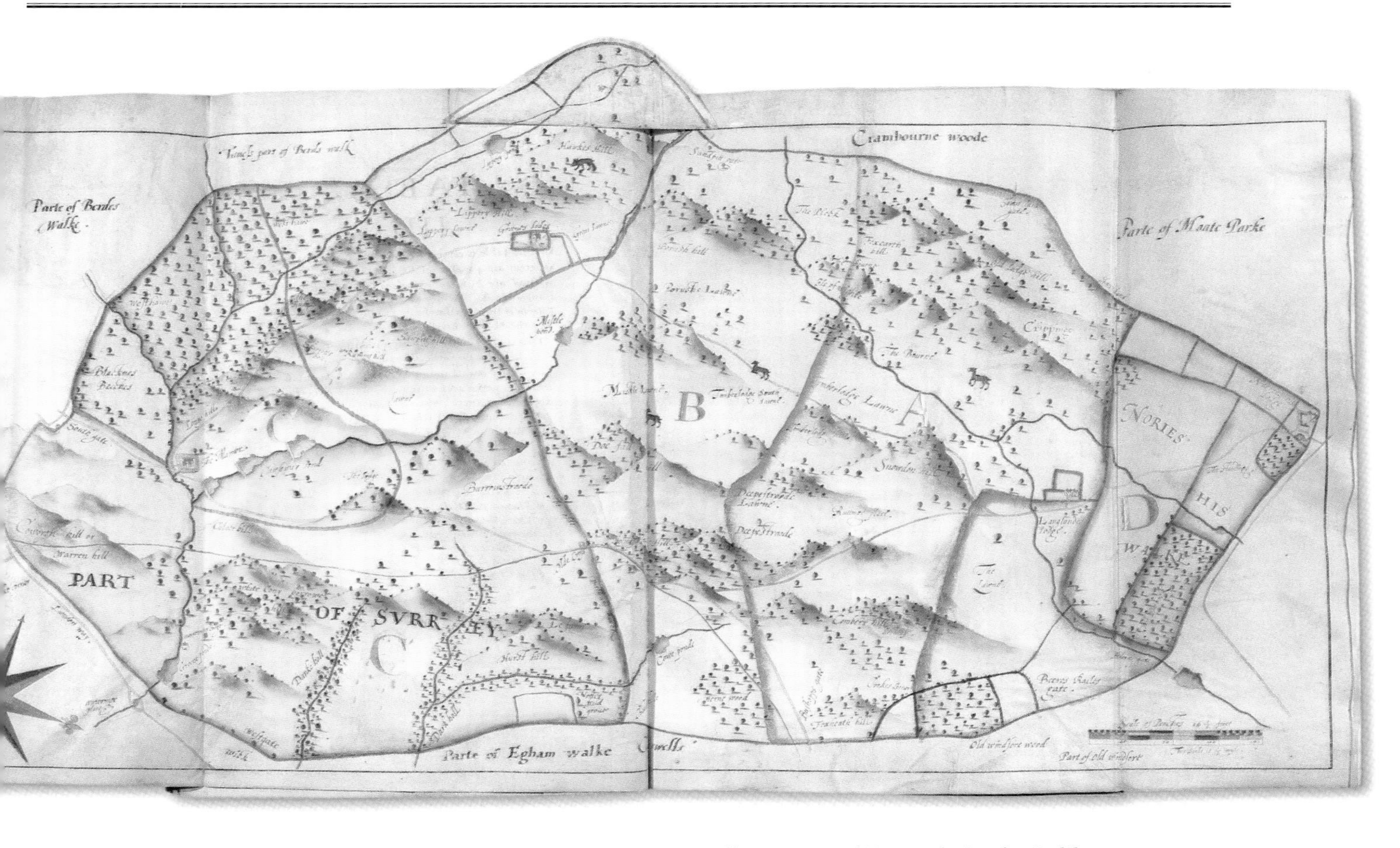

ABOVE ***Norden's Estate Map of Windsor, 1607***
John Norden made very detailed maps of the royal lands. This map indicates relief by using little hills as well as showing rivers, forests, and routeways. The numbers of deer are noted with some care, since they were valuable both as a source of meat and as a source of royal sport. Besides his work as royal surveyor, Norden also published panoramas of London and Westminster.

Another practicing surveyor and mapmaker during this period was John Norden (1548–1625). He produced manuscript maps of Essex, Northampton, Cornwall, Kent, and Surrey, as well as a map of London (see page 116). Norden was also a surveyor of estates, his official title being "General Surveyor of King's Landes and Woods." A rich collection of his manuscript maps is housed in the British Library, including his *Description of the Honor of Windsor* (1607), which is an atlas of estate maps of the royal holdings in Berkshire, Surrey, and Buckinghamshire. The Royal Library at Windsor Castle has another copy, dedicated to King James I. There are over 17 manuscript maps in the atlas, showing individual deer parks, the general layout of each estate, and the names of the keepers. Even the number of deer in the parks is recorded.

BELOW ***Illustrations of Triangulation by Galileo***
These illustrated plates showing triangulation come from a treatise on the use of the compass, Le Operazioni del Compasso Geometrico et Militare, *written by Galileo Galilei (1570–1642). The treatise was published in Padua in 1606 following a dispute with fellow professor Simon Marius (1570–1624). Galileo accused Marius of plagiarizing his proportional compass. Later on, he successfully brought an action against a pupil of Marius, Baldassar Capra, after Marius had returned to Germany.*

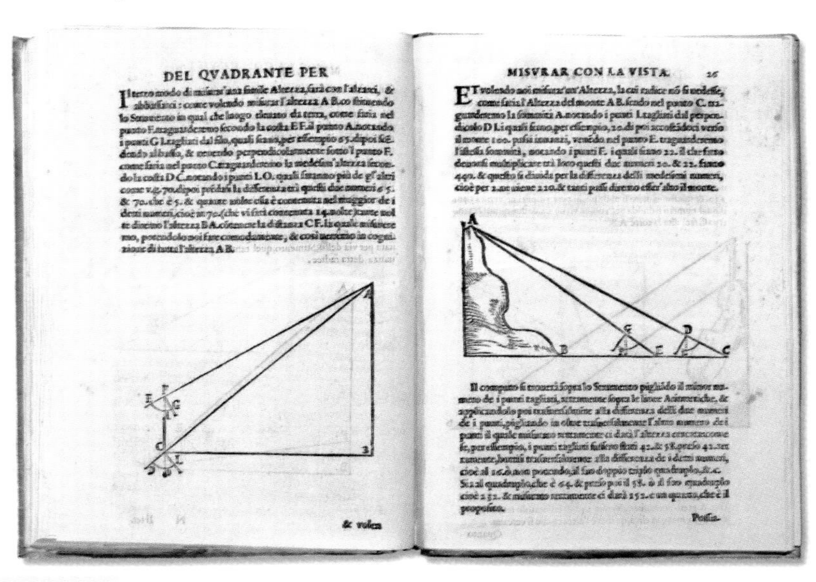
DEL QVADRANTE PER

& volen

MISVRAR CON LA VISTA. 26

Possia.

11

NATIONAL MAPS

Mapping National Territories

National mappings developed in Europe throughout the 16th century as national identities gradually replaced local and feudal ones. National maps came in a variety of forms. For example, in 1539 Olaus Magnus produced a nine-sheet map of Scandinavia. It was the first large-scale regional map of Europe, and one of the first maps to show whole countries as cartographic "units." It was intentionally nationalistic, and the legend states that the aim was to show the "Scandinavian countries and the wonders that exist there."

In Scotland, between 1583 and 1596, Timothy Pont produced very detailed manuscript maps, 77 of which are now housed in the National Library of Scotland. It was a huge undertaking and would form the basis of Willem Blaeu's maps of Scotland in his *Atlas Novus* (1654). At around the same time, Bouguereau was making the first national atlas of France: *Le Théâtre Français* was published in Tours in 1594. The country was covered by 48 maps, many including inserts of town plans. The atlas was quoted as being "for the pleasure of learned men, for the use of martial men and of the King's tax gatherers and treasurers, and for the guidance of merchants." Bourguereau died in 1596, and his partner, Jean Le Clerc, took over the project and saw it through seven editions from 1619–32. In the first edition, a picture of King Henry of Navarre covered the map of France; flick back the portrait and underneath was the map: king and country, nation and sovereign, the body of the country, and the head of the king.

The first national atlas in Europe was produced by Christopher Saxton in 1579. Saxton's work was not just a technical accomplishment. The mapping was uniquely connected to political ends. Since Henry VIII's break with Rome in 1533, England had been rent by religious factionalism. The Crown had shifted from the Protestant evangelism of Edward VI's brief reign (1547–53) to the militant Catholicism of Mary I (1553–8). Elizabeth I's reign (1558–1603) was beset by tensions between Protestants and Catholics at home, and international rivalry abroad.

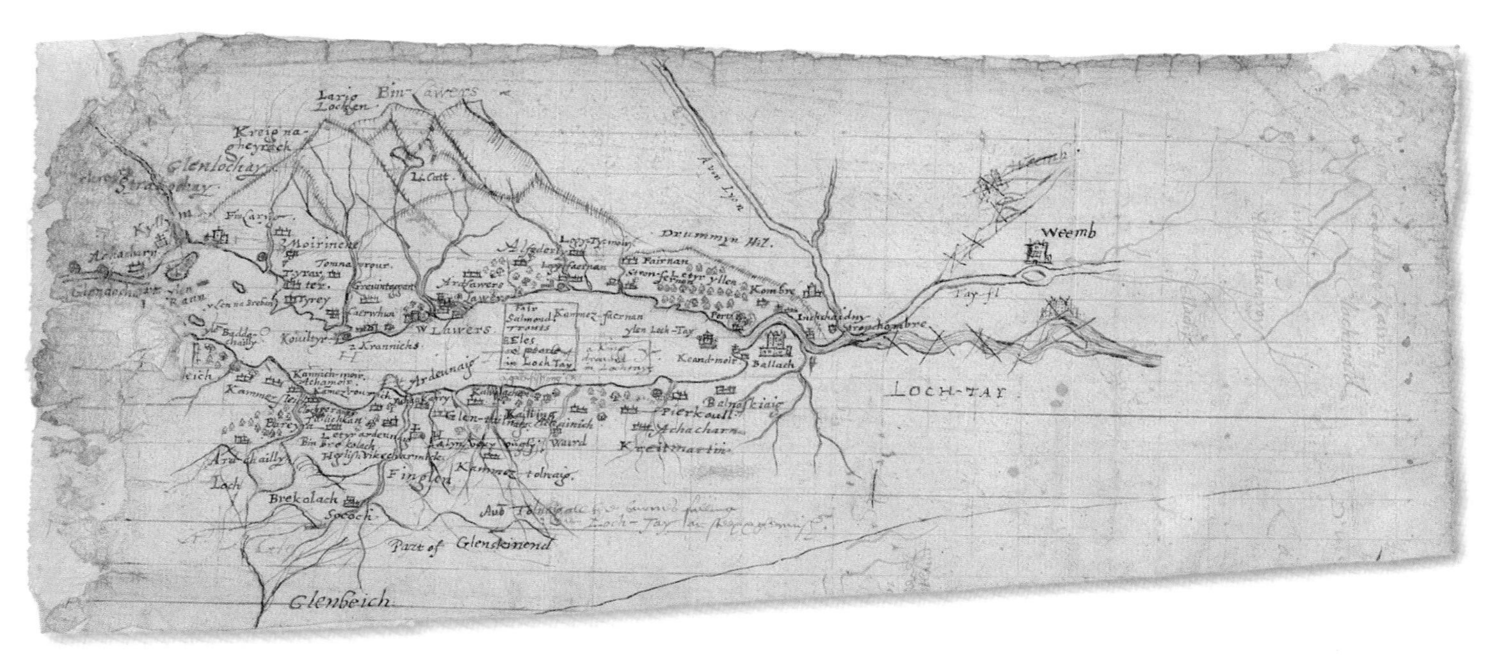

BELOW *Map detail of Dundee, c. 1580–90, by Timothy Pont*
Timothy Pont's detailed maps show in rich detail the geography of late 16th-century Scotland. This map clearly shows the city of Dundee and the other urban centers along the north shore of the River Tay. Note the merchant ship at the mouth of the river.

ABOVE *Map of Loch Tay, c. 1580–90, Timothy Pont*
This Pont map depicts the physical relief around Loch Tay. Rivers are shown flowing into the loch and forests are illustrated around its eastern edge. Pont used many Gaelic place names, and was the first recorder of many features in Scotland's human and physical geography.

A Protestant England under Elizabeth was a complete anathema to the powerful Catholic king of Spain, Philip II. Hence, the disputes of the Reformation and Counter-Reformation, and overt Spanish hostility, marked and defined the Elizabethan era.

Christopher Saxton was born around 1542 in Yorkshire. We know little about the details of his life, other than the fact that he was a surveyor. Surveying was an important skill to have in 16th-century England because there was a very active and fluid land market. The dissolution of the monasteries had created a large pool of land for sale. In 1573 Saxton was directed by Queen Elizabeth I's Secretary of State, William Cecil, to survey and map the counties of England and Wales. Saxton set to work in July of that year, beginning in Norfolk.

The survey lasted until 1578. All the English counties were mapped by 1577, and the Welsh counties by the following year. The resulting maps reflect the turbulent times, in that they take special care to illustrate the lie of the land, in particular any high points. These were then used to create a network of beacons to be lit in the event of an invasion by England's Catholic enemies. This was greatly feared at that time, not least because in 1570 the Pope had decreed that any Catholic had the right under God to kill Elizabeth. Saxton was therefore directed to survey all the southern coastal counties—the most likely to be chosen for an invasion—before proceeding northward.

ABOVE ***Saxton's* Atlas of England and Wales, *1579***
Saxton produced the first atlas of maps of England and Wales. It was a state-sponsored enterprise, paid for and supported by royal approval. As patron of the project Queen Elizabeth appears in this frontispiece in all her regal dignity.

RIGHT ***Lily's* Map of England, *1546***
George Lily's map is one of the first engraved maps of the country. He drew the map while he was in Europe in exile, probably working at the Vatican on cartographic projects. Engraved in Italy, it drew heavily upon a 14th-century source, hence its inaccurate shape.

Saxton's atlas was published in 1579. Its frontispiece shows Elizabeth I as the patron of geography and astronomy. The first map shows the country of England, with no grid. Double-paged maps then follow, showing the individual counties and illustrating rivers, towns, enclosed forests, the homes of local gentry, and county boundaries. Relief is shown in diagrammatic form as little molehills, roughly to scale. In more mountainous counties in the North and in Wales, the molehills are larger! No roads are shown, suggesting that the survey was done from a quick reconnoiter rather than a careful survey. A landmark in English cartography, the atlas was published throughout the 17th century.

BRITANNIÆ INSVLÆ QVÆ NVNC ANGLIÆ ET SCOTIÆ REGNA CONTINET CVM HIBERNIA ADIACENTE NOVA DESCRIPTIO
MARE HIBERNICVM
MARE DEVCALIDONIVM
SEPTENTRIO
CONNACIA
LAGINIA
HVLTONIA
DVBLINVM
ARMACANA METROP
PVRGATORIVM S. PATRICII
MVLA
CVMBRA
ILA
IONA
ARGADIA
ARANA
HEBRIDES INSVLÆ XLIIII
HIRTHA
SCHIA
LEVISSA
MONA
LOQVA
ROSSIA
STRAVERNIA
SOTHERLANDIA
CATHENESIA
MORAVIA
MARIA
BVTHANIA
VITVLVS MARINVS
ORCADES INSVLÆ XXXI
POMONIA
KIRKVALIA
GALLOVIDIA
GLASCO
LAVDONIA
ANGVSIA
EBORACVM
LINCOLNIA
LANCASTRIA
VESTMERLANDIA
CVMBRIA
NORTHVMBRIA
DVNELMVM
FLAMBROGH PROM
ABBROTH PRO
BVTHVANIA PRO
ROMAE, Anglorum studio & diligentia. M. D. XLVI
METROP
EPISCOPATVS
COMITATVS
CASTRA
MILLIARIA
20 40 60 80 100 120 140 160 180 200
ORIENS
54 55 56 57 58 59 60 61 62 63

Regional Mappings in England

During the late Elizabethan and Stuart periods in England maps of the country and the nation abounded. Following Saxton, a tradition of national mapping was established, although not all the projects were as successful as Saxton's. A good example is the efforts of cartographer John Norden.

Norden was born in Somerset in 1548, probably the son of a yeoman. He was a surveyor. He had the idea for a national geography around 1586, and by 1591 had completed a map of Northamptonshire. He sent it to William Cecil (Lord Burghley), with a letter asking him to "consider whether it might be expedient that the most principall townes, Cyties and castles within eurye Shire, should be breefly and expertly plotted out." An official document of 1593 then stated that "John Norden, gent, is authorised and appointed by Her Maiesty to trauayl into the several counties of the realme of England and Wales and to make perfect descripciones, chartes and mappes."

Norden planned to write a comprehensive geography of the country, called *Speculum Britanniae* (Mirror of Britain).

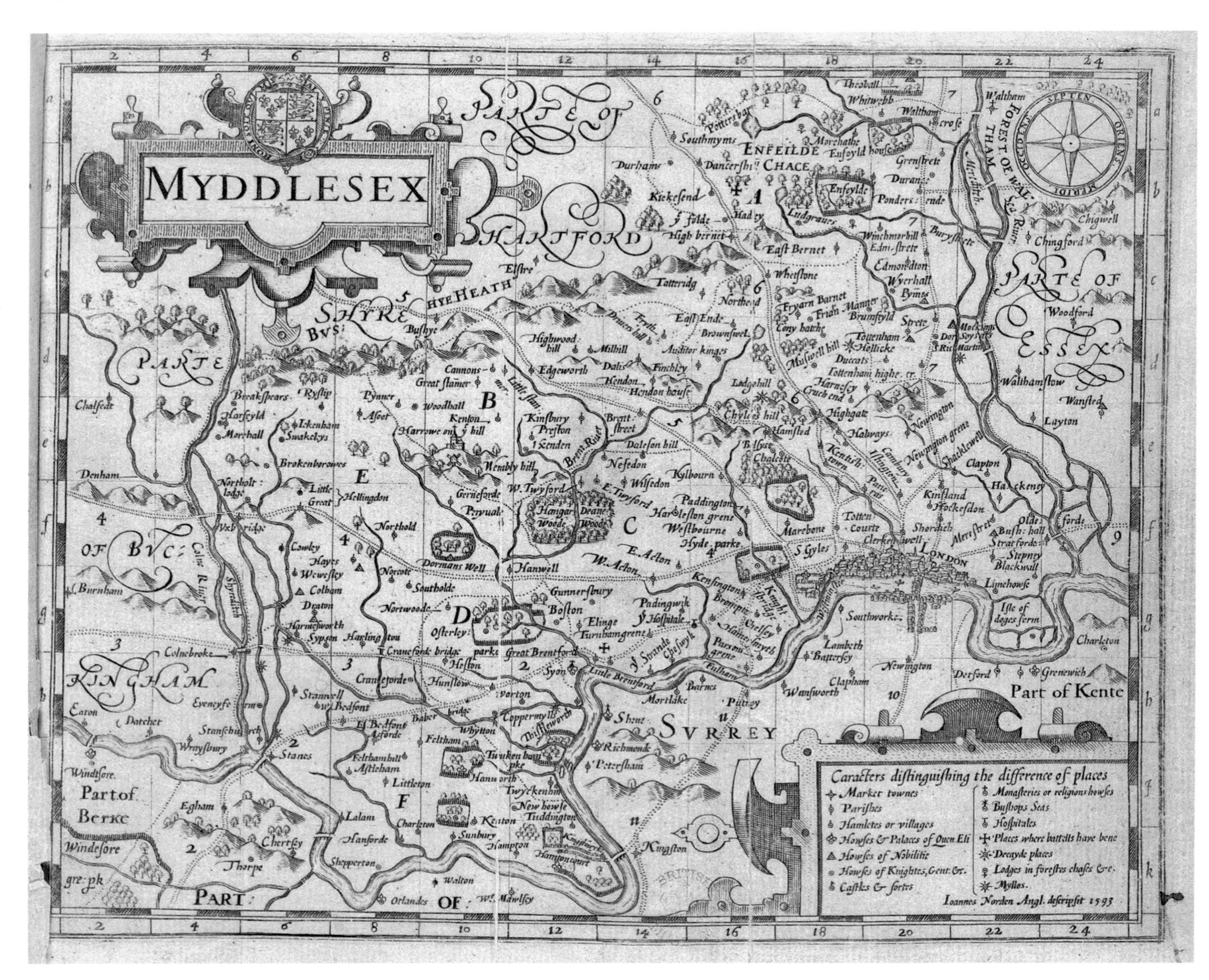

ABOVE **Wiltshire** ***by John Speed, c. 1612***
John Speed's map of Wiltshire is full of detail. In the top left there is a detailed street map of Salisbury, showing the cathedral. In the top right there is a picture of Stonehenge. The borders are filled with text and illustrations. On the left-hand side the coats of arms of local gentry are shown.

LEFT ***John Norden's*** **Myddlesex,** ***1593***
The Norden map of the County of Middlesex shows relief, in the form of little molehills, rivers, roads, and towns. The high-density city of London is almost all on the north bank of the Thames; surrounding villages depicted by Norden, such as Paddington and Kylbourn (now Kilburn), are now the inner suburbs of the expanded metropolis.

However, the project was never completed, and only two counties, Hertfordshire and Middlesex, were published during his lifetime. It started well enough: *An Historicall and Chorographicall Description of Middlesex* was published in 1593 in the form of a small book dedicated to Queen Elizabeth and Burghley. It contained a map of Middlesex, plus two maps of London. The Middlesex map used an index system of letters (a, b, c, etc.) and numbers (1, 2, 3, etc.) to identify points of interest, much as some modern maps do. The maps showed roads, towns, hamlets, and enclosures, and the accompanying text provided an exhaustive history of the areas covered. In 1595, Norden produced a manuscript atlas of the four counties of Middlesex, Essex, Surrey, and Hampshire.

To sustain the project, Norden needed money and patronage, but ran out of both. Burghley died in 1598 and in that same year Norden was forced to publish *An Historicall and Chorographicall Description of Hertfordshire* at his own expense. In it he included an open letter to the queen asking for help with his grand endeavor: "Onlie your Maiesties princelie favor is my hope, without which O my selfe must miserablie perish, my familie in penurie and the work unperformed, whiche being effected, shall be profitble and a glorie to this your most admired Empire." Elizabeth ignored his pleas, but Norden, never one to give up, later approached King James I in 1604. He hoped that

SEPTENTRIO
DIEV ET MON DROYT
PROMONTORIVM HOC IN MARE PROIECTVM CORNVBIA DICITVR
OCCIDENS
MERIDIES
O C E A
Scala Miliarium
Christophorus Saxton descripsit
LEN AERT TER WOORT ANTVER PLANVS SCVLP SIT
PENWITH
KERIAR
MENEGE
TRVRO
TREGNY
ROSELAND
GRAMPOVND
PADSTOW
Padstow hauen
The Gull rock
Pengwinyon poynte
Predannok poynte
Lesard poynte
The Manacles poynt
Helford hauen
Set Anthonys poynt

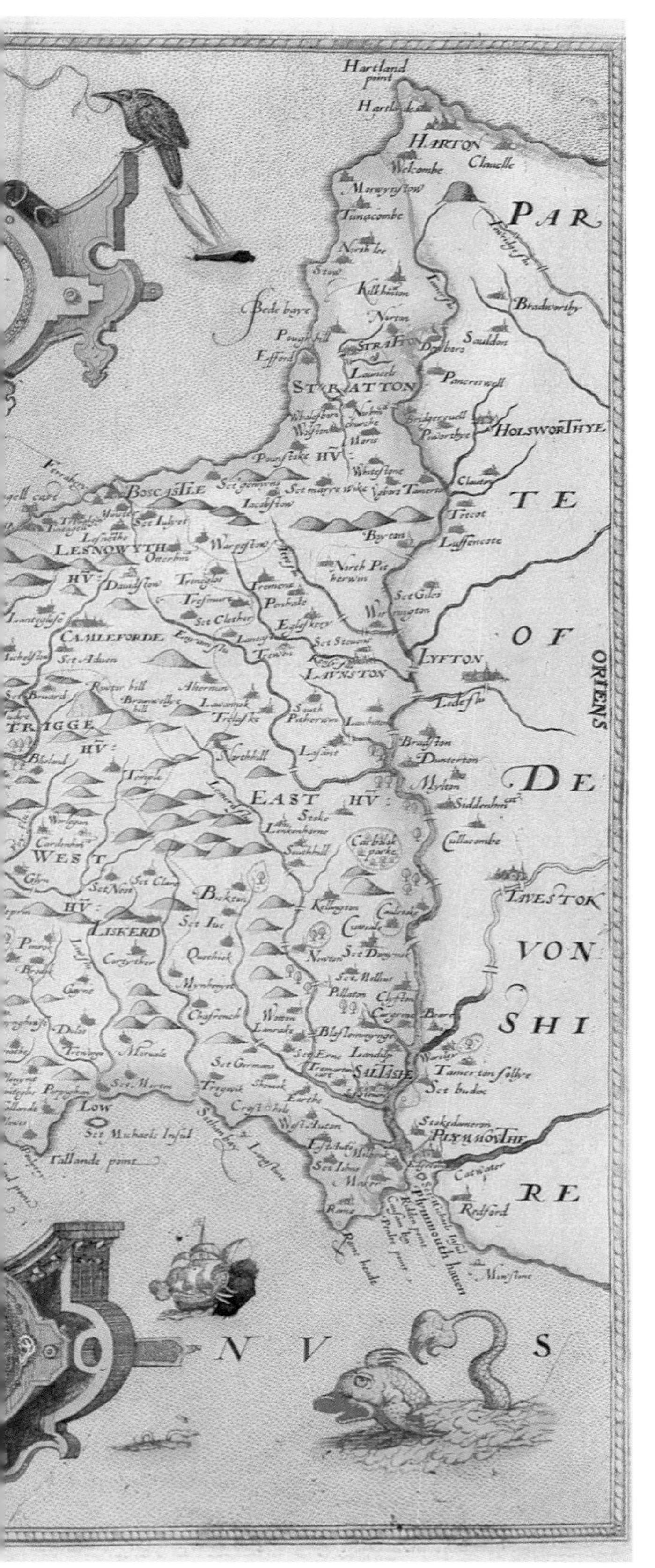

the new king might look more favorably upon his scheme. James, it seems, was no more interested in the proposal than Elizabeth had been—however, Norden did not "miserablie perish in penurie" but was appointed Surveyor of the Duchy of Cornwall for life in January 1605, perhaps in recognition of his efforts to date.

Norden left an important legacy. His books on Hertfordshire and Middlesex raised the level of technical representation in maps. For example, he was aware that different mapmakers were using different yardages to the mile: from 1,120 to 1,760. He chose the 1,760-yard mile and raised the issue of a uniform naming of places at a time when names varied greatly (for example, Bury was also called Berye; Ley also called Leigh). In 1625 Norden published a book called *An Intended Guyde for English Travailers* in which he provided a table of distances between the towns and cities in each county. This remains the standard distance chart and is still used in the UK today.

John Speed (1551–1629) was born in Cheshire and worked in London as a merchant tailor until he obtained a sinecure that enabled him to devote time to historical and geographical studies. The result was *The Theatre of The Empire of Great Britaine*, first published between 1611 and 1612. This was a lavish national atlas, owing much to the work of Ortelius (see pages 122–5). It contained general maps of Scotland, England, and Ireland as well as detailed county maps of England. These drew extensively on the work of Norden and Saxton, and were not gridded, although some copies were later gridded by hand. They show woods, towns (with detailed town maps as inserts), and the coats of arms of local gentry. "Sights of historical interest" such as Stonehenge in Wiltshire are also shown. The atlas contains 50 new town plans, all of which are drawn in bird's-eye view.

The *Theatre* was published in numerous editions, and was expanded over time. The 1676 edition, for example, contained maps of "His Majesty's Dominions" in New England, New York, Carolina, Florida, Virginia, Maryland, Jamaica, and Barbados. A national atlas had become an imperial one.

LEFT **Cornwall** ***from Saxton's atlas, 1579***
Saxton's mapping of England and Wales was undertaken at a time when conflict with Spain was coming to a head; the Spanish Armada would sail in a few years' time. The southernmost counties more susceptible to Spanish attack, such as Cornwall, were mapped first. Saxton mapped towns and rivers but no roads. The necessity of a quick survey precluded the more careful surveying of roads.

Mapping The Renaissance City

In Renaissance times, cities were mapped using three types of view: "prospect" view (from the side); "plan" or "aerial" view (from directly above); and "bird's-eye view" (obliquely from above). In some cases more than one view was used in the same illustration. In prospect and bird's-eye views, the distinction between cartography and art is blurred, and there is no hard and fast divide between aesthetics and accuracy, mapmaker and artist.

During the 15th century many city plans were produced in the form of engravings and woodcuts. In the *Nuremberg Chronicle*, for example, there are prospects of almost 100 cities. Many city prospects were used in a generic way to represent the idea of a city rather than an actual city. They look like real places, with buildings and walls, but much of the detail is imaginary. One exception is the *Peregrinatio in Terrae Sanctam*, which documented a pilgrimage to Jerusalem in 1483–4 led by the Dean of Mainz Cathedral. One of the party was the artist Erhard Reuwich, who illustrated the journey, resulting in very detailed and (for the time) relatively accurate views of the cities en route, such as Venice.

Towards the end of the 1400s, the Italian Francesco Rosselli (*c.* 1445–*c.* 1527) produced prospects of Pisa, Rome, Constantinople, and Florence. At the turn of the century, Jacopo de' Barbari (1450–?), a painter and printmaker, produced a large bird's-eye view of Venice. In it, we look down on the city from the southwest, and are able to see a wealth of accurate detail. The project was commissioned by a Nuremberg businessman and resident of Venice called Anton Kolb, who in 1500 petitioned the Venetian government for monopoly publishing rights. De' Barbari's map is a studio creation, which was assembled from many drawings made in different parts of the city over the course of three years.

Three types of cartographic book were developed in the 16th century: the world atlas, the national atlas, and the city atlas. The first two are still used to this day, but the third is less common—although the modern street map is the nearest equivalent. In 16th-century Europe, cities formed the backbone of economic growth and were the drivers of social change. The creation of a monetary economy, the emergence of a merchant class, and the growth of manufacturing and trade were all made possible by the city. The European city was an important entity in its own right, often with distinct city charters and forms of government, and even though nationalism was by this time firmly established, the "city state" remained an important economic and political unit, conferring economic privileges and social freedoms on its citizens.

Examples of city "maps" produced during the 16th century include an anonymous woodcut prospect of Antwerp (in modern-day Belgium) made in 1515; a bird's-eye view of Augsburg (in modern-day Germany) made in 1521 by Jorg Seld; and a woodcut prospect of Amsterdam (in the Netherlands) made in 1544 by Cornelis Antoniszoon. Hans Lautensack produced a detailed prospect view of

Nuremberg (Germany) in 1552 including inserts that stressed the city's antiquity and appealing to God's favor for municipal success. Lautensack's illustration was used to represent various different cities in many texts published in the 16th century.

RIGHT **Imola** ***by Leonardo Da Vinci, c.1502***
The city of Imola was of vital strategic importance to Leonardo's patron of the time, Cesare Borgia. Leonardo drew sketches of the fortification of the city as well as pacing the streets to gain precise measurements for this beautiful and accurate "aerial" map completed around 1502.

BELOW **Venice** ***by De'Barbari, 1500***
This woodcut map of Venice from 1500 is one of the largest city images of the Renaissance. It shows the high-density city floating on a watery surface. The Barbari illustration depicts the city at the height of its power. The Venetian merchant ships are a significant feature of the map; these ships plied their trade across the seas of Europe and the wider world.

The Great *Theatrum*

One of the signal achievements of Renaissance cartography was the world atlas. Inside its covers, the world was mapped and surveyed. The atlas encompassed the world in one volume. Arguably the first atlas was completed by Abraham Ortelius in 1570. In 1590 Mercator's Atlas *was published. It was so influential that the title was subsequently used to refer to a book of maps.*

ABRAHAM ORTELIUS (1527–98) was born, raised, and died in Antwerp (now in Belgium), and always referred to himself as a citizen of that city. In his day, Antwerp was a thriving, dynamic merchant city. In 1560 it had a population of around 100,000, among whom were almost 600 foreign merchants, making it a place of considerable wealth. The Portuguese had established their spice market there in 1499, the Germans and English traded metals and cloth in the city, and it was a major center for printing and graphic art.

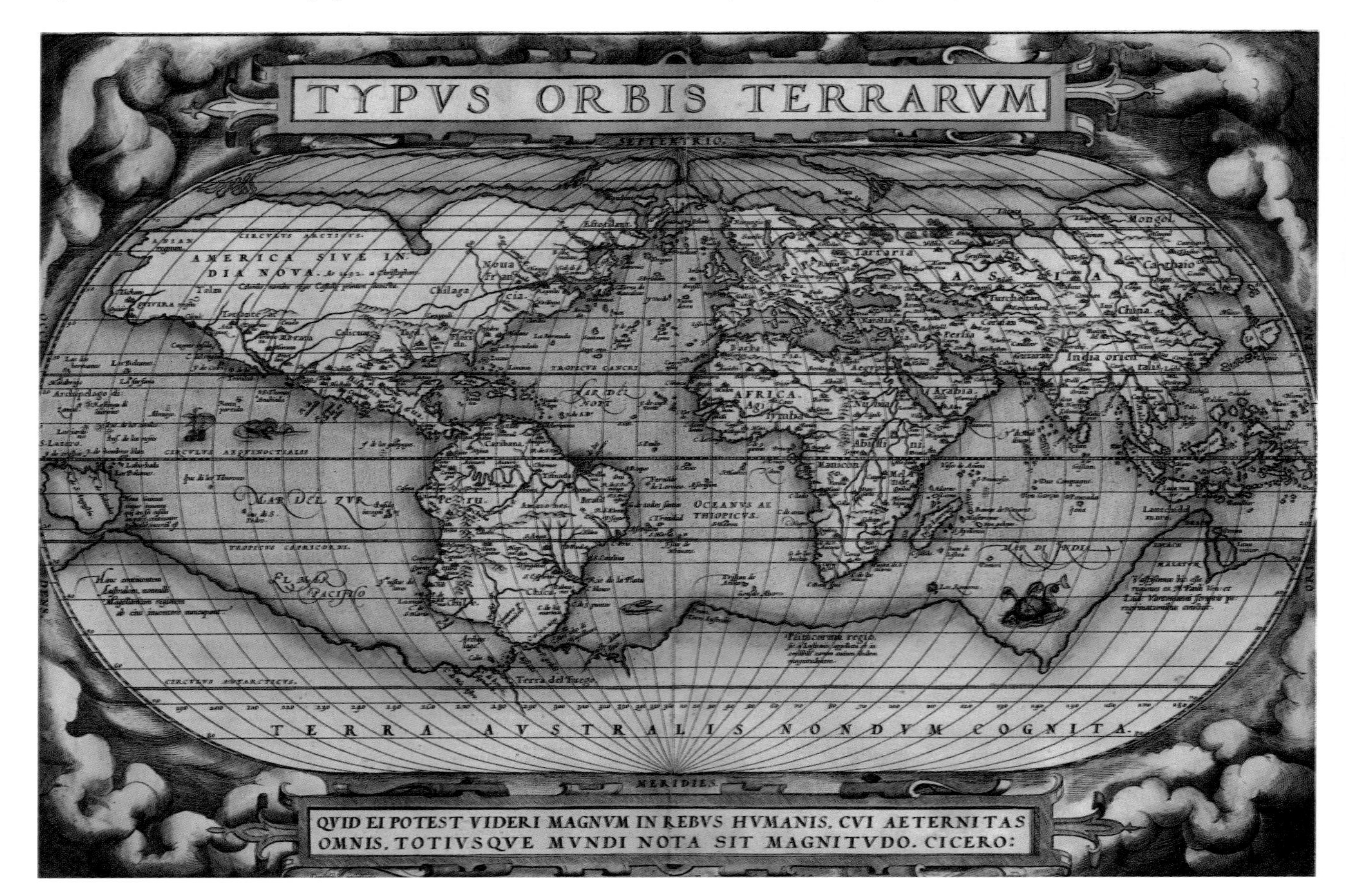

ABOVE ***Single map from Ortelius's*** **Theatrum Orbis Terrarum**
South-east Asia was of major importance to many European traders. This region was the source of valuable spices, textiles, wood, and other resources highly prized in Europe. This map reveals a detailed knowledge of the spice islands of what is now Indonesia. Java and Sumatra appear much larger than India or Japan and this exaggeration reflects their trading importance to Dutch merchants. The cardinal directions are indicated in the map border. The border acts as a picture frame, which is surely no accident: here, the cartographer declares, is a work of art as well as science.

LEFT ***World map from Ortelius's*** **Theatrum Orbis Terrarum**
Ortelius's world map shows the world as known to Europeans in the late 16th century. The New World is known although the size of North America is exaggerated because its western extent is unknown. Europe, Africa, and Asia are more accurately recorded. A large land mass in the south is presented although the map records it as unknown land.

In 1547 Ortelius was a "painter of maps." That is to say, he painted colored maps with watercolor paints, which made the maps more attractive as well as more valuable. He earned his living dealing in maps, coins, and antiquities, and around 1564 he started to make his own maps. At that time, most maps were sold in the form of rolled up parchment scrolls, with the result that anyone wanting to consult several maps simultaneously had to unroll them, lay them out, and hold them down with the necessary weights. Quite apart from being a lengthy and cumbersome exercise, it also required a lot of space. If space was lacking, then each map would have to be unrolled and then rolled up again before the next one was consulted.

A single book, Ortelius concluded, would get round the problem of having to roll and unroll maps, and so he began work on an atlas, which he called the *Theatrum*, in 1566. Ortelius was not simply concerned with providing maps in a

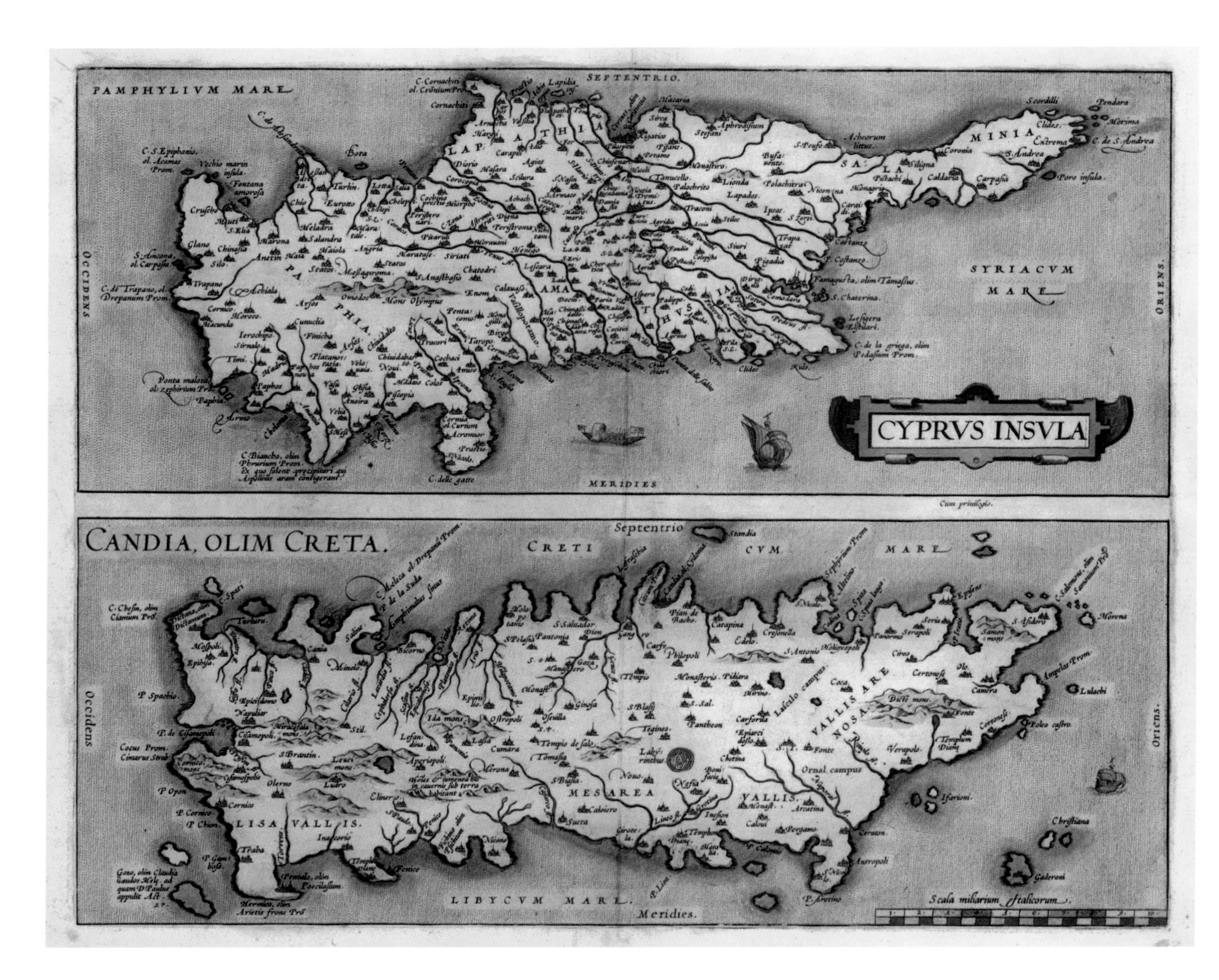

ABOVE *Maps of Cyprus and Crete from Ortelius's* Theatrum
Only the most skillful cartographers were commissioned to provide the highly detailed maps for this atlas, with each map the work of several draftsmen. These maps show towns, rivers, and relief but no roads.

handy book form—he wanted only the very best maps, which he acquired over time from a wide range of skilled cartographers. He graciously acknowledged all of them in every edition of the final work. At the time no copyright law existed, so he was not bound by law to mention anyone. For the first edition 87 names were mentioned, 170 appeared in the 1595 edition, and 182 in the 1603 edition. The world map alone cites 44 cartographers, while 20 were called upon for the map of America. By 1569 this great work was complete, and it went on sale to the public in 1570.

The book was hugely successful and extremely profitable. Between 1570 and 1598, 2,200 copies were sold. The *Theatrum* was first published in Latin and later in Dutch, German, French, Spanish, Italian, and English. Later editions were regularly updated so that while the first edition had only 50 pages, the Italian edition of 1612 had 129. The book continued to be printed as late as 1724, and almost 7,300 copies over 89 editions were eventually printed.

Amazingly, 2,000 copies still exist.

The *Theatrum* was widely respected. Philip II of Spain kept a copy close by him and appointed Ortelius as "His Majesty's Royal Cosmographer" on May 20, 1573. Its success owed as much to Ortelius's canny business practices as it did to the high quality of the product. Ortelius bought his own paper, supplied copper engravings at his own expense, and sold directly to customers, booksellers, and publishers. Deservedly, he gained a very comfortable living from his *magnum opus* and lived the happy life of a wealthy Antwerp burgher until his death in 1598.

The first edition is a stunningly beautiful atlas containing 50 maps. There is little text, as Ortelius believed, in a radical break with tradition, that "the mappe being layed before our eyes, we may behold things done or places where they were done, as if they were at the present and doing." The frontispiece has an elaborate illustration of the continents personified as maidens. Europe is at the top, holding a scepter as a symbol of authority and a rudder with which she steers the affairs of the world. Asia is depicted as an Oriental princess. In her left hand she holds incense, the smoke from which represents oriental mystery. Africa is shown as a black maiden, her head glowing with the heat of the tropics. At the bottom is America, represented as an Amazonian warrior.

ABOVE **Russia and Asia**
A map from Ortelius's first atlas, showing Russia and central Asia. On the left is "Litvania," which corresponds to modern-day Lithuania. The map is decorated with scenes from travelers' tales. The Caspian Sea is shown in the left center of the map.

Many maps in the *Theatrum* are gridded and plotted, though no latitude or longitude indications appear. In some cases the grid lines run through the map, as with the world map; in other cases coordinates are given in the border. Ortelius's map of the world is followed by maps of the New World, Asia, Africa, and Europe. The maps have a standard design: hand-colored icons represent towns, mountains, forests, and so on, and there is little decoration in the margins, and occasional ships and whales in the oceans. What little text there is takes the form of a short passage accompanying each map.

The *Theatrum* marked a revolutionary change in cartography. Perspective rather than narrative dominates. It is the first true embodiment of the geographical gaze and the chorographical eye.

Mercator's *Atlas*

The man who gave us the term "atlas" for a collection of maps is Gerardus Mercator. The maps in his atlas were published over a number of years. In 1585 he published volumes covering France, Belgium, and Germany. In 1589, 22 maps were produced including Italy, Slovakia, and Greece. Mercator died in 1594, at the venerable age of 82, and his son Rumold published all his maps in one volume the following year. Its full title is *Atlas, Sive Cosmographicae Meditationes de Fabrica Mundi et Fabricati Figura* (*Atlas, or Cosmographical Meditations upon the Creation of the Universe, and the Universe as Created*). It is best known simply as Mercator's *Atlas*.

Gerardus Mercator was born on March 5, 1512 in the small town of Rupelmonde, near Antwerp (now in

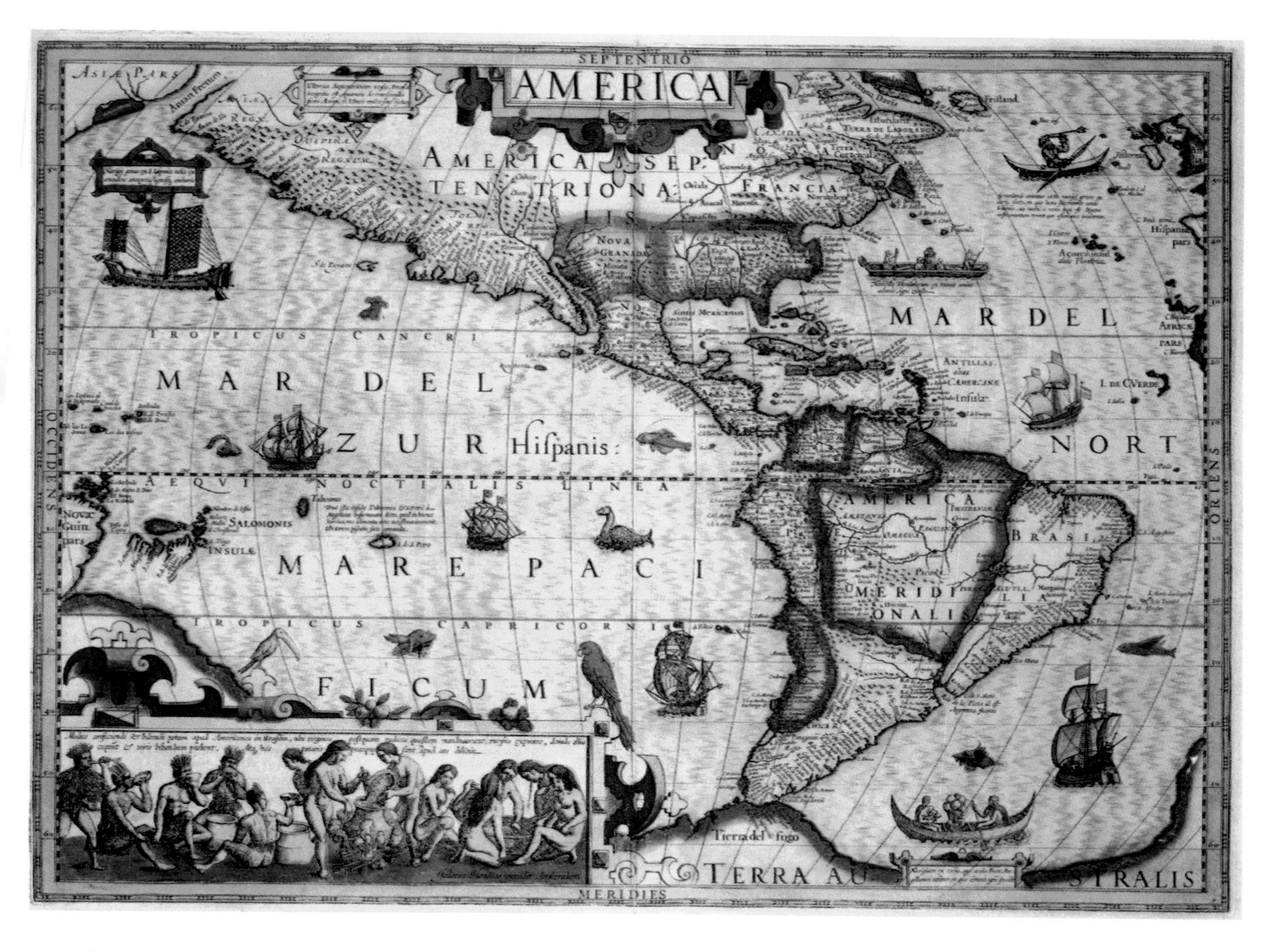

LEFT *Mercator's* **Arctic,** *1595*
This map, created in 1595, is centered on the North Pole. The polar projection gives an interesting view of the northern hemisphere landmasses. Mercator's map is suggestive of a sea channel that would enable circumpolar navigation. The possibility of Northeast and Northwest passages from Europe to Asia prompted sea exploration in the region for the following three centuries.

ABOVE *Mercator's* **America,** *1595*
America was of course first known to Europeans from the shoreline. Further inland knowledge was hazy as can be seen in this depiction of the interior of both South and North America dating from 1595. Maps were also used to tell stories, and illustrations record the indigenous people. European ships and indigenous canoes are depicted in the seas.

Belgium). Christened Gerard Kremer, he later Latinized his name to Mercator—a common, if rather vain, practice among European scholars to give their names associations with the classical learning of the ancient world. Mercator was a deeply religious man, and sustained an interest in theology throughout his life. He wrote numerous theological texts, including commentaries on the letters of St. Paul and the prophet Ezekiel, as well as various biblical chronologies. He made his living as a cartographer, globemaker, and publisher.

His first map was a copper engraving of the Holy Land, made in 1537. In 1538 he published his first world map. Two years later he was commissioned by the merchants of Antwerp to produce a map of Flanders based on earlier surveys. He also conducted surveys for royal patrons, and in 1564 was named official Cosmographer to the Duke of Julich, Cleve, and Berg.

In 1569 Mercator produced a world map using a new projection, known today—and famously—as "Mercator's projection." The world was represented as a square, with the polar regions flattened out to the same extent as the equator. This new approach was found to be invaluable to mariners because, while it magnified the surface area of the poles, it maintained constant compass directions.

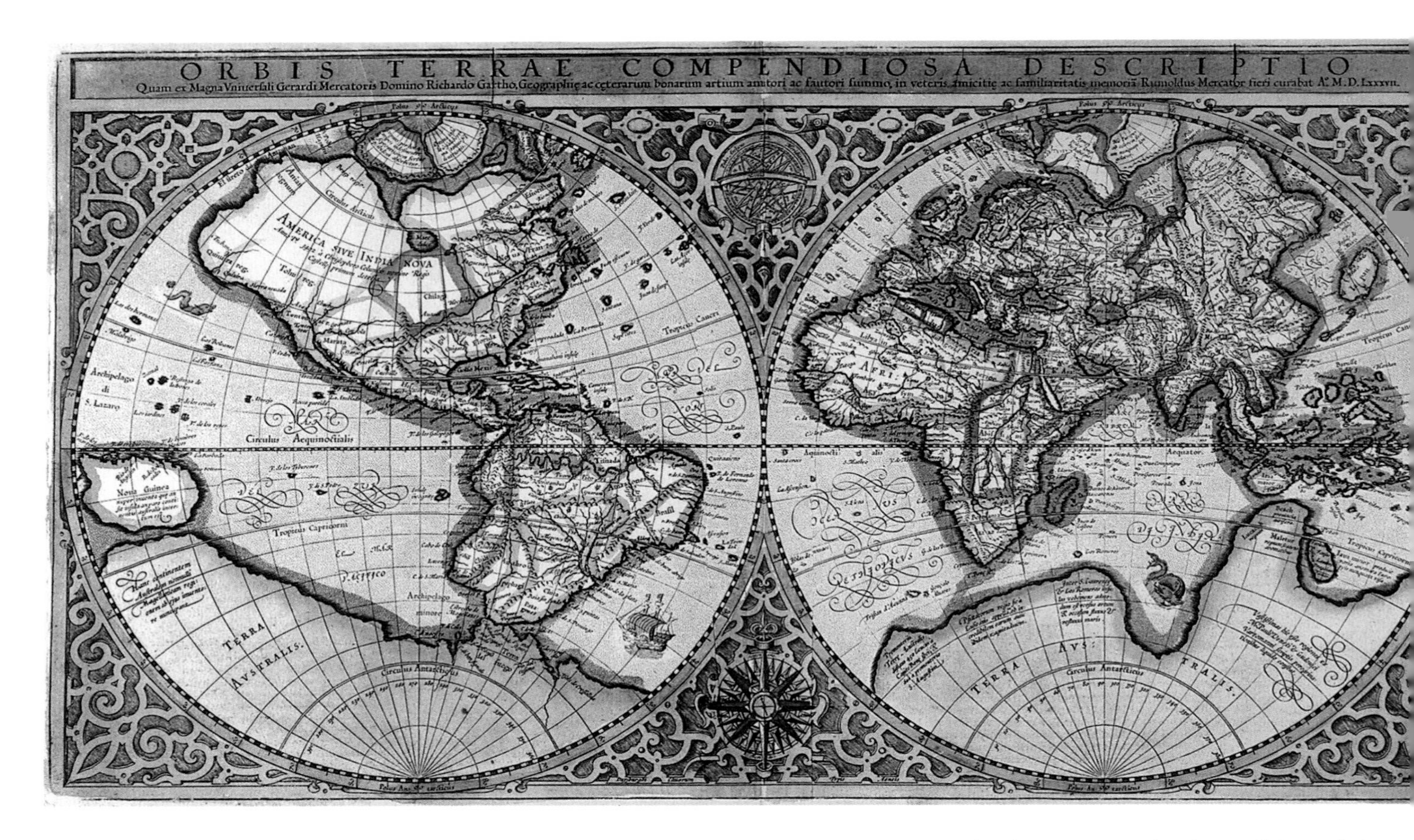

Using the Mercator projection a mariner could plot a line on the map that could be followed by constant compass direction. This was a remarkable scientific and technical accomplishment, and it quickly became the standard projection.

The 1595 *Atlas* is a large book. The frontispiece shows the god Atlas supporting the world between his hands. We are not sure exactly why Mercator or his sons chose Atlas to represent his book of maps. In the introduction there is a 30-page section entitled "The Booke of the Creation and Fabrick of the World" in which Mercator wrote that to know the cosmos is to know the infinite wisdom of God. For Mercator and many of his contemporaries, cosmography was a way of revealing the wonders of God's creation.

The first map in the first edition of the *Atlas* is a double-hemispheric map of the world. The southern latitudes are sketchy: New Guinea is shown, but Australia is yet to appear and is shown as part of the south polar region, called "terra australis." There are maps of Europe, Africa, and Asia (with the Spice Islands exaggerated in size, reflecting their economic significance to Europeans). More detailed maps follow. Each is prefaced by a note on latitude and longitude, and a general geographical introduction. Some of the maps have an index table giving the latitude and longitude of selected cities and towns. The maps are all gridded, using uniform lines of latitude and longitude.

Like Ortelius's *Theatrum*, Mercator's *Atlas* had a modern, serious feel, with modestly decorated borders, and few artistic

OPPOSITE, TOP **Double Hemisphere World Map**
This world map is known as a double hemispheric projection since it consists of representations of the eastern and western hemispheres. The East Indies appear very large, reflecting their trading importance to Europeans. The mapmaker has little sense of the land configuration in the southern latitudes, while western North America has been extended to hazy extremity. This is a relatively inaccurate map, even for its time.

OPPOSITE, BOTTOM ***Portrait of Mercator***
Mercator is a huge figure in the history of cartography. He made maps, globes, and scientific instruments, compiled atlases, and invented cartographic projections. A deeply religious man, he was charged with heresy and jailed for seven months. Later, he moved to Duisberg, Germany, and established a cartographic workshop with his sons.

BELOW **Iceland** ***by Mercator, 1595***
This map of Iceland comes from one of the editions of Mercator's Atlas. *The rocky mountainous nature of the island is well illustrated in this map that depicts relief with shading and figures. Although less accurate than other ways of showing relief it is much more intuitively obvious and revealing at first sight. Note the spouting whale shown to the north of the island.*

flourishes. The key uses literal symbols, and relief is also shown literally—as little hills. Towns are depicted by drawings of little buildings and forests by tree icons. The result is a charming display of geographic data.

Around 1604, the plates of Mercator's *Atlas* were sold to Jodocus Hondius (1563–1611), a Flanders-born engraver and mapmaker who lived in London. After his death, his sons-in-law, Henry and Jan Jansson, published 29 editions of the *Atlas* between 1609 and 1641, as well as 25 editions of a cheaper, "pocket" version, called the *Atlas Minor*, between 1607 and 1638. Editions of the large and small versions were published in Latin, French, German, Dutch, English, and Turkish. The 1630 French edition of the *Atlas Minor* had 643 pages of text. An English version was first published in 1636 and the title was changed to *Atlas, or a Geographicke Description of the Regions, Countries and Kingdomes of the World.* This edition, which featured over 200 maps and now included the New World, also had brief biographies of Gerardus Mercator and Jodocus Hondius. In one illustration Mercator and Hondius are shown sitting at a table together with dividers in their hands, plotting a globe of the world.

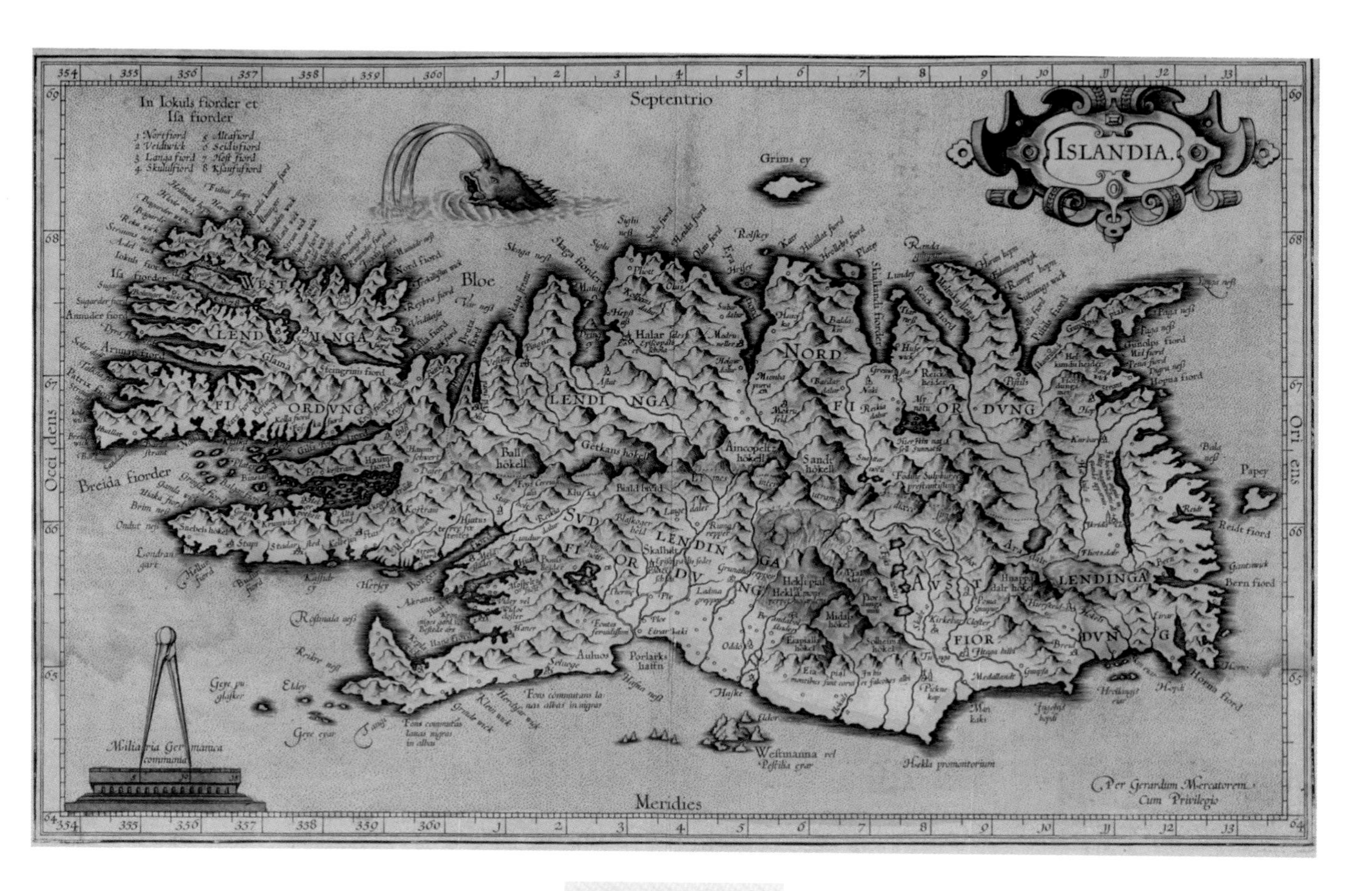

Grand Atlases, Celestial Atlases, and City Atlases

Mercator's *Atlas* became the template for the Dutch "grand atlases" of the 17th century. Their zenith was embodied in the work of Willem Blaeu (1571–1638). Blaeu was a mathematician, astronomer, and instrument maker. Around 1605 he established a printing press near the center of Amsterdam in the Netherlands, where he published various works on navigation, astronomy, and theology. He worked with his son Joan Blaeu (1596–1673), and together they published a magnificent series of atlases. The first appeared in 1630 and consisted of 60 plates, some original, some copied (a year earlier Willem had bought several copperplates from Jodocus Hondius). In 1631 an expanded version was printed, and in 1635 a massive atlas was produced consisting of 208 maps in two volumes, entitled *Novus Atlas*, with an alternative title, interestingly, of *Theatrum*. This was hugely successful, and the Blaeus built upon their

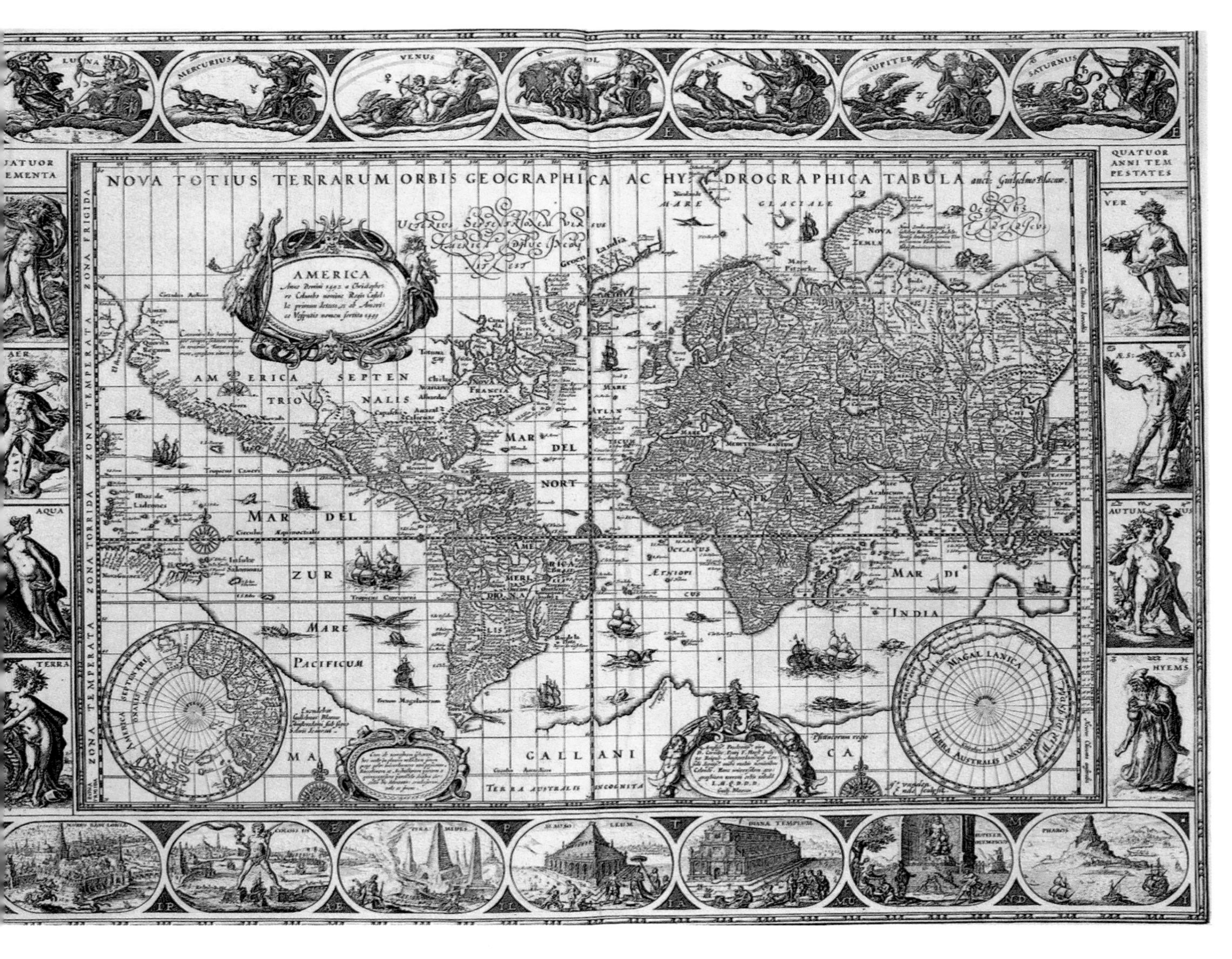

success, Willem becoming the official cartographer to the East India Company. After Willem died, Joan carried on the business and took over from his father at the East India Company. The *Novus Atlas* was expanded to three volumes in 1640, and regularly enlarged in successive printings until six volumes were produced in 1655. Between 1663 and 1665, Joan presided over a new atlas: the massive 600-map *Atlas Major* (sometimes referred to as the *Grand Atlas*). It marked the high point of 17th-century Dutch cartography, and is the largest atlas ever produced.

Atlases continue to be an important part of our view of the world. They are a standard feature of every serious library, and an essential text in schools, colleges, universities, and many workplaces. They remain representative of a major human achievement: the encapsulation of the whole world into one practical volume.

ABOVE *World map from the* Grand Atlas, c. 1665, *by Joan Blaeu*
The atlases of the 17th century were richly decorated. Border panels in this world map depict the four elements, the seven planets, the four seasons, and the seven wonders of the world. Three cartouches and the two polar insets appear in the map, conveniently covering up areas that were probably unknown to the mapmaker.

LEFT Africa *from the* Grand Atlas *by Joan Blaeu*
The grand atlases were richly decorated. Along the sides are depictions of indigenous peoples and along the top are views of cities. The seas are filled with ships and sea creatures, both real and imagined, and in the less well-known interior, creative cartographers would add pictures of animals.

CELESTIAL ATLASES

The publication of terrestrial atlases was accompanied by the production of separate celestial atlases. Often the same publishers were involved. Jan Jansson (1588–1664), a well-known map publisher from Arnhem in the Netherlands, printed the first edition of Andreas Cellarius's *Atlas Coelesti* in 1660, which contains stunning astronomical illustrations. Celestial maps have provided some of the most imaginative flights of fancy. The stellar constellations provide a simple canvas that celestial mapmakers have filled with colorful, imaginative, and fanciful designs. Andreas Cellarius's atlas contains some of the most richly decorated designs. He aimed his work at more than just a narrow range of astronomical specialists. His richly illustrated book was designed for a more general market. Cellarius's atlas was as concerned with aesthetics as with science. The atlas was filled with astronomical diagrams and a wide variety of maps of the heavens, showing both classical and Christian imagery, sun-centered as well as earth-centered universes.

BELOW ***Cellarius Atlas, 1660***
This richly decorated image is a map of the southern sky seen from deep space looking down on the Pacific and Antarctica. The unusual perspective is animated with wonderful illustrations of the constellations. Border decorations are vignettes of astronomers measuring both the earth and the sky.

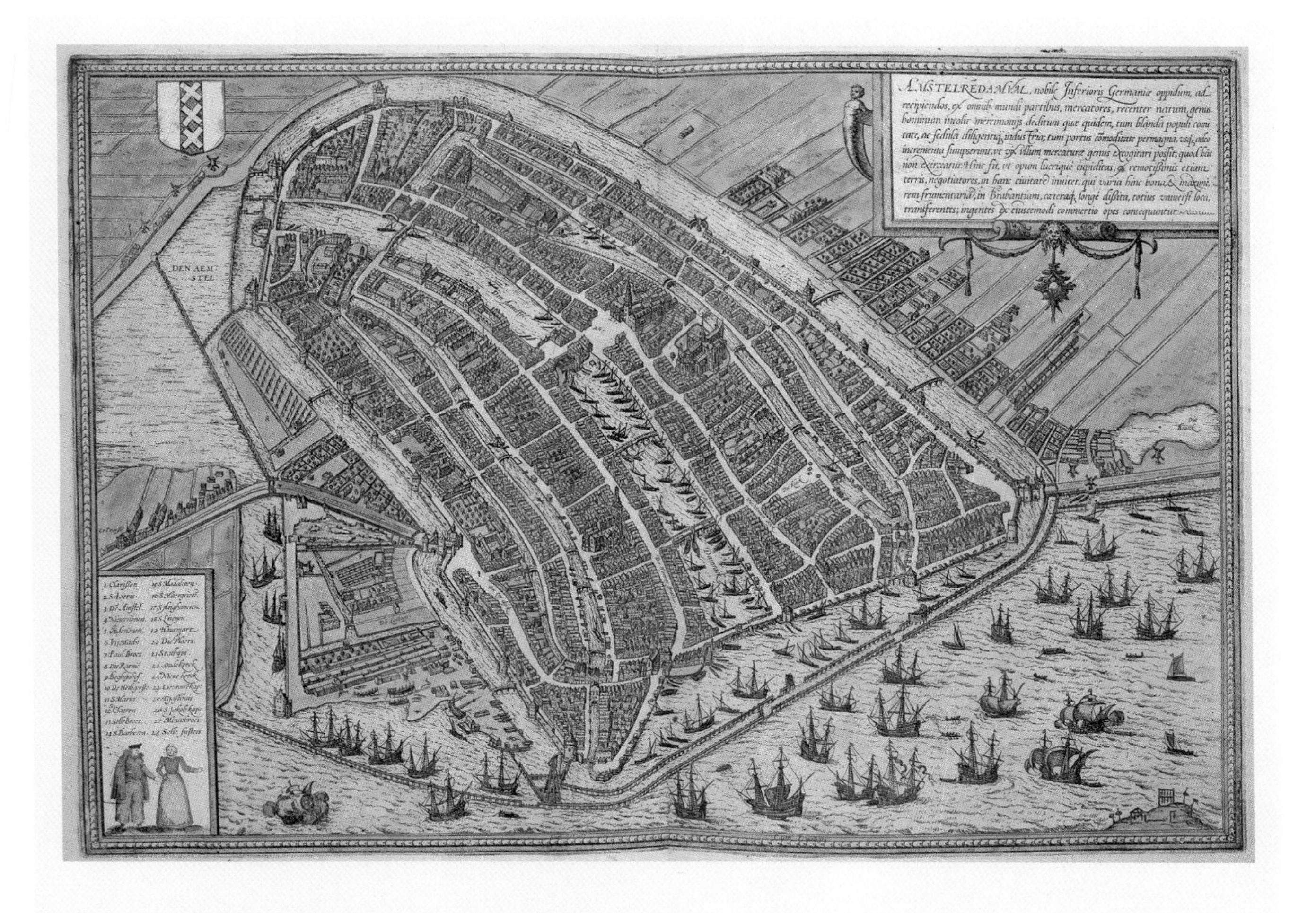

THE *CIVITATES ORBIS TERRARUM*

The first city atlas was called the *Civitates Orbis Terrarum,* and was created by Georg Braun (1541–1622) and Frans Hogenberg (1535–1590) in Cologne, Germany. It was first published in one volume in 1572 and proved so popular that by 1617 it had grown to six volumes containing over 363 urban views of cities throughout the world, with the emphasis on European cities. A total of 46 editions were produced in Latin, German, and French, and many subsequent city atlases were based upon the *Civitates*. This great work provides us with a comprehensive collection of 16th-century urban views and is an invaluable record of the times. Each city has a brief written note detailing its history, situation, and mode of trade. Prospect and bird's-eye views predominate, and even in the plan views the buildings are shown in vertical relief.

In the *Civitates*, the city is not just represented but celebrated. Many of the urban maps were created as representations of civic pride, and many are shown in extraordinary detail, even giving individual street names. In some images, the city in question comes alive, and the range of the atlas is quite amazing, covering as it does such diverse metropolises as Aden, Peking, Goa, Mombasa, and Tangiers.

ABOVE ***The city of Amsterdam from Braun's* Civitates Orbis Terrarum**

This map of Amsterdam highlights the maritime connections of the merchant city which had trading connections all over the world. Ships fill the harbor and the canals. The three wide canals visible in this map still exist.

PART V

Mapping in the Colonial Era

LEFT *The city of Boston, 1887*

Maps as Imperial Claims: The British and French in North America

Colonizing powers map territories under their control. This mapping is not innocent of claims to power and authority; to map a territory is often to claim it. There are many examples, such as the Russian mapping of Siberia, the Belgian mapping of the Congo, and the Dutch mapping of the East Indies. This chapter takes one example: the case of British imperial mapping and empire building, from the early mapping activities in North America to the later imperial mappings in Australia and India.

ONE OF THE BEST examples of the use of maps as a political weapon is the competition for territory in North America between Britain and France in the 17th and 18th centuries.

In 1656 Nicholas Sanson (1600–77), a geography teacher to Cardinal Richelieu and King Louis XIII of France, produced a map of North America called *Le Canada, ou Nouvelle France*: *Canada, or the New France* (see page 139). The map is distorted, but the distortion is revealing. The interior of the country has been truncated so that Lake Erie is shown to be close to the northern boundary of Florida. This distortion minimizes the English territories along the eastern seaboard and maximizes the French claims to the interior. From the mouth of the St. Lawrence River to Florida the territory is clearly marked as French. The French were not only claiming "their" territory but also claiming territory that wasn't theirs, or which was in dispute at that time, or which had not yet been claimed by either side.

Sanson's map set what was to become a familiar precedent. In 1718, a French merchant company founded the city of New Orleans, and the geographer Guillaume Delisle (1675–1726), whose official title was *Premier Geographe du Roi*—chief geographer to the King—produced a map called the *Carte de la Louisiane et du Cours du Mississipi* (see page 138). The English colonies are again compressed along the eastern seaboard. The map is a record of French claims beyond the Appalachians.

Delisle's map was extremely influential and was used as a template for other maps of the region for almost 50 years. Thomas Jefferson had a copy of the map and it was also an important source of information for the Lewis and Clark expedition of 1804–6 that crossed the Rockies to the Pacific.

In direct response to Delisle's map, Herman Moll (*d.* 1732) produced many maps of North America. Moll was born in Germany and came to England in 1678. Living in London he found work as an engraver, bookseller, and geographer. He was the foremost map publisher of the early 18th century, and in 1720 produced *This Map of North America According to ye Newest and most Exact Observations*. In Moll's map the British colonies stretch from the Carolinas to Newfoundland, and the Labrador

RIGHT ***Popple's map of America, 1733***
Popple's map was produced to counter French maps that laid claim to vast territories in North America. The British Government sponsored the map, but was not pleased with the result. The map was disowned in 1755 for not aggressively promoting British claims.

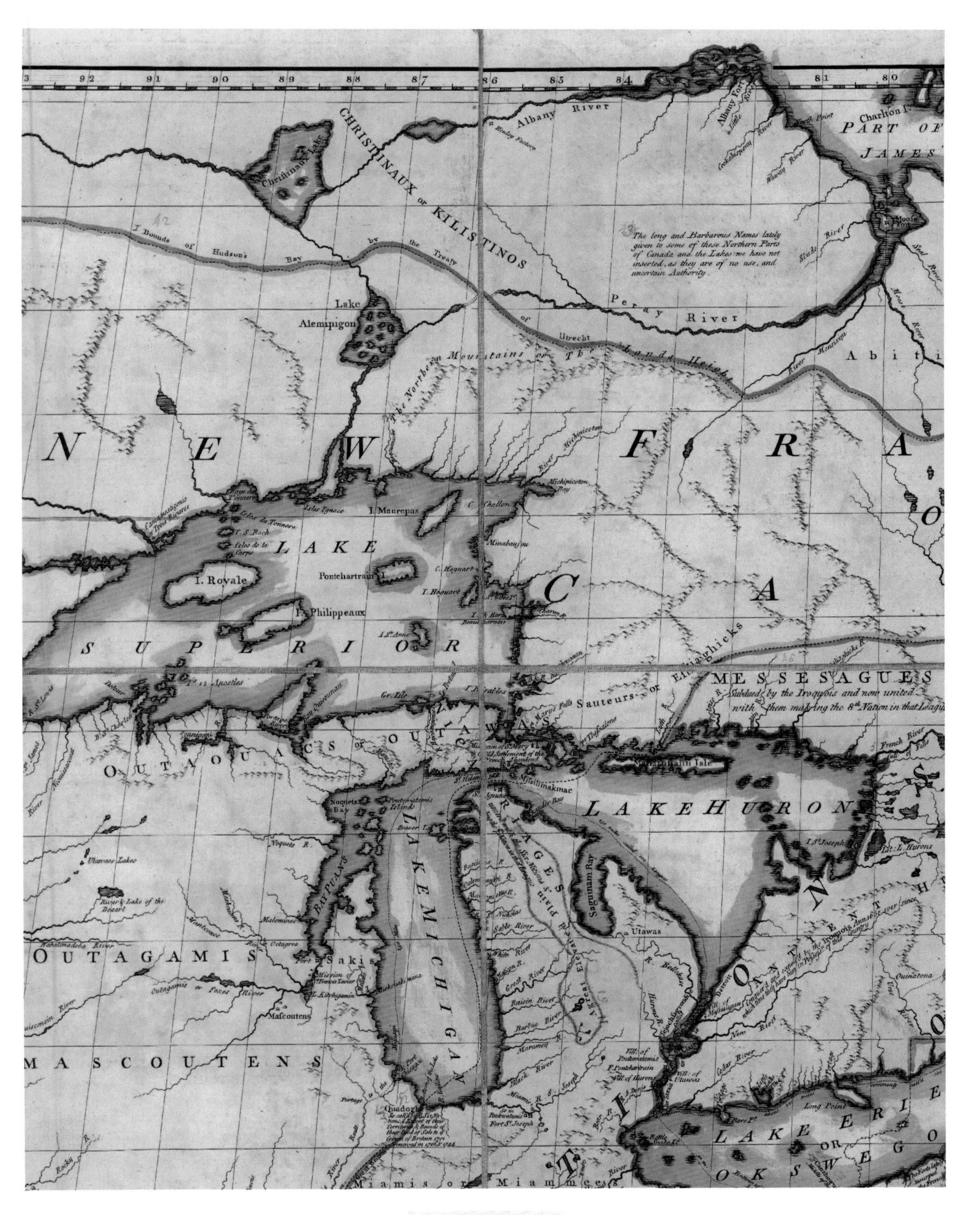
Albany River
CHRISTINAUX or KILISTINOS
Christinaux Lake
Charlton I.
PART OF
JAMES
The long and Barbarous Names lately given to some of these Northern Parts of Canada and the Lakes we have not inserted, as they are of no use, and uncertain Authority.
Bounds of Hudson's Bay by the Treaty of Utrecht
Peray River
Lake Alemipigon
Abiti
NEW FRANCE
LAKE SUPERIOR
I. Maurepas
I. Royale
Pontchartrain I.
I. Philippeaux
Michipicoton Bay
MESSESAGUES
Subdued by the Iroquois and now united with them making the 8th Nation in that League
Sauteurs or
OUTAOUACS or OUTAWAS
LAKE HURON
LAKE MICHIGAN
Missillimakinac
Saguinam Bay
Utawas
OUTAGAMIS
Sakis
Mascoutens
MASCOUTENS
Baye Puans
LAKE ERIE OR OKSWEGO
Long Point
Fort St. Joseph
Miamis or Miammees

The Mapping of Australia

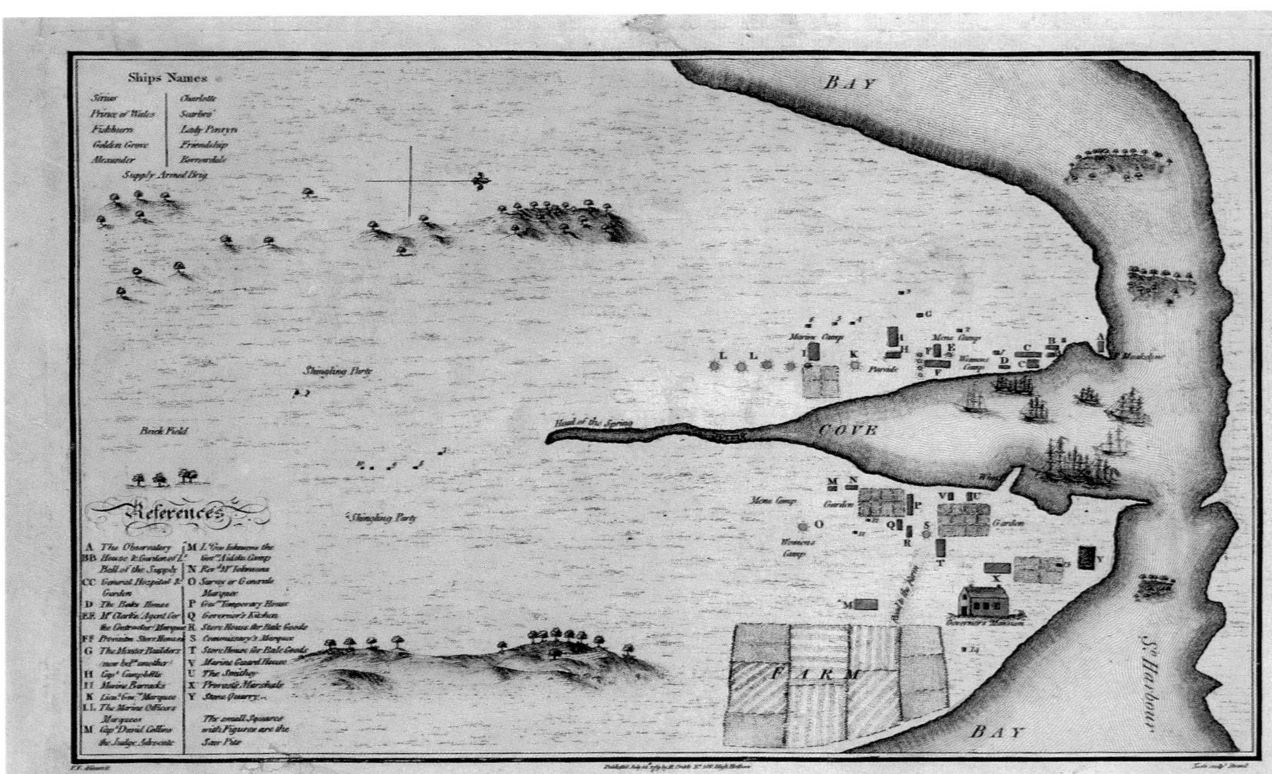
Ships Names
BAY
COVE
References
FARM
BAY
Sketch & Description of the Settlement at SYDNEY COVE PORT JACKSON in the COUNTY of CUMBERLAND taken
by a transported Convict on the 16th of April, 1788 which was not quite 3. Months after Commodore Phillips's Landing there
Sydney Cove lies 3 Leagues to the Northward of BOTANY BAY which is situated in Lat 34 S. Long 151 E.

ABOVE ***Map of Sydney cove, 1778, by Francis Fowkes***
It is probable that transported convict Fowkes was kept below decks until the ship landed in the Harbor—now known as Circular Quay—because from this map there is no indication of the nearby ocean. The land is like a giant whale swallowing the incoming ships.

Australia was completely unknown to the British until Captain Cook landed at Botany Bay in 1770. A map made in 1744 by Emanuel Bowen (*c.* 1720–67), a London engraver, print seller and publisher, shows Australia connected to New Guinea, with no defined eastern coastline. Captain Cook's landing legitimized British control of the new continent, although having laid claim to a land that was not theirs, the British were at something of a loss as to what to do with it. As a result, in its early years, the new colony was used as the distant destination for transported convicts, who had previously been deported to the Americas.

Many maps were made of the new colony. One of the most poignant was drawn by a transported convict called Francis Fowkes, just a few months after the founding of the Botany Bay colony in 1778. The map shows the tiny settlement around what is now Sydney Harbor, and gives no indication of the existence of the Pacific Ocean, perhaps because Fowkes was imprisoned below decks for the duration of the voyage from England.

The gradual mapping of Australia began with the coastline. Matthew Flinders (1774–1814) was responsible for charting the Tasmanian coast between 1798–9. Between 1801–3 he circumnavigated Australia itself, mapping as he went. The result—a map of the entire coastline—was published in 1814.

Exploration and mapping of the interior of Australia was prompted by the need to find more land for farming: the flocks of sheep and herds of cattle needed pasture. Gradually the area inland from Sydney across the coastal mountain ranges was explored and charted, opening up the way for western expansion in the early 19th century.

Much of this work was done under the control of the Surveyor Generals appointed by the British to survey territory, lay out settlements, and divide up the land for farming. John Oxley (*c.* 1785–1828) was appointed Surveyor General in 1812 and devoted much time and effort to following rivers inland, searching for suitable pasture. His successor, Thomas Mitchell (1792–1855), undertook four expeditions into the interior, building upon the work of Oxley.

Later, other explorers such as Edward Eyre, Ludwig Leichardt, and Charles Sturt mapped the remaining territory of Australia.

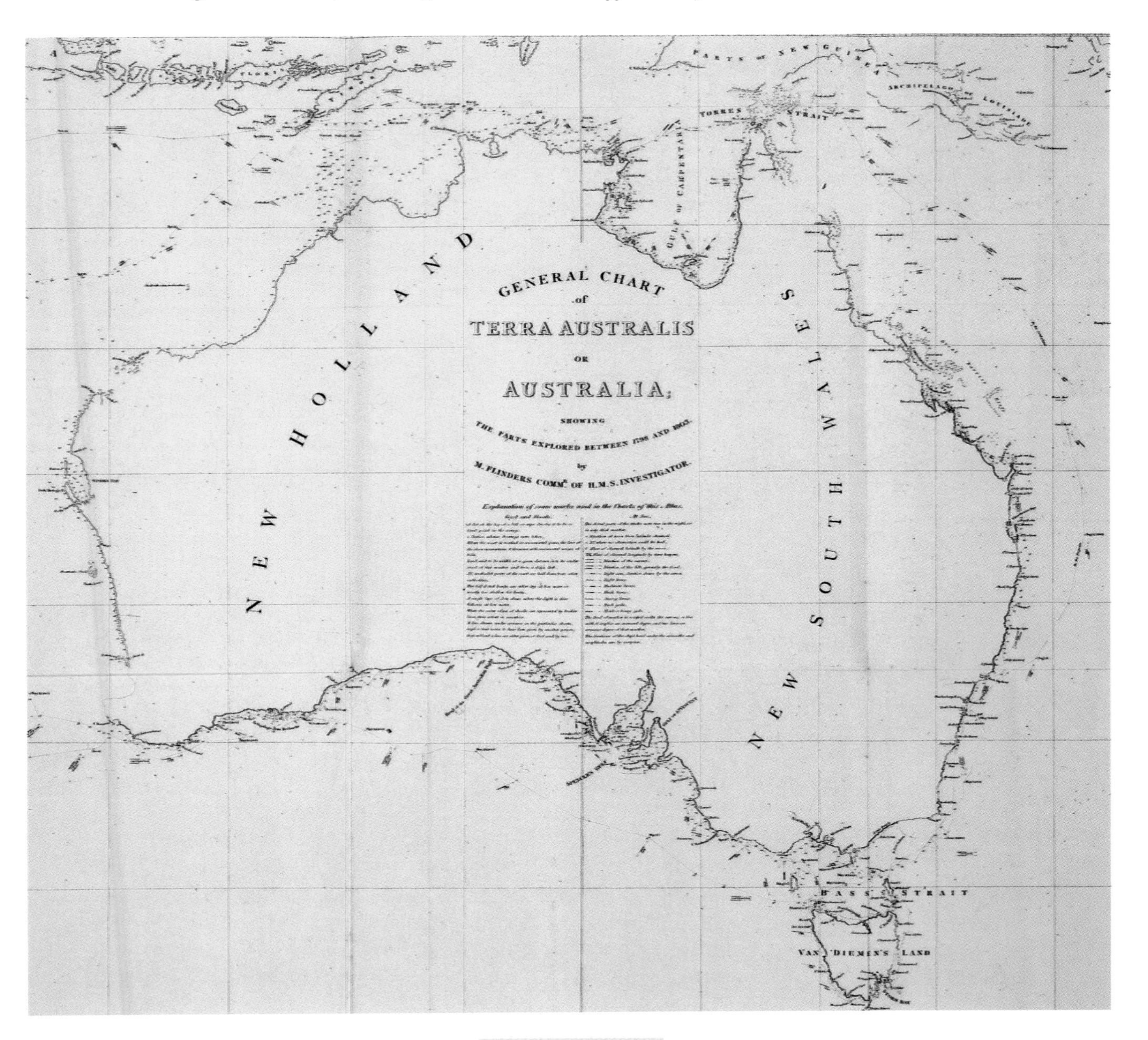

BELOW **Terra Australis c.** ***1814, by Matthew Flinders***
While from the early 16th century, various maps and charts of different sections of the Australian coastline had been made, the picture was not complete until Matthew Flinders sailed and mapped his way around the island continent.

The Mapping of India

India had become part of the trading empire of England in the early 17th century when the British East India Company began trading on the west coast of the subcontinent. Direct contact was restricted to the coastal trading ports of Calcutta, Madras, and Bombay, and along the major rivers. Maps made of India during the mid-18th century show the interior as a blank, annotated with: "A great expanse of country about which we have no exact knowledge."

As British power extended over India, the colonists needed more accurate maps and the East India Company employed mapmakers such as James Rennell (1742–1830), whose first commission at the age of 21 was to map the Ganges River and the surrounding region of Bengal. The result was the *Bengal Atlas*, published in 1779. Rennell went on to make one of the first accurate maps of the whole subcontinent, called the *Map of Hindoostan* and published in 1782.

Though vital, Rennell's work was far from accurate, being in effect a rough and ready survey carried out in difficult conditions. It soon became apparent to the East India Company that they needed to map the whole of India, and do so in greater detail. As a result, an army engineer called William Lambton (*c.* 1756–1823) undertook the Herculean task of mapping the entire country—an endeavor that would eventually be called the "Great Trigonometrical Survey."

Funded by the East India Company, Lambton imported the most accurate surveying instruments of the day from Britain, and in 1802 began measuring a baseline for all his subsequent measurements. Lambton took extraordinary

BELOW ***George Everest in India***

This sketch made by Godfrey Thomas Vigne in 1834 shows George Everest in the foreground supervising the construction of an observation tower. These 60-foot (18-meter) towers allowed the triangulation measurements across the vast landscape of India.

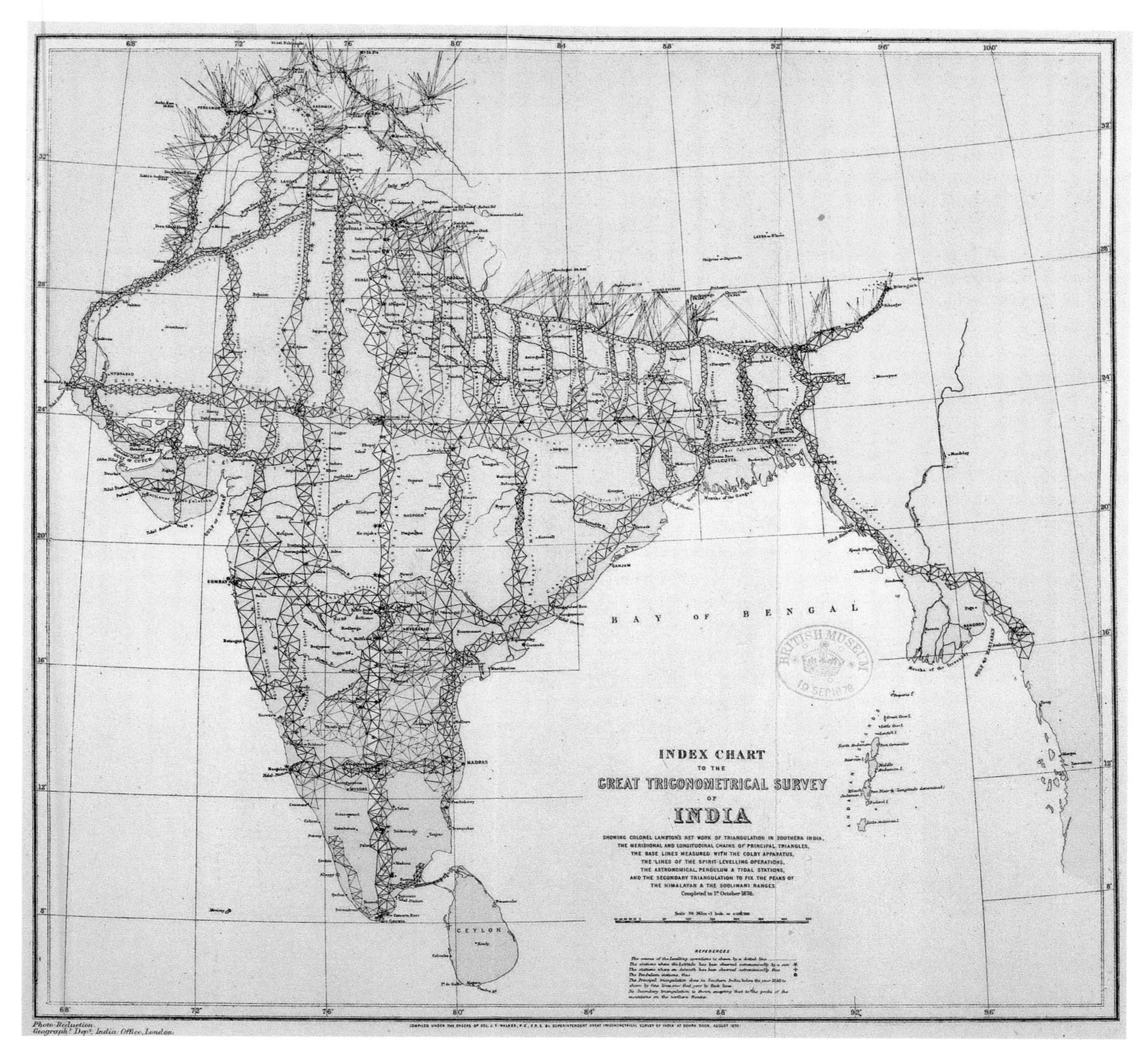

care with this baseline since it was the foundation on which the whole survey would be constructed. He spent 57 days making 400 measurements to ensure its accuracy. From this known baseline he swept through the country surveying the land in great sweeping triangles. In many cases he used existing buildings as his triangulation points, but where nothing suitable existed he built special towers, some of which still stand as testimony to this great survey.

After four years of work, Lambton had surveyed most of the southern peninsula. George Everest succeeded in constructing the central spine of the survey—a series of interlocking triangles that stretched 1,600 miles (2,500 km) along the length of the country. The survey was completed in 1837 and subsequent surveys further extended the detailed mapping of India northward toward the Himalayas. Everest retired in 1843, and his successor proposed in 1856 that Himalayan "Peak XV" be named after him, as indeed it was: Mount Everest.

ABOVE ***The* Great Trigonometrical Survey of India,** *1837*
This map shows the great swathes of measurement taken throughout the Indian subcontinent. The land was inscribed with an imperial presence, and imperial power was now buttressed by more accurate spatial information.

The Mapping of Africa

Until the 19th century, European knowledge of Africa was limited to a narrow coastal strip. While there was trading with the interior, the slave trade being the prime example, the Europeans in the main stuck to the coast. The so-called "opening up" of Africa involved three elements: the exploration of the interior, territorial appropriation, and the search for the source of the Nile River.

In 1816, John Barrow, an important figure in the British Admiralty, advocated the exploration of "blank" areas of the world. Expeditions were duly sent to the Arctic to search for the Northwest Passage, and to Africa to map the full course of the Niger River. Various attempts were made, but it was not until 1831 that Richard and John Lander successfully managed to follow the Niger to its source.

BELOW **The River Ruvuma and Dr Livingstone's Route on his Last Journey,** ***1872***
In August 1872 Livingstone made his last journey. In what is now central Tanzania, he and a band of hired porters crossed the Kalongosi River and headed toward Lake Bangweulu. Terminally ill and carried on a litter, Livingstone got lost. He died in April 1873. His heart was buried under a tree, his body embalmed and returned to Britain. He is buried in Westminster Abbey.

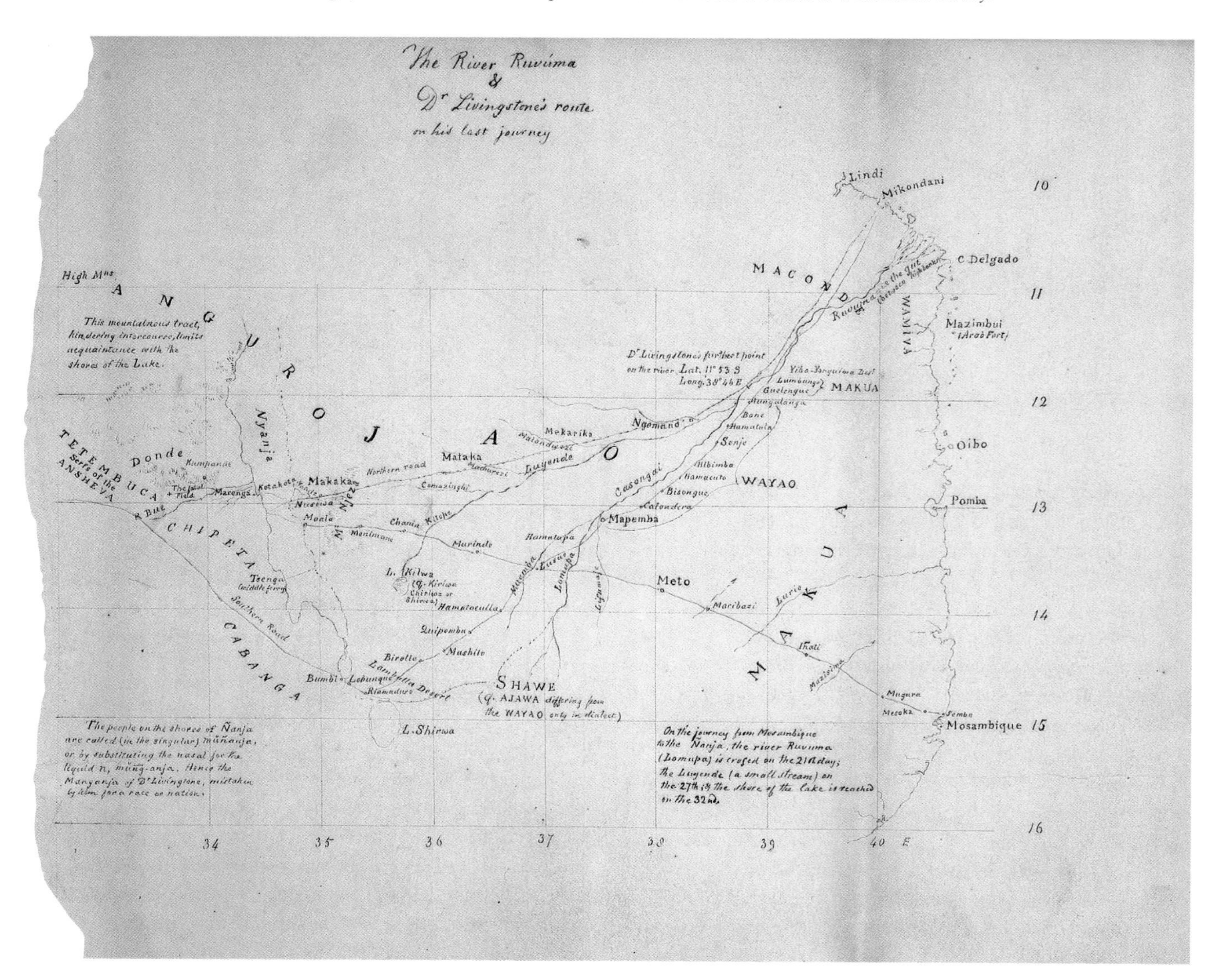

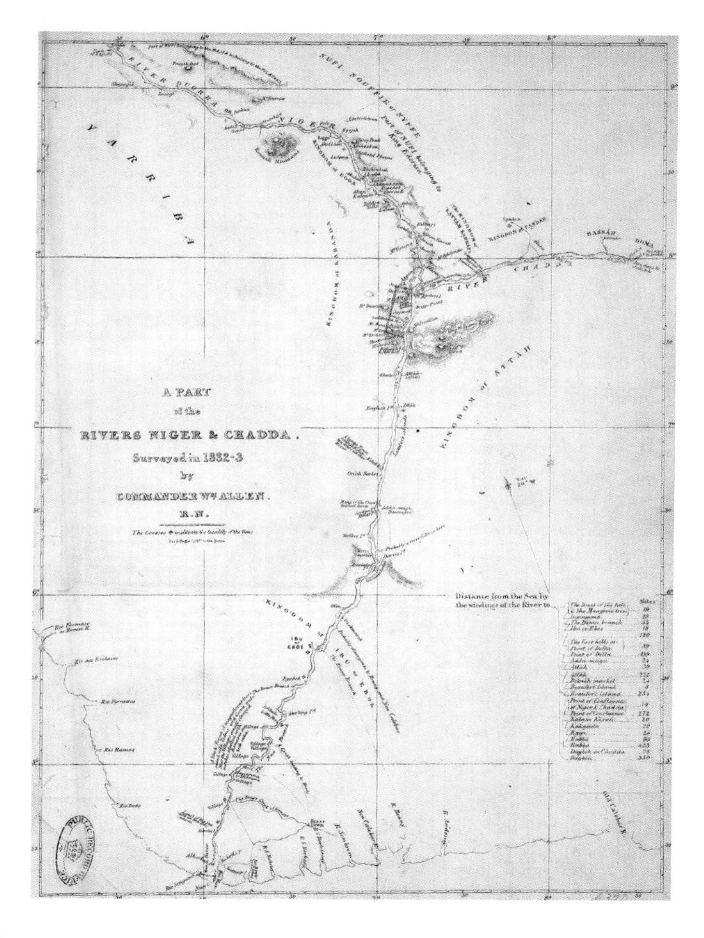

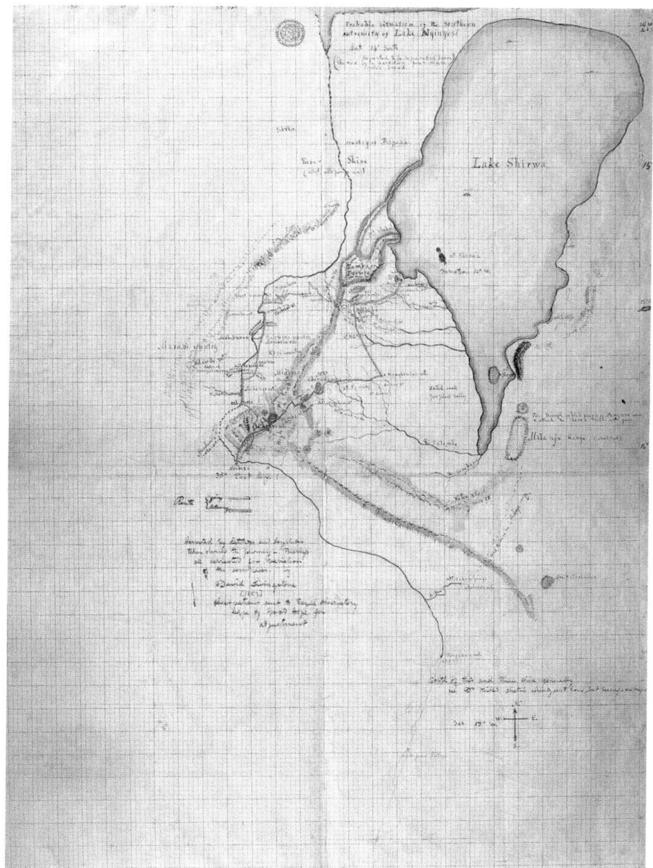

ABOVE LEFT **A part of the Rivers Niger & Chadda,** ***1841***
Europeans mapped the rivers of Africa as vital trading routes with the interior. This map was part of a report made in 1841.

ABOVE RIGHT ***Lake Shirwa, 1859, by Livingstone***
David Livingstone made manuscript maps of the lake system of central Africa.

In southern Africa there was no equivalent to the search for the Niger, but instead a steady expansion northward from the Cape Town area. The English missionary David Livingstone (1813–73), traveled through much of central Africa and in 1849 he crossed the Kalahari Desert. In 1851 Livingstone reached the Zambezi River, and between 1854 and 1856 managed to cross the entire continent. Throughout his remarkable travels, he charted and mapped the land, greatly adding to the growing bank of cartographic knowledge.

In the east, some exploratory mapping was undertaken as part of the search for the source of the Nile River. In 1856 the Royal Geographical Society in London sponsored expeditions to this end, and in 1857 the explorers Richard Burton (1821–90) and John Hanning Speke (1827–64) managed to discover Lake Tanganyika, in east central Africa. Speke believed that the source of the Nile was Lake Victoria, but Burton disagreed and an ugly controversy ensued. Speke returned to Africa in 1860 and confirmed his finding. Livingstone was then sent by the Royal Geographical Society to verify Speke's claim, and promptly went missing for almost three years. The British explorer and journalist Sir Henry Morton Stanley (1841–1904) was sent by the *New York Herald* to search for Livingstone. He found him at Ujiji and they explored Lake Tanganyika together. David Livingstone died of dysentery in 1873.

The European exploration of Africa was not simply a scientific exercise, but an integral part of what later became known as the "scramble for Africa." In 1877, the Royal Geographical Society produced a map of Africa that asserted a claim to territory on the basis of the priority of exploration. From 1884 to 1900, the European powers claimed vast swathes of territory in the African interior. The continent was divided up between the competing powers with boundaries set by imperial cartographers, often with inadequate information. Arbitrary lines and imperial compromises left a continuing legacy in the national boundaries of postcolonial Africa.

Cartography and the Enlightenment

In the last quarter of the 17th and the first quarter of the 18th century, considerable progress was made in cartography and surveying. The Enlightenment preoccupation with cataloguing the world and classifying knowledge was reflected by and embodied in the mapping of the world.

A CENTRAL FIGURE of the English Enlightenment was Edmund Halley (1656–1742), the well-known astronomer who, in 1705, identified the comet that now bears his name. Halley was also a mapmaker, producing several maps including a star chart and a map of the trade winds of the world. In 1698 Halley was commissioned by the British Royal Navy to determine longitude. Commanding a small ship called the *Paramore*, he made many observations of the compass variation from magnetic north and summarized his work in a map produced in 1700.

On the other side of the English Channel, the French were also pursuing an active mapping program. Louis XIV's finance minister, Jean-Baptiste Colbert, ordered an accurate map of France to be made. Jean Picard (1620–82) was given the task of choosing an accurate measure. He concentrated on measuring one degree of latitude, by measuring the distance between Sourdon and Malvoisine in Picardy. He then took an accurate astronomical fix from the star, the Knee of Cassiopeia. The project took two years from 1668 to 1670. Picard's work was 40 times more accurate than any previous measurements, and the result was a

THE ENLIGHTENMENT

The Enlightenment—also called the Age of Reason—was a period of great scientific and intellectual progress that occurred in Europe and the United States during the 18th century. It had its foundations in the 17th century when scientists and thinkers such as Newton, Locke, Pascal, and Descartes began openly questioning accepted beliefs.

The Enlightenment was represented in Europe by such thinkers as Voltaire, Rousseau, Montesquieu, Adam Smith, Swift, Hume, Kant, and Lessing; and in America by Paine, Jefferson, and Franklin. What linked all these figures was a rejection of established religious authority, a profound belief in individual liberty and equality, and a rational, scientific approach to dealing with social and political issues.

Enlightenment ideals were also adopted by several rulers, known as "enlightened despots," including Catherine II of Russia, Frederick II of Prussia, and the Holy Roman Emperor Joseph II. The writers of the United States constitution were greatly influenced by the ideas of the Enlightenment.

ALEXANDER VON HUMBOLDT

Friedrich Wilhelm Heinrich Alexander von Humboldt (1769–1859) was born in Berlin, Germany, and studied at the Universities of Frankfurt, Göttingen, Hamburg, and Freiburg. He was fascinated by the physical world, and traveled widely. In 1799 he went to South America, where he gathered 60,000 plant specimens and made many maps. In his later years he undertook a 9,000-mile (14,500-km) trip to Siberia. His travel journal consisted of 34 volumes.

Humboldt's maps included "cartograms": maps that display statistical information in a diagrammatic form. His map of the Ecuadorean volcano, Chimborazo, combines altitude with vegetation type, showing how vegetation differs with increasing altitude. He drew the first "isothermic" map, showing temperature variation. Maps in Humboldt's hands were used to present a wide range of empirical material. He was arguably the greatest Enlightenment scientist and one of the most accomplished cartographers the world has ever seen.

striking increase in the accuracy of geographic coordinates. Picard moved to Paris where he collaborated with Jean-Dominique Cassini (1625–1712) and worked on calculating the precise coordinates of French cities. Picard also produced a 40-page pamphlet in which he described his surveying work. First published in 1671, it was called *The Measure of the Earth*. It is a model of scientific elegance and simple writing.

Cassini's son, Jacques (1677–1756), took over the task of mapping France begun by his father and Picard. He worked on the project with his son, César François-Cassini de Thury (1714–84), developing a system of triangulation to cover large areas. The resulting map was filled with topographic detail and produced as an atlas in 1791 by César's son, Jacques-Dominique Cassini (1748–1845).

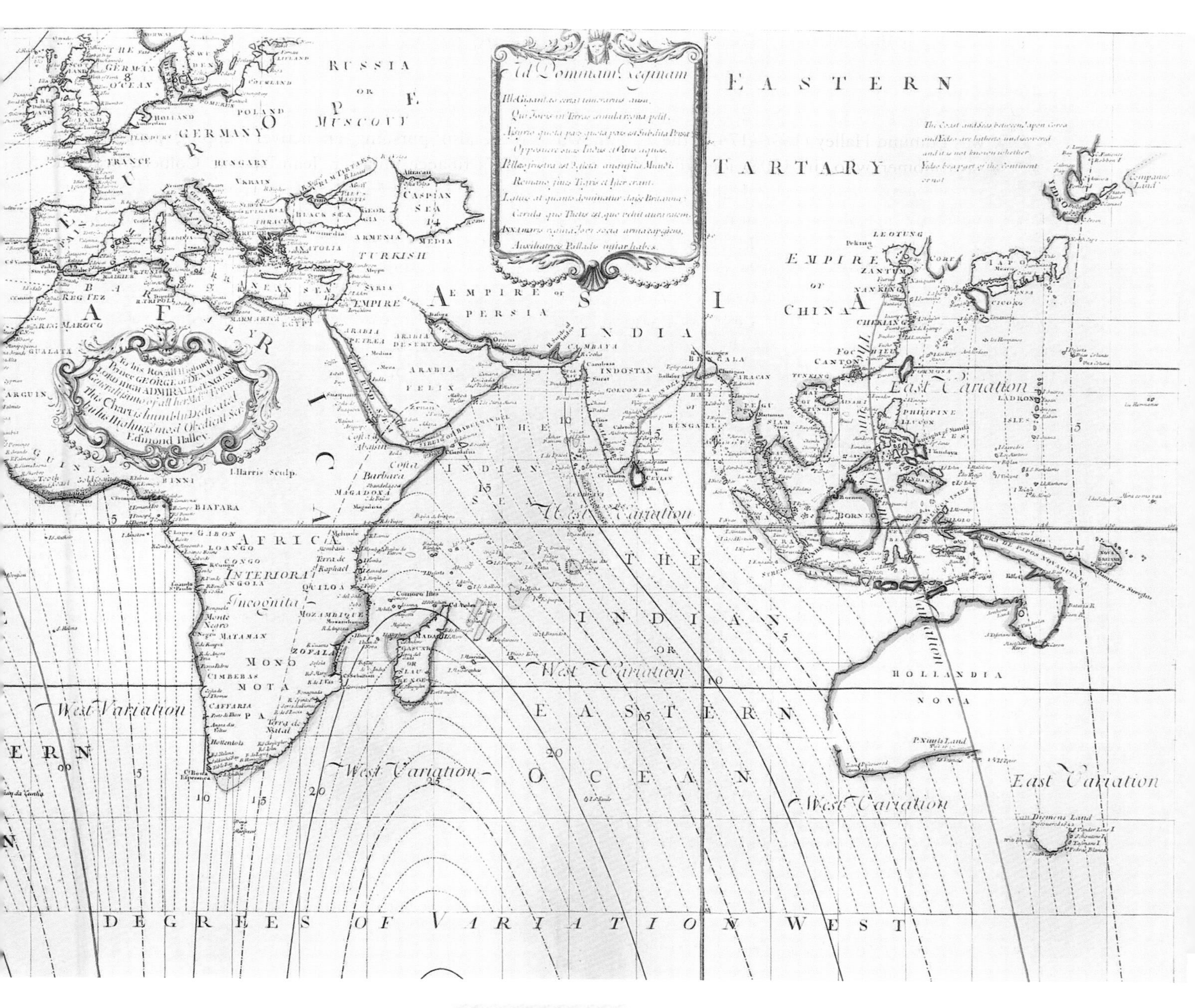

BELOW ***World variation chart,1702, by Edmund Halley***
This map by the astronomer Edmund Halley draws upon his own findings as well as the work of Dutch East India Company navigators. It shows the variation in degrees from geographical north in the southern Indian and Atlantic oceans. This was vital information for accurate wayfinding.

Mapping The Enlightenment City

In 18th-century Europe, urban growth dramatically increased as a number of national powers, including Britain, France, Russia, and Italy, embarked upon lavish city building programs. The European Enlightenment city was carefully planned by the rich and powerful as a symbol of their nation's strength and sophistication. The maps of these new cities were equally large and lavish.

In 1739, a bird's-eye view map of Paris, France, was commissioned by Michel Etienne Turgot (1690–1751), the chief administrator of the city. The work was carried out by cartographer Louis Bretez, who was provided with a pass giving him complete freedom of movement in order to make the necessary sketches. As a result, he was able to map both public and private buildings. The map consisted of 20 sheets, bound as an urban atlas that, when spread out, covered an impressive 12 x 8 feet (3.6 x 2.5 m). The map is orientated toward the east so that the viewer can see the entrance to the city churches, which face west. It is one of the most comprehensive urban mappings of the 18th century.

In 1746, only seven years after the Paris map was produced, John Rocque (d. 1762), a French Huguenot émigré—who was persecuted in France for being a Protestant and therefore moved to England—published another large map, this time of London. Rocque was a surveyor and mapmaker who produced large-scale maps of English towns, each undertaken as a commercial enterprise funded by wealthy patrons and subscribers. A particularly generous donor would find the map dedicated to them. Merchants and local business people would often provide the funds to underwrite the costs of surveying, mapmaking, and printing; Rocque's map of Bristol, for example, was dedicated to the merchant companies in the city. Rocque's London map was completed in 1744 and covered 24 sheets. When put together, the sheets formed a single map measuring 7 x 13 feet (2 x 4 m). The map is a plan view with some images added in three dimensions, such as ships in the Thames River, and trees in the surrounding countryside. In it we see a dense, tightly bound city with green fields and orchards still within reasonable distance of the center.

LEFT ***Excerpt from the Turgot/Bretez map of Paris, 1739***
The perspective of the map allows us to feel that we hover above the city with a privileged vantage point. The city is carefully spread out below us for our visual pleasure and empowerment.

OPPOSITE, ABOVE ***Rocque's map of London, 1744***
While the map of Paris is an attempt to provide a three-dimensional sense of the city this map of London uses a plan perspective. While accurate, it gives less accessible reading of the city. The city is flattened out in the plan view.

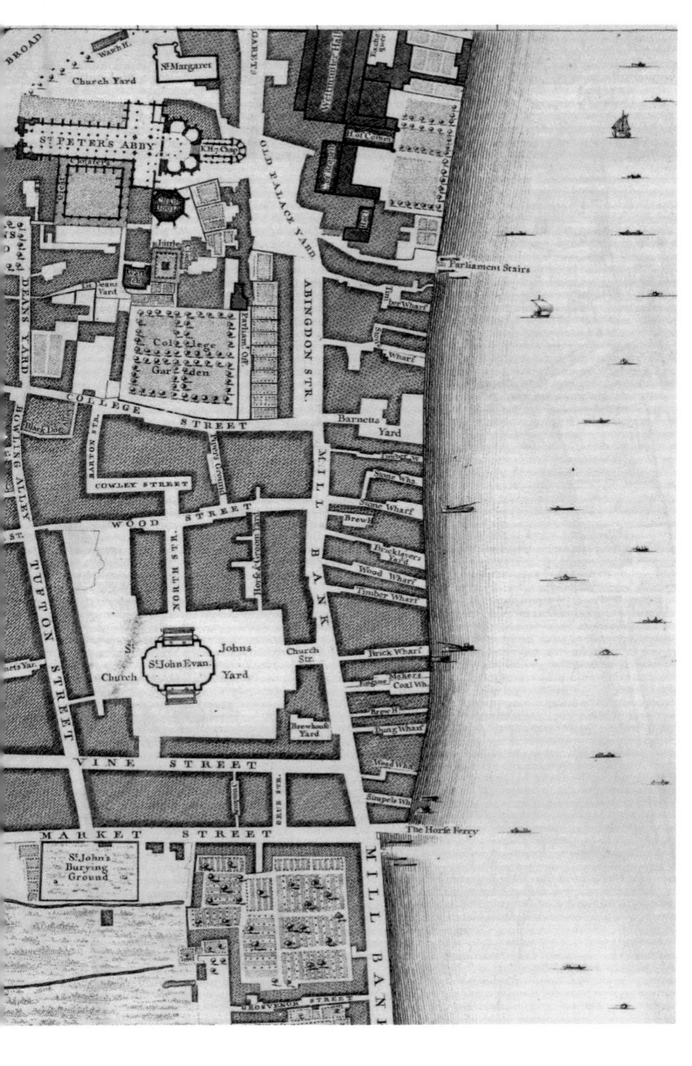

FIRE INSURANCE MAPS

One of the most comprehensive and detailed urban mappings during the 18th century was undertaken by insurance companies, which needed accurate maps to determine the likelihood of city fires and calculate the level of insurance premium to be paid by the residents. No civic fire service existed, hence the need for "fire insurance." A map of London made by Richard Horwood for this purpose between 1792 and 1799 lists every building in the city center.

In the United States, many fire insurance maps were produced and updated between 1852 and 1968. The Sanborn Company published highly detailed urban maps listing every building, frequently subdividing property in multi-dwelling structures, and giving construction details. By the 1950s more than 12,000 areas had been mapped.

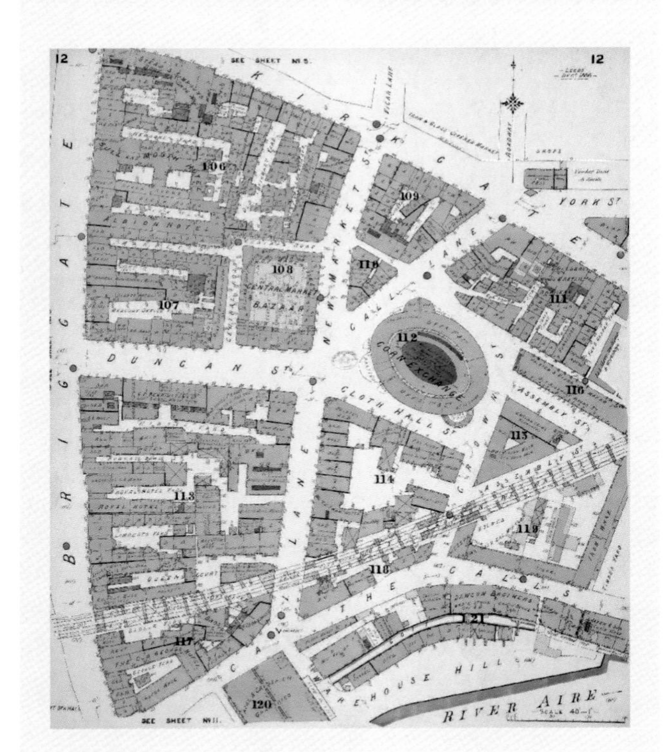

ABOVE ***Goad Map***

Goad maps are the British equivalent of the US Sanborn maps. They were used to calculate insurance premiums but they provide a marvelous historical record of different land uses within cities and give us an opportunity to plot significant land use changes over time.

Two years after the London map was printed, an impressive map of Rome, Italy, was produced under the supervision of the Italian surveyor and architect Giambattista Nolli (*c.* 1692–1756). The map provided a detailed view of Rome's streets, buildings, public and private outdoor spaces, and selected interiors such as St. Peter's and the Pantheon. Nolli began his survey of the city in 1736, and in 1748 was finally able to present his great plan view of Rome to Pope Benedict XIV.

Grand urban maps were not restricted to western Europe. When Peter the Great established the city of St. Petersburg in 1703 he also founded the Imperial Academy of Sciences, which in 1753 commissioned its geography department to produce a map to celebrate the city's fiftieth anniversary. The work was undertaken by geographer and cartographer Ivan Fomich Truskott (1721–86) and the resulting plan map was distributed to all the major European capitals.

Creating National Identity in the Early US Republic

The American Revolution resulted in political independence for a new country but cultural independence was more difficult to attain. The North American colonials had forged a distinctive culture as a result of the diverse migrants who had settled in the New World, but before the revolution this was the result of pragmatic adjustment, and had not been a conscious endeavor.

THE NEW AMERICA already had a popular geographical work, produced in England and named after its author. *Guthrie's Geography*, first published in 1769, continued to be popular and was published in successive editions as late as 1842. The work grew with each new edition, and by 1795 (the fifteenth edition) had 956 pages and 25 maps, with chapters on planets, empires, climate, and the history of nations. The largest section described the different countries of the world.

However, because *Guthrie's Geography* originated from the period of British colonization of North America, it was written from the British perspective, and even in the 1793 edition the "United States" is not actually named. The individual states have indistinct boundaries, the size of Canada is exaggerated, and the new republic is given little prominence. Having recently lost its American colonies, the British Crown was not about to give the upstart new republic any significance whatsoever. The "United States" was depicted as merely a small part of "North America."

RIGHT *Maps of US States in* Carey's American Atlas, *1795*
There was no standardized scale or key used in Carey's atlas so each state is represented at a different scale with different keys. This map of Vermont, for example, pays more attention to the political subdivisions of the state than its mountainous terrain.

OPPOSITE *Maps of US states in* Carey's General Atlas, *1796*
Situated between New York State and Rhode Island, the small state of Connecticut is easily represented in a single sheet. By the time of the maps the Native Americans of the region had all been subdued.

THE AMERICAN REVOLUTION AND DEVELOPMENT OF THE UNITED STATES

The American Revolution was the struggle of the 13 colonies that became the United States of America for independence from Britain. By the 1750s, British rule had become increasingly unwelcome to many colonists. The British government tried to impose taxes on the colonies, in part to pay for defending the colonies against the French and Native Americans, provoking increasingly violent rebellion. Britain responded by passing several laws limiting the colonies' political freedoms.

The colonists formed the Continental Congress to coordinate their response, and hostilities between the two sides broke out in 1775. On July 4, 1776, the Continental Congress adopted the Declaration of Independence. After initial setbacks for the colonial forces, they finally achieved victory in 1781. The Treaty of Paris in 1783 recognized the United States as a nation.

During the 19th century, settlers moved westward into the American interior, extending the western frontier of the United States. The United States purchased Louisiana from the French in 1803, and in 1845 annexed Texas, causing a war with Mexico. US victory in this war led to the acquisition of California and most of the present-day southwest USA. The Pacific northwest was added by a peaceful settlement with Britain. Additional territory was gained with the purchase of Alaska (1867), the annexation of Hawaii (1898), and the conquest of Spanish territories, such as Puerto Rico and Guam, in the Spanish-American War (1898).

In 1794, an Irish immigrant to the United States called Mathew Carey (1760–1839) attempted to set the record straight by publishing *Guthrie's Geography* with a new text, more favorable to the new republic. He also had new maps drawn for the book, and these subsequently formed the basis of the first proper atlases of the republic: the *American Atlas*, published by Carey in 1795 with 21 maps, and the *General Atlas*, also by Carey, published in 1796 with 47 maps. Carey used Philadelphia as his prime meridian of longitude, as well as London.

Both the *American Atlas* and the *General Atlas* contained maps of the different states, bringing them all

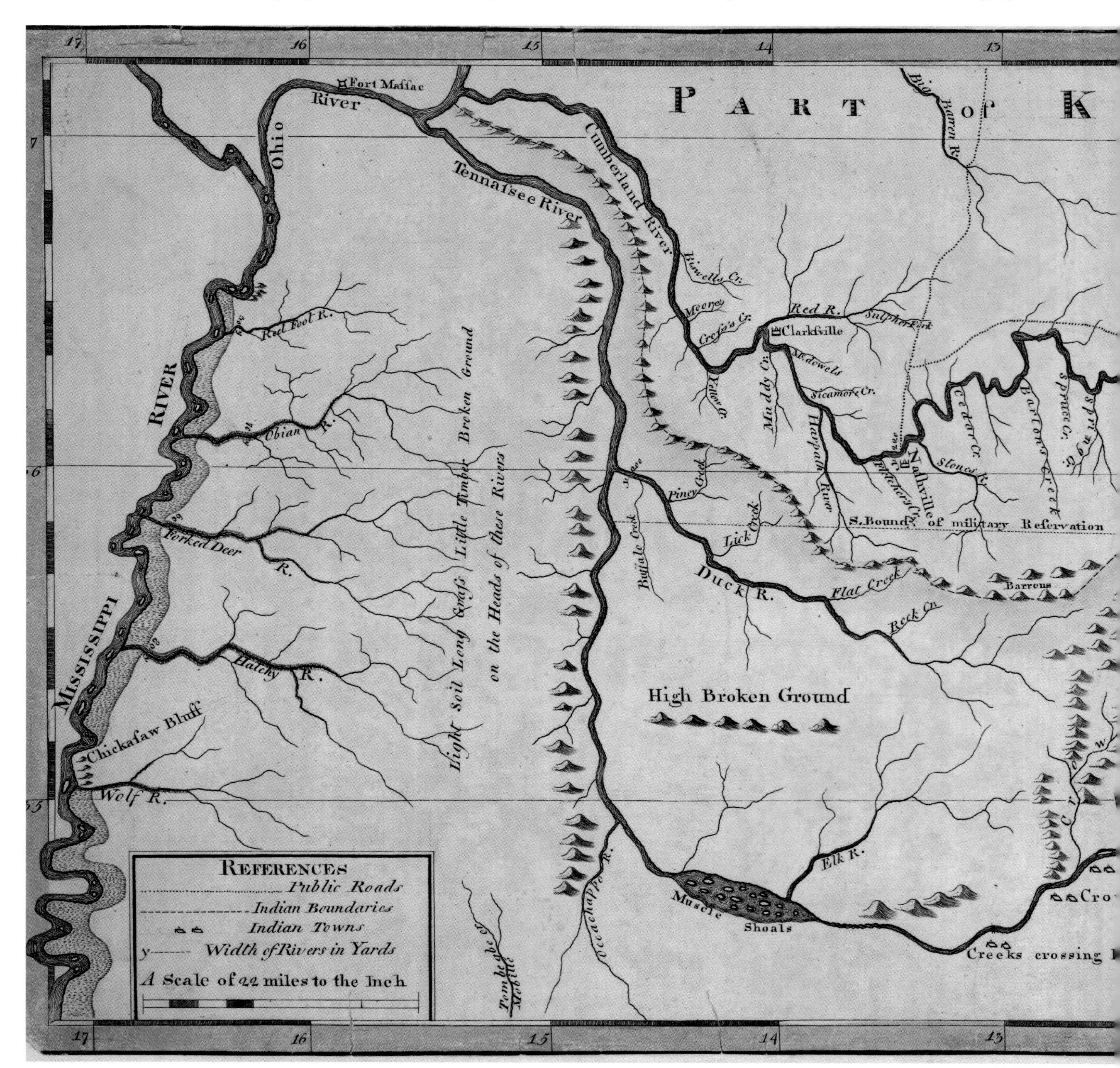

together in one volume for the first time. This was no mean feat in those days, as it implied a coherence of political outlook between the states that did not necessarily exist in reality. It is not too fanciful to suggest that both books assisted in the unification of the new independent states, placing the emphasis more on "united" and less on "states."

BELOW *Map of Tennessee by Mathew Carey*
This is a cruder representation than the maps of Vermont and Connecticut. The map shows more of a frontier territory, less settled by whites, with a remaining Native American presence.

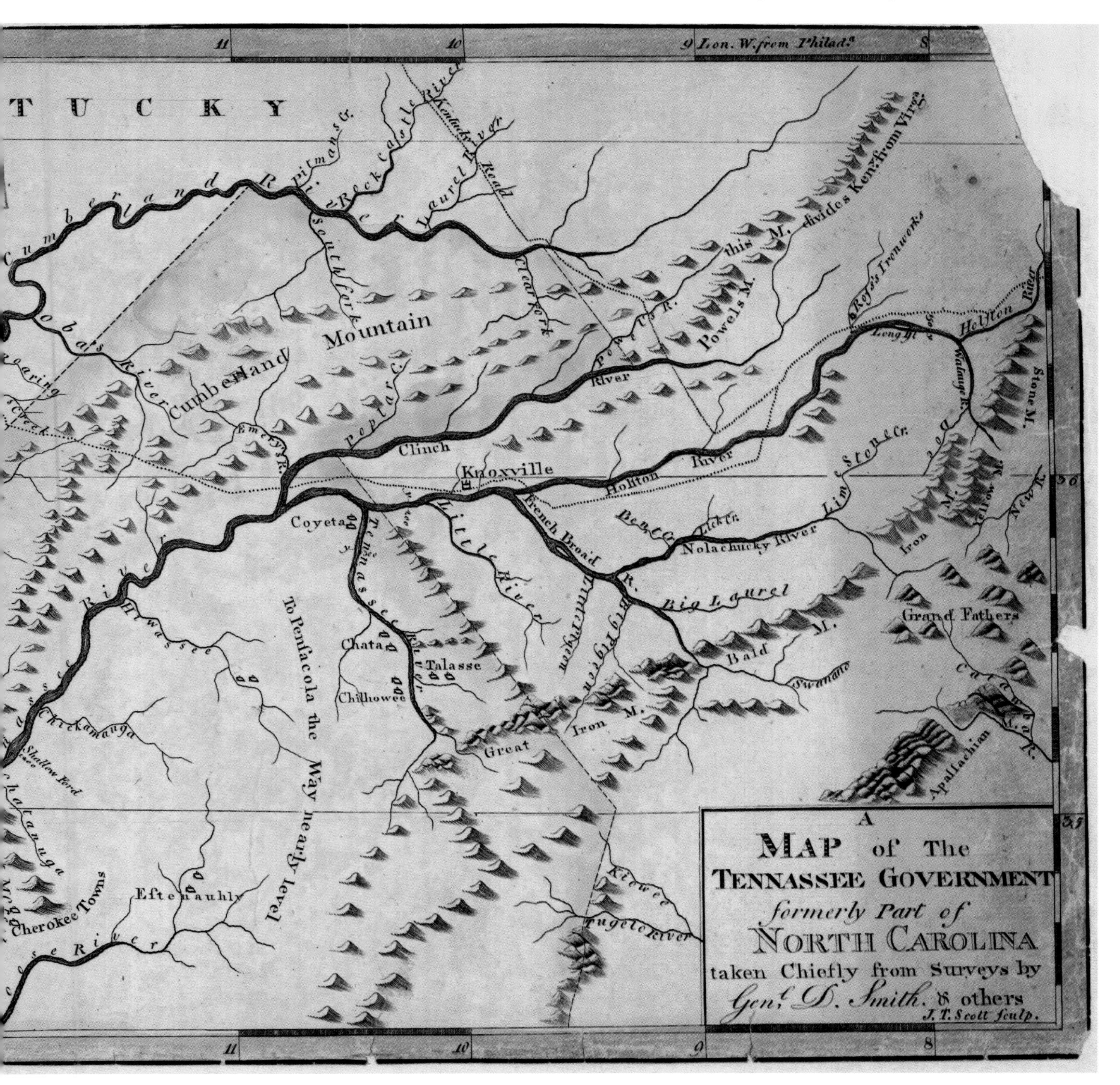

New National Geography for a New Nation

A central figure in the creation of a national geography for the United States in the first half-century after the revolution was John Melish. Born on June 13, 1771 in Methven, Scotland, he was apprenticed to a cotton merchant in Glasgow who traded with the West Indies and the United States. In 1811 he settled in Philadelphia, where he remained for the rest of his life and became an important figure in the city's vigorous book and map publishing business. Melish wanted to write a national geography of his adopted country, and published a number of diverse geographical works including *A Description of the Roads in the United States,* in 1814, and *The Traveller's Directory* in 1816. This was a small pocketbook designed for the amusement of the general reader and the enlightenment of the traveler. It contained a geographic description of the land, a gazetteer, and road maps. It provided information on each state, including situation, boundaries, extent, area, "face of country" (i.e. physical geography), rivers, minerals, soil (with special reference to fertility), produce, climate, and—for each county—the number of townships and the population of the chief towns.

Melish also published maps. His 1812 *Travels* contained eight maps, all drawn by him in a fine, elegantly understated style. This was the beginning of his career as a mapmaker and map seller. By the end of the decade he had an establishment that employed over 30 people and had developed a catalogue of over 60 maps, covering individual states, cities, the United States as a whole, and the world. He published his first large-scale map of the United States in 1813 at a scale of 1 inch to 100 miles (2.5 cm to 160 km), which was priced at $1, and sold well.

In the course of his geographical studies, Melish was frequently led to regret the fact that there was no map in existence that provided an overview of the entire United States territory. He determined to rectify this situation, and embarked upon a project in 1820 to produce a beautifully engraved large-scale map that was designed to be hung on a wall as a public statement of a nation in the making. This map is full of the promise of the new West as perceived at that time: vacant, inviting, ready to be populated (despite the fact that it was already populated by Native

Americans). The general statistical table, located in the bottom left-hand corner of the map, gives area and population, plus number of inhabitants per square mile. The current population is given as 18,629,903, yet Melish asserts that the continent is capable of supporting some 500 million people! Expansion was on the way, and Melish's map helped to give it impetus.

BELOW ***Detail of map of USA by John Melish, 1813***
John Melish was a prolific mapmaker who made many maps of the entire country. These were acts of geographical description that celebrated the United States. In his writings and maps Melish promoted continued westward expansion.

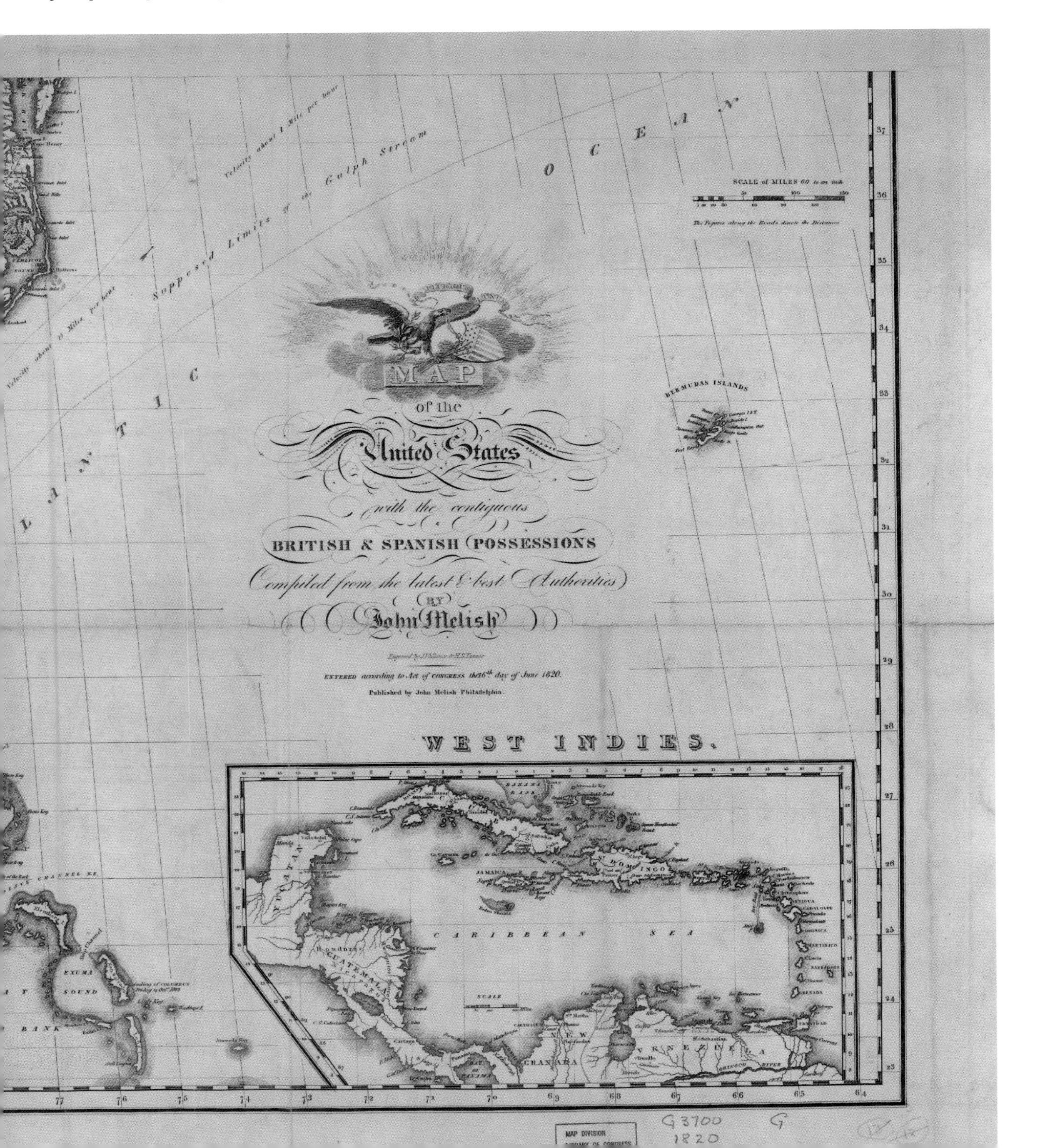

Surveying The National Territory

Before expansion could properly take place, the new nation of the United States of America needed to understand what lay in the blank space to the West—called "unexplored territory" on maps published in the late 19th century. The answer was to conduct surveys and make maps.

From 1800 to 1838, much of the mapping of the national territory was undertaken by the military on an informal, ad hoc basis, concerned in the main with basic exploration and national land claims. The resulting maps were essentially claims to territory. Federal mapping was a spasmodic affair. Survey teams were sent out on an irregular basis with differing aims, methods, and agendas. The most famous is the Lewis and Clark expedition.

In 1838 the Army Corps of Topographical Engineers was established by Congress and charged with the exploration and development of the continent and the construction of a scientific inventory of the land, with particular attention to the problems of transportation. For the remainder of the 19th century, the mapping of the West remained intimately connected with military control, investment opportunities, and transport improvements. John Charles Fremont led three major surveys in 1842, 1843, and 1845 to the Rocky Mountains, Oregon, and California. The United States and Mexico Boundary Survey was undertaken between 1848 and 1853, and utilized the skills of geologists, botanists, surveyors, and naturalists.

THE LEWIS AND CLARK EXPEDITION

The Lewis and Clark expedition of 1804–6 inaugurated the exploration of the American West. Promoted by Thomas Jefferson, Lewis and Clark were to explore up the Missouri River, across the Rocky Mountains, and on to the Pacific Ocean. The goal was to find out more about the area, establish a route to the Pacific and strengthen the US claim to the territory. They set out on May 14, 1804, eventually reaching the Pacific coast in November, 1805. It was a momentous journey that resulted in a far more accurate overview of the Rocky Mountains and the American West as a whole.

In March 1853, Congress authorized a government survey of all principal rail routes. The Corps of Topographical Engineers was instructed to find the most sensible railroad route from the Mississippi to the Pacific. The survey came under the control of the Secretary of War, Jefferson Davis, who sent out four main parties: a northern survey concentrating on the 47th and 49th parallels; a survey of the 38th parallel; and two surveys along the 35th parallel—one from the west and one from the east. The result was a widening of botanical, zoological, and geological knowledge, and the creation of a detailed topography of the West.

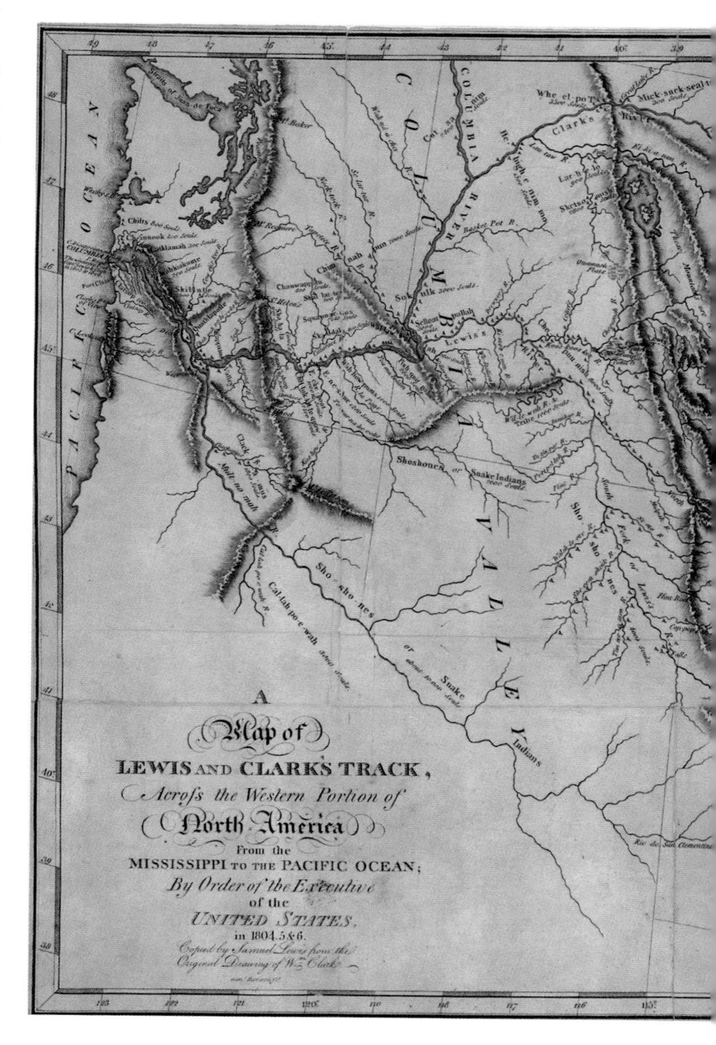

RIGHT ***From Lewis and Clark's notebooks***
The notebooks of Lewis and Clark are full of detailed descriptions as well as maps and diagrams. Many of them drew upon information gleaned from local Native Americans. The sketch shows the three forks of the Missouri, close to present-day Three Forks, Gallatin County, Montana.

BELOW ***The Lewis and Clark Expedition, 1804–06***
The discoveries of Lewis and Clark were the basis of a more accurate small-scale map of the western mountain region. This 1810 map both records and celebrates the Lewis and Clark expedition. It shows the whole route from St. Louis to the mouth of the Columbia River.

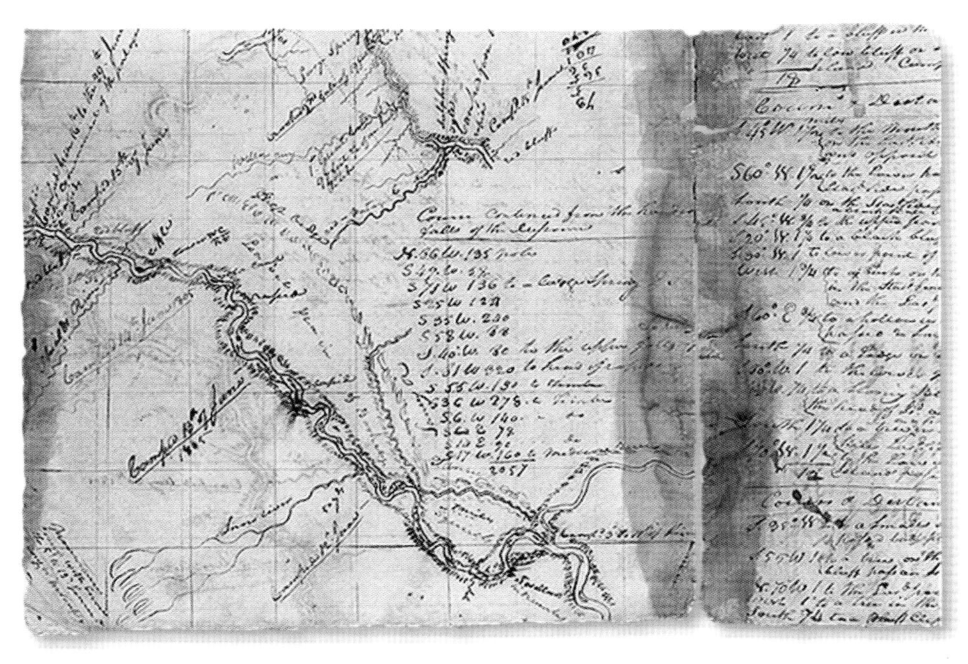

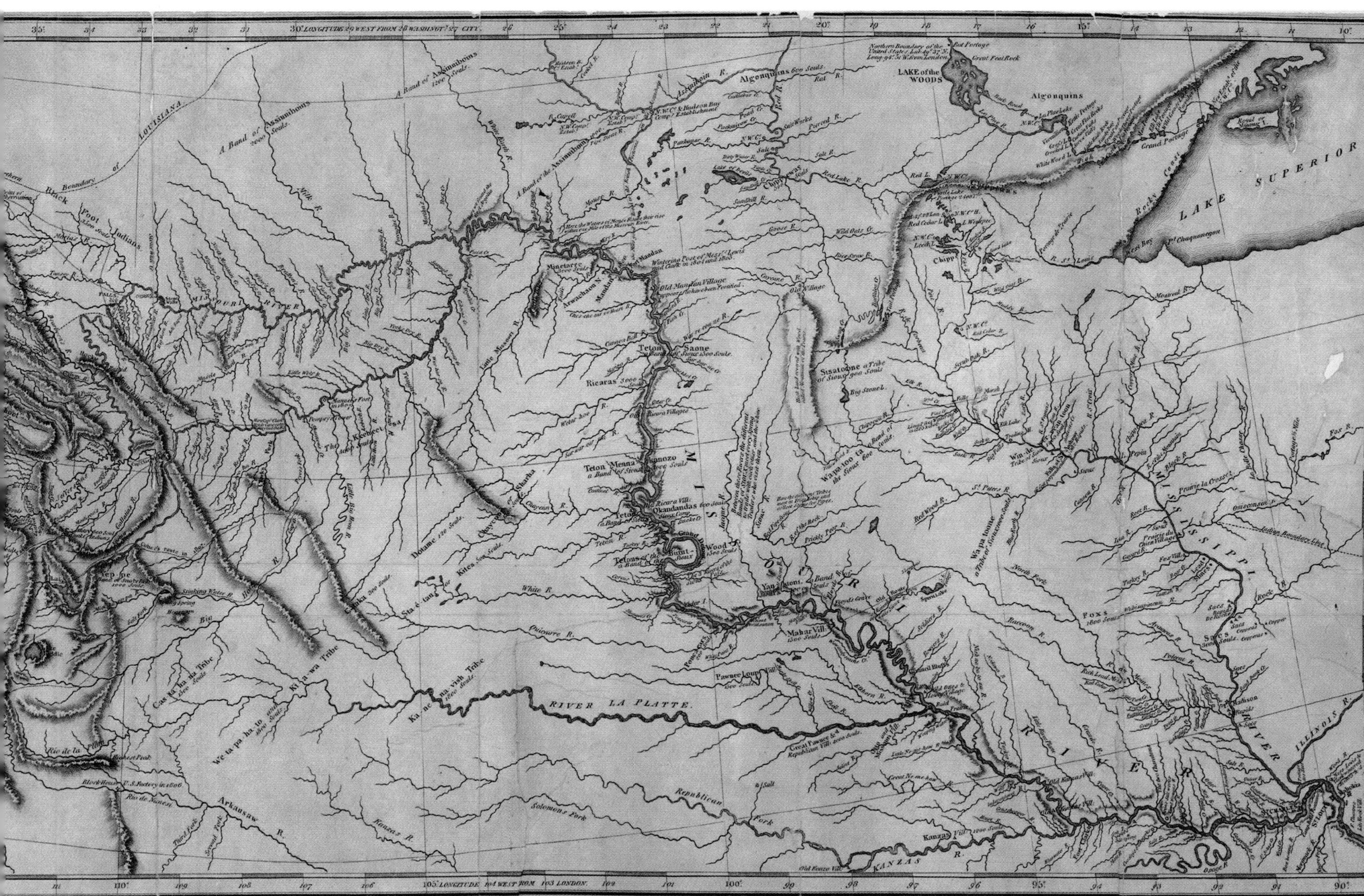

The Great Surveys

The mapping of the new continent was interrupted by the Civil War (1861–65). After the war, the federal government undertook further surveys of the West that were to set new standards of mapping and result in the formation of the United States Geological Survey. Four large surveys were funded by Congress and are commonly named after their principal leaders (King, Wheeler, Hayden, and Powell). The journalistic reporting and artistic illustration of these great surveys were reproduced in the expanding magazine and book trade, and greatly influenced Americans' perception of the West.

Clarence King (1842–1901) led his survey along the 40th parallel between 1863 and 1873, covering a large area and focusing primarily on the geological structure of the land. The Wheeler Survey, led by Lieutenant George Wheeler (1842–1905), covered a huge area over the period 1863–73, including California, Colorado, Montana, Idaho, Nebraska, Nevada, New Mexico, Utah, and Wyoming. Wheeler produced the first contour maps of the region and also produced 27 land classification maps that showed the different types of land use.

Ferdinand Hayden (1829–87) also led his expedition into Colorado (1873–76). He was a geologist whose scientific surveys provided valuable data on the geology, botany, and zoology of the West. Hayden felt that his primary responsibility was to publicize and promote the West. His reports and maps helped to bring the grandeur of the Rocky Mountains and the Yellowstone region to wider public attention.

John Wesley Powell (1834–1902) undertook two surveys, beginning in 1869 when he traveled down the Colorado River. In 1871 Powell set out again, with federal backing, north of the Grand Canyon. In 1878, he published his report on *The Arid Regions of The United States*. Thus, by the end of the 1870s, the West had been comprehensively explored, mapped, described, and classified.

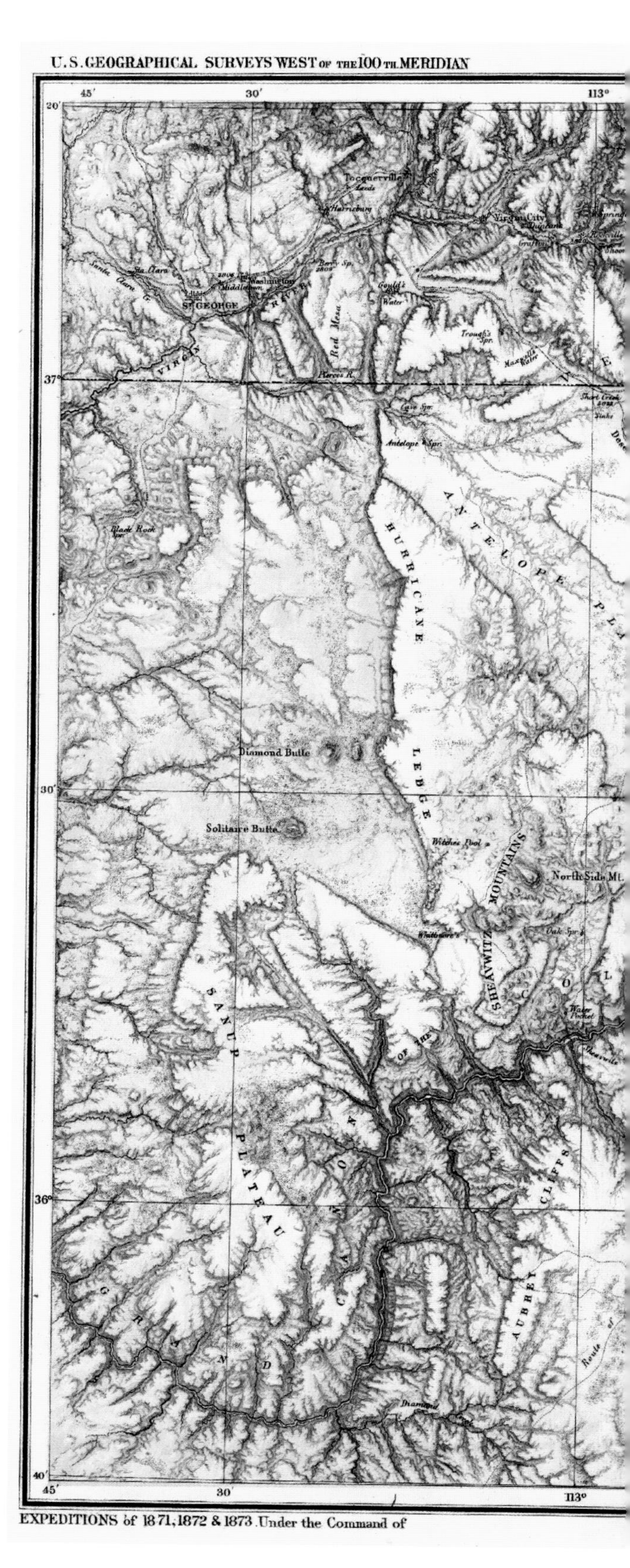

RIGHT *Map from the Wheeler Survey, 1871*

The Wheeler Survey covered a huge area, including parts of California, Colorado, Montana, Idaho, Nebraska, Nevada, New Mexico, Utah, and Wyoming, over the period 1863–73. The survey produced the first contour maps of the region, 27 land classification maps, and detailed topographic maps such as the one shown here.

PARTS OF NORTHERN & NORTH WESTERN ARIZONA & SOUTHERN UTAH, ATLAS SHEET No 67.
30′
112°
30′
111°
37°
36°
Kanab
Paria
Nipple Pk.
16 Mile Spring
NINE MILE VALLEY
HOUSE ROCK VALLEY
House Rock Spr.
PARIA PLATEAU
Jacobs Pool
BUCKSKIN OR KAIBAB PLATEAU
KANAB CAÑON
Tenney's Gulch
POWELL'S PLATEAU
Mesa Butte
WHITE MESA
PAINTED DESERT
COLORADO CHIQUITO
RED BUTTE
BREAKS
El Vado de los Padres
Soap Spr.
Water
Weyss, Herman & Lang, Del.
Scale 1 inch to 8 miles or 1 : 506880
1st. Lieut. Geo. M. Wheeler, Corps of Engineers, U.S. Army.

Mapping National Communities

During the last decades of the 19th century, the great mapping of the West was accompanied by the production of city, county, and state atlases. Technological improvements in printing, such as mechanized printing and cheaper paper, made such atlases more economical to produce, and hence more widely available to the general public. Atlases of individual cities were produced by commercial companies, which raised money from subscriptions, and then undertook field surveys and analyses of tax records and property lists to produce an atlas of the city that listed all the main buildings as well as the individual property owners.

A basic unit of local government in the United States was, and still is, the county. Prior to 1847, county maps were generally produced as wall maps, to a standard scale of 1 inch to 1 mile (2.5 cm to 1.5 km). While impressive for public display, such maps were hardly practical. The demand for something less expensive and more portable

THE UNITED STATES GEOLOGICAL SURVEY

The United States Geological Survey was created by an Act of Congress in 1879. Its initial brief was to map public lands, paying particular attention to land classification, geological structure, and mineral resources. The first director was Clarence King (see page 160) and under his leadership the Survey concentrated on the mineral resources of the land. The second director, John Wesley Powell (see also page 160), shifted the emphasis to mapping the entire country.

The Geological Survey is now the foremost national mapping agency in the United States, producing a range of maps of different scales for different uses. To date, the Survey has made some 55,000 maps and taken almost 250,000 aerial photographs. In 1997 the organization began work on updating the national atlas of the United States.

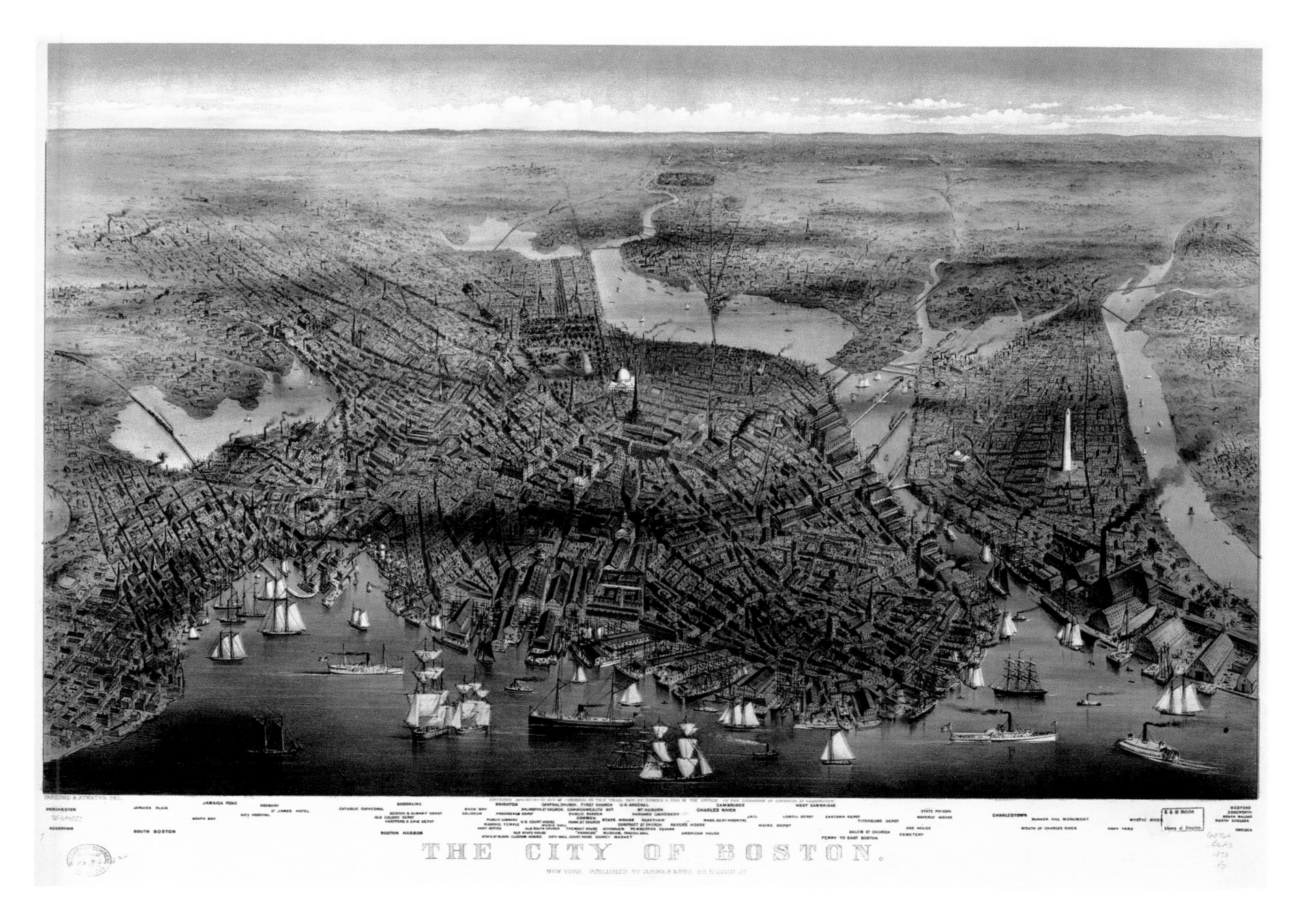

ABOVE **The City of Boston,** *1887*
Boston has always been one of the larger cities in the United States with important trading links to the Caribbean and Europe. It was also the center of intellectual activity with such famous schools as Harvard and MIT.

LEFT **Bird's Eye View of Phoenix Arizona,** *1885*
Compared to the dynamic metropolis of Boston, Phoenix at the time of this map has yet to develop into the laid out grid square. The extensive growth of Phoenix would have to wait for the second half of the 20th century.

led to the development of county atlases; their "golden age" occurred between 1850 and 1880, when they reached their peak of detail and elaborate design. Over 5,000 different county atlases were produced, and their coverage was particularly strong in the northeast and Midwest. Because they showed not only the land and the buildings, but also the landowners, these books served to bind together and represent whole communities. To own one, and be named in it, increased a person's sense of belonging.

The average cost of producing a county atlas was between $10,000 and $15,000. The main expense lay in the printing and marketing. Despite this, it was a lucrative business—on average 1,000 copies of each county atlas were sold, resulting in receipts of around $25,000. While not all landowners bought a copy, some, and especially those with full-page spreads, bought more than one to distribute to friends and clients. A clear profit of at least $10,000 was not unusual. One publisher, Alfred Andreas, made an impressive profit of $17,000 on his *Atlas of Peoria County,* published in 1878.

State atlases were also made. Prior to the Civil War you could purchase atlases for South Carolina, New York, and Maine. After the war, from 1866 to 1890, more than 20 state atlases were produced. Many of these included some of the earliest and best thematic maps. For example, the *State of Illinois Atlas* included maps of presidential elections, geology, climate, and railroads. The *Atlas of Massachusetts* had thematic maps and discussions of topography, history, railways, geology, climatology, the census, and even school districts.

Francis Walker's Statistical Atlas

National atlases do not just cartographically represent nations, they legitimize and justify nations. To map a nation is to give it justification and legitimacy. And what national atlases portray also reveals much about power within the national society.

One important early national atlas that tells us much about the changing depiction of a nation was published in the 1870s. In the early censuses in the United States, there were few maps. In fact not a single map was used until the 1850 census, which had a crude map of drainage basins. The 1860 census used only six maps. In the first volume of the *Report of the 1870 Census*, however, 12 demographic maps were presented. These maps and the 1874 *Statistical Atlas of the United States* were the brainchild of Francis Walker (1840–97). He was a "social commentator"; nowadays we would call him a social scientist, with an interest in statistics and maps.

The statistical analysis of social data was a recurring theme in all Walker's work, and the *Statistical Atlas* of 1874 is one of the earliest attempts to present census data in map form. It contains 44 maps and 16 illustrations, accompanied by social data on health, immigration, religion, ethnicity, economic trends, and population distribution and density. The maps and diagrams are discussed in detail by Walker in his introduction, where he provides a section on how to read them, drawing attention to understanding the intensity of shading, the distinction between absolute and relative proportions, and the need to see the diagrams together to make the right links.

Walker was writing at a time when social science, social control, and social surveillance were all emerging as important new discourses of a nation experiencing rapid urbanization and large-scale immigration. The sense of searching for the locations and causes of social disorder, very broadly defined, lies at the very heart of Walker's statistical rendering of the nation. Although called a national atlas, many of the social data maps show only the country east of the 99th meridian. This is the ultimate in East Coast bias. There is a section containing Pacific maps that shows the western littoral but contains only ten maps, all on one page, which show population, including ethnic maps of the Chinese population. Obviously this is an insignificant area for Walker, and he makes no mention of this bias in his introduction.

Even from a distance of well over one hundred years, the atlas is an incredibly sophisticated display of social statistics. This census was the first to introduce the practice of identifying the center of population. Walker identified the center and it has been depicted in subsequent censuses, with its steady westward progression reflecting westward expansionism and settlement.

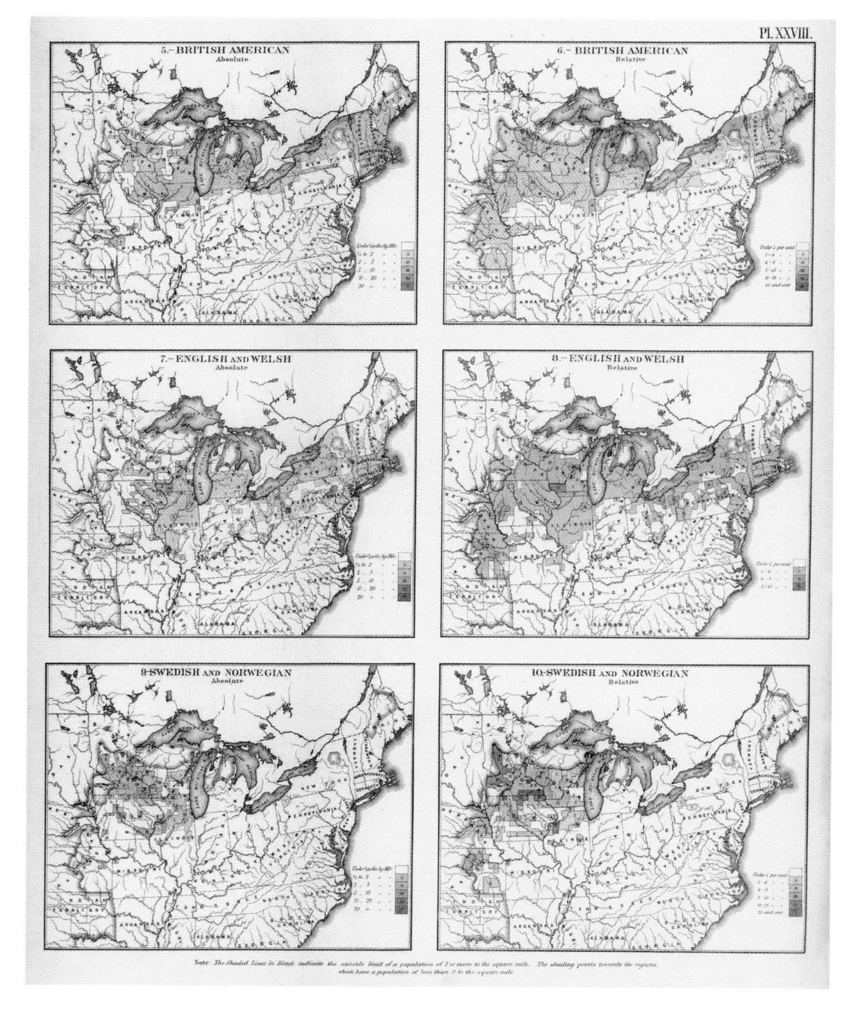

RIGHT *Table from Francis Walker's* Statistical Atlas,*1874*
Walker used a variety of statistical diagrams to display social data. He was particularly interested in social statistics that reflected deviance, delinquency, and social difference. Here is a table that records school attendance.

OPPOSITE *Maps from Francis Walker's* Statistical Atlas,*1874*
Mapping the degree and location of different racial and ethnic groups has been an important feature of the US Census. Using data from the 1870 census, Francis Walker mapped the distribution of different nationalities. Notice the concentration of Scandinavians in the upper Midwest.

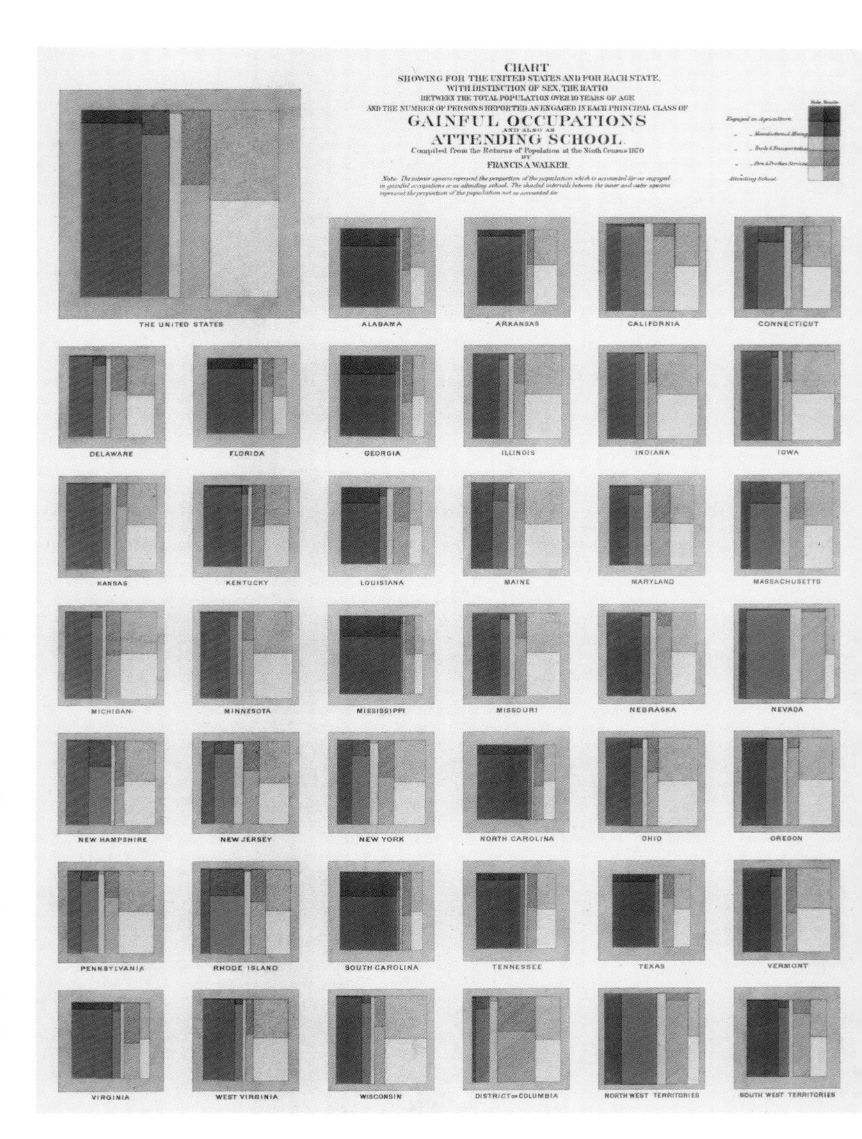

The *Statistical Atlas* is an excellent example of the cartographic presentation of national social statistics. Throughout the nineteenth century there had been a growing use of national thematic maps. Before the development of sophisticated statistical techniques such as multivariate and regression analysis, maps and graphical displays provided a useful and revealing way of presenting data and possible causal connections. The map became a statistical method and a device often employed in the analysis of crime and disease. Contributions to the atlas came from many departments of the federal government and a dozen or so of the day's prominent "men of science," including geologists, geographers, and botanists.

Mapping the nation was not just an inventory but one way to search for connections and identify sources of disorder, especially crime and disease. As superintendent of the 1870 Census, Walker added tables on school attendance, illiteracy, pauperism, and crime, and among the social categories he included were the blind, deaf, dumb, insane, and idiotic. The 1874 *Atlas* also has a section entitled "The Relations of Race and Nationality to Mortality," written by Walker, where he draws attention to "the deficiency of foreign children." Deaths from various causes are disaggregated by age and gender. He also has a map on the "afflicted classes"—the blind, deaf mutes, the insane—all disaggregated by age, gender, race and nationality. By identifying the dependent, the delinquent, and the disabled, Walker is identifying sources of difference, sites of potential disorder.

Francis Walker's *Atlas* was one of the earliest national atlases and prompted the compilation of other atlases based on census data. Walker's legacy continued into the 20th century. After Walker the US census would use maps and diagrams in its tables on a regular basis, and the centerof population would become a standard measure.

GERRYMANDERING

The term "gerrymandering" refers to the manipulation of constituency or state boundaries so as to give undue influence to a party or class. It derives from the efforts of Governor Elbridge Gerry of Massachusetts in the United States. In 1812 he enacted a law that consolidated all the Federalist Party supporters into just a few districts, while the supporters of Gerry's party, the Democratic-Republicans, were spread out over many districts. In this way, he ensured an election victory for the Democratic-Republicans. The resulting maps of the electoral districts were said to resemble the shape of a salamander—hence the term "gerrymander."

16

CARTOGRAPHIC ENCOUNTERS

Maps of Southeast Asia

There are two forms of colonial cartographic encounter: the depiction of indigenous peoples and how indigenous peoples helped in the making of the maps of the imperial-colonial powers. The first refers to how local people were represented; the second to their role in cartographic representation. This chapter looks at indigenous mapping before the arrival of the colonizers, and how cartography changed as a result of the coming together of two cultures.

THERE ARE FEW SURVIVING old maps from Southeast Asia, and none exist at all that were produced before the 16th century. However, if we extend our definition of maps a longer perspective is possible.

Many of the temples and palaces constructed in the region were built as cosmological maps of the universe. Like all centralized agricultural societies around the world, the cities were sites of administrative, political, and religious significance.

The city of Angkhor in northwest Kampuchea was constructed between the 9th and 15th century. The city was orientated around a central temple, the great Hindu temple of Angkhor Wat, which was built in the 12th century. The central temple in all such cities signified Mount Meru, regarded as the *axis mundi* (the center of the world) of Hindu cosmology. The temple not only housed religious events but was itself a "document" of religious significance. It was a map of the world, or at least a map symbol.

While cosmological maps abound in Southeast Asia there are also examples of more mundane maps. The Shan map, currently housed in the library of the University of Cambridge in the UK, depicts a rural area along the disputed Chinese–Burmese border. The map was created by local people, following an order from the British superintendent for the area, H. Dalby, in 1859. It is orientated with south at the top. The area in yellow is China, while the large red and small black areas are Burmese states under the control of the British. The map shows both plan and bird's-eye features. The river is shown in plan form

while the mountains are shown in an oblique perspective, which is more effective at depicting relief. The bright colors demarcate the different political areas very sharply. The green circular symbols are probably villages.

The Shan map is a particularly interesting example of how political boundaries are affected by geomorphological changes. The river is the slow-moving and meandering Nam Mao, which has changed its course over the years. This should have been the obvious political boundary, but its shifting nature is revealed by the political boundaries that are shown on the map, which reflect the course of the river as it would have been many years before. The map is also interesting because it is an example of a very common type of cartographic encounter; British colonial officials commissioned the map from local people for their own broader geopolitical purposes. The local and the imperial are connected in a shared cartographic project: local knowledge is being used by an imperial power for the advancement of its own ends.

Batik is a technique developed in Southeast Asia that involves the dyeing of cloth. The patterns are formed by covering part of the cloth in wax so that they will not receive the color. The wax is boiled off and reapplied in a different pattern. Another color is then applied. In this way, skilled craftspeople can create multicolored, richly patterned designs. Maps come in many forms, so it is no surprise to discover batik maps from this region of the world. The layering technique is perfectly apt for mapmaking: maps are, after all, a series of layers and a sequence of decisions about what to leave in and what to take out.

Maps of Southeast Asia come in a variety of forms. They range over the centuries and show a wide range of influences. Hindu, Buddhist, and Muslim iconographies appear in maps of this region. From the 16th century the European influence is evident in the adoption of certain Western cartographic conventions. The maps of Southeast Asia, like the culture in which they were embedded, range widely in style and conception.

LEFT ***Angkhor Wat Hindu temple***
The city and its buildings not only housed people and events, they were a map of the cosmos. The city was planned as a symbolic universe centered on the pyramid temple. The city is a map of the universe that provides a link between the sacred and the mundane, the universal and the particular.

FOLLOWING PAGE ***The Shan map of the Chinese-Burmese border, 1859***
A map produced at the behest of the colonial power by the local people; who benefits from such information? The answer is not always obvious. The 19th century saw bloody conflict in the area, with the Shan people fighting the Burmese, and the Burmese fighting the British. Local Burmese warlords, or dacoits, periodically launched ferocious campaigns of violence against the Shan. Perhaps this map was not produced grudgingly, but in the hope of protection from attack.

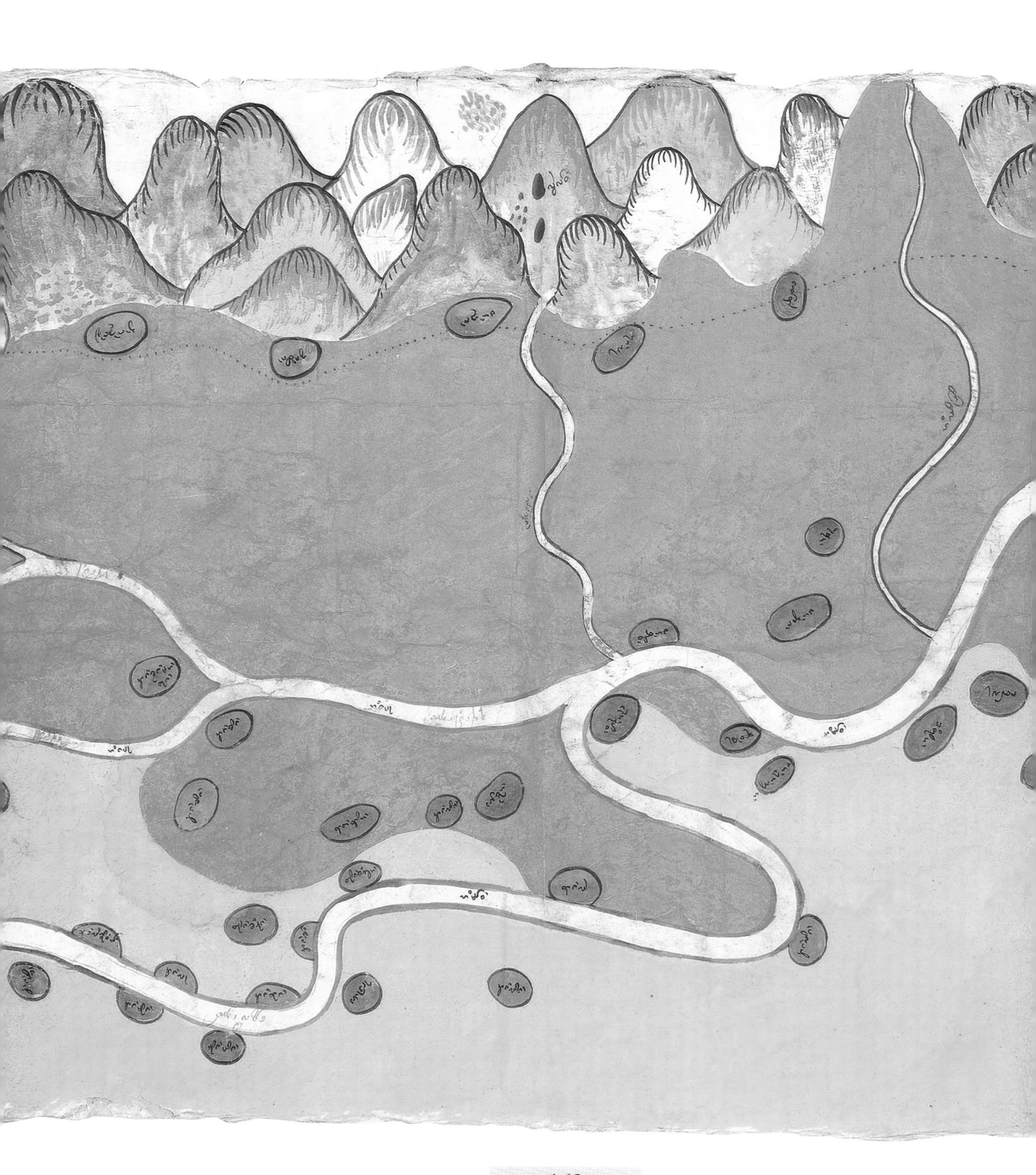

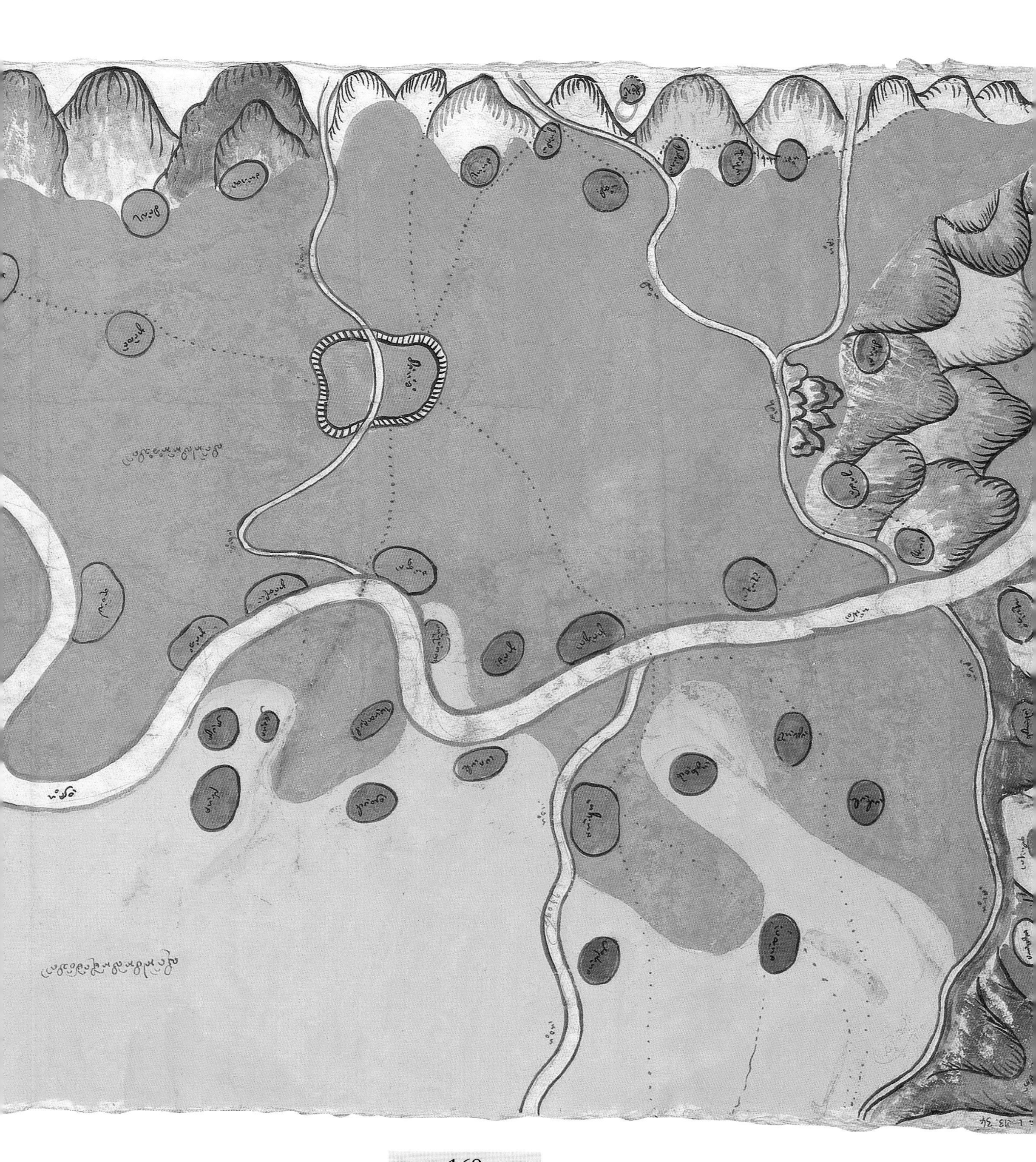

Maps of Central Asia

Many early Tibetan maps are cosmographies—models of the universe. They were designed as points of meditation and contemplation rather than as mirrors of exact geographic reality. As a traditional theocratic society, where religious influence and political power went hand in hand, mapping the spiritual realm was as important as mapping the terrestrial plane. Maps were bound by a convention of representation: red represented sacred places while white was used to show profane places. Many Tibetan maps took the form of a mandala, a symbolic diagram of the universe. A typical pattern would consist of a square surrounded by concentric circles. Inside the square, more concentric circles contain images of divinities. The outer circles represent initiation, illumination, cognition, and spiritual rebirth.

There are also examples of more pragmatic mappings. For example, the Tibetan government commissioned maps of the border regions with India. There were also routeway maps, many of which were pictorial rather than plan-view in design. Maps for pilgrims making journeys of religious devotion combined both religious and pragmatic concerns. Itinerary maps, with pictures of the towns and villages, enabled pilgrims to follow the necessary routes.

Tibetan maps were influenced by Chinese cartography and later by European cartographic conventions. A collection of maps now held in the British Library—the Wise Collection—shows both local and European mapping conventions. Made in the 19th century, between 1844 and 1862, these maps were drawn with black ink and watercolor on European paper. As Central Asia was an important geopolitical area for competing imperial powers, the maps were probably commissioned by a British officer for military intelligence, but made by an indigenous mapmaker.

Mongolia was a more secular society than Tibet. The remaining evidence indicates a mapping tradition more concerned with the terrestrial realm than the spiritual. No Mongolian maps exist from before the 18th century. Most of the remainder date from the mid-19th century and consist of large-scale manuscript maps depicting tribal regions and pasture areas. Richly annotated, they are now believed to have been commissioned by imperial China to restrict the movement of nomadic pastoralists and to prevent border disputes between different peoples. The tight demarcation of the maps does indeed indicate restriction.

BELOW *Map of the Tsa-Ri region, c. 1900*
This cotton scroll map shows a mountainous area between the India–Tibet border region along the upper Subansiri River. It is a picture map that shows the river, topography, and buildings from a bird's-eye perspective. Monasteries, forts, and villages are represented along the valley. Picture maps such as this were a common feature of Tibetan cartography. The precise dating of the map has proved difficult, but it is likely to have been made sometime in the late 19th or early 20th centuries.

Indigenous Maps of Sub-Saharan Africa

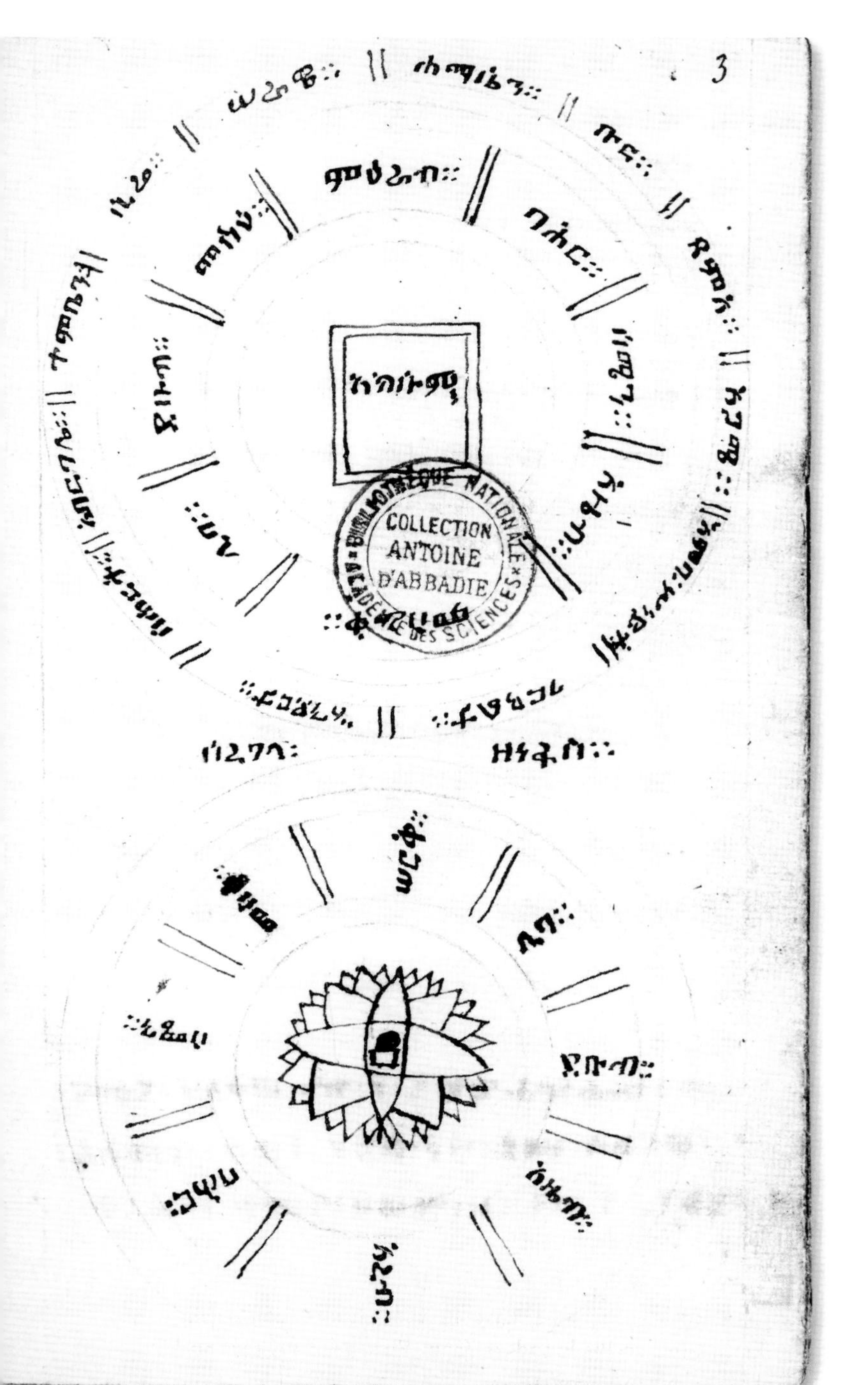

A rich multitude of mapping styles can be found in sub-Saharan Africa, and a good example is the "circle maps" of Tigray, Ethiopia. Centered on the ancient kingdom of Aksum, which flourished over 1,500 years ago, the maps show the region as a series of concentric circles divided into different sections. The pattern is reminiscent of Muslim cosmological maps. These maps connect real places with primary mathematical divisions. Adding to their complexity are their multiple orientations: some circles are orientated toward the north, others toward the west.

Mapmaking was often an important part of initiation ceremonies in Africa. During the initiation of the Luba people, who live in a region of what is now the Democratic Republic of Congo, elders drew white-lined maps on the black walls of the meeting house showing the whole region: river systems, chiefdoms, and ancient migration paths. These *lukala* maps were traditionally very abstract, but contemporary designs since the 1980s show a more figurative style.

In the early years of the European colonization of the continent, many maps were produced by indigenous peoples for European explorers, travelers, and colonial administrators. Only a few such maps survive. For example, in 1824, the English explorer Hugh Clapperton (1797–1837) wanted to plot the course of the Niger River. The Sultan of Sokoto in West Africa, Mohammed Bello, gave Clapperton a map of the country that later appeared in the explorer's account of his travels, published in 1826. Centered on the

LEFT ***Tigrean circle map, 1859***
The city of Aksum is in the rectangular area in the center of the top circle, surrounded by a circle showing eight directions, and an outer circle depicting the 14 provinces of the region. The bottom figure is a wind rose. It is ironic that this facsimile bears the stamp of a colonial power!

RIGHT ***Plan of King Njoya's Kingdom, Cameroon, 1912***
The king decided to make a map of his kingdom in 1912. Twenty topographers checked the work of 60 surveyors who visited every village in the country. The survey stopped only during the rainy season. The walled city of Fumban is at the center of the map.

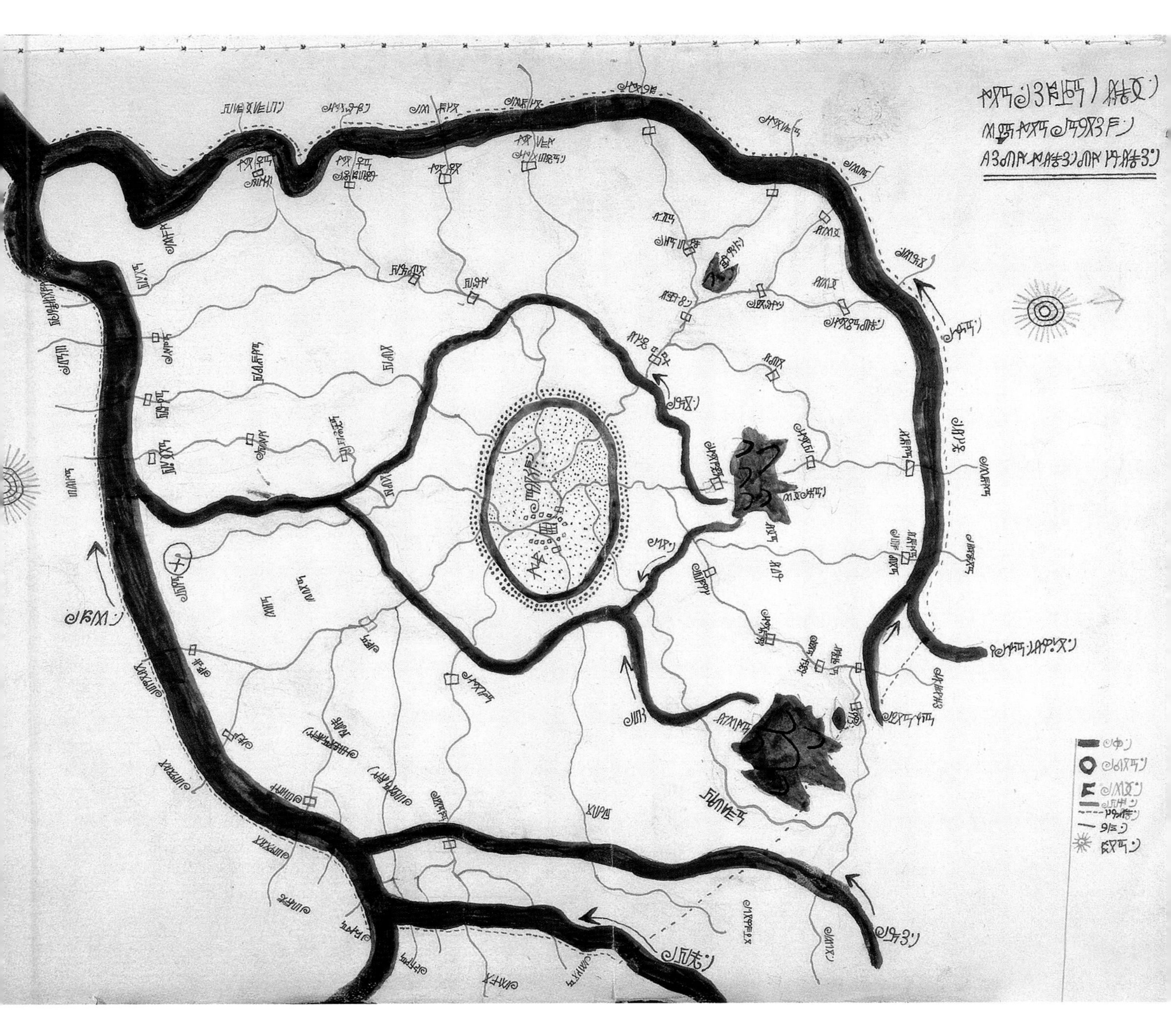

sultan's base in Sokoto, the map shows the Niger River flowing from west to east, rather than north to south, into the Atlantic. It turns out that the wily sultan was withholding information from Clapperton on the correct assumption that the more Europeans knew about the local geography, the more this knowledge would enable them to take power over the region.

In 1912, King Njoya (*c.* 1875–1933) undertook an ambitious survey of his kingdom of Bamum, in Cameroon, employing some 60 surveyors. The resultant map exaggerated the size of the capital, Fumban, and extended the territory of the kingdom into a pleasing square shape. Presented to the British in 1916, the map centers on the royal capital. The rising sun is shown on the left of the map and the setting sun on the right, with the result that south is at the top of the page. The map of King Nyoja's kingdom is both a survey and a claim to sovereignty—at that time, King Njoya was seeking to present a case in the face of competing imperial claims to his kingdom from European powers and members of his own court.

Ottoman Cartography

The early Ottoman Empire (*c.* 1400–1800) produced a variety of different types of map. Unfortunately, few survive from before the 16th century.

As custodians of a large, sprawling, and expanding empire, the Ottomans were involved in armed conflict with a variety of foes, and their maps were vital strategic weapons. Military maps were of particular importance, especially as the Ottoman Empire extended its reach into western and eastern Europe. Plans of cities besieged by the Ottomans include Belgrade, Kiev, and Vienna. There are also battle plan maps from the Battle of Prut in 1711 and maps showing Russian Army maneuvers along the empire's eastern European edge in 1768–69.

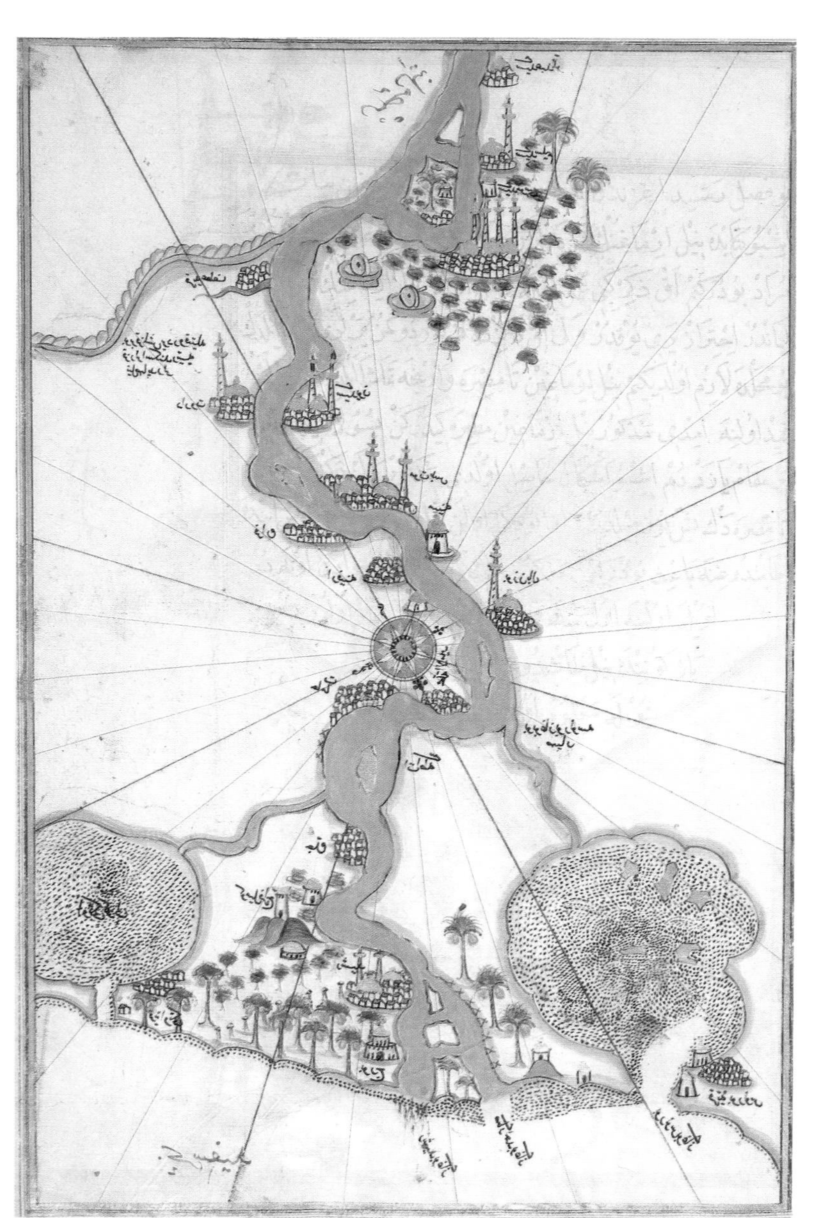

Cartography was also a scholarly enterprise for the Ottomans. From the mid-15th to the mid-17th centuries, scholars translated the standard geographical works from Arabic and Persian into Ottoman Turkish. They then turned their attention to translating and adapting European works.

Ottoman world maps are similar to Arabic maps in their circular composition and geometric structure. Among the very few examples of regional maps to survive, the Vatican Library in Rome, Italy, has an unusual map of the Nile River drawn on cloth, perhaps created by the Ottoman mapmaker Evliya Celebi (d. 1684).

An important Ottoman contribution to cartography comes from the illustrated histories that were designed to record the power and achievement of the Ottomans. First initiated by Sultan Mehmed II after the conquest of Constantinople in 1453, they were first illustrated around 1537. Painters specializing in miniatures were brought from Persia and the town views then developing in Europe were also sources of inspiration. With their eclectic mix of eastern and western art and culture, these illustrations reached their innovative peak under Sultans Murad III (1574–95) and Mehmed III (1595–1603).

Topographic illustrations figure largely in these pictorial histories in the form of itineraries and town views. An illustrated account of Suleyman the Magnificent's military campaign in Persia and Iraq from 1533 to 1555, for example, was the subject of an illustrated history completed in 1564 that depicted the towns traveled to in the campaign. An illustration of Istanbul is represented in a bird's-eye view, with great attention to detail. While drawing upon European

LEFT ***Chart of the Nile, c. 1521, by Piri Re'is***
This map is orientated with south at the top. The deltaic river mouth of the Nile is shown at the bottom of the map. It combines a plan view to depict the course of the river with a bird's-eye view to show the major buildings along its banks. In 1516–17 Piri Re'is sailed to Cairo along the Nile during the Ottoman campaign against Egypt.

THE OTTOMAN EMPIRE

The Ottoman Empire was a vast one, extending into Asia, Europe, and Africa. It was established in the 13th century by Osmanli or Ottoman Turks. The Ottoman Empire began as one of several small Turkish states in Asia Minor. The Ottomans gradually absorbed their neighboring states, and in the 14th century they began to expand into territory belonging to the Byzantine Empire, conquering Constantinople in 1453 and adopting it as the Ottoman capital.

The Ottoman Empire reached the height of its power in the 16th century. Selim I (ruled 1512–20) assumed the Caliphate (leadership of the Muslim world) with his victories in Syria, Palestine, Algeria, and Egypt, while his son Suleyman the Magnificent (ruled 1520–66) brought much of the Balkans, Hungary, and Arabia under Ottoman control. Suleyman's navy dominated the Mediterranean, attacking the coasts of Italy, Greece, and Spain.

After Suleyman's death, the Ottoman Empire began to decline. Its institutions failed to modernize and its rulers fell into corrupt and decadent ways. The powerful nation states arising in Europe formed alliances to hound the Ottoman Empire out of the continent. The decline in the organization of the empire led to a series of military defeats. Control of Greece and Egypt was lost in the early 19th century. During that century the Ottoman Empire gradually lost its economic independence, and came to depend entirely on foreign investment and loans.

Most of the remaining European territories were lost in the Balkan Wars of 1908, and the Ottoman Empire finally disintegrated in 1918 following its defeat by the Allied forces in the First World War.

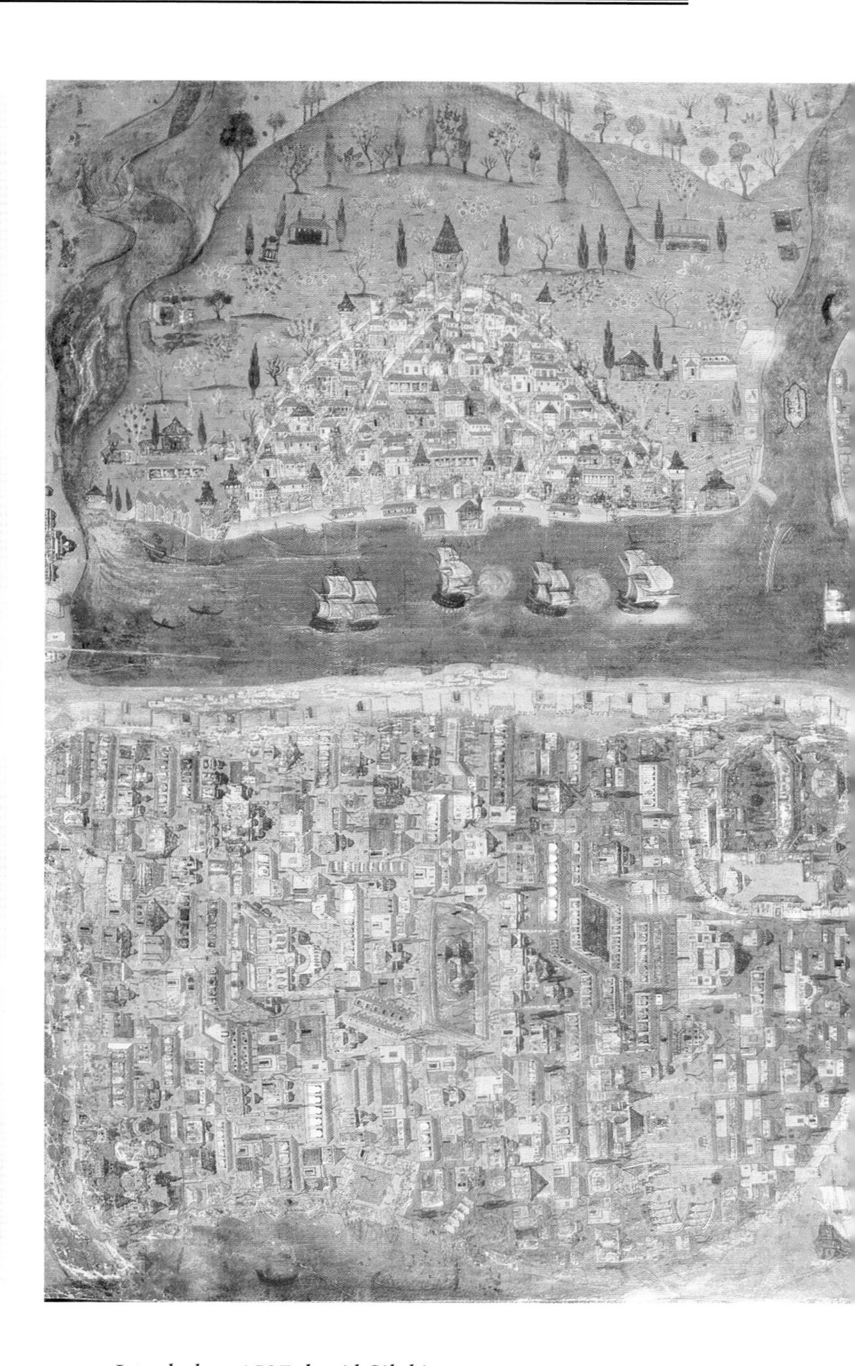

ABOVE ***Istanbul, c. 1537, by Al-Silahi***
This bird's-eye view of Istanbul pinpoints major buildings in the city. The domes of Hagia Sophia are clearly visible in the middle left. Ships are depicted sailing along the Golden Horn toward the Bosphorus strait.

image-making techniques, this illustration highlights the Islamic sites, including the great Hagia Sophia mosque in Istanbul. Other cities shown in this history include Baghdad and Aleppo, and geographical features such as gorges, rivers, and roads are also included.

When the Ottoman Empire expanded into western Europe, illustrated histories recorded the path of its European campaigns. The maps and plans of these illustrated histories combined both the delicacy of Ottoman miniature painting with the artistic perspective of western Europe in delicate, yet accurate depictions of places.

Ottoman cartography was not restricted to the land. The pirate turned admiral Piri Re'is (*c.* 1470–1554) produced the *Kitab-i bahriye* (*Book of Maritime Matters*) around 1521. It contains almost 200 sea charts, and represents the beginning of a maritime cartographic legacy that mapped the Mediterranean and the wider world beyond.

17

UNIVERSAL MAPPING

Ruling the Waves

By the 18th century European scientific explorations, often closely tied to imperial ambitions, were extending their reach across the world. Universal mapping programs sought to map the oceans, record distant continents, and catalogue the urban condition.

BY THE LATTER PART of the 17th century, The Netherlands were in decline and the home of marine mapping had shifted to Britain and France, as had military and mercantile maritime power.

The English instrument maker and navigation teacher John Seller (*c.* 1630–97) began work on a sea atlas which he called *The English Pilot.* It consisted of four volumes covering the coasts north and south of the Zuider Zee, plus Oriental and Western navigations. Volume 1 was published in 1671. *The English Pilot* was reprinted throughout the 18th century, and the maps and charts became increasingly accurate. The 1749 version of Volume 4, published by the British Board of Navigation, for example, included detailed sailing instructions, sea charts, maps of compass variation, and detailed harbor charts stretching from Hudson Bay to the Amazon.

By the end of the 18th century, British maritime dominance had been well established. In 1793, the Hydrographic Office was formed to coordinate the mapping of the oceans, and the Royal Navy commenced an extensive mapping program, which was stimulated by international rivalry, war, and the need to provide accurate information to maintain naval superiority and commercial transactions. For Britain, as the center of a far-flung empire, the charting of the oceans was absolutely vital for the maintenance of power and commerce. By 1914, the Admiralty had produced over 2,000 charts covering most of the world.

The French had their own maritime mapping program. The *French Neptune*, by Romein de Hooge (1645/6–1708) is heavily indebted to the earlier Dutch sea atlases. Produced in 1693 it contained detailed sea charts of the

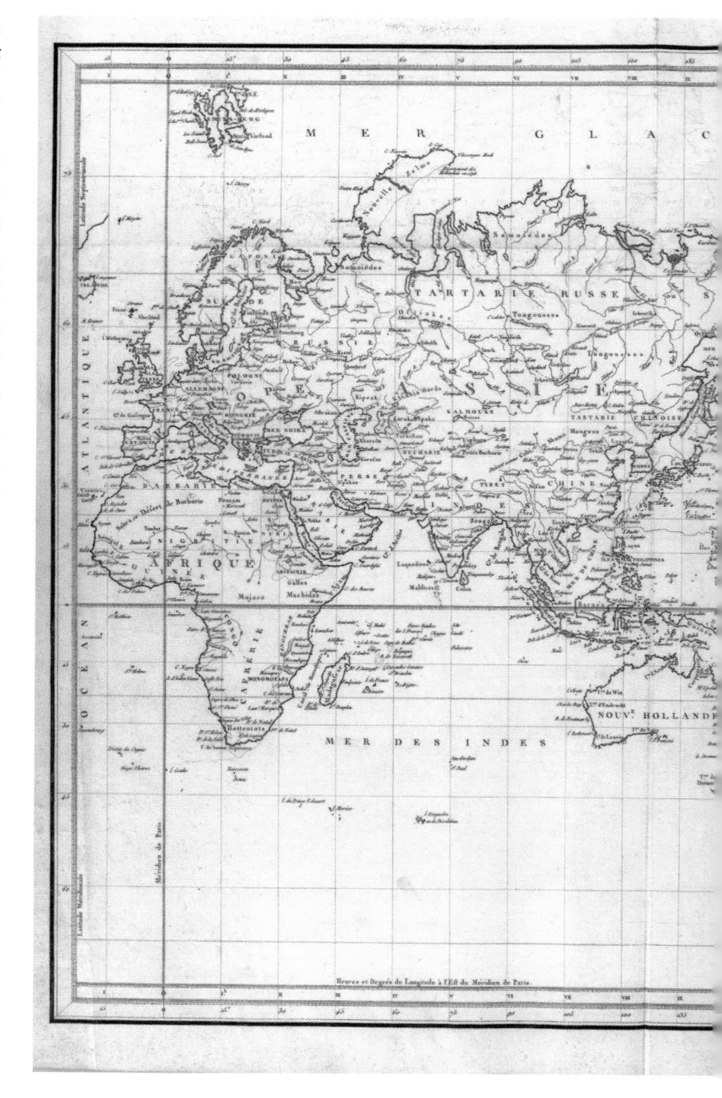

French coastline. Later, French expeditions, such as the 1785–88 voyage around the world of Jean-François de la Perouse (1741–88), generated vital maritime information that was translated into a sea atlas that included a world map with his route marked in red.

RIGHT ***Satellite maps of El Nino, 1995***
The climatic phenomenon of El Nino, when the trade winds slacken or even reverse, was named by early Spanish settlers in South America. The disruption occurs around Christmastime—hence El Nino, the "boy-child." La Perouse missed a major El Nino event by five years; crossing the Pacific would have been very difficult without the trade winds blowing normally, from the southeast to the northwest in the southern hemisphere.

BELOW ***World map, from La Perouse's voyage***
La Perouse's voyage began in 1785. He sailed across the Atlantic around Cape Horn to the Pacific Northwest, Hawaii, China, Japan, Russia, and Australia. He died in the Solomon Islands but his records survived.

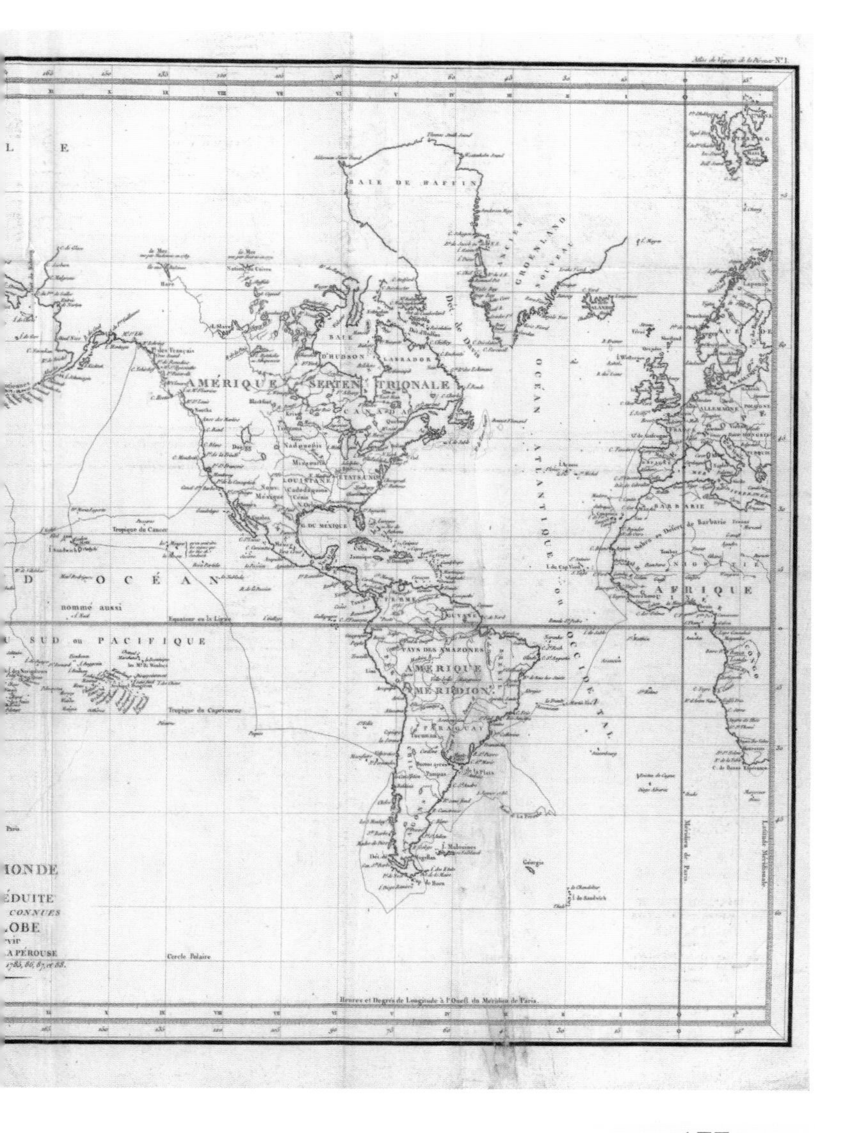

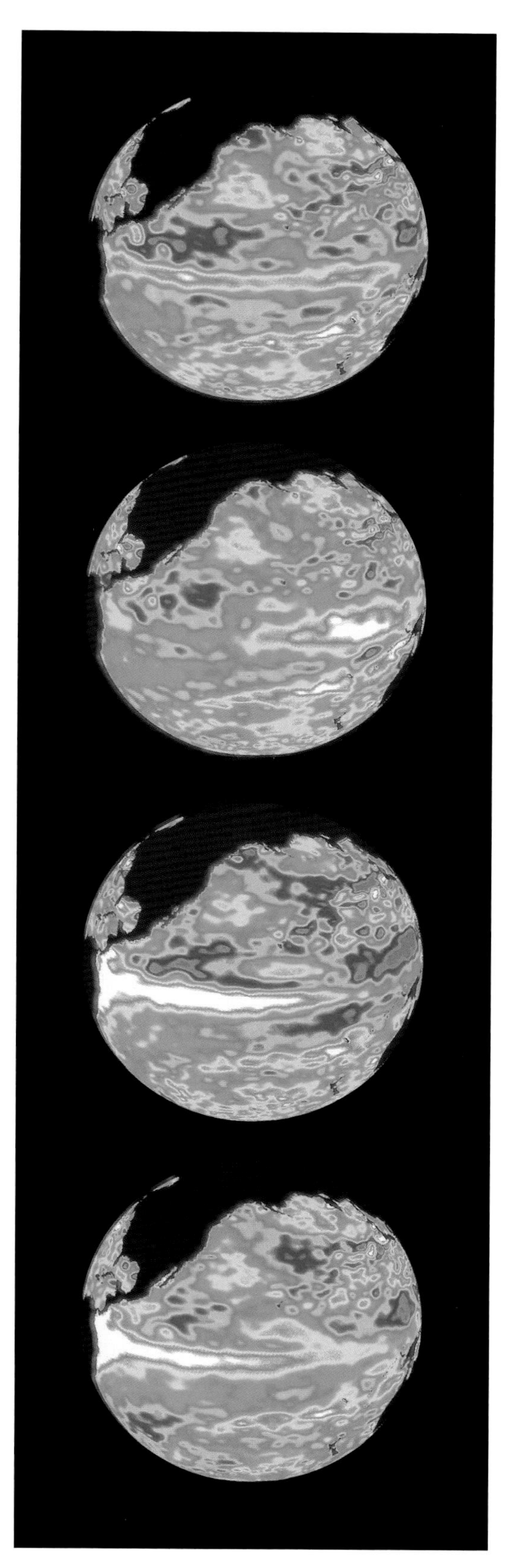

Mapping Antarctica

Until the beginning of the 16th century it was widely believed that there was a great southern continent to match the great mass of land in the northern hemisphere. The world map from the 1482 Ulm edition of Ptolemy's *Guide to Geography*, for example, shows a continuous landmass right across the southern hemisphere. Almost 100 years later, the world map in Ortelius's 1570 atlas showed a huge continent called "Terra Australis." Gradually, as explorers traveled farther south, a more accurate picture began to emerge. The 1714 "polar projection" map made by Guillaume Delisle shows the world following the discoveries of Tasman, but before any clear picture of the polar ice cap had been formulated. The British navigator and mapmaker Captain James Cook (1728–79) completed the first circumnavigation of Antarctica between 1772–75, sailing in the *Resolution*. On this voyage he also charted Easter Island and discovered New Caledonia, the South Sandwich Islands, and South Georgia Island.

Cook was a meticulous navigator and mapmaker. He discovered Australia for the British and almost single-handedly rewrote the geography of the Pacific.

The 19th and early 20th centuries saw the beginnings of the exploration of the interior of the polar landmass. American, French, and British expeditions were dispatched to find the South Pole. Charles Wilkes discovered Wilkes Land in 1840, Dumont d'Urville discovered Terre Adelie, and from 1839–43 James Ross named the Ross ice shelf Ross Island, and the Admiralty Mountain Range. In 1893 John Murray produced a map of Antarctica for the Royal Geographical Society in London that stimulated new interest in surveys and led to intensive mapping of that region. The 20 years between 1894 and 1914 saw a large number of Antarctic expeditions create more accurate maps of the great ice continent.

CAPTAIN JAMES COOK

James Cook (1728–79) was an explorer, navigator, and mapmaker who discovered much of the Pacific for Britain. From humble origins he joined the navy in 1755 and was soon mapping the coasts of eastern Canada. He was no mere functionary; he wrote a paper for the Royal Society on a solar eclipse he had witnessed and was chosen by that organization to command an expedition to Tahiti to study the transit of Venus across the sun. After witnessing the transit he sailed the *Endeavour* on to New Zealand and then to Australia, where he landed at Botany Bay, just south of present-day Sydney. The *Endeavour* returned to England in 1771. Cook captained another expedition that left the following year and reached the Antarctic Circle before sailing to Tahiti, Tonga, and the Easter Islands, finally returning home to England in 1775, when he was awarded a gold medal by the Royal Society. In 1776 he led an expedition to find the Northwest Passage, the fabled route from the North Atlantic through to Asia. He sailed east around the Cape of Good Hope, discovering the Hawaiian Islands in 1778 on his way to Alaska. Unable to find the Passage, he returned to Hawaii, where he was clubbed to death by hostile islanders.

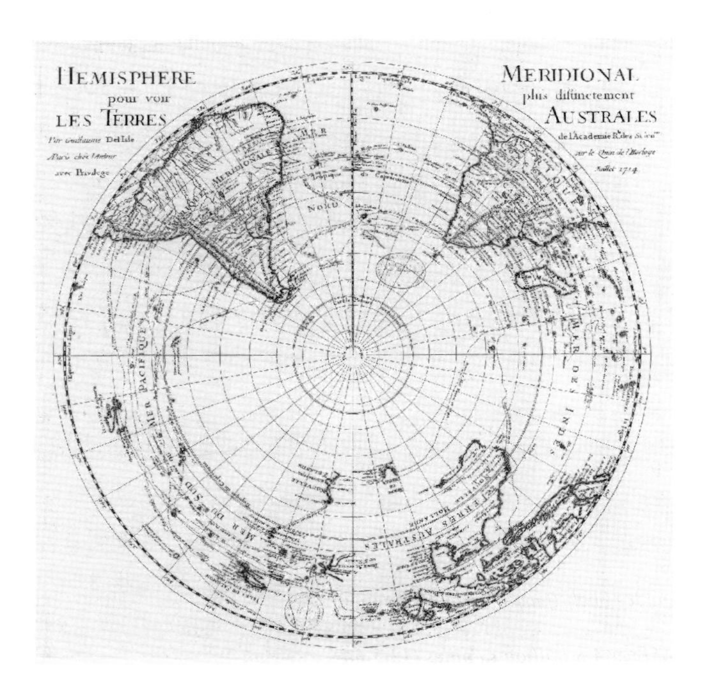

LEFT **Polar projection, *1714*, by *Guillaume Delisle***
This early 18th-century map records the southernmost tips of South Africa and South America; it is less definite about Australia and shows no Antarctica. The gaps would be filled over the next 200 years.

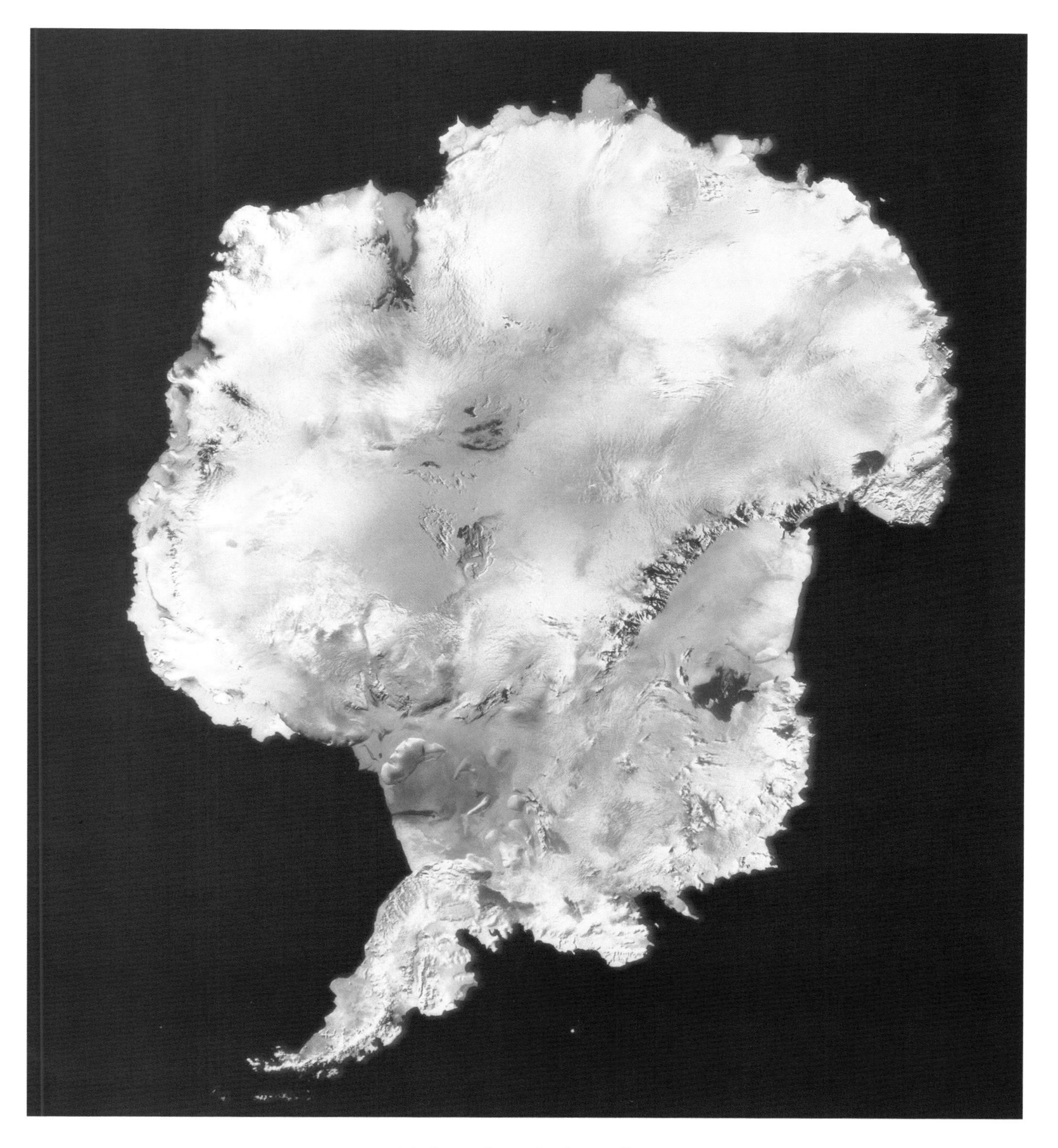

ABOVE ***Modern enhanced-color satellite image***
The colors in this satellite image of Antarctica are enhanced to accentuate the variations in the large-scale structure of the ice cover over the continent. Most of the ice seen here covers land, with the exception of the Ross Ice shelf (brown tint below center) and the Ronne Ice Shelf (purple tint left of center). Just below the center is the line of Transantarctic Mountains. The permanent ice cover is over 9,842 ft (3,000 m) thick near the centre of the continent, and covers a total area of over 4.8 million sq miles (12.5 million sq kms).

19th-century City Maps

In the 19th century, as the costs of map production reduced and urban populations increased, a thriving market for city maps developed. Many maps were produced, but perhaps the most remarkable were the work of the "Society for the Diffusion of Useful Knowledge" (SDUK). The Society was founded in England in 1826 by a "group of gentlemen," which included the Lord Chancellor, Henry Peter Brougham (1778–1868), with the purpose of furnishing "the means of instruction to those who are desirous of acquiring it, and to excite the desire of those who are indifferent to it." The Society became a chartered institution in 1832, and was a typically Victorian phenomenon, embodying the ideals of high moral purpose and ethical edification. Map publication was an important part of the Society's mission: the plan was to produce a series of 200 maps of the great cities of the world. Each would be sold for a shilling (in black and white) and for a shilling and sixpence (in color). Not surprisingly, the Society ran into financial problems in the 1840s, finally going under in 1843, but the maps continued to be published well into the next decade.

BELOW ***SDUK map of Vienna, 1833***
The area of parks and fortifications around the old city, the Ringstrasse, is clearly visible. Elaborate public buildings appeared in the Ringstrasse soon after the map was published.

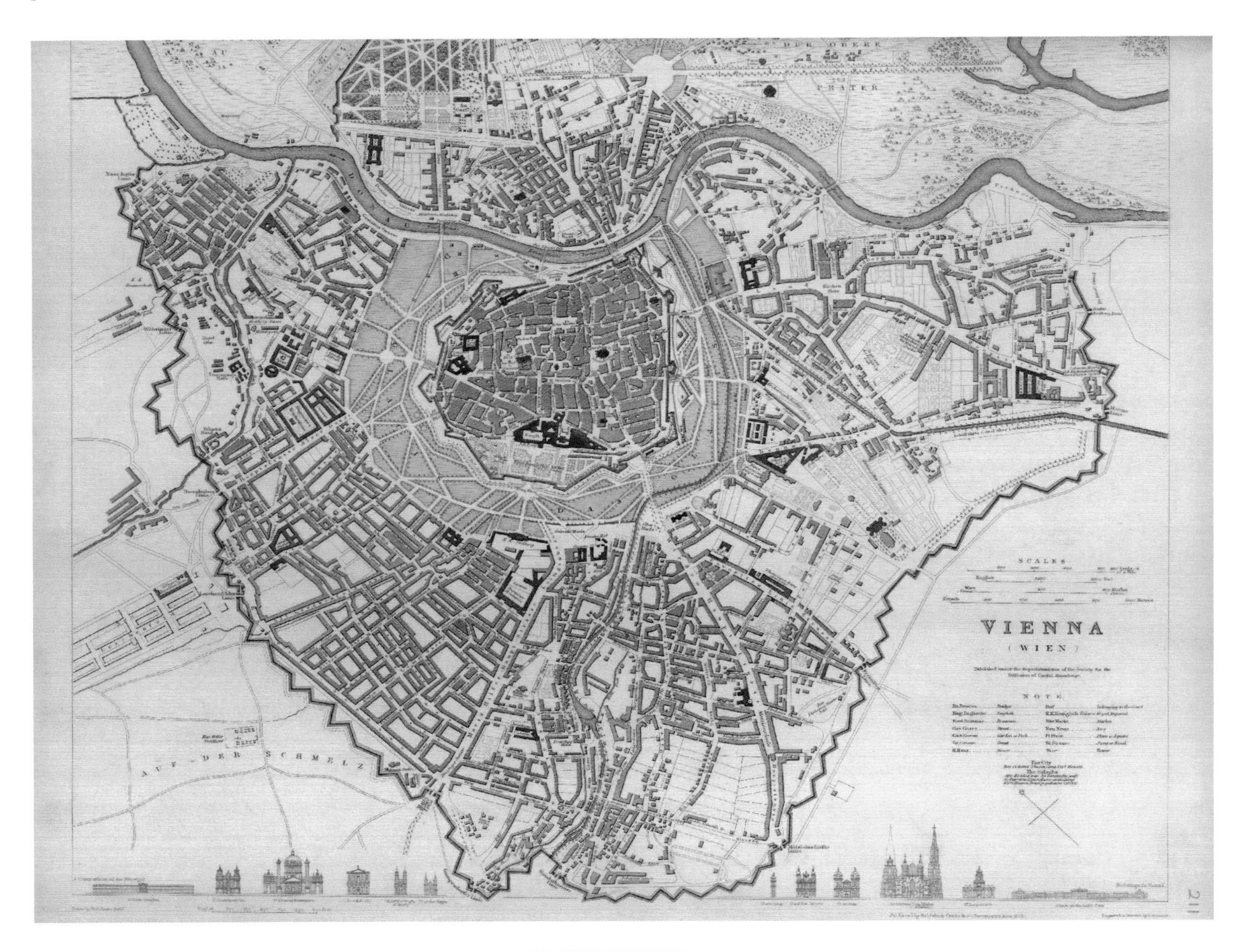

LEFT ***City plan of Topeka, USA, c. 1865***
The grid was an important feature of many cities in the American Midwest. This bird's-eye view shows the strong grid pattern of streets that guided the growth of this city. The grid has yet to be filled in, so the city looks more like a promise to be fulfilled than an existing reality.

The Society's city plans are elegant and simple in design, benefiting as they do from the crisp lines of steel engravings. They are highly simplified in appearance, and although rendered in plan view, they also contain bird's-eye views of certain neighborhoods and individual buildings. Public buildings are extremely well documented, reflecting the early Victorians' strong sense of civic purpose.

All the Society's maps were produced between 1830 and 1843, and they provide a unique glimpse of an urban world on the eve of massive industrial growth. The maps cover cities from Calcutta to Moscow and St. Petersburg to Boston, and represent a revealing "snapshot" of each one. The map of New York, for example, made in 1840, shows that urban development had yet to fill the grid plan that was laid down over the island of Manhattan. The urban frontier stops at the edge of Madison Square, with few buildings above 28th Street. The map of Vienna, made in 1833, shows a green parkland area around the city center that within 25 years would be transformed into the famous "Ringstrasse" of public buildings. In total, the SDUK maps constitute a comprehensive overview of the state of the city in the first half of the 19th century.

Bird's-eye-view city maps had fallen out of favor with cartographers. However, the form was revived in the 19th century, especially in the United States and Canada, where bird's-eye city plans were extremely popular. Between 1865 and 1900, nearly 5,000 different urban images were printed: a total of some 2,400 towns, cities, and even hamlets. The reason for this explosion of mapmaking was the introduction of lithography, which dramatically reduced the cost of printing. Lithography was invented in 1798 by the German engraver Aloys Senefelder (1771–1834).

The new maps were produced in the following way: a newspaper article would announce the arrival of the mapmaker or artist, often accompanied by his agent and publisher. He would then draw the city in perspective from a street plan and spend some weeks sketching in notebooks, while the agent would hustle for subscribers in the local community. A quick mapmaker could do more than ten towns a year. Local townspeople and their businesses could buy advertising space in the illustrated borders that decorated each new town map.

These images provide a fantastically detailed record of 19th-century American and Canadian cities. They range from the almost naive painting style of the image of Newport, Rhode Island, published by Galt and Hoy in 1878, to the 1877 image of Boston, showing a teeming, high-density city, packed and overflowing.

One of the most impressive single images is the bird's-eye view of Chicago made by James T. Palmatary in 1857. The four-sheet lithograph shows the Chicago River disgorging marine traffic into the Greta Lake and an urban fabric stretched tight across the grid. The image is unique because the great fire of 1871 destroyed many of the buildings shown.

NEW YORK.
SCALE OF FEET
1000 500 0 1000 2000 2640 feet = ½ mile
JERSEY CITY
NEW JERSEY RAILROAD
Canal Basin
POWLES HOOK
ELLIS OR BUCKING ISLAND
Fort Gibson
HUDSON RIVER
Proposed Pier & Basin
Albany Steam Boats
Albany Basin
Corporation Dock
North Battery
NEW YORK
HARBOUR
Castle Clinton or Garden
BATTERY
BROADWAY
PARK
CHATHAM STREET
BOWERY
Chapel Street
St. John's Park
U. S. Revenue Office
Whitehall St.
Castle William
GOVERNORS OR NUTTEN ISLAND
FORT COLUMBUS
S. Battery
EAST RIVER
Ferry
Catharine Slip
Market St.
Rutgers St.
Governeur Slip
BUTTERMILK CHANNEL
Cornels Mill Pond
CITY OF BROOKLYN
LONG ISLAND RAILROAD
MAIN STREET
FULTON STREET
NAVY YARD
Lit. Dock
CORLEARS HOOK
Navy Yard Ferry
Williamsburgh Ferry
WALLABOUT BAY

LEFT ***SDUK map of New York, 1840***

This map is orientated with west at the top of the page and east at the bottom. The grid pattern for the streets across the island of Manhattan was laid out in 1811. This map shows the extent to which the city was still concentrated in the southern tip of the island and across the East River into Brooklyn. Urban development was moving slowly northward up the island to fill in the spaces of the grid.

NDISE MART
LA SALLE
CLARK
OHIO
GRAND AVE
DEARBORN
ILLINOIS
HUBBARD
KINZIE
LA SALLE
CLARK
LAKE
DEARBORN
STATE
WABASH
WACKER DR
DEARBORN
STATE
MICHIGAN AVE
WABASH
Chicago
RANDOLPH
WASHINGTON
MICHIGAN AVE
MADISON
STETSON
WATER
LAKE

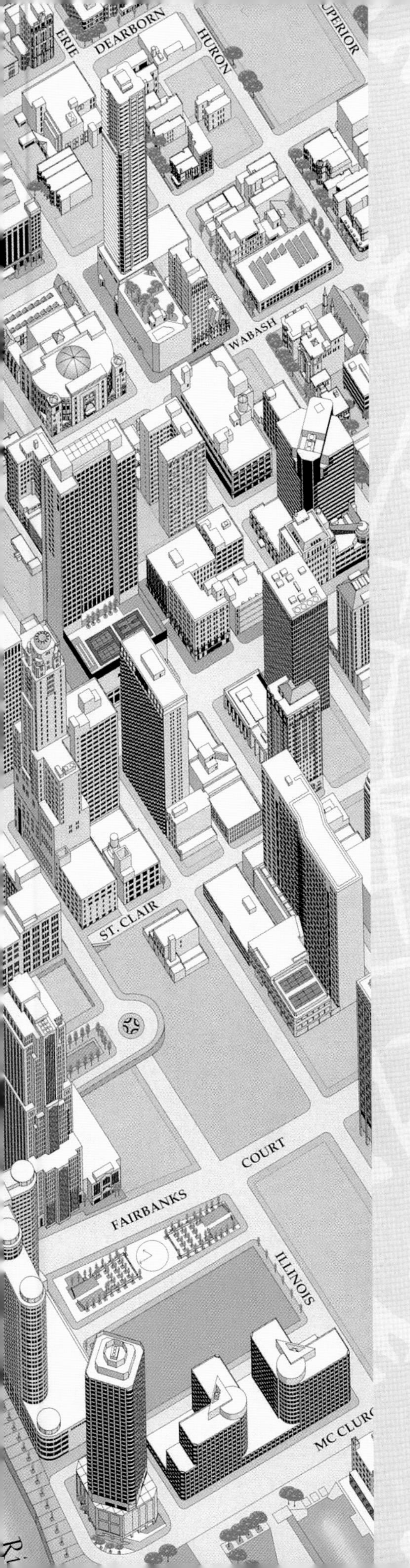

PART VI

Mapping the Modern World

LEFT *Contemporary axonometric map of Chicago, after Hermann Bollmann*

18

THEMATIC MAPS

Routeways and Flows

A distinction can be made between absolute space—the space of carefully calibrated latitude and longitude, and relative space—the space of thematic values, such as routeways, flows, and areal surfaces. Part of the language of maps is to show relative values, resulting in what are called "thematic maps."

THE WORD "ITINERARY" comes from the Latin for "journey." There has long been a connection between maps and journeys, and itinerary maps are the most common form of direction giving. If stopped by someone in the street who asks directions to a specific place, we tend to tell the person how to get there with a variant on the "turn left at the church, second right at the traffic lights" style of directions. Such directions can be called a "verbal itinerary map." Non-verbal itinerary maps constitute one of the earliest forms of map: for example, a map that shows routes and roads only.

Road maps have always been an essential element in the construction of national economies, both ancient and modern. The first English road maps were made by John Ogilby (1600–76) in 1675. They were produced as thin strips noting landmarks on either side of the road. The strips were produced at the same scale. Up to six strips were printed on one page. The strip map proved popular and is still used today. The Automobile Association in the USA provides strip maps for members requesting itinerary maps from stated origin to destination points.

More recent route maps reflect the changing nature of transportation technology. Route maps of subway systems and motorways give us an image of the paths to follow across and through the urban landscape. The major airlines now use maps of their routes to show their connections.

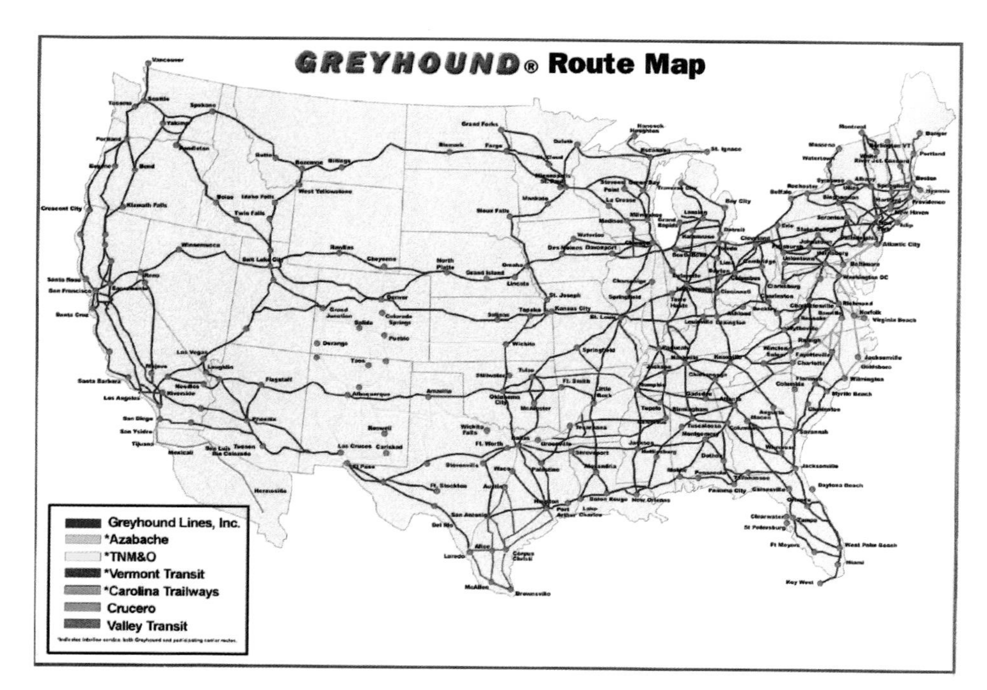

RIGHT *Road maps, 1675, from John Ogilby's* Britannia
Using a strip map travelers could make their way along popular routes. The map identified towns and features along the roadway. The little circles on this map are compass roses. A form of strip map is still used by motorists.

LEFT ***Contemporary Greyhound bus route map, USA***
Greyhound buses travel to over 3,700 destinations. A map that showed so many stops would be of far less use to the traveler than a straightforward list. This simplified route map does little more than suggest some interchanges and invite the intrepid to take to the open road: "Go Greyhound—and leave the driving to us." There is no city hierarchy; Washington D.C. gets the same symbol as Butte.

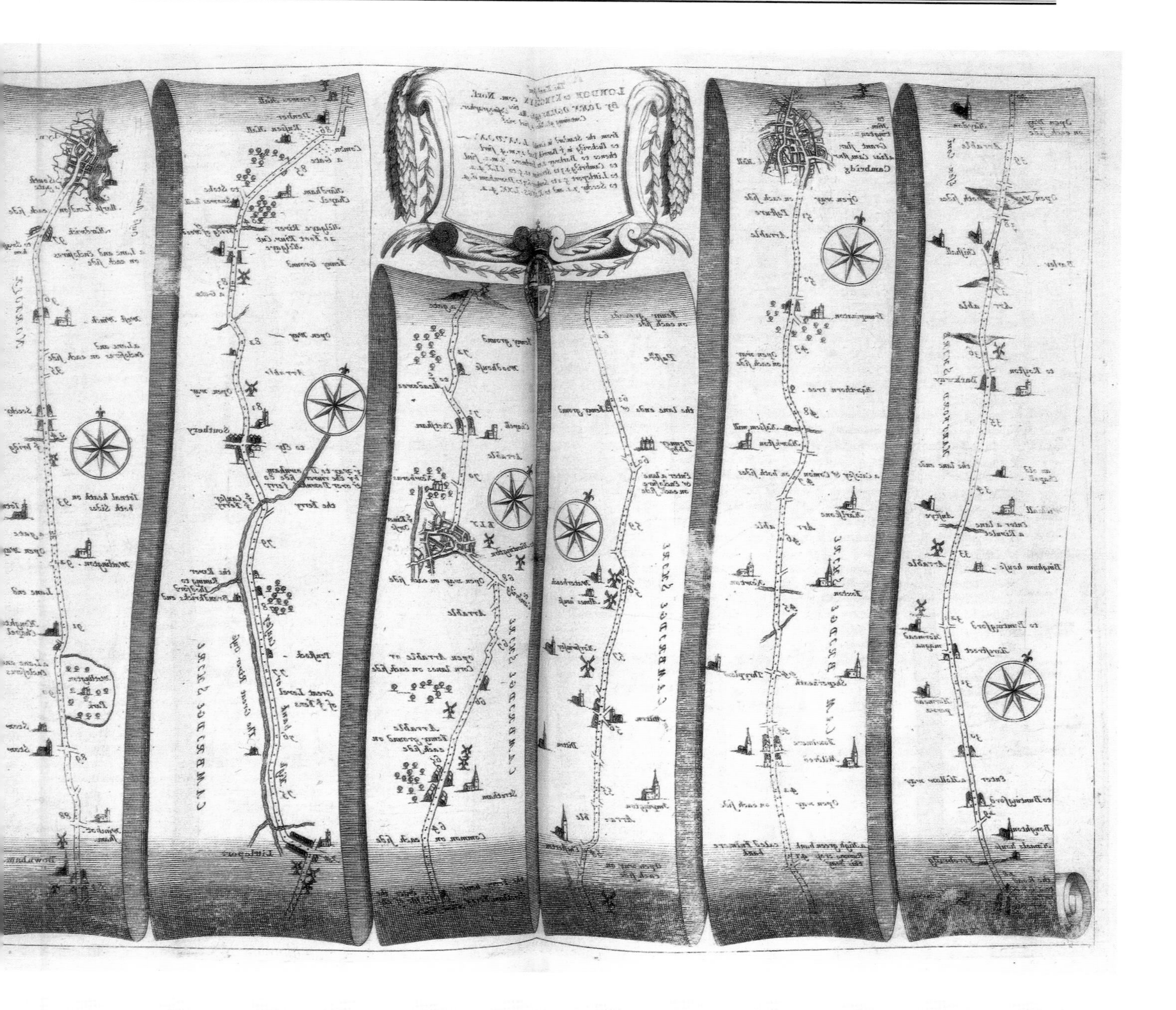

MENTAL MAPS

While not possessed of the extraordinary navigation skills of birds, insects, and even mammals, it is clear that the creation and refinement through experience of mental maps is an integral, perhaps instinctive, part of human thought processes.

Mental maps come in many different forms. Mental images are unique to each individual, and each person's map of the world is partial and selective. For example, while we may live in a city, we probably have a good mental map of only a tiny part of it. It will be based on the following elements: paths, edges, nodes, districts, and landmarks. Paths are the routes we follow to get around, edges are the boundary markers between different districts, and nodes are places of concentrated activity such as shopping areas. Districts are named areas of the city and landmarks are any easily recognizable features. Traveling through Washington, D.C., for example, the Capitol and the Washington Monument act as convenient and highly visible landmarks that help me orientate myself and ensure I am traveling in the right direction.

Hierarchies and Surfaces

Hierarchies, large and small, important or less important, can be represented on maps. A small dot can represent a village, a larger one a town, and an even larger one a city. The proportion of the dots can also be calculated mathematically, using whatever type of data they are designed to represent: population, crime rates, anything—from the level of pollution to the number of wild swans. Many modern maps show urban settlements both proportionately and as part of a stepped hierarchy, with separate symbols used to represent various size levels such as "less than 10,000," "10,000–100,000," and so on, up to over 5 million for world maps.

The commonest way to define the surface of the earth is by the use of color. Different colors can be used to represent anything: political divisions of territory; climate; topography; and so on. Map scale is a factor: for example,

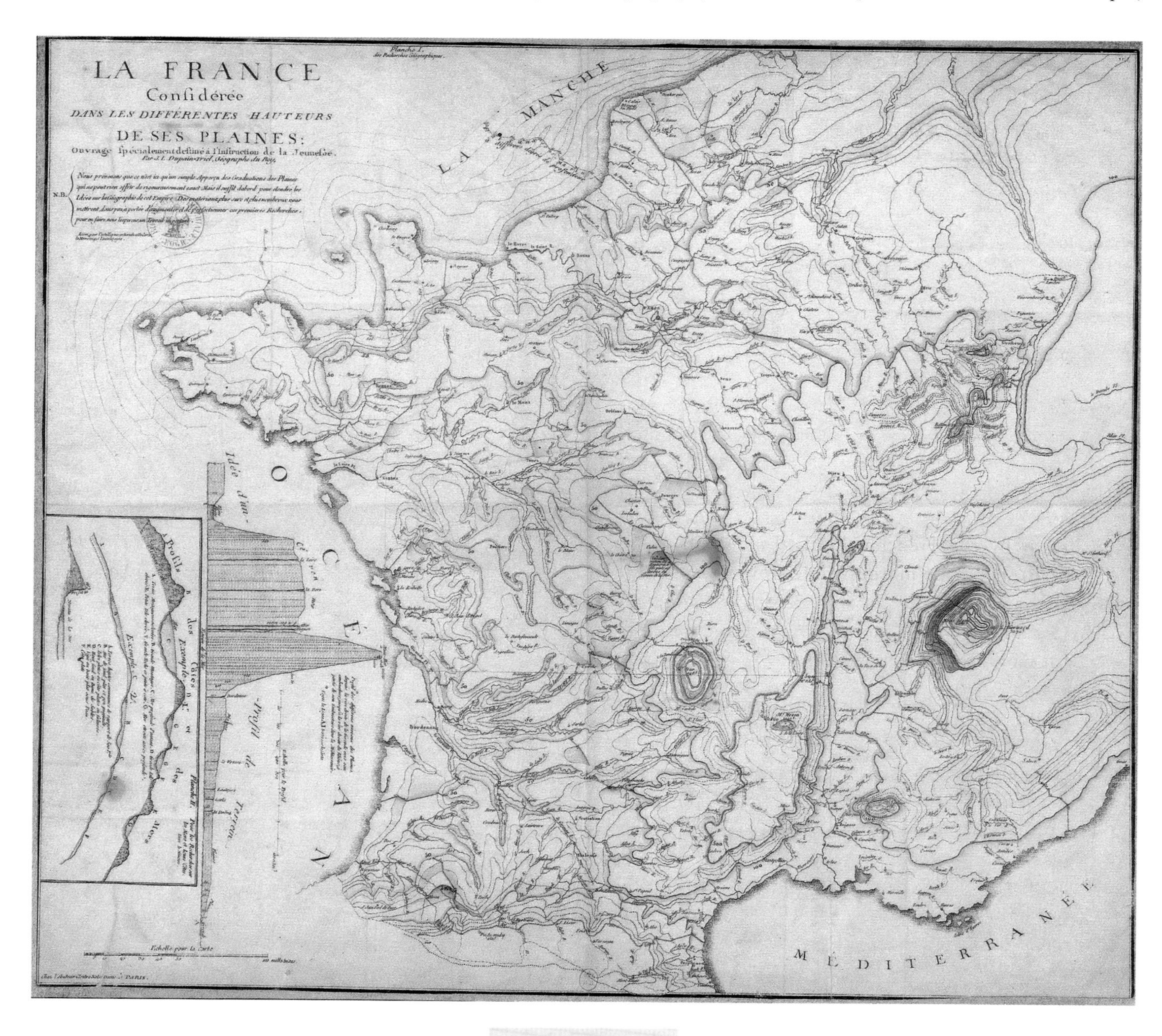

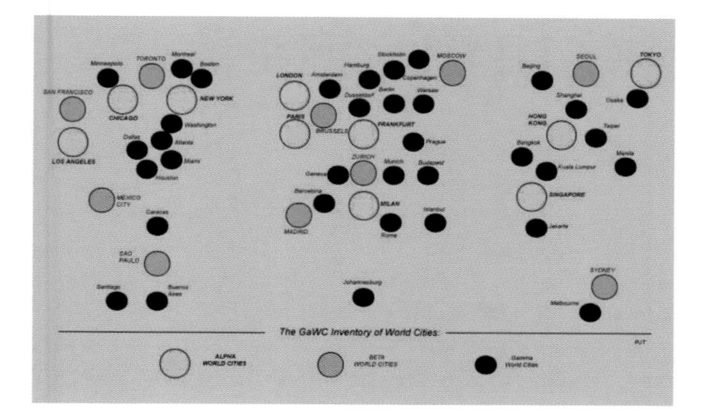

ABOVE ***Contemporary analysis of world cities***
This web map distinguishes between different levels of the global urban hierarchy. A threefold division identifies the most important, major, and minor global cities. A variety of information about each city can be accessed by clicking on the city icon. But this city roster is not based merely on population size: an attempt has been made to define global economic importance. Calcutta is defined as a "mega-city" but not a "world city"; Zurich is a "world-city" but not a "mega-city."

LEFT ***Contour map of France, 1791, by Dupain-Triel***
This is one of the earliest contour maps of France. Contour lines identify height, and the closer the contour lines the steeper the slope. Note the relief profile of the country on the left-hand side of the map.

small-scale maps of the entire world use color to represent different types of land such as mountains and deserts. In a large-scale map of a small area, devices such as contours, shading, and the use of symbols can be used to great effect.

The movement of people and animals can also be shown on a thematic map. This is commonly known as the mapping of flows. Good examples of this type of map are those drawn by the Frenchman Charles Joseph Minard (1781–1870). He made more than 42 flow maps covering such diverse subjects as the volume of wine exported from France, cotton imports to Europe, and the origin and destination of immigrants. The nature of the data being represented sometimes forced Minard to change a map's space from absolute to relative. For example, in order to fit in the thick flow lines representing commerce through the narrow English Channel in many of his maps, he widened the Channel out of proportion to the land.

In 1861, Minard produced his greatest work: a map of Napoleon's Russian campaign (1812) that overlays a geographical map with statistical information and graphics. A huge range of information is included, such as the changing size of the army, its position over time, the direction of its movement, and the temperature during the long retreat from Moscow.

THE LONDON UNDERGROUND MAP

One of the most recognizable thematic maps is that of the London Underground. Residents of the city as well as visitors soon learn to navigate their way around the underground network using this remarkable and memorable map.

The map was first devised by Harry Beck (1903–64), an electrical draftsman, who submitted the first draft in 1931. Unlike its predecessors, which were overly complex and difficult for travelers to understand, the map is entirely unrelated to the geography of the city itself. It is wholly schematic in design, pulling apart the stations that are close together in the center of the city and drawing together those in the suburbs.

Initially, Beck's plan was considered too radical, because it distorted the distances between the stations, but in 1933 his idea was accepted and the first "Beck map" was published. Beck was paid the heady sum of £5 for his design, and continued to refine and modify the map until his death in 1964.

The map is a classic example of thematic cartography, and has become a symbol of the city itself. It is reproduced over 60 million times each year, in various forms, by private companies other than the London Underground. In 1997, the artist Simon Paterson used the design as the basis for his painting called *The Great Bear*, in which he used the basic design but changed the names of the stations to philosophers, soccer players, politicians, and figures from history.

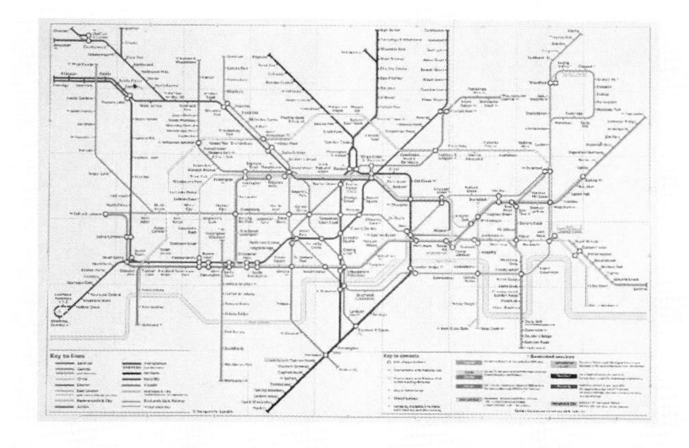

ABOVE ***London Underground map by Harry Beck***
One of the most famous and most recognizable maps in the world. Beck also designed electrical circuitry and the influence is obvious.

Mapping Social Difference

Mapping demographics does not only mean presenting population levels; many other characteristics of human society can be mapped. Between 1845 and 1852, the German publishing company Justus Perthes, produced a series of maps under the general title *Physikalischer Atlas* (*Physical Atlas*). The author was Heinrich Berghaus (1787–1884), a professor of applied mathematics at the Berlin Academy of Architecture. His world maps depicted ethnic categories, forms of government, religions, and what he termed "spiritual constitution." The "Christian" lands are depicted as having the most spiritual constitution, and the "heathen" lands as experiencing "the minimum, or complete darkness of the soul." This was a clear demonstration of the perceived superiority of Christianity over other religions and these maps represent an early, and rather extreme, example of sociological mapping.

The rapid growth of towns and cities in the 19th century was often a cause for alarm among middle- and upper-class commentators. Many people were worried by the breakdown of traditional lifestyles that occurred when people moved away from close-knit rural communities to the anonymity of the city. Karl Marx (1818–83) noted the appalling conditions in which many poor people lived in those cities. However, he also saw the rapid growth of industrial cities and the way in which they brought workers together as a potential source of revolutionary change and a cause for optimism. Whether viewed as a cause for celebration or concern, the development of the city was a popular topic and resulted in various attempts to map this new phenomenon.

As cities increased in size, the rich and the poor communities tended to be separated into different neighborhoods, and "urban segregation" became a subject of cartographic interest. For example, the 1841 census of Ireland provided the basis for a whole series of maps concerning social characteristics, including one of the city of Dublin that color coded the streets as "first class," "high class," "second class," and "third class"—the latter being deemed to be inhabited by "artisans, huxters, and low population."

A similar type of classification was adopted by Charles Booth (1840–1916), a rich shipowner and social commentator. He wrote a study of London in 1889 entitled *Life and Labour of the People in London*. This 17-volume work contains a number of maps depicting social classification. The "worst" areas are said to be inhabited by the "very poor," and Charles Booth further characterized these people as "lowest class" and "vicious, semi-criminals."

The maps provide us with an interesting picture of urban life in the 19th century, because the classifications used, and their underlying ideology, tell us much about the world view of middle- and upper-class commentators of the day. For many of them, cities were social volcanoes that could erupt at any time, and urban mapping was an attempt to predict where the "social seismic activity" was strongest, and the threat of anarchy from the local population the most extreme.

The mapping of social difference can also have a direct effect on the people being mapped. A good example of this is the decision by the United States government in the 1930s to underwrite mortgages for house purchase, in an attempt to relieve the effects of the Great Depression. In 1936 a national inventory was undertaken to establish the creditworthiness of different neighborhoods, which were rated from "A" to "D" on a map with corresponding colors of green, blue, yellow, and red. Grade A neighborhoods were considered to be "up and coming" and in demand; Grade B areas were good; Grade C areas were dominated by ageing buildings in need of repair and were "infiltrated" with "lower-grade populations"—a code for blacks, Jews, and foreign immigrants, and Grade D areas were evaluated as "poor-quality housing" with an "undesirable population."

The maps and accompanying text were sent to banks and mortgage lenders, with the result that loans were not granted to people seeking housing in areas graded D, and rarely to those wishing to live in Grade C areas. "Red" areas were therefore starved of federally protected mortgage funds. Denied the lifeblood of mortgage finance, conditions in many inner-city neighborhoods got progressively worse, widening the gap between rich and poor areas. This mapping exercise represented a federal endorsement of the prejudices held by the white, middle-class real-estate industry, and continued to exert its unfair influence right through to 1965, when the practice was very belatedly ended by the Department of Housing and Development.

The mapping of social difference continues. Census data allow government and private companies to identify rich and poor areas. This information is often used by private companies to target advertising campaigns and leaflet distributions. Credit companies use the postal zip codes to target pre-approved credit card applications. Addresses in a city are used to screen job applicants, credit applications, mortgage requests. The mapping of the city is not innocent of important economic and social implications. Certain areas of the city also take on informal categories as locals learn to distinguish between good and bad areas, safe and unsafe districts, our kind of area and not our kind of area. Mapping social difference can generate social difference.

LEFT ***Map of London poverty 1898-99, by Charles Booth***
Charles Booth undertook an extensive survey of London social conditions that he then mapped. A seven-color classification was used from the lowest class in black through the very poor in light blue, mixed populations in purple, fairly comfortable in pink, middle class in red, and the wealthy upper class depicted in yellow. This map shows a wealthy part of the city with the very wealthy living close to the more prestigious areas of public space.

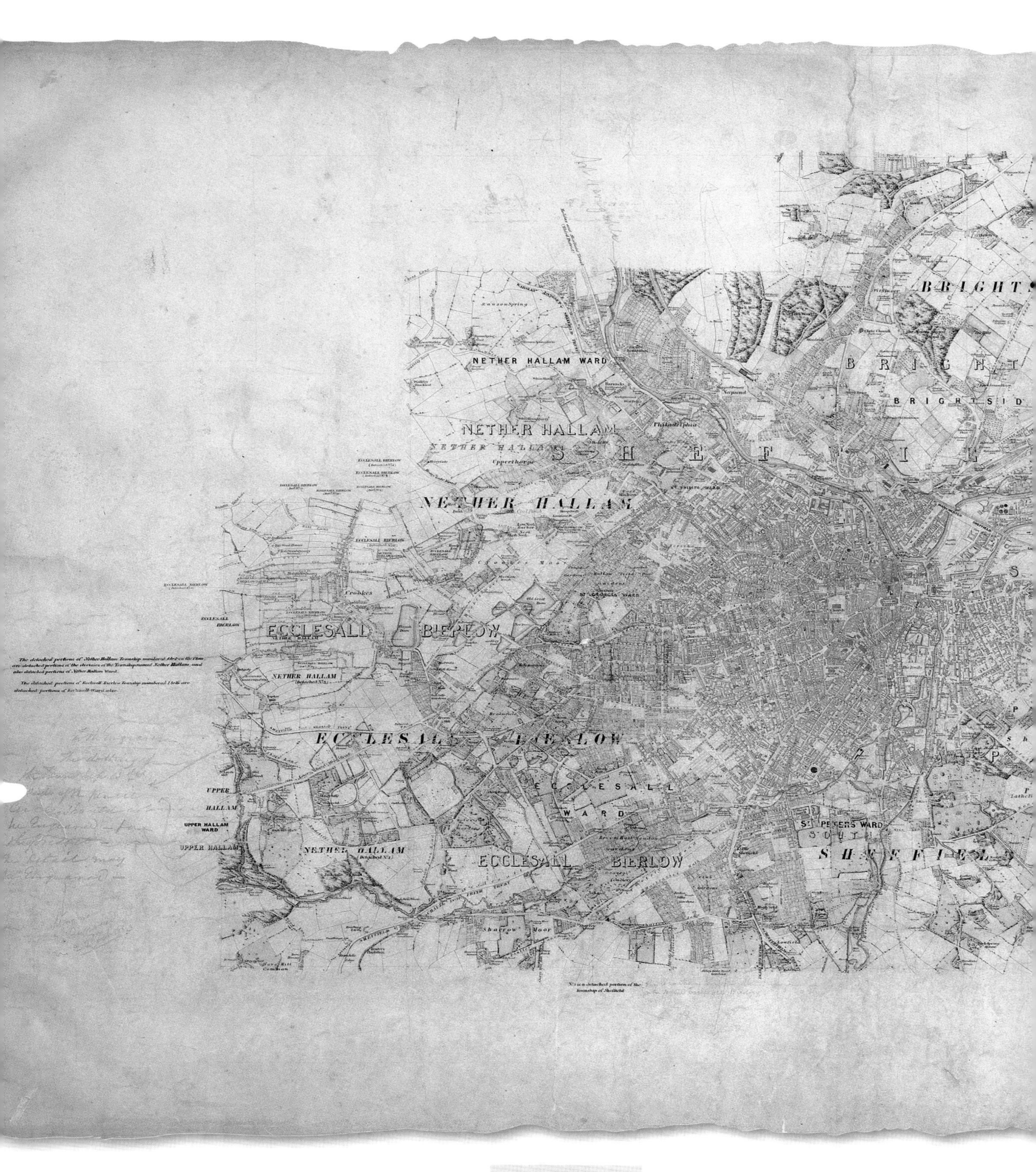
NETHER HALLAM WARD
NETHER HALLAM
NETHER HALLAM
SHEFFIELD
NETHER HALLAM
ECCLESALL BIERLOW
NETHER HALLAM
ECCLESALL BIERLOW
ECCLESALL
WARD
ECCLESALL BIERLOW
UPPER HALLAM
UPPER HALLAM WARD
UPPER HALLAM
ST. PETERS WARD
SOUTH
SHEFFIELD
BRIGHTSIDE
ST. GEORGES WARD
Crookes
Philadelphia
Upperthorpe
Sharrow Moor

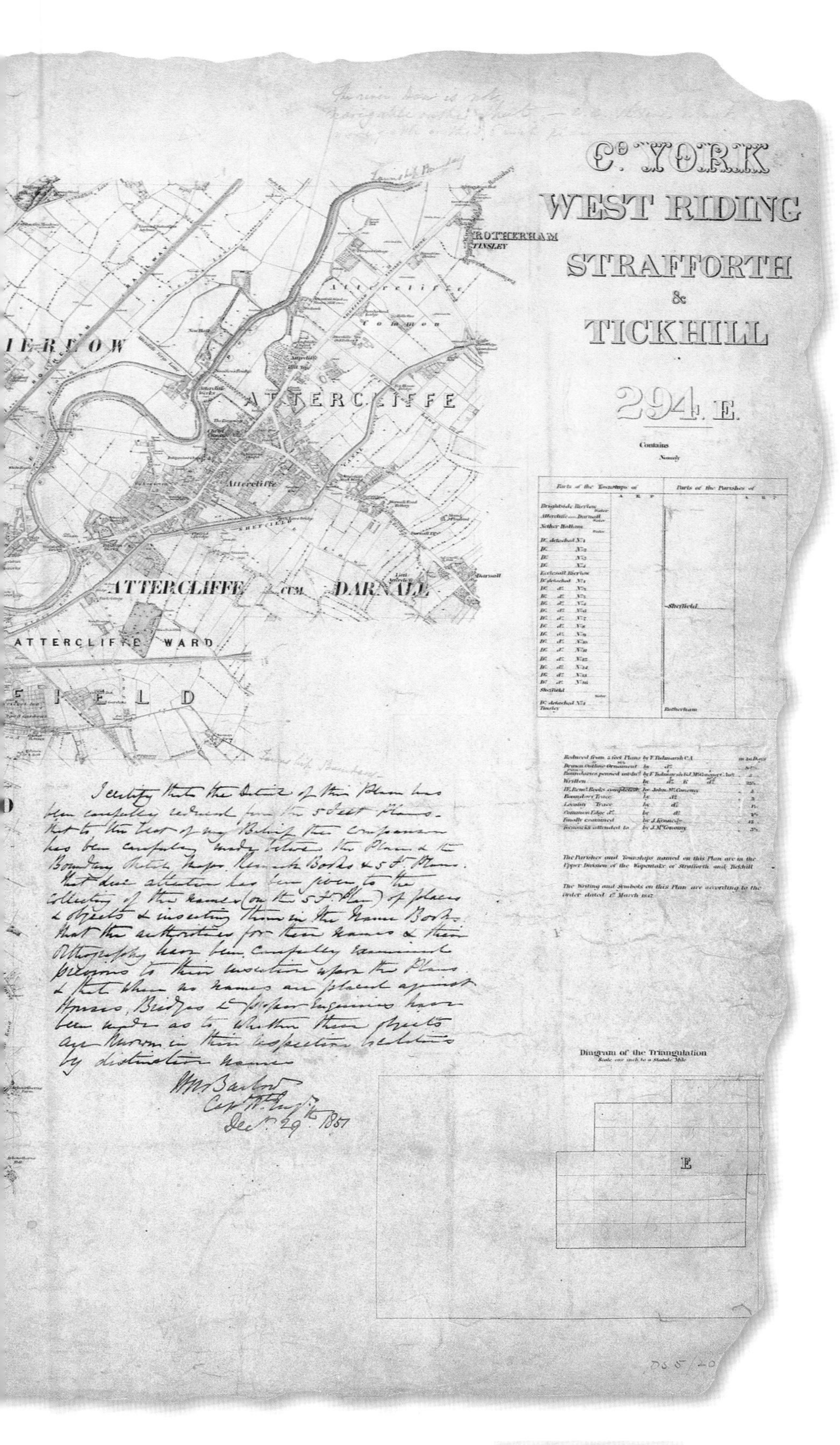

LEFT *Ordnance Survey map, c. 1850*

In the 1840s, concern in Britain over its rapidly growing cities led the Ordnance Survey to map those cities in northern England with a population of 4,000 or more. A scale of 1:1,056 was used. Later, in the 1850s, an even more detailed mapping, at the scale of 1:528, was published for 18 more cities. Here is an example of the steel-producing city of Sheffield. The maps provided the authorities with detailed plans of cities that could be centers of social radicalism, and perhaps even revolution. These maps also provided commercial publishers with the base for a whole range of town plan maps.

Mapping Disease and Mapping Morality

The mapping of disease also began during the 19th century. Rapid industrialization, an increase in urbanization, and the emergence of new social classes created a ferment of social change and concern, with the result that the authorities began to collect and centralize social data for analysis. Maps were used as a way of plotting, and hence understanding, social change and its consequences. A particular concern was public health, and in Britain the Poor Law Commission published its *Report on the Sanitary Condition of the Labouring Population* in 1842. The report included two maps of housing types and incidence of disease in Leeds and Bethnal Green, London.

Maps were also used to "plot" diseases and epidemics. A worldwide cholera epidemic began in India in 1817, and US mapmaker Henry Schenck Tanner (1786–1858) produced *A Geographical and Statistical Account of the Epidemic Cholera from its Commencement in India to its Entrance into the United States* in 1832, in which he wrote:

"Among the infinite variety of publications on the Epidemic Cholera, there is none, I believe, which gives any satisfactory account of the geographical progress, and statistical details of the subject ... the gradual extension of the pestilence; its localities; the period of its commencement and termination; the number of human beings which have been subjected to its attacks, and those who become its victims, and other statistical facts were either wholly disregarded ... or given in such a loose and unconnected manner as to render a reference to them at once irksome and unprofitable."

Tanner was not quite accurate. A number of maps at global, national, and local levels was produced. However, few of them appeared in print until later. Tanner's book consists of a series of tables listing the number of cases reported, duration in days of the "pestilence," and the number of deaths in different localities, by country. A world map then shows the diffusion of the epidemic from India in 1817. Tanner also produced a more detailed map of the United States and New York that shows the sites where cholera had broken out by means of small red dots. This map has a detailed chart of the diffusion of the illness, showing how the disease spread geographically.

One of the most famous medical maps was drawn by John Snow (1813–58), a London doctor. He was convinced that cholera was communicated by contaminated water, and in 1855 he published *On the Mode of Communication of Cholera*, which contains two maps. The first shows two areas of London served by two different water companies that used different sources for their water supply. While the area served by one company had death rates due to cholera of only 5 per 1,000, the other had rates of 71 per 1,000. Snow's second map plotted the distribution of cholera cases and showed that they clustered around particular pumps—for example, people using the water pump in Broad Street were more likely to go down with cholera. It was indeed the correct argument.

The term "moral statistics" first appeared in an essay written in 1833 by the French statistician André-Michel Guerry (1802–66). The term refers to levels of crime and poverty, among other social phenomena. "Crime" maps first appeared in France in 1829 when Balbi (1782–1848) and Guerry used data from 1825 to 1827 to plot, for each of the *départements* in the country, the incidence of crime in relation to "educational instruction." Their maps were therefore mapping crime and seeking to explain its causes. In 1864 Guerry went on to produce sophisticated maps of types of crime such as murder, rape, "theft by servants," and suicide. His work was read and admired in Europe and the United States. Thanks to Guerry, "mapping morality" became a legitimate branch of the science of cartography.

Today, "geographic profiling," like psychological profiling, is an important part of law enforcement. It assumes that criminal activity is "place specific" and that criminals like to use known areas, usually some distance from their homes. It is believed that if a series of similar crimes are plotted, they may reveal a single criminal's "hunting ground" and perhaps the person's current location.

RIGHT *Snow's maps of Cholera cases, 1865*
Snow's second map plots the distribution of cholera cases. Notice the heavy frequency around the water pump in Broad Street in the middle of the map. From this data Snow was able to pinpoint the source of the disease. The pump was sealed off and infection rates in the area plummeted.

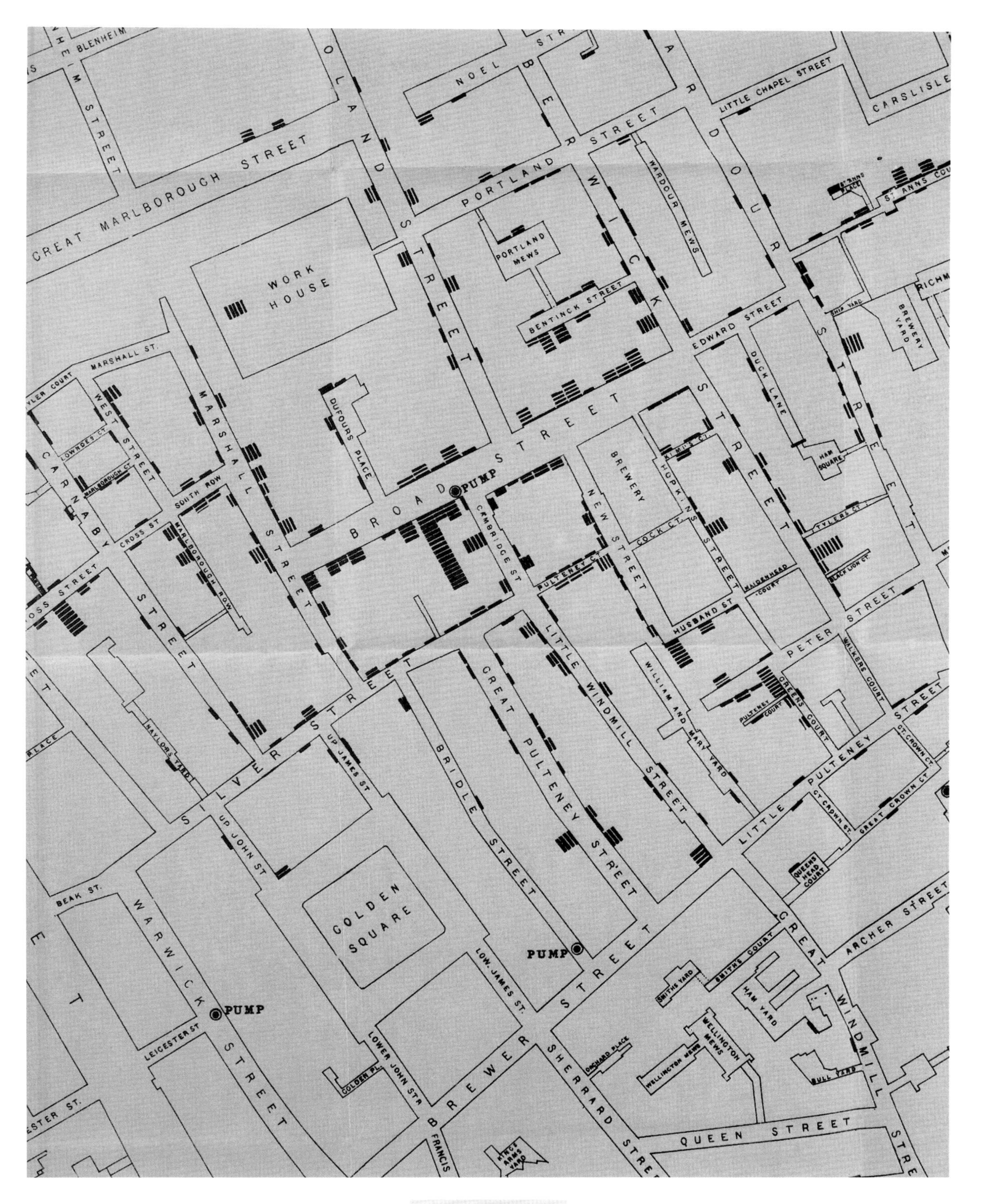
BLENHEIM
NOEL
LITTLE CHAPEL STREET
CARSLISLE
GREAT MARLBOROUGH STREET
PORTLAND STREET
WORK HOUSE
PORTLAND MEWS
BENTINCK STREET
WARDOUR MEWS
EDWARD STREET
SHIP YARD
BREWERY YARD
MARSHALL ST.
TYLER COURT
WEST STREET
LOWNDES CT.
MARLBOROUGH CT.
CARNABY
MARSHALL STREET
DUFOURS PLACE
BROAD STREET
PUMP
SOUTH ROW
CROSS ST.
MARLBOROUGH ROW
CAMBRIDGE ST
NEW STREET
BREWERY
HOPKINS STREET
COCK CT.
PULTENEY CT.
DUCK LANE
HAM SQUARE
TYLERS CT.
BLACK LION CT.
MAIDENHEAD COURT
HUSBAND ST
PETER STREET
WALKERS COURT
LITTLE WINDMILL STREET
GREAT PULTENEY STREET
WILLIAM AND MARY YARD
PULTENEY COURT
GREENS COURT
SILVER STREET
UP JAMES ST
UP JOHN ST
BRIDLE STREET
NAYLORS YARD
LITTLE PULTENEY STREET
GT. CROWN CT.
GREAT CROWN CT.
QUEENS HEAD COURT
ARCHER STREET
GREAT WINDMILL
GOLDEN SQUARE
BEAK ST.
WARWICK STREET
LOW. JAMES ST.
PUMP
SMITHS YARD
SMITHS COURT
HAM YARD
WELLINGTON MEWS
PUMP
LEICESTER ST
LOWER JOHN STR
GOLDEN PL.
BREWER STREET
ORCHARD PLACE
BULL YARD
QUEEN STREET
FRANCIS
KINGS ARMS YARD

RIGHT *Map from* **Report on the Sanitary Conditions of the Labouring Population,** ***1842, by Edwin Chadwick***

In Britain in 1834 the Poor Law Commission was established in response to fears of poor public health in the urban areas. Edwin Chadwick, the secretary of the board, published an analysis in 1842 that included two maps of housing types and incidence of disease in the city of Leeds and in Bethnal Green, London. On this map of Leeds the darker the color the "less clean" the district.

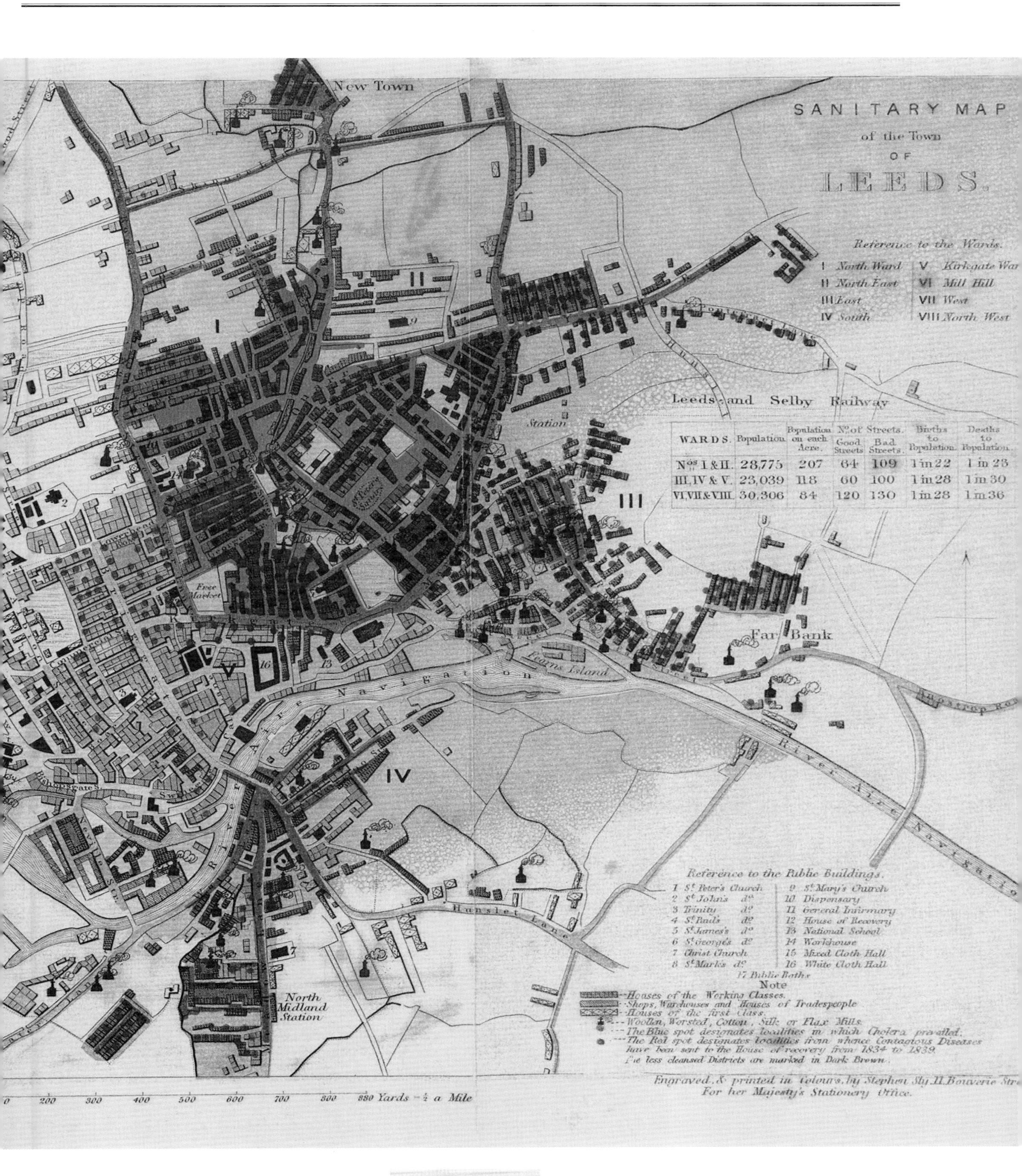

SANITARY MAP
of the Town
OF
LEEDS.
Reference to the Wards.
I North Ward
II North East
III East
IV South
V Kirkgate War
VI Mill Hill
VII West
VIII North West
New Town
Leeds and Selby Railway
Station
Free Market
Far Bank
Fearns Island
Aire Navigation
River Aire Navigation
Hunslet Lane
North Midland Station
I
II
III
IV
V
WARDS.	Population.	Population on each Acre.	No. of Streets. Good Streets	Bad Streets.	Births to Population.	Deaths to Population.
Nos I & II.	28,775	207	64	109	1 in 22	1 in 23
III, IV & V.	23,039	118	60	100	1 in 28	1 in 30
VI, VII & VIII.	30,306	84	120	130	1 in 28	1 in 36
Reference to the Public Buildings.
1 St Peter's Church
2 St John's do
3 Trinity do
4 St Paul's do
5 St James's do
6 St George's do
7 Christ Church
8 St Mark's do
9 St Mary's Church
10 Dispensary
11 General Infirmary
12 House of Recovery
13 National School
14 Workhouse
15 Mixed Cloth Hall
16 White Cloth Hall
17 Public Baths
Note
Houses of the Working Classes.
Shops, Warehouses and Houses of Tradespeople
Houses of the first Class.
Woollen, Worsted, Cotton, Silk or Flax Mills.
The Blue spot designates localities in which Cholera prevailed.
The Red spot designates localities from whence Contagious Diseases have been sent to the House of recovery from 1834 to 1839.
The less cleansed Districts are marked in Dark Brown.
Engraved, & printed in Colours, by Stephen Sly 11 Bouverie Str
For her Majesty's Stationery Office.
200 300 400 500 600 700 800 880 Yards = ½ a Mile

Mapping Geology, Climate, and Weather

In 1793 the English surveyor William Smith (1769–1839), who surveyed areas where canals were to be built, noted that rocks were laid down in layers. The fossils in one layer were often different from those in other layers. He considered the possibility of following these layers of fossils and thus mapping the rock structure. For the next 20 years he traveled Britain by stagecoach and on foot, taking notes and identifying fossils and rocky outcrops with a view to making a map of the country's geology.

William Smith's first map was a geology of the land around the city of Bath—and it was the first geological map ever made. Smith's crowning achievement was a geological map made in 1815, *A Delineation of the Strata of England and Wales, with Part of Scotland*, which shows the rock strata in different colors. For the time, it was astonishingly accurate. Following Smith's example, geological mapping became an important aspect of 19th-century cartography, particularly in the light of the new-found and greatly increased need for fossil fuels during the Industrial Revolution.

A distinction can be made between climate and weather. "Climate" refers to characteristic patterns of precipitation, temperature, and so on, whereas "weather" refers to the conditions over shorter time periods. Both have been mapped extensively since the 12th century in the form of world maps showing the different climatic zones. However, true meteorological mapping is closely tied to the Age of Reason and the dominance of science and scientific inquiry that began in the 17th century.

The first meteorological chart was drawn by the astronomer Edmund Halley (1656–1742) in 1688 and depicts the trade winds in the equatorial regions of the world. In 1817, the physical scientist Alexander von Humboldt (1769–1859) developed the concept of isotherms—showing lines on maps or charts linking points where the temperature was the same at any given time, or that experienced the same mean temperature for a given period. This gave rise to isothermic maps. The mapping of temperature is now an integral part of our understanding of weather and climate.

ABOVE **A Delineation of the Strata of England and Wales, with Part of Scotland, *1815, by William Smith***
One of the earliest geological maps, this is an amazingly accurate map for its time. William Smith began working on it in 1805, basing it on his extensive surveys throughout the British countryside. Soon after its publication, Smith was sent to a debtors' prison and was made homeless. Happily, in recognition of his achievement, the king later rewarded him with a lifetime pension.

Mapping the weather and the climate has the enormous benefit of increasing our ability to predict violent weather patterns, such as storms, hurricanes, and tornadoes, that can cause huge damage to property and potential loss of life. Three types of map are used for this purpose. The first are maps of the historical occurrence of these phenomena, which allow meteorologists to identify any patterns of recurrence that may exist. The second type are maps showing predicted future activity, and the third type are maps showing how, for example, a hurricane originates and develops, and the course that it takes as it moves across the surface of the earth.

The daily weather map has become an accepted part of our lives and is one of the most pervasive cartographic images in the world. The very first weather maps were a set of storm maps that were published in the United States in 1846. Such maps caught on and quickly became common in Britain and France.

By the end of the 19th century weather maps were used all over the world. In recent years weather maps have become extremely sophisticated, and nowadays they incorporate sky cams, satellite, and radar images. To view the nightly weather forecast is to witness a rich array of contemporary weather mapping techniques.

ABOVE ***Contemporary map showing ozone depletion***
This image, produced from NASA satellite imagery, shows ozone levels in the southern hemisphere. The pale blue area is the thinning of the ozone level above the South Pole. Constant satellite data can be used to make animated dynamic maps of ozone thickening and thinning.

BELOW ***Computer-generated map of the Pacific Ocean***
This map of the Pacific ocean picks out the underwater topography. The edges of the plates that constitute the earth's surface are shown in light blue. The edge of one plate runs parallel to the coast of South America. The plates are moving apart at a rate of around 6 inches (15 cm) per year.

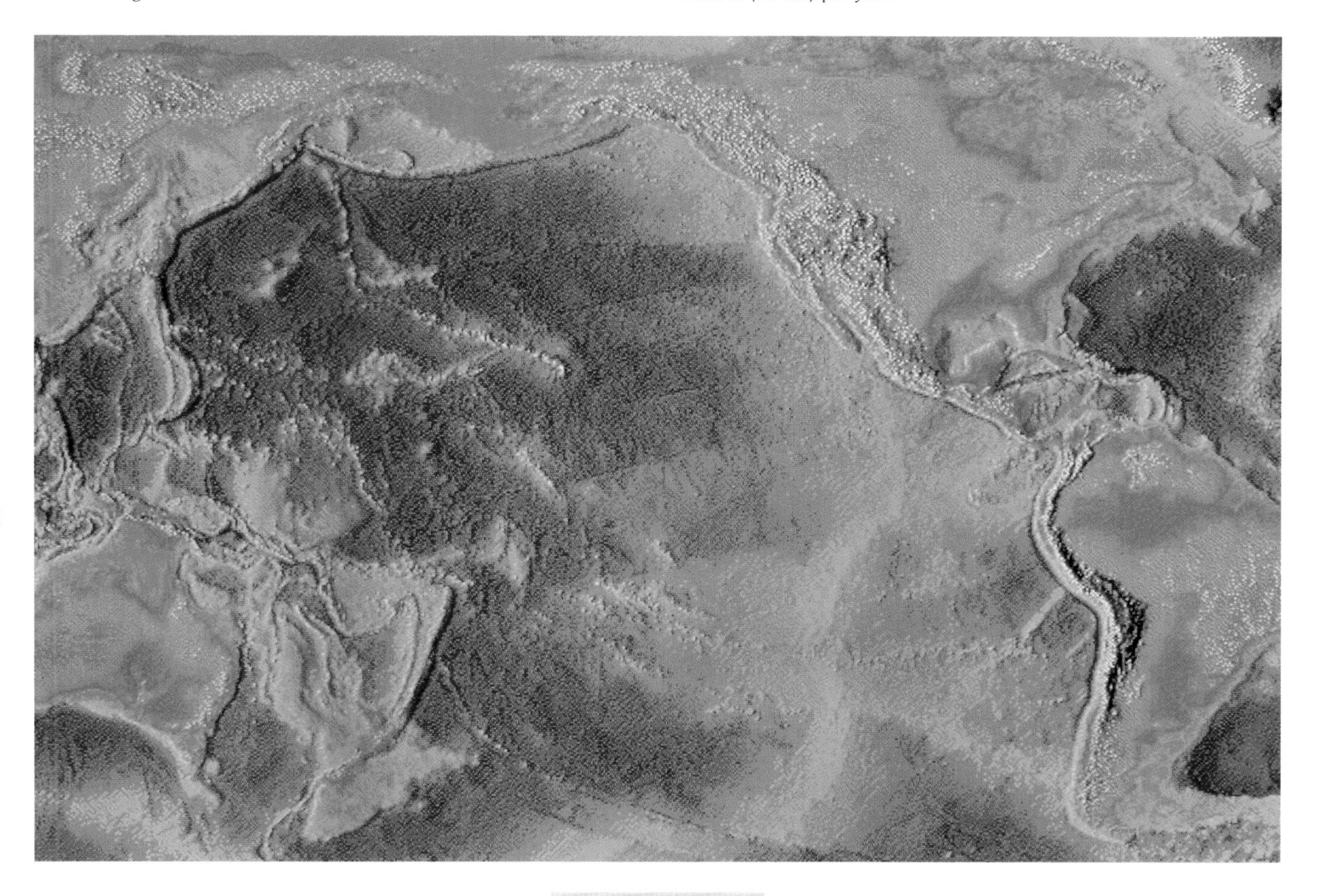

Pl. XIII.
PACIFIC OCEAN
WASHINGTON
OREGON
CALIFORNIA
NEVADA
UTAH
WYOMING
COLORADO
NEBRASKA
KANSAS
DAKOTA
ARIZONA
NEW MEXICO
TEXAS
INDIAN TERRITORY
LOWER CALIFORNIA
GULF OF CALIFORNIA
LLANO ESTACADO OR STAKED PLAIN
EXPLANATION OF COLORS.
EOZOIC
PALEOZOIC
CAMBRIAN AND SILURIAN
DEVONIAN
CARBONIFEROUS AND PERMIAN
MESOZOIC
TRIASSIC AND JURASSIC
CRETACEOUS
CENOZOIC
TERTIARY
ALLUVIUM
VOLCANIC
Note: There may be some Metamorphic Paleozoic formations included in the Atlantic portion of the Eozoic. In the western portion the Metamorphic Mesozoic formations are only partially separated from it. The Paleozoic System and the Cenozoic system are not subdivided west of 100° W. Long. Greenwich, except in the case of a few Post tertiary lacustrine areas and deltas.
C.H.

LEFT Geological Map of the United States, ***1874, by Hitchcock and Blake***

Geological mapping was widely promoted in the 19th-century United States by federal and state governments. Accurate geological maps were seen as an important form of resource inventory, a vital prerequisite for mineral exploitation and mining developments. This small-scale map of the entire country gives a useful summary of the geological structure. There are many stories to be drawn out from such a map. Pittsburgh's position, character, indeed its very existence—and Andrew Carnegie's steel empire established from within it—are, quite literally, built upon the primeval forests of the carboniferous period, and the coal that they became.

19

MAPS AND POWER

Maps as a Means of Surveillance

As asserted elsewhere in this book, land and sea maps reflect and embody political power. They can and have been used as a means of surveying, and hence understanding, the land; as a means of propaganda; and in times of war and peace, as a means of marking out and agreeing (or disputing) the boundaries between one territory and another.

MAPS HAVE OFTEN been used as a means of surveillance. For example, Philip II of Spain (ruled 1556–98), like many Renaissance monarchs, was much taken with cartography as a means to visualize and embody his territories. As the Spanish Empire expanded (the Spanish Empire, under Philip II, would be the first on which the sun never set). Philip was unable to visit all the lands under his control, and used maps for this purpose instead. For example, he commissioned a complete map of the Iberian peninsula from the cartographer Pedro de Esquivel and the result was the 21-sheet "Escorial Atlas." Made to the detailed scale of 1:430,000, it was to date the most detailed survey of mainland Europe ever undertaken.

Mapping is also associated with the fear of losing power. After the failed 1745 uprising when certain Highland clans joined Bonnie Prince Charlie's attempt to reclaim the throne of Britain for his father, the government embarked on a bloody and repressive strategy to avoid any further recurrence of social unrest. Part of this strategy involved producing a map of the whole of Scotland. prior to this official mapping had neither been encouraged nor widely promoted in Britain but in the wake of this rebellion, in which the Highland army had marched as far south as 100 miles (160 km) from London, the central authorities were willing to undertake a massive military survey.

William Roy (1726–90) mapped the whole of Scotland at an incredibly detailed scale so that the government could see the entire territory. The information he provided made it easier for the authorities to work out how to control the population, and plan any counter-offensives in the event of further rebellion. The map was kept securely in the King's Royal Library in London because of its military value, and as a result it was not seen by other mapmakers until the early part of the 19th century. This provides an exaplanation as to why maps of Scotland in the late 18th century were poor, certainly not as accurate as Roy's map. Roy's survey led to the foundation of what is now known as the Ordnance Survey, one year after his death.

In the 19th century the authorities were concerned that the rapid growth of cities in Britain presented the possibility of massive social unrest. The cities concentrated the working class into tight communities that were not so bound to the established order as the agricultural regions of the country. There was a mapping of northern cities with a population of more than 4,000, at a scale of 1:1,056. The first map, produced in 1843, showed the city of St. Helens. In 1855, a mapping at the scale of 1:500 for all cities was begun and by 1892 all British cities with a population of more than 4,000 had been mapped at this detailed scale. The maps gave the authorities detailed plans of cities that might develop into centers of social unrest and perhaps even revolution. Subsequently, these maps provided commercial publishers with the basis for a whole range of town plans.

RIGHT ***Map of Scotland, 1775, by William Roy***
Shaken by the rebellion that nearly overthrew the Crown, the British Government undertook a very detailed survey of Scotland led by William Roy. The level of detail is apparent in this map of the area around Edinburgh. Such maps would have provided invaluable information in the wake of another rebellion.

LEITH
Bonnington
Powderhall
Pilrig
Dowcraigs
Northmains
Lochend
Abbeyhill
Restalrig
Jocks Lodge
Southmains
Road to Berwick
Arthur Seat
mill
Diddiston
Northmains
E. Diddiston
Magdalen Pans
Turnpike
South Mains
Mains
Brunstane
Niddry mills
Pepper Mill
Kings Meadow
Inch
Craig Millar Castle
Niddry
Southmains
Causewayhead
Libberton
Libberton Kirk
Greenend
Bank
Caldcotts
Edmiston mains
Edmiston
Mountainhall
Shawfair
Middlefield
Hiltons
Sunnyside
Carney
Stankend
Woolmound
Good Trees
Gillmerton
Drum
Newton Kirk
Manse
Newton
mountain
Sudhouse
House of Gillmerton
Todhill
Claybarns
Mains
Old Kirk
North Esk Water
Eastpark
Grange

Drawing the Line

Reduced to its simplest form, cartography involves drawing lines. Whether it be on stone, canvas, paper, ceramics, or a computer screen, it is an important part of making maps. But drawing lines on maps is not an act innocent of wider political and deeper social significance.

In the late 15th century, there was increasing competition between Portugal and Spain for colonial territories in the Americas and Asia. In 1493, Pope Alexander adjudicated the dispute with a line drawn 100 leagues west of the Cape Verde islands. Spain was given all the unclaimed land west of the line, Portugal all the unclaimed land to the east. Neither side was happy, and at a meeting of diplomats at Tordesillas in northern Spain on June 7, 1494, the line was moved 270 leagues west, to between 48° and 49° west of Greenwich. The Treaty of Tordesillas, as this agreement was called, drew an arbitrary line across the surface of the earth that enabled the Portuguese to claim what is now Brazil and parts of Africa, including present-day Mozambique, and Angola, and India. Spain received papal sanction to claim most of the Americas. Thus did a line on a map alter the course of history in the coming centuries.

Countries draw lines between themselves; lines on a map become borders. Drawing national boundaries is a vital part of nation building. When the new nation of the United States emerged from British colonial rule, the drawing of boundaries was an important cartographic exercise. At the discussions prior to the Treaty of Paris of 1783, the British and American negotiators used the detailed map of

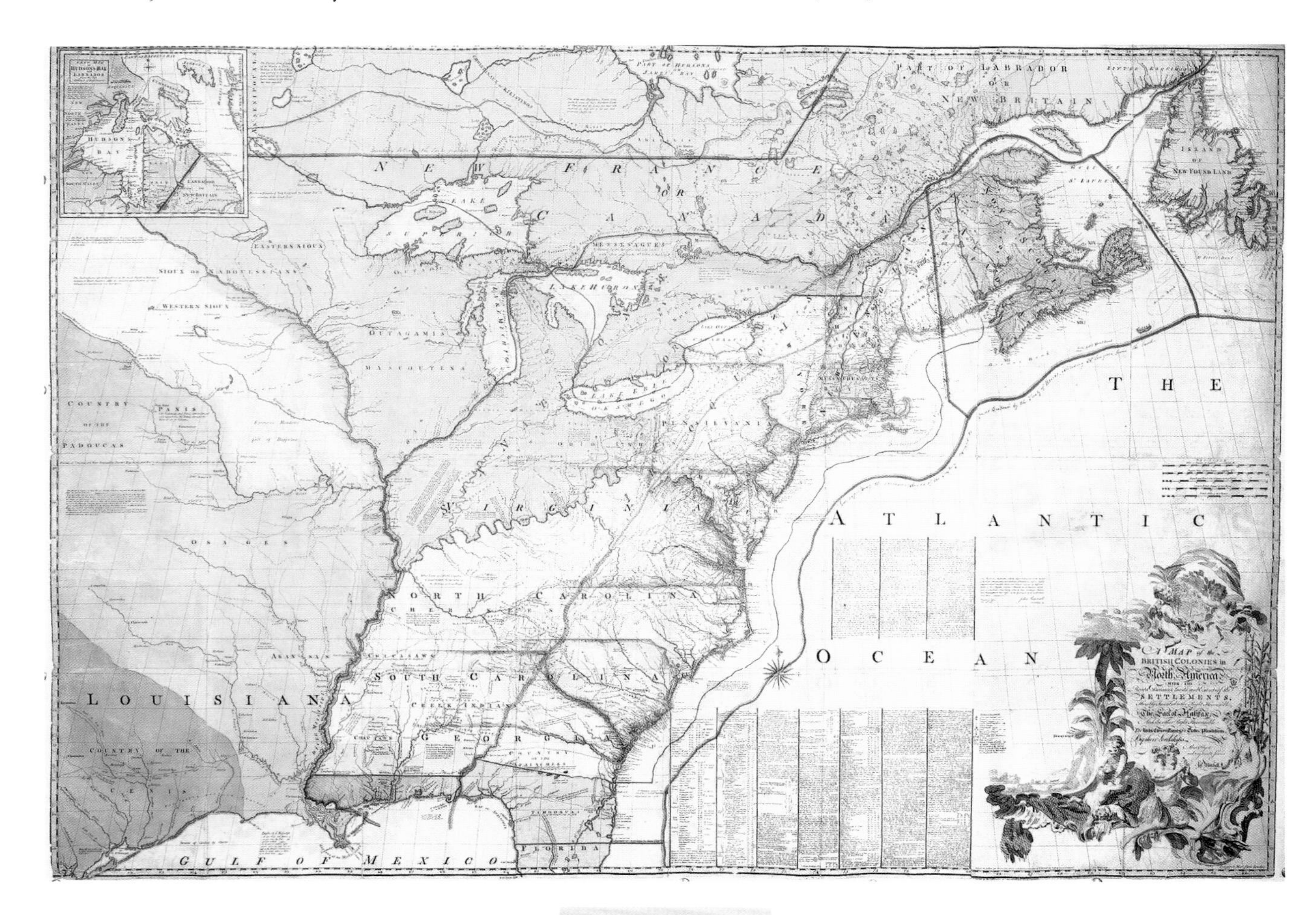

BELOW ***Mitchell's map of North America, 1775***
The red lines that cover this map were drawn by negotiators at the Paris Peace Conference to divide up the continent after the American War of Independence.

North America first produced by John Mitchell in 1755. A copy of the map used at the meeting is covered with red lines that demarcate the boundaries between the United States and Canada, which was then British. Because the final treaty line of 1783 was considered more favorable to the United States, public access to the map was forbidden by the British government until 1896.

Some boundaries use lines from cartographic projections. For example, many of the borders that divide the countries of postcolonial Africa were actually drawn by colonial cartographers who had never visited those places. As a result, many borders are uncharacteristically straight and take no account of local geography at all. For instance, part of the border between Namibia and South Africa falls along the 20° line of longitude, and the border between Libya and Egypt tracks the 25° line of longitude.

At a more local level, drawing lines on maps reflects and embodies power relationships. A 17th-century Japanese map of Nagasaki was used to dictate where people lived. The lines on the map affected who lived where.

Lines on maps can have effects on the ground. International boundaries can shape different national destinies and national borders mark off territory. The lines on a map can shape reality.

LEFT UNMIBH *Map of Croatia-Bosnia, 2001*

The boundaries drawn on this map were used to separate out the different ethnic groups in the region. After years of ethnic cleansing and destruction it is hoped that the new boundaries will bring some stability and long-term peace to a troubled region.

THE POSTCOLONIAL DIVISION OF COUNTRIES IN AFRICA

In 1945, all of Africa, apart from Egypt, Liberia, and Ethiopia, was under the control of European powers, and in every part of the continent there was a great desire for independence. During the 1950s, Libya, Sudan, Morocco, Tunisia, Ghana, and Guinea achieved self-rule as the European rulers either decided or were forced to withdraw from their African colonies.

The trend continued in the 1960s with independence for Cameroon, Senegal, Madagascar, Zaire, Somalia, Nigeria, Algeria, Uganda, Zambia, Botswana, and many other countries. Mozambique achieved independence in 1975, followed by Zimbabwe in 1980 and Namibia in 1990. Finally, African self-rule was achieved in South Africa in 1994, following a peaceful transition from white minority rule.

The newly independent governments of Africa inherited borders that had been created by Europeans in the 1880s. With the exception of Somalia, these borders had been drawn up with no regard to the boundaries between different ethnic groups, linguistic variations, and religious divisions. Some national boundaries even cut across the grazing grounds of cattle-owning peoples.

However, there was general agreement among the African leaders to retain these artificially constructed borders. The leaders attempted to create a sense of national unity, but this proved difficult as the new countries contained many conflicting interests, usually based on old tribal and ethnic divisions. As a result the postcolonial years have been marked by political instability and frequent changes of government.

In some cases divisions have led to conflict. Sudan and Chad, for example, are divided between an Arab Muslim north and an African Christian south, causing bloody civil wars in both countries. In Uganda, similar problems were caused by a divide between the Baganda of the south and Acholi in the north. Nigeria has three main divisions: the Muslim north, Ibo east, and Yoruba south, and this led to a major civil war in 1967.

Maps as Propaganda

All maps tell lies: they are selective with the truth, they exclude, they generalize, they exaggerate. Whether some lie more than others is debatable, but when maps use selectivity and exaggeration to present specific arguments they move into the realm of propaganda. There is always, of course, a strong element of relativism in operation here: while your maps are certainly propaganda, mine are completely accurate.

There are the more obvious propaganda maps that tend to appear during times of intense rivalry and conflict. An early Thai map, for example, which purports to show different national areas, represents one nation better than another nation. During the struggle for global dominance between Britain and Germany in the late 19th century many German maps showed British imperial designs for dominance; the British Empire was often depicted as a set of dangerous tentacles strangling the globe.

In the summer of 2002, when the Arab-Israeli conflict in the Middle East was especially violent, a pro-Israeli lobby paid for an advertisement that appeared in US newspapers showing a map of the area with the word "Palestine" over the present State of Israel. The banner headline was: "If the Arabs really want peace with Israel, they must renounce this map." The advertisement was making a claim for Israel's right to exist, but significantly failed to show Israel's occupation of the West Bank.

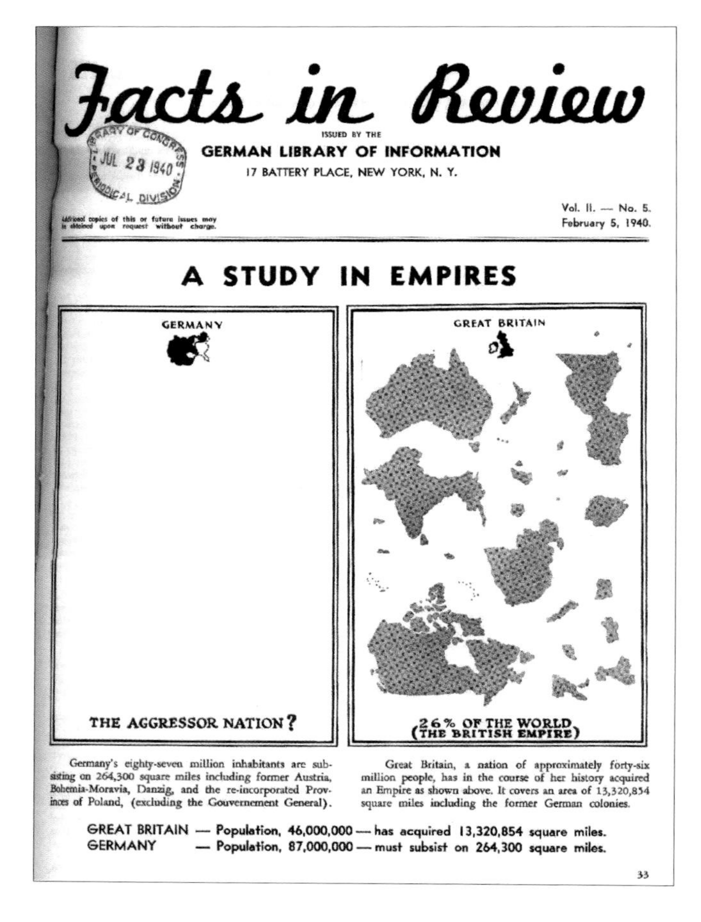

Facts in Review

ISSUED BY THE
GERMAN LIBRARY OF INFORMATION
17 BATTERY PLACE, NEW YORK, N. Y.

Additional copies of this or future issues may be obtained upon request without charge.

Vol. II. — No. 5.
February 5, 1940.

A STUDY IN EMPIRES

Germany's eighty-seven million inhabitants are subsisting on 264,300 square miles including former Austria, Bohemia-Moravia, Danzig, and the re-incorporated Provinces of Poland, (excluding the Gouvernement General).

Great Britain, a nation of approximately forty-six million people, has in the course of her history acquired an Empire as shown above. It covers an area of 13,320,854 square miles including the former German colonies.

GREAT BRITAIN — Population, 46,000,000 — has acquired 13,320,854 square miles.
GERMANY — Population, 87,000,000 — must subsist on 264,300 square miles.

33

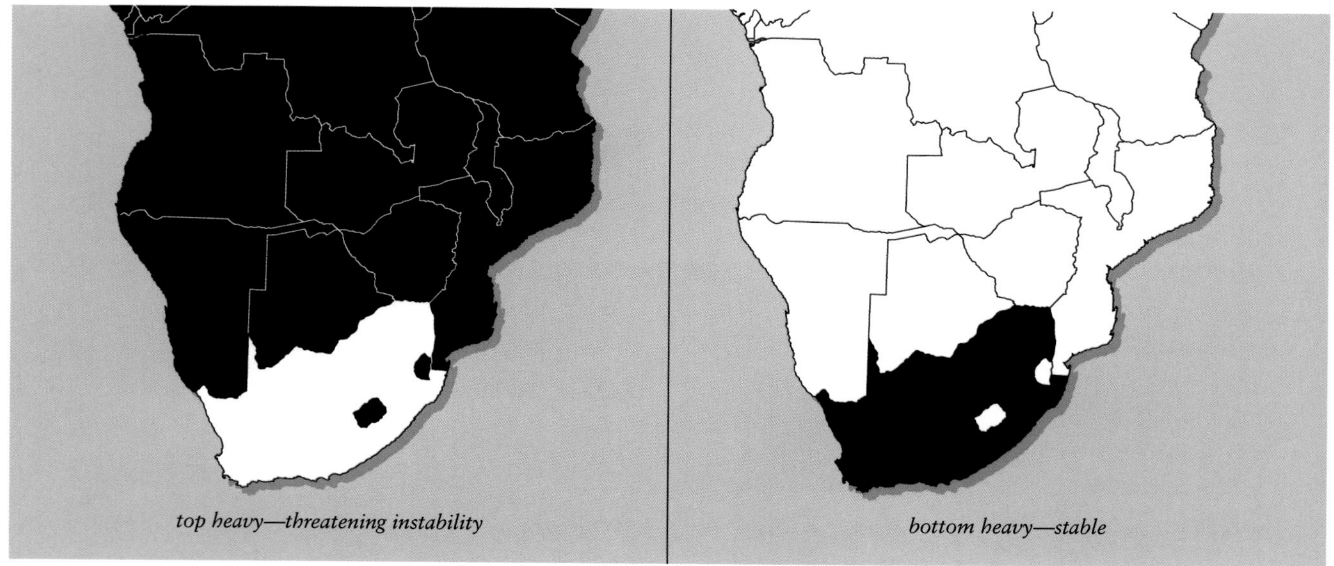

top heavy—threatening instability

bottom heavy—stable

The map highlighted an extreme Palestinian position yet failed to show that Israel's occupation of the West Bank was a major cause of tension. The map promoted a positive view of Israel as a vulnerable country and a "negative" Arab position.

Even cartographic projections can express a political message, if sometimes inadvertently. A good example is the Mercator projection, which was a particular favorite of the British in the late 19th and early 20th centuries. This is hardly surprising, as this projection exaggerates the size of Canada and Australia and even the UK, so that when the British Empire was colored in red, it seemed far larger than it actually was.

Similarly, during the Cold War, Mercator projections were popular in the West because they exaggerated the size of the Soviet Union, making it appear more threatening. In contrast, a world map with its projection centered on the North Pole would show that the US and their western allies appear to surround and threaten the Soviet Union.

Disputed territories frequently result in different maps of the same place. For example, Indian maps will show the territory of Kashmir as part of India, while maps made in Pakistan will show it as part of that country. Similarly, maps produced by the Argentine government in the 1970s showed the Falkland Islands as part of Argentina, when in fact they were part of the United Kingdom.

So we can see, from just a few isolated examples, that it is essential to view all maps with a critical, some might say cynical, eye. This is vital if we are to read between the "cartographic lines" and get at the truth of the map. Who drew it, and why? When did the person draw it and for whom? Like any historical document, maps are made by people in power, who have many interests to serve beyond that of the "truth."

TOP LEFT ***Wartime propaganda map, 1940***
This pro-German cartogram contrasts a small Germany with a vast and imperial Britain. The diagram was used to persuade people in the US not to support Britain in its war with Germany.

LEFT ***Contemporary "propaganda" maps***
The difference in the shading on these two maps of Africa alters the perception of what is shown. The map on the left, showing the weight of countries pressing on South Africa, looks unstable, while the map on the right conveys the opposite impression.

RIGHT **The Turkish Fleet Routed, c. *1580, by Dante Ignazio***
This painting in the map gallery of the Vatican in Rome, Italy, depicts the Battle of Lepanto, in which a Christian fleet defeated a Turkish Islamic force intent on conquering Cyprus. Although Cyprus was surrendered to the Turks two years later, the map was made as a form of propaganda in order to boost the morale of Christians.

Maps and the Military

In order to wage war effectively it is essential to know where you are and where your enemies are. Hence the making of maps for military purposes occupies a large and important role in the history of cartography. The connection between the military and mapmaking in the UK, for example, is embodied in the organization known as the Ordnance Survey, the origins of which lie in William Roy's military survey of Scotland (see page 202). In 1801 the Ordnance Survey became the national mapping agency of the UK, responsible for surveying and for map publication. The Ordnance Survey played a huge role in British life in terms of its role in producing maps of different scales for different purposes. Control shifted from military to civilian authorities only in 1977.

BELOW ***Zone maps, Second World War***
Map like this were produced by the Allies during the Second World War to guide the bombing campaign of German cities. The map pinpoints a range of targets, including the central city, utilities, and industrial centers. The campaign caused heavy civilian casualties.

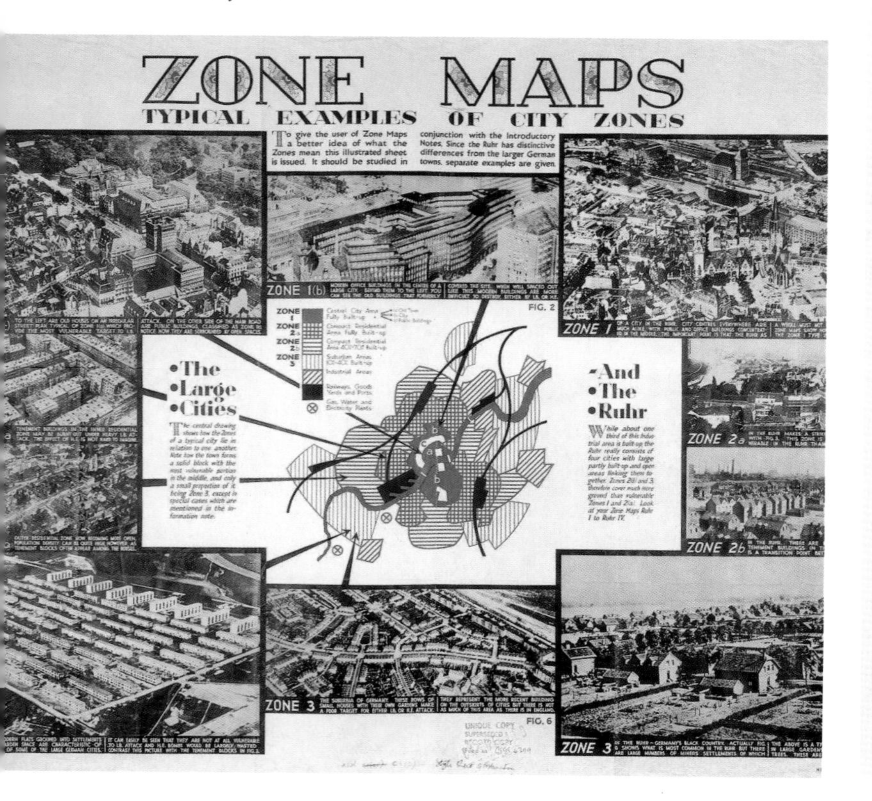

MAPPING IN ADVERSITY

ABOVE ***Map of Kovno Ghetto***
This paper map of the Kovno Ghetto was made by the inhabitants of the ghetto along with other written and statistical documentation of the horror.

In 1941, the German Army invaded Lithuania, and on June 24 they captured the city of Kovno. Within a few weeks, all the local Jews—some 30,000 of them—had been rounded up and incarcerated in a ghetto, where the housing was poor and there was no running water. In November 1943, the ghetto was reclassified as a concentration camp, and on July 8, 1944, the Germans began a six-day liquidation program of the remaining people. By the time the Soviet Army entered the city on August 1, only a few people remained alive.

During this dreadful time, the population of the ghetto bore witness to their oppression through writing, photography, painting, the meticulous recording of statistics, and—amazingly—the drawing of maps. The boundaries of the ghetto were mapped by its inhabitants, as were police precincts. The Kovno maps bear witness to the atrocity.

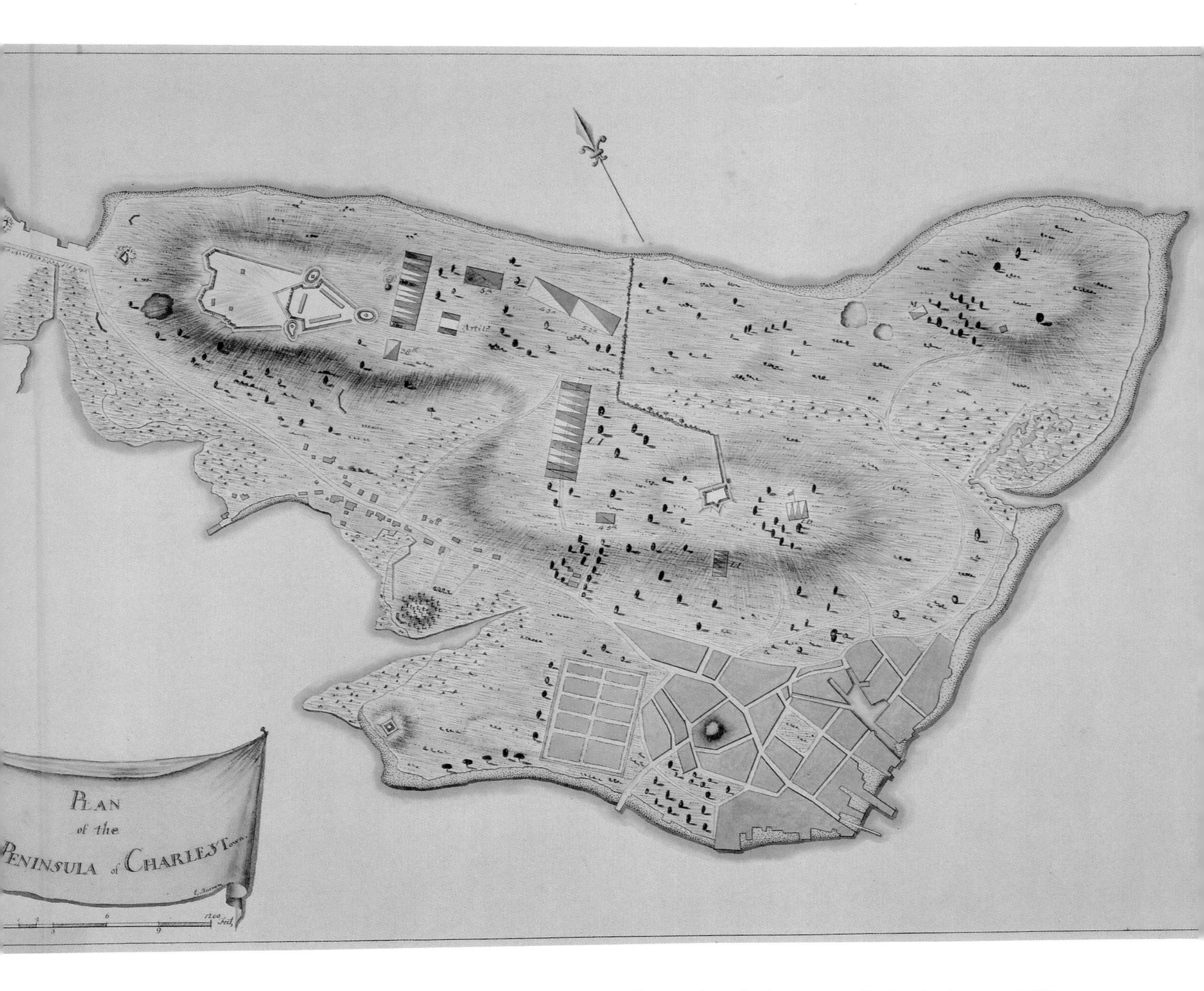

War promotes map production. An estimated 60 million maps of the Western Front were produced in the First World War. During the Second World War, a wide variety of maps were produced, including maps made of the Normandy beaches and surrounding countryside to aid the Allied invasion of France that began on D-Day, June 6, 1944, and zone maps made for Allied aircraft to guide the bombing of German cities.

The mapping of military campaigns is also an important part of the history of cartography. Battles have been described through maps. Since at least the eighteenth century, printed battle maps have played an important role in the public discussion of military affairs. In 18th-century

ABOVE ***Military plan of Charlestown Peninsula, Boston, 1775***
The Charlestown peninsula is directly opposite Boston Harbor. In June 1775, it was taken over by anti-British forces who occupied the hill in the middle of the area called Bunker's Hill. The British bombarded the high terrain, landed troops, and eventually occupied the Hill, but at a cost of very heavy losses.

Britain, periodicals published articles describing colonial struggles and imperial rivalries. The accompanying maps provided the domestic audience with an understanding of overseas events. A map published in 1745 showed the Battle of Louisberg, in what is now northeastern Cape Breton Island. With its three-scale map and detailed notation, the map provides a good coverage of the event.

20

CARTOGRAPHY IN CONTEMPORARY SOCIETY

Fakes and Forgeries

In today's society, it is as important as ever to regard maps with a critical eye. Are they genuine? Who created them and for what purpose? In some cases it has been discovered that maps have been forged. And in the era of mass political participation, maps have sometimes been used as a propaganda tool. Nowadays, the creation of maps has been revolutionized by computers and the Internet, and the development of remote sensing from satellites.

IN 1965, *TIME MAGAZINE* revealed the discovery of an ancient map, which it described as "by far the most important cartographic discovery of this century." The map, drawn in ink on calfskin, became known as the Vinland Map. It showed the coast of northwest Europe and part of the coast of North America, and was thought to have been made around 1440. The map also contained written statements in Latin, one of which, located beside a large island in the west, reads, "the companions Bjarni and Lei Ericksson discovered a new land, extremely fertile and even having vines, the which island they named Vinland." Here at last was possible evidence of what scholars had suspected for many years: that the Vikings had sent expeditions to North America before the time of Columbus.

The map was discovered by a bookseller in Barcelona, Spain. He found it in a manuscript entitled *Tartar Relations*, which recounted an expedition to central Asia in the 13th century. In 1957, the map was bought by a New Haven dealer for US$3,500, who in turn showed it to the curator of maps at Yale University, Alexander Vietor, who secured Yale's right of first refusal. In 1959, the map came up for sale and an anonymous donor bought it for Yale for US$1 million. Yale promoted a book on the map, called *The Vinland Map and the Tartar Relations*, which was published the day before Columbus Day in 1965.

A number of scholars were skeptical. Gerald Crone, the map curator at the Royal Geographical Society in London, carried on a vigorous correspondence in the London *Times* and the *Geographical Journal*. Eva Taylor, another English academic, thought that the geography of the map was too new for the 15th century and she was the first to openly call it a fake. At a conference held at the Smithsonian Institute in 1966, several scholars raised the possibility of the map being a forgery. In 1972, a chemical analysis was carried out on the map, which revealed that while the parchment was old enough to be genuinely 15th century, the ink dated from no earlier than the 1920s.

Why would someone fake this map? The people who had made money from its sale had not made it, so simple avarice was not the reason. In 2002, the historian Kirsten Seaver made a case for the German Jesuit priest Josef Fischer being the maker of the map. Fischer was a recognized map expert, and believed that the Vikings had been to North America before Columbus. He was also an expert in map forgeries, having written an article on false Renaissance world maps. Closer examination of the Vinland Map revealed that some of the legend has a strong Roman Catholic tinge. For example, one section notes that "Eric, legate of the Apostolic See and Bishop of Greenland" had visited Vinland. In other words, the Catholic Church was in on the discovery. Fischer had, perhaps, tried to counter 1930s Nazi anti-Jesuit propaganda by making a map that showed that Catholics had been involved in North American exploration and discovery. It is a convincing theory, but the truth will probably never be known.

MAP THEFT

Gilbert Bland Jr was an antiques dealer from southern Florida, United States, who, on December 7, 1995, was caught trying to steal a number of ancient maps from the George Peabody Library in Baltimore, Maryland. It soon became evident that Bland had stolen maps from many other university collections, including the University of Chicago, Northwestern University, the University of Washington, the University of Virginia, the University of British Columbia, and the University of Rochester.

Bland acted under a number of aliases. Posing as a researcher, he would take out atlases and other books with maps and remove the maps using a razor blade. He then hid the maps on his person and left undetected until the day when a security guard at the Peabody Library noticed something suspicious about his actions. Bland was eventually found guilty of map theft.

Recent years have seen a number of map thefts. Maps are particularly vulnerable to theft because they can easily be ripped out of books. The map trade is in itself also partly to blame since the breaking up of old atlases and rare books to take out and sell maps is a common practice. Single maps, ripped from ancient atlases, are the lifeblood of the map trade.

The recorded cases are only the tip of the iceberg. The Library of Congress probably lost hundreds of thousands of dollars worth of rare maps until stricter security was put in place. In part, map thefts occur because of lax security in many libraries. People have been able to take out rare books undisturbed, and unnoticed. Now, many libraries operate more stringent security in order to protect their rare possessions.

LEFT ***The Vinland Map forgery***
This world map was originally believed to have been drawn in the 15th century. While the parchment is over 500 years old, the ink used to draw the map dates from the 1920s. A German Jesuit priest, Josef Fischer, is the likely forger.

Cartoversies

The Peters projection was named after the German mapmaker Arno Peters (b. 1916). It was developed in the 1970s as a new way of looking at the world, an orientation that, it was often argued, overcame the traditional exaggeration of the size of rich countries compared to poor countries. Peters used an equal area projection.

However, there are criticisms of the Peters projection. First, it was not all that original. The projection had been devised in 1855 by the Scotsman James Gall (1808–95), who wrote at the time of his projection and his other mathematical innovations, "All that I would ask, is that when it be used, my name be associated with it." And even Gall drew from a longer tradition of equal area map projections. In 1722, the Swiss-born mathematician Johann Heinrich Lambert (1728–77) had proposed an equal area projection.

The second is that it did not achieve its desired objective. A number of other projections, such as the Goode projection, provide the same sense of area without the shape distortion of the Peters projection. The Goode projection is closer to global reality and thus more accurately portrays the location and size of poor tropical countries. As the cartographer Arthur Robinson noted of the Peters projection, "The landmasses are somewhat reminiscent of wet, ragged, long winter underwear hung out to dry on the Arctic Circle." A map projection devised in 2002, the Hobo-Dyer projection, is an equal area map, with land masses in truer proportion but more accurate in shape than the Peters map.

The Peters projection became fashionable because it was used by its supporters to demonstrate what they believed were the failings of the Mercator projection, which tended to exaggerate the size of more temperate regions compared to tropical regions. The Mercator projection was initially designed to aid navigation, but had become, by the

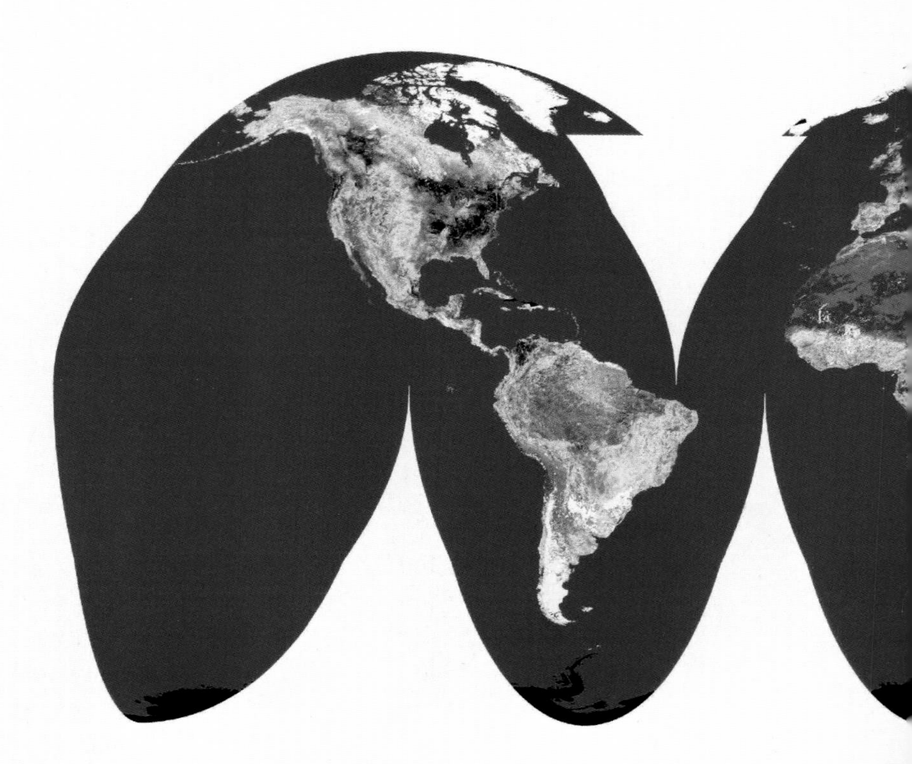

This global image was produced by the U.S. Geological Survey, National Mapping Division, EROS Data Center in cooperation with the Committee on Earth Observation Satellites (CEOS), International Geosphere-Biosphere Program (IGBP), National Aeronautics and Space Administration (NASA), National Oceanic and Atmospheric Administration (NOAA), European Space Agency (ESA), Commonwealth Scientific and Industrial Research Organization of Australia (CSIRO), and key Advanced Very High Resolution Radiometer (AVHRR) ground receiving stations from throughout the world.
1000 0 1000 3000
1000 0 1000

OPPOSITE, TOP **Peters world projection**
Touted as an advancement over Eurocentric maps of the world, the so-called Peters projection still has biases. It extends the length of South America and Africa and distorts their surface area.

RIGHT **Goode projection**
While this Goode projection has the obvious distortion of four quasi-elliptical shapes rather than a single area it is extremely useful for displaying global scale data as it minimizes the surface area and shape distortion of the earth's surface compared to the Peters projection.

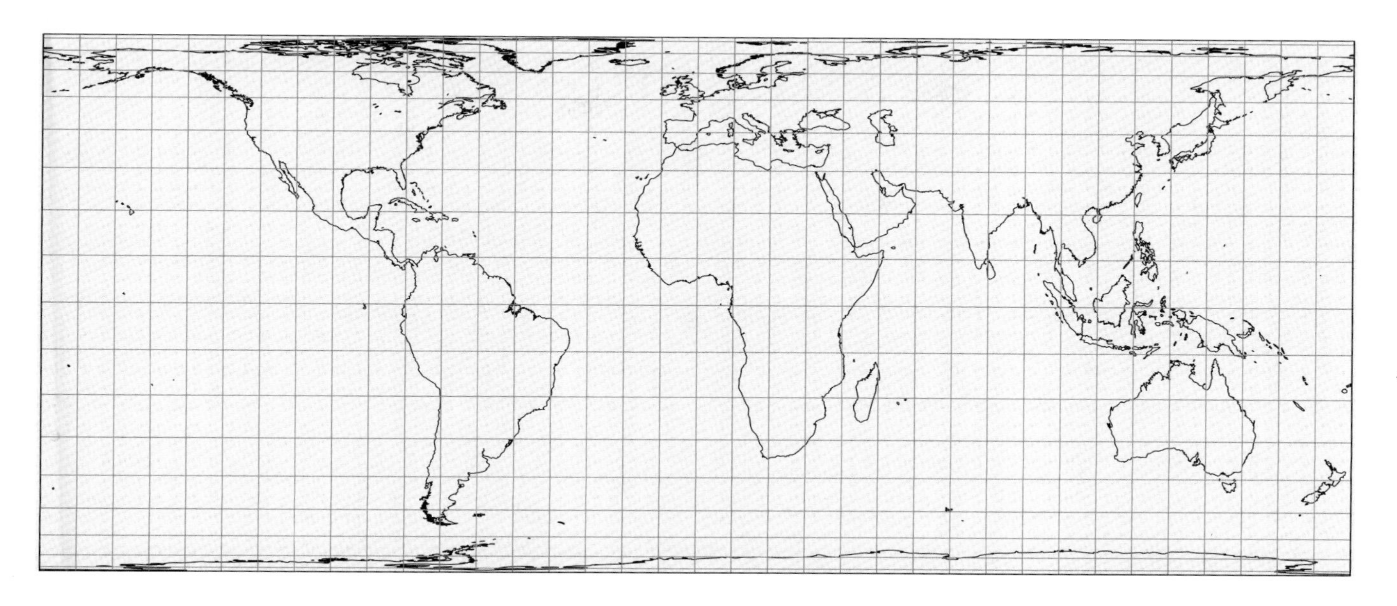

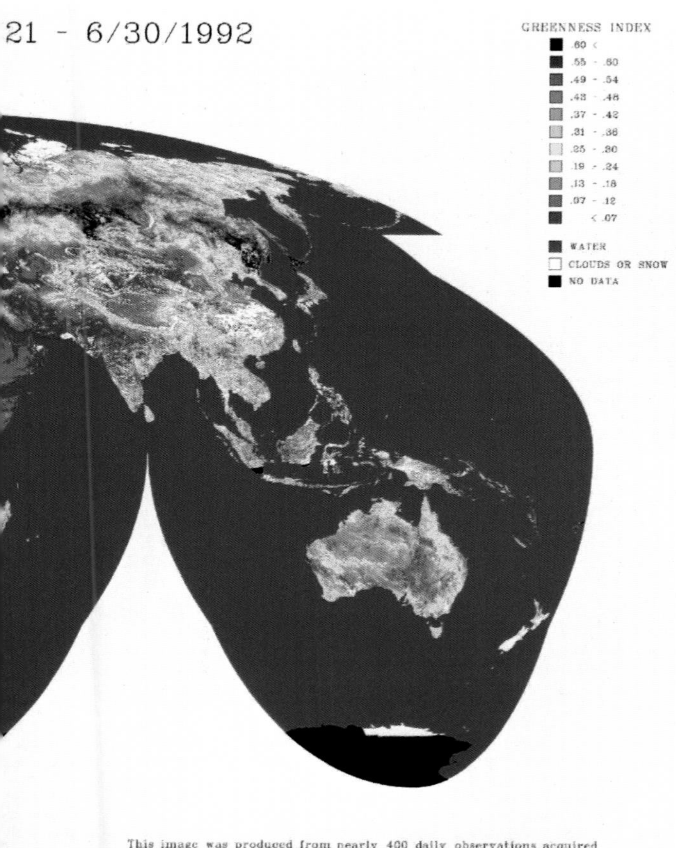
21 - 6/30/1992
GREENNESS INDEX
.60 <
.55 - .60
.49 - .54
.43 - .48
.37 - .42
.31 - .36
.25 - .30
.19 - .24
.13 - .18
.07 - .12
< .07
WATER
CLOUDS OR SNOW
NO DATA
This image was produced from nearly 400 daily observations acquired by the worldwide network of ground data receiving stations and NOAA during the period of June 21 - 30, 1992. The imagery was processed in accordance with the standards described in the International Geosphere Biosphere Program (IGBP) Report #20. The data are calibrated to reflectance (channels 1 and 2) and brightness temperature (channels 3,4, and 5). No atmospheric correction has been applied. The data are geometrically registered using ground control and mapped to the Goodes Interrupted Homolosine projection. The data are composited using normalized difference vegetation index maximum value compositing. Subsequent cloud screening was based on a thermal threshold value. The vegetation index values are color coded to represent major global vegetation patterns.

19th century, the most widely accepted world projection. However, professional cartographers were well aware of the bias in the Mercator projection, and in the 20th century it began to fall out of fashion because it presented such a Eurocentric view of the world. The Peters projection achieved its appeal because it was hailed as a non-Eurocentric representation of the world at a time of increased awareness of global inequality.

Less a sophisticated piece of cartography, the Peters projection was more an advertising campaign. Peters trained as a journalist and essentially campaigned for "his" projection. He held a press conference in 1973 in Berlin, Germany, complete with a slick brochure. He worked at getting the endorsement of the World Council of Churches, Christian Aid, The United Nations Educational, Scientific, and Cultural Organization (UNESCO), and the United Nations Children's Fund (UNICEF). The projection became the cartographic projection of choice among non-governmental, left-wing, and Christian charitable organizations. The West German government also heavily promoted the Peters projection. Professional scholars in West Germany and around the world argued against the simplistic arguments and made the points that it was not original and that it was not a good map. But by then the projection had taken on a life of its own making.

In one sense the Peters controversy ignited public interest in map projection. In another sense, the fact that a journalistic hustler was able to claim something that was not his and was not accurate even by his own standards, since many poor countries were still underrepresented by the projection, demonstrates a general lack of cartographic literacy in society.

Cartography Today

Contemporary cartography is a rich area of activity, and more modern maps, dating from the last third of the 20th century onward, can be said to have three characteristics that distinguish them from "traditional" maps.

The first is that modern maps can be made using computers. Mapmaking has become technically sophisticated, but at the same time it has also become more impersonal. While we can often name the mapmakers of past times, the identities of most modern cartographers remain hidden. There are some exceptions. The maps made by Richard Edes Harrison for *Time* magazine during the Second World War had a distinctive personal signature, but such cases are rare.

The second characteristic is that maps are now an integral part of what are known as geographical information systems (GIS). The growing memory capacity of computers has allowed a whole array of data to be used with software to store, manipulate, and generate geographic data such as altitude readings, temperatures, zip codes, and population characteristics, to name but a few. Because the management and display of geographic data is of vital concern to governments and private firms, GIS has become big business. Such data now play a part in thousands of national and corporate decisions, such as where to build schools and hospitals. In order to build schools, for example, it is necessary to know a range of things: the

IMAGES FROM SPACE

ABOVE ***Earth photographed by Apollo 17***
The first image of the earth from space reinforces the sense of one world and a shared planet.

In 1968 one of the first photographs of the earth was taken from space from Apollo 8. It shows a shadowed earth above a lunar landscape. In 1972 Apollo 17 took a full picture of the earth. These images were a great technical achievement and of enormous cosmological significance. The earth is revealed as a fragile, blue and white dot shimmering in an inky blackness. The images reinforce the sense of one world, a singular home of humanity, small and vulnerable. It is possible that they played a direct part in shaping a new, global consciousness and ecological awakening. The images speak to one world and a shared common future.

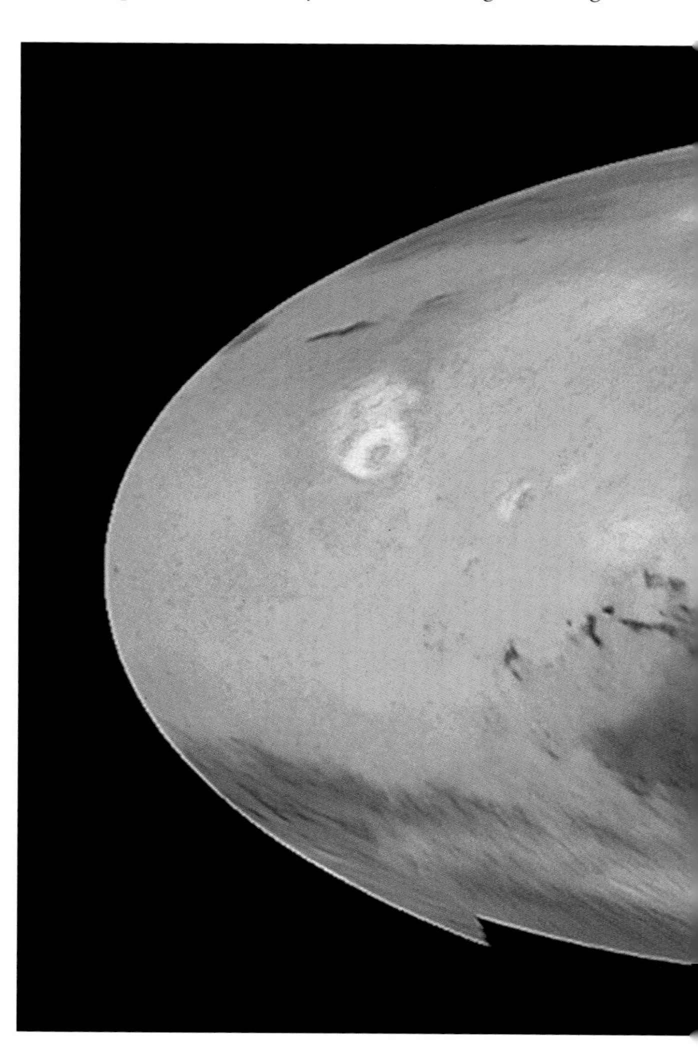

characteristics of the populations of different areas in order to identify where there is greatest demand, a land use map to pinpoint where specifically schools can be built; and maps of roads and highways to show the accessibility of different possible school locations. All this geographic information needs to be stored and analyzed in a coherent system so that the best location is chosen.

RIGHT ***Contemporary Landsat satellite image of China***
This Landsat image shows the Great Wall of China using different spectral wavelengths. The longer wavelengths are better at penetrating cloud cover. The different wavelengths register different phenomena, allowing multiple and slightly different pictures of the same location. Landsat images are useful in mapping land cover and land use changes and taking pictures of inaccessible areas.

BELOW *Mars*
While traditional cartography has been restricted to making maps of the earth, improved technology has allowed a mapping of the nearer planets in our galaxy. This is an image of one of our nearest neighbors, Mars; ready for, say, a Hammer projection.

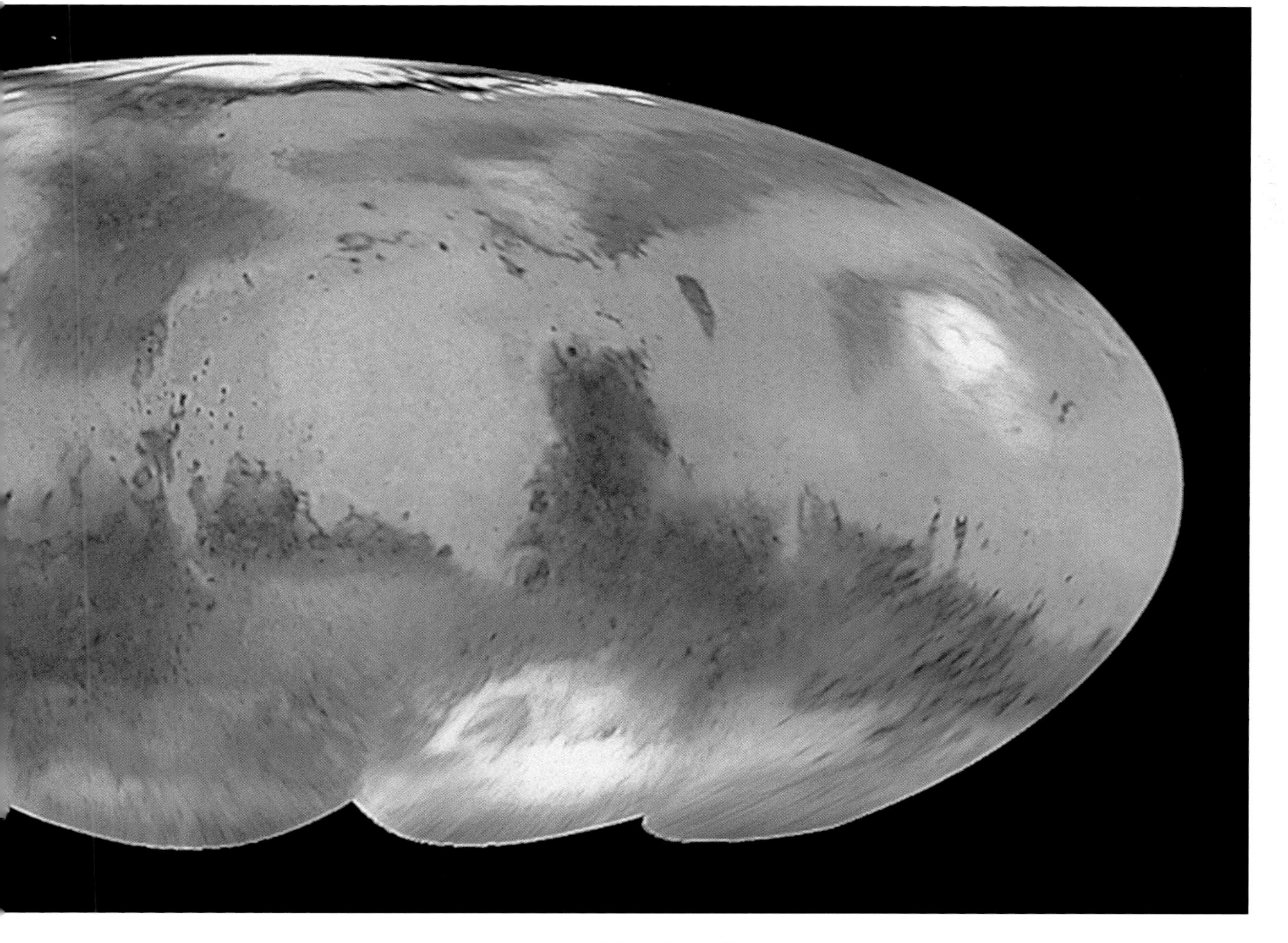

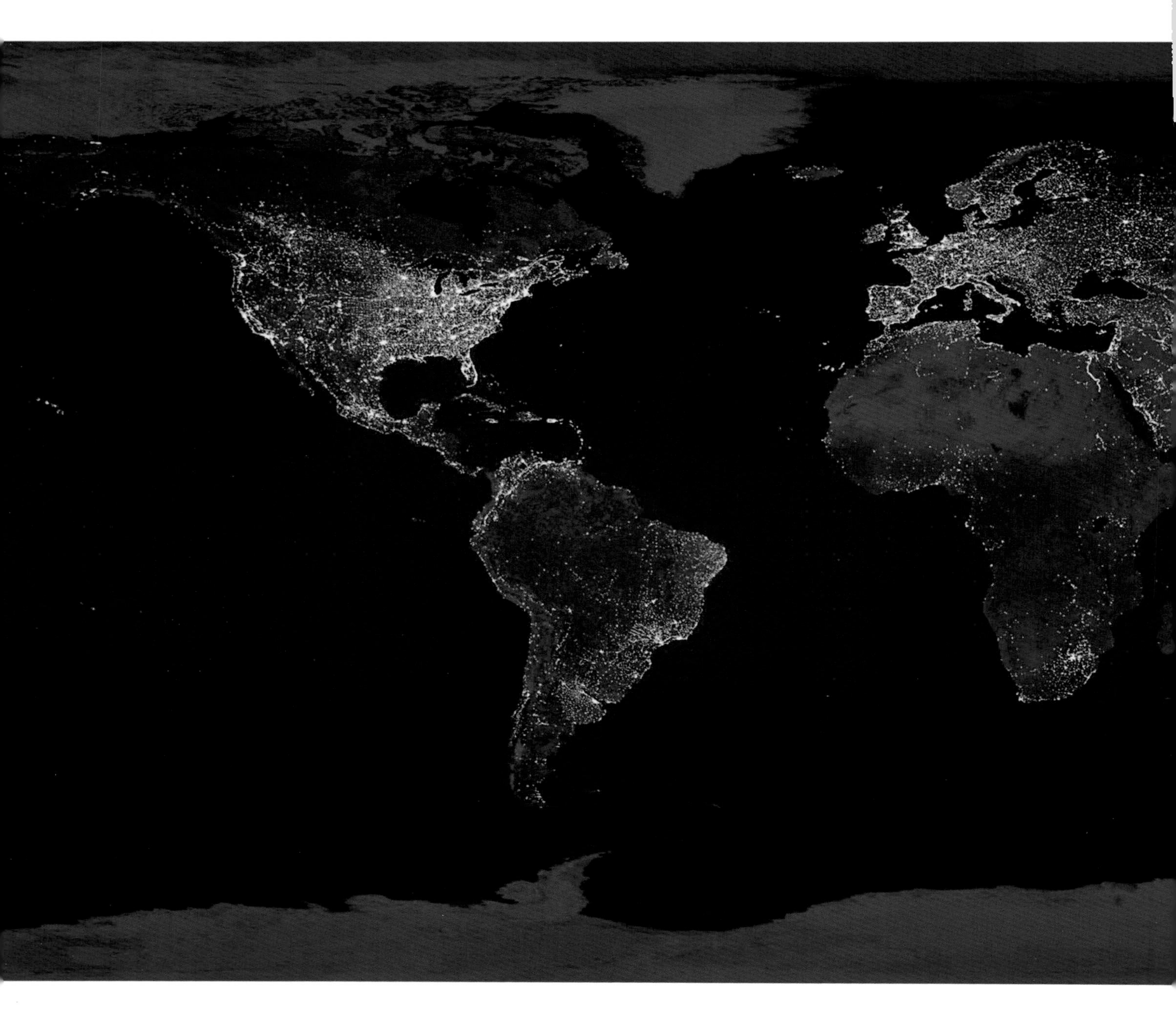

The third characteristic of contemporary cartography is the use of remote sensing techniques. Traditional cartography used data collected from field surveys that was then plotted onto maps. Contemporary cartography uses a wider range of, in many cases, automatic data collection. Aerial photography is an important element in modern mapmaking, and has been used extensively since the end of the Second World War when more sophisticated techniques were developed. Planes and satellites are fitted with cameras that are programmed to take certain photos at certain points in the journey. *The Home Planet*, published in 1988, is an atlas that uses photographs from space to represent the world.

Aerial photography is an extremely useful way of collecting data, but there are drawbacks—for example, cloud cover can inhibit data collection. Satellites, in contrast, provide constant monitoring and can penetrate cloud cover because they are using the whole of the electromagnetic spectrum. Remote sensing from satellites was first developed by the US military and the satellites that have the most detailed pictures are still under military control. However, satellites are now commonly used to collect data

LEFT ***Contemporary map showing urbanization, NASA/the Goddard Space Flight Center***
This composite image of city lights picks out the larger more populous cities of the world. Thus Australia only appears as a band of coastal light with a western outlier in the city of Perth.

from the earth. Each satellite is fitted with sensors that are able to pick up electromagnetic information from the earth. The sensors can be targeted to focus on specific bands of the electromagnetic range, allowing them to collect data on specific phenomena—for example, weather patterns and land use. There are currently three types of satellite sensor: metereological sensors, ocean sensors, and land observation sensors. Among the various modern land observation systems is Landsat, which was the name given to a satellite first launched by the US agency NASA (National Aeronautics and Space Agency) in 1972. Subsequently other satellites were launched, each one numbered sequentially and becoming progressively more sophisticated in the type and degree of information they could gather. In 1999 Landsat 7 was launched; it is a satellite capable of observations at extremely high resolution (i.e. very detailed), allowing highly accurate monitoring of land use across the world.

Remotely sensed data such as that collected by Landsat have greatly enhanced our understanding of land use patterns. We now have more solid information on the rates of deforestation, desertification and urban growth in all parts of the world. The satellites are eyes in the sky that allow us more accurately to measure, map, and predict global land use change. Satellite data has also allowed us to adopt a more global perspective in mapping and monitoring land use changes. In February 2000, the space shuttle *Endeavor* scanned the earth's surface with radar signals to produce the most comprehensive and accurate topographic map of the world to date.

Satellites are also used in providing accurate location data. Where we are is one of those basic questions that is more easily answered now through the use of GPS (global positioning systems). Satellites that circle the earth can be used to plot our location.

The study of maps has been revolutionized by the Internet, and many libraries have put their cartographic collections on the web, greatly increasing access to them by academics and the general public alike. There are also numerous websites devoted to the history of cartography.

The Internet also allows users easy access to navigation programs that will provide a route map for practically any journey the user wishes to make, anywhere on the globe, in great detail—down to the very street he or she wishes to visit. Maps from the whole world over can be accessed by one person sitting at a computer, a fact that may still astonish us today, as it would Ptolemy.

Further Reading

Allen, P. (2000) *Mapmakers Art*. Barnes and Noble

Bagrow, l. (1964) *The History of Cartography*. Watts and C.

Berthon, S. and Robinson, A. (1991) *The Shape of The World*. Rand McNally

Black, J. (1997) *Maps and Politics*. Reaktion

Brody, H. (1997) *Maps and Dreams: Indians and the British Columbia Frontier*. Waveland Press

Brotton, J. (1977) *Trading Territories: Mapping the Early Modern World*. Reaktion

Brown, L.A. (1977) *The Story of Maps*. Dover

Carlucci, A. and Barber, P. (2001) *The Lie of The Land*. British Library

Cosgrove, D. (ed) (1999) *Mappings*. Reaktion

Delano-Smith, C. and Kain, R. J. P. (1999) *English Maps: A History*. British Library

Dorling, D. and Fairbairn, D. (1997) *Mapping: Ways of Representing The World*. Pearson

Driver, C. (1988) *Early American Maps and Views*. University Press of Virginia

Goss, J. (1993) *The Mapmakers Art*. Rand McNally

Harley, J. B. (2001) *The New Nature of Maps*. Johns Hopkins University Press

Harley, J. B. and Woodward, D. (1987–) *The History of Cartography*. University of Chicago

Harvey, M. (2000) *The Island of Lost Maps*. Random

Harvey, P. D.A. (1991) *Medieval Maps*. British Library

Haywood, J. et al., (2001) *Atlas of World History*. Barnes & Noble

Elliot, J. (1987) *The City in Maps*. British Library

MacEachren, A. M. (1995) *How Maps Work*. Guildford

Monmonier, M (1991) *How To Lie With Maps*. University of Chicago

Short, J. R. (2000) *Alternative Geographies*. Pearson

Short, J. R. (2001) *Representing The Republic*. Reaktion

Snyder, J. P. (1993) *Flattening The Earth: Two Thousand years of Map Projections*, University of Chicago

Turnbull, D. (1993) *Maps Are Territories*. University of Chicago

Thrower, N. (1996) *Maps and Civilization*. University of Chicago

Whitfield, P. (1994) *The Image of The World*. British Library

Whitfield, P. (1995) *The Mapping of The Heavens*. British Library

Whitfield, P. (1996) *The Charting of The Oceans*. British Library

Wigal, D. (2000) *Historic Maritime Maps*. Parkstone

Wilford, J. N. (2002) *The Mapmakers*. A. A. Knopf

Winchester, S. (2001) *The Map that Changed the World*. Viking

Wood, D. (1992) *The Power of Maps*. Guildford

The most important academic journal on the history of cartography is *Imago Mundi*

WEBSITES

www.auslig.gov.au/
National mapping division of Australia. Find an aerial photograph of any area of the country.

www.earthamaps.com/
DeLorme Cybermaps. Search by place-name for U.S. city maps, with zoom facility.

http://earthtrends.wri.org/
World Resources Institute. Mapping of energy resources, agriculture, forestry, government, climate and other thematic maps.

http://ihr.sas.ac.uk/maps/
History of cartography; no images, but search by cartographic topics to many other links.

www.lib.utexas.edu/maps/
Vast map collection at the University of Texas, historical and modern, including maps produced by the CIA.

www.lib.virginia.edu/exhibits/lewis_clark/
Information on historic expeditions, including Lewis and Clark.

www.lindahall.org/pubserv/hos/stars/
Exhibition of the Golden Age of the celestial atlas, 1482-1851.

http://memory.loc.gov/ammem/gmdhtml/
Map collections 1500-1999, the Library of Congress; U.S. maps, including military campaigns and exploration.

www.nationalgeographic.com/maps
The National Geographic site; includes historic mapping and simple black-and-white maps of all the countries of the world.

www.ordsvy.gov.uk/
Site of one of the oldest national mapping agencies; search and download historical and modern maps of the U.K.

http://scarlett.libs.uga.edu/darchive/hargrett/maps/
University of Georgia historical map collection; maps from the 16th to the early 20th century.

http://.topozone.com/
Search by place-name or latitude and longitude for all areas of the U.S. Maps at various scales.

www.un.org/Depts/Cartographic/
United Nations cartographic section. Search by country and by different UN missions worldwide.

http://mapping.usgs.gov/
U.S. national atlas and much more, including satellite images.

imageswww.worldatlas.com/
World atlas and statistics about all countries of the world.

Index

Acknowledgments

1 Bodleian Library, Oxford; 2 Stapleton Collection/Corbis; 6–7 The British Library; 8 BP/NRSC/Science Photo Library; 9 Phil Schermeister/Corbis; 10t Dean & Chapter, Hereford Cathedral; 10b, 11, 12t The British Library; 12bl, 12br, 13 www.ordsvy.gov.uk (Ordnance Survey holds an extensive archive of historical mapping); 14t, 14b The British Library; 15 © ODT Inc. Amherst, MA; 16–17 The British Library; 18 Andromeda Oxford Limited; 18–19 David Rumsey Collection; 19 Glasgow University Library; 20 The British Library; 21 © National Maritime Museum, London; 24l, 24r, 25 The British Library; 26l, 26r co op. Archeologica Le Orme dell' uomo; 27 © The Field Museum, Chicago; 28–29, 29 Natal Museum; 30–31 James Q. Jacobs; 31 Kevin Schafer/Corbis; 32, 33 Pitt Rivers Museum, Oxford; 34 © Old Mick Walangkari Tjakamarra, 1973; Licensed by the Aboriginal Artists Agency, Sydney/National Gallery of Australia; 35 Penny Tweedie/Corbis; 36–37 Gianni Dagli Orti/Corbis; 39, 40–41 © The British Museum; 41 © The President and Fellows of Harvard College; 42 © The British Museum; 43 Bodleian Library, Oxford; 44, 45 V & A Picture Library; 47 Gianni Dagli Orti/Corbis; 48 Bettmann/Corbis; 48–49 © The British Museum; 50 Marc Levoy, Digital Forma Urbis Romae Project, Stanford University/© Comune di Roma, Eugenio La Rocca; 50–51 Österreichische Nationalbibliothek Bildarchiv; 52 The British Library/The Bridgeman Art Library; 54–55 Adam Woolfitt/Corbis; 56–57 The Huntington Library, Art Collections, and Botanical Gardens, San Marino, California/Powerstock; 59, 60, 61 The British Library; 62–63 Museo Naval, Madrid; 64, 65 The Huntington Library, Art Collections, and Botanical Gardens, San Marino, California/Powerstock; 66–67 Bodleian Library, Oxford; 69 The British Library; 70, 71, 72–73 Bodleian Library, Oxford; 74t © The British Museum; 74b, 75, 77, 78, 78–79 The British Library; 79 Archivo Iconografico, S.A./Corbis; 80–81 The British Library; 82–83 Bettmann/Corbis; 84–85, 86–87 © The British Museum; 88–89 The British Library; 90 Public Record Office, Kew; 91 Werner Forman Archive; 92–93 The British Library; 94, 95 Library of Congress; 96 Mitchell Library/State Library of New South Wales; 97 The British Library; 98–99 John Carter Brown Library, Boston University, MA, USA/The Bridgeman Art Library; 100, 101 © National Maritime Museum, London; 102 The British Library; 103 Royal Geographical Society, London, UK/The Bridgeman Art Library; 104–105, 106l The British Library; 106r Paul Almasy/Corbis; 107l, 107r The British Library; 108, 109t, 109c AKG London; 109b Courtesy of the Historic Cities Research Project (http://historic-cities.huji.ac.il) The Hebrew University of Jerusalem, Dept. of Geography; 110t, 110c, 110b The Science Museum/Science & Society Picture Library; 111t The Royal Collection © 2003, Her Majesty Queen Elizabeth II; 111b The Science Museum/Science & Society Picture Library; 112–113, 113 National Library of Scotland; 114 Glasgow University Library; 114–115, 116, 117, 118–119 The British Library; 120–121 Harry Ransom Humanities Research Center, The University of Texas at Austin; 121 Scala Group S.p.A; 122, 123, 124, 125 Library of Congress; 126, 127 Stapleton Collection/Corbis; 128t Rosenwald Collection/Library of Congress; 128b Bettmann/Corbis; 129 Corbis; 130, 131, 132, 133 The British Library; 134–135 Library of Congress; 137 Maryland State Archives; 138 Bibliothèque Nationale de France; 139 Bibliothèque Nationale Québec; 140, 141 Library of Congress; 142 Mitchell Library/State Library of New South Wales; 143 Dixson Library/State Library of New South Wales; 144, 145 The British Library; 146, 147l Public Record Office, Kew; 147r Royal Geographical Society, London; 149 © National Maritime Museum, London; 150 The British Library; 151l Birmingham Central Library; 151r The British Library; 152, 153, 154–155, 156–157, 158–159 Library of Congress; 159 Courtesy of the Beinecke Rare Book & Manuscript Library, Yale University; 160–161, 162, 163, 164, 165 Library of Congress; 166–167 Kevin R. Morris/Corbis; 168–169 Cambridge University Library; 170–171 © The British Museum; 172 Bibliothèque Nationale de France; 173 Public Record Office, Kew; 174 The Walters Art Museum, Baltimore; 175 Topkapi Palace Museum, Istanbul, Turkey/The Bridgeman Art Library; 176–177 David Rumsey Collection; 177 NASA/Science Photo Library; 178 Bibliothèque Nationale de France; 179 NRSC LTD/Science Photo Library; 180 Birmingham Central Library; 181 Corbis; 182–183 Birmingham Central Library; 184–185 Ludington Limited; 186 Greyhound Lines, Inc.; 187 The British Library; 188 Bibliothèque Nationale de France; 189t www.lboro.ac.uk/gawc/citymap; 189b London Transport Museum; 190–191 The London School of Economics; 192–193 Public Record Office, Kew; 195, 196–197 The Wellcome Trust; 198 The Geological Society of London; 199t NASA/Science Photo Library; 199b Dr. Fred Espenak/Science Photo Library; 200–201 Library of Congress; 203, 204 The British Library; 205 B.C. Biega; 206 Library of Congress; 207 Scala Group S.p.A; 208l The British Library; 208r Yad Vashem Film & Photo Archive, Collection Avraham Tory/U.S. Holocaust Memorial Museum Photo Archives; 209 Alnwick Castle, Northumberland, UK/The Bridgeman Art Library; 210–211 Courtesy of the Beinecke Rare Book & Manuscript Library, Yale University; 212–213 Stocktrek/Corbis; 214 NASA; 214–215 Stocktrek/Corbis; 215 NASA/Science Photo Library; 216–217 NASA.